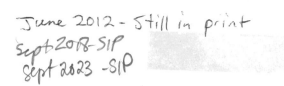

COMPLEX
PROBLEM SOLVING
The European Perspective

COMPLEX PROBLEM SOLVING

The European Perspective

Edited by

PETER A. FRENSCH
University of Missouri at Columbia

JOACHIM FUNKE
University of Bonn, Germany

LEA LAWRENCE ERLBAUM ASSOCIATES, PUBLISHERS
1995   Hillsdale, New Jersey   Hove, UK

Lawrence Erlbaum Associates, Inc., Publishers
365 Broadway
Hillsdale, New Jersey 07642

Library of Congress Cataloging-in-Publication Data

Complex problem solving : the European perspective / edited by Peter
A. Frensch, Joachim Funke.
   p.   cm.
Includes bibliographical references and index.
ISBN 0-8058-1336-5 (cloth : alk. paper). — ISBN 0-8058-1783-2
(paper : alk. paper)
1. Cognitive neuroscience. 2. Cognitive science. I. Frensch,
Peter A. II. Funke, Joachim.
QP360.5.C66 1995
153.4'3—dc20   95-4455
                                                      CIP

Books published by Lawrence Erlbaum Associates are printed on acid-free
paper, and their bindings are chosen for strength and durability.

Printed in the United States of America
10 9 8 7 6 5 4 3 2 1

We dedicate this book to Donald E. Broadbent who suddenly and unexpectedly passed away during the final stages of the project. He was both an initiator and a very active contributor to the complex problem-solving scenes in Europe and North America, and was, perhaps more than anybody else, familiar with, and comfortably working within, the two approaches. Donald Broadbent will be deeply missed.

Contents

Contributors

Jens F. Beckmann, Psychologisches Institut, Universität Leipzig, Tieckstr. 2, D-04275 Leipzig, Germany

Dianne C. Berry, Department of Psychology, University of Reading, Earley Gate, Whiteknights, Reading RG6 2AL, England

Berndt Brehmer, Department of Psychology, University of Uppsala, Box 1854, S-751 48 Uppsala, Sweden

Donald E. Broadbent (deceased), Department of Experimental Psychology, University of Oxford, South Parks Road, Oxford, OX1 3UD, England

Axel Buchner, FB1—Psychologie, Universität Trier, Universitätsring 15, D-54286 Trier, Germany

Dietrich Dörner, Lehrstuhl Psychologie II, Universität Bamberg, Markusplatz 3, D-96047 Bamberg, Germany

Peter A. Frensch, Department of Psychology, University of Missouri-Columbia, 210 McAlester Hall, Columbia, MO 65211

Joachim Funke, Psychologisches Institut, Universität Bonn, Römerstr. 164, D-53117 Bonn, Germany

Uwe Funke, Lehrstuhl für Psychologie, Universität Hohenheim, Institut 540 F, D-70593 Stuttgart, Germany

Jürgen Guthke, Psychologisches Institut, Universität Leipzig, Tieckstr. 2, D-04275, Leipzig, Germany

Oswald Huber, Psychologisches Institut, Universität Fribourg, Route des Fougères, CH-1701 Fribourg, Switzerland

Rainer H. Kluwe, Institut für Kognitionsforschung, Universität der Bundeswehr, Holstenhofweg 85, D-22043 Hamburg, Germany

Josef F. Krems, Institut für Psychologie, Universität Regensburg, Universitätsstr. 31, Gebäude PT, D-93053 Regensburg, Germany

Robert J. Sternberg, Department of Psychology, Yale University, Box 208205, New Haven, CT 06520-8205

Alex J. Wearing, Department of Psychology, University of Melbourne, Parkville, Victoria 3052, Australia

Preface

Imagine your typical 5-year-old sliding all over the living-room floor while feverishly using her Lego building blocks to construct the world's biggest mansion. And imagine the engineer at the Chernobyl Nuclear Power Station thinking of all possible ways to stop the greatest atomic disaster from happening. Both the 5-year-old and the seasoned engineer engage in complex problem solving (CPS). At an abstract level, we might define complex problem solving as thinking that

> ... occurs to overcome barriers between a given state and a desired goal state by means of behavioral and/or cognitive, multistep activities. [In CPS,] the given state, goal state, and barriers ... are complex, change dynamically during problem solving, and are intransparent, [and] the exact properties of the given state, goal state, and barriers are unknown to the solver. CPS implies the efficient interaction between a solver and the situational requirements of the task, and involves a solver's cognitive, emotional, personal, and social abilities and knowledge. (Frensch & Funke, this volume)

Clearly, complex problem solving, defined in this way, is ubiquitous, even though the results of such problem solving are, gratefully, not always as important as they were in the Chernobyl example mentioned earlier. However, not every task we face gives rise to complex problem solving. Rather, at least according to our definition, a problem must be (a) novel, (b) complex, (c) dynamically changing over time, and (d) intransparent before we can legitimately call our dealings with the problem "complex problem solving." CPS, thus, is not a straightforward extension of "simple" problem solving (SPS), that is, problem solving involving relatively simple problems such as choosing the "right" clothes for a festive occasion. Instead, CPS and SPS are qualitatively different. For example, SPS frequently serves to overcome a single barrier; CPS, in contrast, deals with a large number of barriers that coexist simultaneously. Because there are multiple barriers, a single cognitive or behavioral activity may not be sufficient to reach the goal state. Rather, a well-planned, prioritized, set of cognitions and actions may need to be performed in order to get closer to the desired goal state.

Complex problem solving, then, is a topic that deserves our all attention, and certainly the attention of experimental psychologists—if only for the potentially disastrous consequences of problem solving gone awry. Why, however, do we need an entire volume dedicated to European research on CPS? The answer is twofold: First, we need such a book because much of the existing, original European research has been published exclusively in non-English-language journals or books and has not been accessible to North American scholars—with the exception of those of us lucky enough to be familiar with several languages. And second, we need such a book because European research on CPS has a flavor that is quite different from that of most of the research conducted in North America. That is to say that both the theoretical and empirical approaches to studying CPS have been quite different in Europe and North America during roughly the past two decades.

A little bit of history: Both the North American and the European approach to studying CPS originated from the realization (which occurred sometime during the mid-1970s) that empirical findings and theoretical concepts that had been derived from simple laboratory problems are not generalizable to more complex, real-life problems. Even worse, it appears that the processes underlying CPS in different domains are different from each other. These realizations have led to rather different responses in North America and Europe.

In North America, initiated by the work of Herbert Simon on learning by doing in semantically rich domains (e.g., Anzai & Simon, 1979; Bhaskar & Simon, 1977), researchers began to investigate problem solving in separate natural knowledge domains (e.g., physics, writing, chess playing). Frequently, these researchers focus on trying to understand the development of problem solving within a certain domain, that is on the development of expertise (e.g., Anderson, Boyle, & Reiser, 1985; Chase & Simon, 1973; Chi, Feltovich, & Glaser, 1981). Domains that have attracted rather extensive attention in North America include such diverse fields as reading, writing, calculation, political decision making, managerial problem solving, lawyers' reasoning, mechanical problem solving, problem solving in electronics, computer skills, and game playing.

In Europe, two main approaches have surfaced during the past two decades, one initiated by Donald Broadbent (1977; see Berry & Broadbent, this volume) in Great Britain and the other one by Dietrich Dörner (1975; see Dörner & Wearing, this volume) in Germany. The two approaches have in common an emphasis on relatively complex, semantically rich, computerized laboratory tasks that are constructed to be similar to real-life problems. The approaches differ somewhat in their theoretical goals and methodology, however. The tradition initiated by Broadbent emphasizes the distinction between cognitive problem-solving processes that operate under awareness versus outside of awareness, and typically employs mathematically well-defined computerized systems. The tradition initiated by Dörner, on the other hand, is interested in the interplay of the cognitive, motivational, and social components of problem solving, and utilizes very complex computerized scenarios that contain up to 2,000 highly interconnected variables.

Thus, North American research on CPS has typically concentrated on examining the development of expertise in separate, natural knowledge domains. Most of the European research, in contrast, has focused on novel, complex problems, and has been performed with computerized, sometimes highly artificial tasks. Much of the North American work has been summarized in a volume edited recently by Sternberg and Frensch (1991) whereas the European research has, thus far, not been systematically and extensively reviewed. The present volume focuses exclusively on the European approach, and can thus be considered a companion volume to the Sternberg and Frensch book. Included are contributions from researchers in four European countries: Sweden, Switzerland, Great Britain, and, primarily, Germany, both the former West Germany and the former East Germany. The distribution of contributors, we believe, rather accurately reflects where the bulk of the empirical research on CPS has been conducted in Europe.

The contributions to this volume center around five main topics. The first three chapters are *introductory* chapters that provide definitions and describe the various theoretical frameworks and empirical approaches that have been offered thus far. Frensch and Funke (chap. 1) compare various definitions of CPS and discuss the different traditions that have developed in Europe and North America. They also offer a, rather general, theoretical framework that aims at integrating the existing CPS research. Buchner (chap. 2) discusses both the empirical approaches and the important theoretical models that have been developed in Europe. He argues that there are two main approaches to empirically studying CPS in Europe. The one approach searches for individual differences in CPS and uses naturalistic scenarios as research tool; the other approach aims at understanding two main components underlying CPS, namely the processes of knowledge acquisition and of knowledge application, and uses precisely described, but rather artificial, task environments as methodology of choice. Dörner and Wearing (chap. 3) describe a rather ambitious general theoretical model of CPS that is not limited to describing the role of cognitive variables in CPS, but focuses also on the role of motivational and emotional variables.

The second group of chapters deals with *general topics* in CPS research, such as the role of feedback on task performance, implicit learning processes, and the relation between CPS and decision making. Brehmer (chap. 4) presents a series of experiments that demonstrate the differential effects of different types of feedback on CPS. He argues that delay of feedback negatively affects subjects' performance, and further, that it is very difficult for subjects to re-deploy resources during the course of CPS. Berry and Broadbent (chap. 5) deal with dissociations between what people can actually do and what they can verbalize about their actions, and argue that different types of knowledge may be independently acquired and used during complex problem solving. Huber (chap. 6) bridges the gap between CPS research and classical decision making research. In a series of experiments, he demonstrates the importance of task variables on the decision process. If one follows his reasonable assumption that complex problems can be decomposed into smaller subproblems, then the theory behind his results could be useful in explaining at least some CPS processes as well.

The third group of chapters deals with *differential aspects* of CPS, such as intelligence, cognitive flexibility, and personnel selection. Beckmann and Guthke (chap. 7) analyze the relation between CPS and intelligence. They call for a new conceptualization of intelligence as "learning ability," and empirically demonstrate the relation between learning ability and problem solving performance. Krems (chap. 8) discusses the relation between CPS and cognitive flexibility, the latter being a precondition for the former. Cognitive flexibility refers to the ability to modify hypotheses during diagnostic reasoning and trouble-shooting, and is analyzed in terms of expert-novice differences. Uwe Funke (chap. 9) reviews how basic CPS research can be, and has been, fruitfully applied to personnel selection and training.

A fourth group of chapters deals with *methodological issues* in CPS. Joachim Funke (chap. 10) reviews experimental approaches to studying CPS where the contributions of the person, the task situation, and the interaction between the person and the task situation were systematically manipulated. He also discusses when it is appropriate to use experimental methods in CPS research, and how this can be done more effectively. Kluwe (chap. 11) discusses when and for which purpose single case studies are an appropriate methodological tool for studying CPS. He also criticizes some earlier applications of single case studies thereby making use of considerations that come from philosophy of science.

The last topic, *evaluation*, consists of a single chapter. Here, Sternberg (chap. 12) compares the North American and the European approaches to studying complex problem solving, and places both approaches within a common theoretical framework. Sternberg argues that the North American and the European approach constitute just two out of many possible conceptions of expertise.

This volume is the result of an international cooperation that started two years ago with the idea of bringing the European research on complex problem solving to the awareness of American scholars. We hope that the contributions to this volume will be both informative and comprehensive. According to an old saying, quoted by Dietrich Dörner (1983), psychologists give answers to questions that nobody has asked, and provide no answers to the questions that have been raised. We believe—foolheartedly some might argue—that research on complex problem solving is one area where this rather pessimistic view of psychological research does not apply.

We thank the many people who have worked hard to make this book possible. First, and foremost, we are very grateful to the scholars who generously gave of their time to write chapters for this book. Judith Amsel and Kathleen Dolan of Lawrence Erlbaum Associates were very helpful in getting the project off the ground and provided support during all stages. Lisa Irmen (University of Bonn) was responsible for formatting draft versions, indexing, etc., and provided excellent feedback to each and every chapter. The Abteilung Allgemeine Psychologie at Bonn University and its chair, Jürgen Bredenkamp, and the Department of Psychology at the University of Missouri-Columbia with its chair Tom DiLorenzo provided both financial and moral support whenever needed. Last but not least: this cooperative effort could never have been produced this quickly and efficiently without the existence of the Internet and email. A big thank you to our computer guys who made file exchanges and mailing so easy.

REFERENCES

Anderson, J. R., Boyle, C. B., & Reiser, B. J. (1985). Intelligent tutoring systems. *Science, 228*, 456–462.

Anzai, K., & Simon, H. A. (1979). The theory of learning by doing. *Psychological Review, 86*, 124–140.

Bhaskar, R., & Simon, H. A. (1977). Problem solving in semantically rich domains: An example from engineering thermodynamics. *Cognitive Science, 1*, 193–215.

Broadbent, D. E. (1977). Levels, hierarchies, and the locus of control. *Quarterly Journal of Experimental Psychology, 29*, 181–201.

Chase, W. G., & Simon, H. A. (1973). Perception in chess. *Cognitive Psychology, 4*, 55–81.

Chi, M. T. H., Feltovich, P. J., & Glaser, R. (1981). Categorization and representation of physics problems by experts and novices. *Cognitive Science, 5*, 121–152.

Dörner, D. (1975). Wie Menschen eine Welt verbessern wollten [How people wanted to improve the world]. *Bild der Wissenschaft, 12*, 48–53.

Dörner, D. (1983). Empirische Psychologie und Alltagsrelevanz [Empirical psychology and its importance for daily life]. In G. Jüttemann (Ed.), Psychologie in der Veränderung. Perspektiven für eine gegenstandsangemessene Forschungspraxis (pp. 13–29). Weinheim: Beltz.

Sternberg, R. J., & Frensch, P. A. (Eds.). (1991). *Complex problem solving: Principles and mechanisms.* Hillsdale, NJ: Lawrence Erlbaum Associates.

COMPLEX PROBLEM SOLVING
The European Perspective

PART ONE

INTRODUCTION

Definitions, Traditions, and a General Framework for Understanding Complex Problem Solving

Peter A. Frensch*
University of Missouri at Columbia, USA

Joachim Funke
University of Bonn, Germany

*Peter Frensch is currently at the Max Planck Institute for Human Development and Education, Berlin, Germany.

INTRODUCTION

Many of our daily activities involve problem solving of some sort. For example, we decide what to wear in the morning, which route to take to get to our office, which job-related duties to perform in which sequence once we arrive at our office, what to have for lunch, and so on. Of course, not all problem solving is alike. There are problems that can be solved with a few mental steps, and there are problems that require extensive thinking. There are problems that we have never encountered before, and there are problems we are familiar with. There are problems that have very clear goals, and there are problems where the goals are far from clear. Problems, then, can be distinguished on any number of meaningful dimensions, and the solution processes, the mental steps we engage in when solving a problem, may differ widely for different types of problems.

Given the multidimensionality of a problem, it may not come as a surprise to discover that different researchers, all claiming to study the phenomenon of problem solving, have on more than one occasion wholeheartedly disagreed with each other's conclusions. For example, many of those studying expert problem solving have maintained that experts typically use a forward-working (from the givens to the goal) approach to problem solving, whereas others have argued that experts work backward (from the goal to the givens). This apparent contradiction can be resolved if one considers the type of task that has been studied by the different researchers. It turns out that those claiming that experts prefer a forward-working approach have used problems that their experts were relatively familiar with, whereas those claiming the opposite tended to use tasks that were relatively novel for their experts (Smith, 1991). Thus, any general conclusion regarding expert problem solving, and indeed any conclusion regarding problem solving in general, can only be meaningful if we can all agree on what constitutes a problem and what constitutes problem solving.

In the first section of this introductory chapter, therefore, we present definitions of the terms *problem* and *problem solving* that have been offered in the past, and discuss why these definitions differ. In the second section, we discuss the main differences between the current North American and European mainstream approaches to studying problem solving, and argue that the differences between the two approaches are at least partially due to differences in how problem solving is defined. Finally, in the third section, we discuss how selecting a definition of problem solving constrains a theory of problem solving, and describe how a general theoretical framework for understanding problem solving that is based on the definition adopted within the European tradition, might look like.

DEFINITIONS OF PROBLEM SOLVING

"When I use a word," Humpty Dumpty said in a rather scornful tone, "it means just what I choose it to mean—neither more nor less." (Lewis Carroll, 1935, p. 119)

According to Webster's New Twentieth Century Dictionary (1983), a definition is "an explanation or statement of what a word or word phrase means or has meant." In the first section of this chapter, we present and compare various statements of the meaning of problem solving that have been offered in the past. We ask why we need an explicit definition of problem solving at all, and discuss why existing definitions differ. Finally, we present our thoughts on whether we can ever agree on a general definition of problem solving.

Explicit Definitions

Researchers in the area of problem solving have long been troubled by the absence of agreement on the exact meaning of many of the basic terms used (e.g., Smith, 1991). Among these basic terms are *expert, novice, heuristic, problem,* and even *problem solving* itself. Consider, for example, some of the better known definitions of problem solving that have been offered in the past:

- Problem solving is defined as any goal-directed sequence of cognitive operations. (Anderson, 1980, p. 257)
- . . . problem solving is defined here as a goal-directed sequence of cognitive and affective operations as well as behavioral responses for the purpose of adapting to internal or external demands or challenges. (Heppner & Krauskopf, 1987, p. 375)
- What you do, when you don't know what to do. (Wheatley, 1984, p. 1)

These definitions are examples of literally dozens and dozens of definitions that continue to be offered in the literature. Most of the definitions that one encounters in the literature differ primarily on three dimensions. First, they differ in terms of their *semantic content,* that is, in which actions and thoughts are classified as problem solving. To take two examples from the aforementioned, affectively coping with the loss of a close relative, for instance, would be considered problem solving by Heppner and Krauskopf, but would not be considered problem solving by Anderson. Second, the definitions differ in how fuzzy their *boundaries* are. The boundary of Anderson's definition is clearly more precise, or less fuzzy, than the boundaries of the definitions presented by Heppner and Krauskopf or Wheatley. What exactly is meant, for instance, by Heppner and Krauskopf's "internal or external demands or challenges?" And what exactly does Wheatley's "what you do" include and exclude? And finally, the definitions differ in terms of their *category size*, that is, in how many events are classified as problem solving.

If we find it difficult to define *problem solving*, then perhaps we can at least agree on a definition of the more basic term *problem*. The following are some of the commonly cited definitions of *problem*:

- A problem exists when the goal that is sought is not directly attainable by the performance of a simple act available in the animal's repertory; the solution calls for either a novel action or a new integration of available actions. (Thorndike, 1898, cited by Sheerer, 1963, p. 118)

- A problem occurs . . . if an organism follows a goal and does not know how to reach it. Whenever a given state cannot be converted into the desired state directly through the activation of obvious operations, thinking is needed to construct mediating actions. (Duncker, 1935, p. 1; translated by the authors)

- A question for which there is at the moment no answer is a problem. (Skinner, 1966, p. 225)

- A problem is a stimulus situation for which an organism does not have a ready response. (Davis, 1973, p. 12)

- A problem is a "stimulus situation for which an organism does not have a response," . . . a problem arises "when the individual cannot immediately and effectively respond to the situation." (Woods, Crow, Hoffman, & Wright, 1985, p. 1)

- A person is confronted with a problem when he wants something and does not know immediately what series of actions he can perform to get it. (Newell & Simon, 1972, p. 72)

- Whenever there is a gap between where you are now and where you want to be, and you don't know how to find a way to cross that gap, you have a problem. (Hayes, 1980, p. i)

As in the case of problem solving, it should be readily apparent that the one and only, universally accepted definition of what constitutes a problem does not exist. Most of the definitions in the literature appear to differ again on primarily three dimensions: (a) their semantic content, or more precisely, a focus on either the absence of a task-relevant *response* or the absence of a task-relevant *thought* that would lead to a solution for the task at hand, (b) the fuzziness of their boundaries, and (c) their category size, that is, in how many tasks are classified as problems.

For example, the definitions provided by Thorndike, Davis, and Woods et al., respectively, focus on the absence of an observable response, whereas most of the remaining definitions focus on the absence of a nonobservable thought or cognition. Thus, a known, yet complicated mathematical equation that requires hours to be solved and thus may not lead to an observable response for a long time, may be classified as a problem according to some definitions, but may not constitute a problem according to other definitions.

On the other hand, however, most, if not all, of the definitions just given do appear to share an important component, namely a focus on the *distance* between the task and the solver, rather than a focus on the nature of the task itself. That is, a problem is said to exist only if there is a gap between task and solver, or a barrier between the state given in the actual situation and the goal state in the head of the problem solver. A problem is not defined by task features, but rather by the interaction between task requirements and solver, that is, by the interaction between task characteristics and person characteristics. In general, gap definitions imply that the same task may constitute a problem for one solver, but not for another, whereas task definitions assume that a given task either constitutes, or does not constitute, a problem for all solvers.

Explicit Versus Implicit Definitions

The impression that all definitions of *problem* share a common aspect, namely a focus on the task-person interaction, quickly disappears, however, when we consider implicit, in addition to, explicit definitions of a problem. By an explicit definition, we mean a definition that is articulated in writing, or is at least stated verbally. Thus, all of the examples given previously constitute explicit definitions of problem and problem solving, respectively. By an implicit definition, in contrast, we mean an operational definition that one uses in one's research. Ideally, the implicit definition is accompanied by, and consistent with, an explicit definition. However, frequently the implicit definition is the only definition a researcher uses, and worse, on occasion, the implicit definition used may not be consistent with the explicit definition that one subscribes to.

By their very nature, implicit definitions are hidden and can be discovered only if one carefully examines the details of the research performed under the heading of problem solving. For instance, historically, much of what is generally considered problem-solving research has been concerned with subjects' performances on classroom tasks that are well-structured (e.g., "what does 15×16 equal?"). For these tasks, subjects typically do not immediately know the correct answer, although they know how to get the answers, that is, how to solve the task. Such tasks would not be considered problems according to any of the explicit definitions previously discussed. However, by using these tasks in what is labeled as *problem-solving research*, one implicitly defines *problem* in terms of task characteristics.

Thus, explicitly, problems have been defined in terms of the interaction between task and individual; implicitly, however, problems frequently have been defined in terms of their task properties. If we accept the explicit definitions of *problem solving*, then research that has used exerciselike tasks cannot be relevant to our understanding of problem solving. The extensive literature on routine versus non-routine problem solving (Davis, 1985), for instance, would not belong to the area of problem solving. If we accept the implicit definitions, in contrast, then any theoretical treatment of problem solving that is based on an explicit definition cannot adequately cover our empirical findings (except in the unlikely case that both explicit and implicit definitions are identical in scope and content). For instance, much of what we know about the performance of novices on exercises and most of what we know about expertise would not accurately be included in problem-solving theory because most of the work to date has compared the performance of novices and experts on the solution of tasks that can only be considered exercises for the experts.

To summarize, definitions of *problem solving* and *problem*, both explicit and implicit, differ widely. Some definitions focus on the interaction between task characteristics and observable behavior, other definitions focus on the interaction between task characteristics and nonobservable cognitions, whereas still other definitions focus on task characteristics alone. In addition, definitions differ in their category size and in how precise, or how fuzzy, their boundaries are.

Why Do Definitions Differ?

Why is it that psychologists do not seem to be able to agree on definitions of *problem* and *problem solving*? After all, physicists appear to agree on the meaning of an atom, and mathematicians seem to have no quarrel with the meaning of an equation. But then, is it even necessary to subscribe to a common definition? Why not simply accept a variety of different definitions? Why not interpret a researcher's findings simply on the basis of the, explicit or implicit, definition provided by the researcher?

We believe that in order to meaningfully discuss these questions, it is helpful to distinguish between two aspects of a definition: (a) its purpose, and (b) its perceived usefulness. The primary purpose of a definition, we submit, is to facilitate accurate communication among all people who use the defined term. Whether or not a definition meets its purpose is directly related, for example, to how clearly the definition distinguishes between aspects that are to be included and those that are to be excluded. In this regard, the better defined the boundaries of a term, that is, the less fuzzy the boundaries, the better a definition meets its purpose. For example, Anderson's (1980) definition of *problem solving* contains clearer boundaries than Wheatley's (1984) definition. Therefore, Anderson's definition is a better definition than Wheatley's if one applies the purpose criterion.

However, the primary reason for why one particular definition is favored over another one, we argue, is not that the one definition meets the purpose criterion and the other one does not. Rather, the reason for why one particular definition is favored has to do with what we call the *perceived usefulness of definitions*. By usefulness, at least in the context of theoretical and empirical psychological research, we mean the extent to which a definition allows meaningful generalizations to be drawn. An advantage on the purpose criterion does not automatically translate into an advantage on the usefulness criterion. Consider the following example. Assume *problem* is very narrowly defined such that it includes only addition problems (e.g., 2 + 1). Further assume that we find empirically that second graders perform worse on these problems than third graders (hardly a surprise here). Note that although our narrow definition would score high on purpose because it very clearly specifies which tasks are considered problems and which ones are not, the definition would not allow us to generalize our findings to tasks other than simple addition problems. Thus, the usefulness of our definition would be severely limited. In general, the usefulness of a definition varies with the number of instances that are covered by the definition and over which meaningful generalizations are possible.

The Perceived Usefulness of a Definition

We argue that, again in the context of psychological research, meeting the purpose criterion is a prerequisite of a useful definition. Before a definition can be useful, one needs to be clear about what its boundaries are. Once the purpose criterion has been met, however, that is, once a definition has been formulated that has precise boundaries, what matters is the definition's usefulness. We further argue that the usefulness of a definition is not an objective property of a definition in the sense that a given definition is judged as more or less useful by everyone in the field. Rather, researchers differ in how useful they judge a definition. We believe that the perceived usefulness of definitions, on the one hand, is a consequence of a researcher's prior knowledge, beliefs, and theoretical goals, and, on the other hand, is primarily responsible for the variety of definitions we observe in most areas of psychology, including the area of problem solving.

The Role of Theoretical Goals

Hunt (1991) recently distinguished among three different goals that one may have in mind when studying problem solving, namely the extraction of scientific, engineering, or humanistic explanations. When the goal is to extract scientific explanations of problem solving, the focus is on the observation of empirical laws and the formulation of simple, but general principles from which the empirical laws can be deduced. Questions of interest for those interested in extracting scientific explanations of problem solving, are, for example, "Which cognitive processes are performed in which sequence to arrive at the solution of a problem," or "How are solutions to previous problems stored in our memory?"

When the goal of studying problem solving is to extract engineering explanations, in contrast, one is primarily interested in generating instructions that are useful for solving a particular set of problems. Thus, potentially interesting questions would be, "Does positive feedback facilitate problem solving?" or "How can we best structure the problem-solving context such that the probability of successful problem solving is optimized?" In general, scientific and engineering explanations differ in that scientific explanations search for general principles explaining the process of problem solving, whereas engineering explanations search for principles that increase the likelihood of success in problem solving. Although engineering principles might be derived from scientific principles, they need not be. In fact, we know a good deal about how to structure the environment such that success at problem solving is increased, without knowing why our methods work.

Humanistic explanations, finally, are personal interpretations of events such that the events make sense to us. Thus, humanistic explanations of the events described in a piece of art differ widely across interpreters, as do humanistic explanations of why it is that our paper was rejected by a prestigious journal, to use an example that is closer to home.

How is the perceived usefulness of a definition affected by theoretical goals? We argue that a definition is perceived as useful only if the definition is consistent with one's theoretical goals. If one's goal is to establish a scientific explanation, for example, then a definition of problem solving focusing on the cognitive operations by which a goal is accomplished (e.g., Anderson, 1980) is perceived as useful. If, in contrast, one's goal is to extract an engineering explanation, then any useful definition will probably need to focus on the interaction between problem solver and the environmental context that increases the likelihood of success. If one's goal is to generate a humanistic explanation, then a definition of problem solving may need to focus on the achievement of a subjectively meaningful interpretation of a situation to be perceived as useful.

In summary, what one wants to know about problem solving, that is the theoretical goals, determines to a certain extent whether or not one perceives a definition of problem solving as useful. Theoretical goals that one may have are not limited to the ones mentioned previously, of course. For instance, if one is interested in a scientific explanation of problem solving that considers the neurophysiological substrates of problem solving, then a definition focusing on the cognitive processes would be rather meaningless. Instead, one would probably want to define problem solving in terms of the neurophysiological processes that occur while one engages in a certain type of behavior.

The Role of Beliefs

The perceived usefulness of a definition is affected by one's prior beliefs just as much as it is affected by one's theoretical goals. With prior beliefs, in this context, we mean primarily beliefs that determine how one goes about generating scientific, engineering, or humanistic explanations of problem solving. The effect of prior beliefs may be most evident in scientific explanations. Researchers differ, for instance, in the extent to which their theorizing considers the behavioral, cognitive, or neurophysiological level. If one holds the belief, for example, that theories should be stated primarily in terms of observable behavior, then a definition of problem solving in terms of cognitive operations would not be perceived as useful (see definitions by Davis, 1973; Skinner, 1966; Thorndike, 1898; Woods et al., 1985, previously mentioned). If, in contrast, one holds the belief that psychologically meaningful theories should be formulated at a neurophysiological level, then definitions in terms of both observable behavior and cognitive operations would be perceived as meaningless.

One may argue that our discussion of the effects of prior beliefs is obsolete, given our discussion of theoretical goals because different prior beliefs lead to different theoretical goals. That is, if one's prior belief is that humans can best be understood only at a behavioral level, for instance, then one's theoretical goal will be to formulate scientific explanations at a behavioral level. Thus, the effect of prior beliefs on accepting a definition as useful would be an indirect one, mediated, so to speak, by theoretical goals. Although this may indeed frequently be the case, we argue that it need not always be the case. Different prior beliefs may lead to the same theoretical goals, and the same prior belief may still lead to the formulation of different theoretical goals. For example, even though some researchers may disagree on the proper level at which theorizing should occur, they may agree on using the experimental method for generating scientific laws. Conversely, even though researchers may agree on what constitutes the proper level of theorizing, they may yet disagree on how to extract scientific knowledge.

The Role of Prior Knowledge

Definitions are not static concepts that, for a given set of prior beliefs and theoretical goals, remain unchanged over time. Rather, definitions are very dynamic concepts that change as new knowledge becomes available.

To take a decidedly nonproblem-solving example, today's definitions of *music* would normally include what is labeled as rock and roll. But imagine a person who never heard this sort of music before; very likely, the definition of this person would label rock and roll as noise. Similarly, definitions of *art* would change dependent on a person's prior knowledge of Pablo Picasso's work. Prior knowledge thus places constraints on what is perceived as a meaningful definition.

This general principle has been rather obvious in the area of problem solving as well. Not too long ago, it was thought that any problem solving might be accomplished by a limited set of procedures. That is, it was argued that a limited number of general algorithms—sequences of mental steps that are guaranteed to arrive at a solution if a solution exists—might suffice to solve any problem of any kind (Groner, Groner, & Bischof, 1983). Groner et al., for instance, described how Raimundus Lullus, a Spanish philosopher in the 13th century, searched for a general algorithm that would produce every truth. Both Descartes (Adam & Tannery, 1908) and Leibniz (Gerhardt, 1880) also seemed to have believed that algorithms could be found that would solve at least all mathematical problems, perhaps even philosophical problems. Gödel (1931), eventually, put to rest the search for an universal algorithm by showing that certain mathematical problems could not be solved by any algorithm.

More recently, researchers have been searching for heuristic methods, rather than algorithms, that would be capable of solving problems of any kind (e.g., Duncker, 1935; Newell, Shaw, & Simon, 1958; Polya, 1945). Heurisms are general problem-solving procedures that do not guarantee that a solution is found if it exists. Heurisms merely increase the probability that a solution is found. Work on artificial intelligence, however, has more and more led to the conclusion that general heuristics are typically too general to be helpful for any but novel problems (e.g., Newell, 1983). Thus, the prevailing opinion at this time is that many problems cannot be solved by utilizing a small number of domain-general heuristics, but rather can only be solved by using domain-specific knowledge and procedures.

Can We Ever Agree on a Universal Definition of Problem Solving?

It follows from our discussion that different researchers will agree on a definition only if the definition is perceived as useful by all of them. Whether or not the definition is perceived as useful, in turn, is constrained by the prior beliefs, knowledge, and goals of the researchers. This implies that we can agree on a definition of problem solving only to the extent that we can agree on the constraints that are to be placed on the formulation of the definition.

Some constraints, we believe, are more readily acceptable to most researchers than are others. For instance, prior knowledge constraints are relatively easy to accept because they are directly based on empirical research and are affected by opinion only to a limited degree. On the other hand, beliefs on how to best theorize about the human mind are probably tightly entrenched in researchers' thinking, and nearly impossible to change. Researchers' theoretical goals also differ, and might even change over time. Realistically, we cannot expect to find an universally accepted definition of problem solving. What we can expect to find, however, is a limited number of meaningful definitions that differ systematically in terms of the theoretical goals and beliefs that are held by their subscribers.

In summary, we distinguish between a definition's purpose and its perceived usefulness. The purpose of a definition is to facilitate accurate communication. A definition is perceived as useful if meaningful generalizations can be drawn across the cases, or instances, subsumed by the definition. We argue that generalizations are meaningful if they are consistent with what we (a) already know about the entity that is to be defined, and if they are consistent with, (b) our prior beliefs and, (c) our theoretical goals. We do not claim, of course, that these are the only variables affecting whether one perceives a definition as useful or not. Our general point is simply that different definitions exist because the perceived usefulness of a definition varies across people in a systematic way.

In the next section, we present definitions of problem solving that have been offered by the contributors to this volume, and discuss the theoretical goals that underlie these definitions. Our discussion serves three purposes. First, it serves as an illustration of our general point that different researchers adopt different definitions of problem solving because they differ in their theoretical goals and beliefs. Second, it allows us to clarify which topic the research described in this volume is exactly concerned with. Third, it allows us to compare the mainstream approach chosen by many European researchers with the mainstream approach chosen by many of their North American counterparts. To foreshadow our main point: We argue that the definitions adopted by many of the European and North American researchers differ, at least in emphasis, and that consequently the two areas of research are concerned with different phenomena that overlap only partially. The two approaches are thus best considered complementary.

DEFINITIONS OF PROBLEM SOLVING: THE EUROPEAN APPROACH

The Contributors' View

We asked all of the contributors to this volume to provide us with a short definition of *complex problem solving* (CPS) as they use the term in their chapter. Following are, in alphabetical order, their occasionally somewhat shortened and edited answers.

Beckmann & Guthke. CPS represents a class of task demands the cognitive mastery of which calls for the recognition of causal relations among the variables of a system.

Berry. Deciding whether a task should be considered as being complex or not, seems to be a relative rather than an absolute issue. Some tasks seem to be complex when compared with many traditional experimental problem-solving tasks. In these cases, the large number of variables and their interconnectivity, the intransparency, the time lags, and the large number of goals to be met all contribute to task complexity.

Brehmer. I am concerned with peoples ability to handle tasks that are complex, dynamic (in the sense that their state changes both autonomously and as a consequence of the decision makers actions), and opaque (in the sense that the decision maker may not be able to directly see the task states or task structure).

Buchner. CPS is the successful interaction with task environments that are dynamic (i.e., change as a function of the user's interventions and/or as a function of time) and in which some, if not all, of the environment's regularities can only be revealed by successful exploration and integration of the information gained in that process.

Dörner. CPS concerns the behavior of people or groups of people in complex, dynamic, and intransparent situations where the exact structure and properties of the situations are relatively unknown. The complex problem solver permanently elaborates on her goals and constructs hypotheses about the (unknown) structure of the domain. He or she makes decisions and needs to control the results.

U. Funke. The main objective of applying paradigms of CPS research for personnel selection is to use more complex, meaningful, integrative, and realistic tasks requiring higher order thinking processes and skills. Personnel selection and training applications adopt research paradigms as a technology and lack a common definition of CPS.

Huber. CPS is the task of optimizing one or more target variables of a system by a series of decisions. The system consists of several variables, there are several alternative actions. Information about the system or system states is incomplete (e.g., not available or probabilistic) or delayed. A time component may be involved.

Kluwe. 1. Referring to the task environment, complex problems may be characterized by a large number of interrelated components (or variables); 2. Referring to the problem space, complex problems may be characterized by a large number of different cognitive operations that are necessary for searching through the problem space (e.g., the number of steps of a program simulating solution search). 3. Complex problems, finally, may be decomposed into smaller subproblems.

Krems. A problem is called "complex" when goal-state and initial-state are clearly described, and when there is (a) no precise definition of the problem space (not complete) and/or (b) no precise definition of the operators available (what can be done). Both (a) and (b) depend on domain-specific features (e.g., the context, the number and connectivity of relevant variables) and on the level of expertise (amount of knowledge about the domain-specific features). In general, I use the term CPS as more or less equivalent to problem solving in semantically rich domains or in knowledge-rich tasks.

Although the definitions presented previously are all different from each other in some respects, they share some important characteristics. For example, all definitions describe problem solving as a cognitive, rather than behavioral or neurophysiological, activity. This should not surprise us, given that most researchers in this volume are interested in scientific or engineering explanations of problem solving. That is, they are interested in the mental steps underlying problem solving (e.g., Berry & Broadbent, this volume; Brehmer, this volume; Huber, this volume; J. Funke, this volume), in how problem-solving performance can be improved (e.g., Brehmer, this volume), or in how to best select people such that they can deal with known task demands (e.g., U. Funke, this volume). Furthermore, all researchers represented in this volume subscribe, at least implicitly, to the Information-Processing framework as the theoretical framework within which to formulate general psychological principles.

What may appear surprising, however, is the consistent lack of an emphasis on the interaction between problem and solver. That is, most definitions do not appear to be gap definitions; rather, most definitions define a problem in terms of the task specifications a solver faces. For example, Brehmer defines a problem as a task that is "complex, dynamic, . . . and opaque." Similarly, Kluwe states that a problem consists of a "large number of interrelated components." Berry refers to a relativistic point of view that, nevertheless, is restricted by task attributes. The emphasis on task features, rather than the task-solver interaction, is even more obvious when we consider implicit definitions of problem solving. For example, many of the contributors to this volume, and indeed most of those performing contemporary problem-solving research in Europe, use complex computerized scenarios as their problems. Because these problems are novel, subjects do not typically differ in terms of the background knowledge they bring to bear on the tasks. Thus, any influence of prior knowledge is minimized, and the researchers' main interest is in how task characteristics affect problem solving.

The reason for the apparent emphasis in European research on task specifics, rather than on the task-solver interaction, is perhaps best understood historically. Therefore, a brief excursion into the recent history of problem-solving research is in order.

Historical Roots

Beginning with the early experimental work of the Gestaltists in Germany (e.g., Duncker, 1935), and continuing through the 1960s and early 1970s, research on problem solving was typically conducted with relatively simple, laboratory tasks (e.g., Duncker's X-ray problem; Ewert & Lambert's, 1932, disk problem, later known as Tower of Hanoi) that were novel to subjects (e.g., Mayer, 1992). Simple novel tasks were used for various reasons: They had clearly defined optimal solutions, they were solvable within a relatively short time frame, subjects' problem-solving steps could be traced, and so on. The underlying assumption was, of course, that simple tasks, such as the Tower of Hanoi, captured the main properties of real problems, and that the cognitive processes underlying subjects' solution attempts on simple problems were representative of the processes engaged in when solving "real" problems. Thus, simple problems were used for reasons of convenience, and generalizations to more complex problems were thought possible. Perhaps the best known and most impressive example of this line of research is the work by Newell and Simon (1972).

During the Gestaltists days and the 1960s and early 1970s, the prevailing definitions of problem solving at least implicitly contained three assumptions: (a) the theoretical goal was to understand the cognitive processes of a person solving a problem, (b) cognitive processes were guided by internal goals, and (c) perhaps most importantly, the cognitive processes were essentially the same for all kinds of problems. Problems were typically defined such that they represented situations for the person that could not be solved by the mere application of existing knowledge; thus, problems were typically domain-general, or knowledge-lean (e.g., VanLehn, 1989).

However, beginning in the 1970s, researchers became increasingly convinced that empirical findings and theoretical concepts derived from simple laboratory tasks were not generalizable to more complex, real-life problems. Even worse, it appeared that the processes underlying CPS in different domains were different from each other. These realizations have led to rather different responses in North America and Europe.

In North America, initiated by the work of Simon on learning by doing in semantically rich domains (e.g., Anzai & Simon, 1979; Bhaskar & Simon, 1977), researchers began to investigate problem solving separately in different natural knowledge domains (e.g., physics, writing, chess playing) and gave up on their attempt to extract a global theory of problem solving (e.g., Sternberg & Frensch, 1991). Instead, these researchers frequently focus on the development of problem solving within a certain domain, that is on the development of expertise (e.g., Anderson, Boyle, & Reiser, 1985; Chase & Simon, 1973; Chi, Feltovich, & Glaser, 1981). Areas that have attracted rather intensive attention in North America include such diverse fields as reading (Stanovich & Cunningham, 1991), writing (Bryson, Bereiter, Scardamalia, & Joram, 1991), calculation (Sokol & McCloskey, 1991), political decision-making (Voss, Wolfe, Lawrence, & Engle, 1991), managerial problem-solving (Wagner, 1991), lawyers' reasoning (Amsel, Langer, & Loutzenhiser, 1991), mechanical problem-solving (Hegarty, 1991), problem solving in electronics (Lesgold & Lajoie, 1991), computer skills (Kay, 1991), and game playing (Frensch & Sternberg, 1991).

The European Situation

In Europe, two main approaches surfaced, one initiated by Broadbent (1977; see Berry & Broadbent, this volume) in Great Britain and the other one by Dörner (1975, 1985; see also Dörner, Drewes, & Reither, 1975; Dörner & Reither, 1978; see Dörner & Wearing, this volume) in Germany. The two approaches have in common an emphasis on relatively complex, semantically rich, computerized laboratory tasks that are constructed to be similar to real life problems. The approaches differ somewhat in their theoretical goals and methodology, however. The tradition initiated by Broadbent emphasizes the distinction between cognitive problem-solving processes that operate under awareness versus outside of awareness, and typically employs mathematically well-defined computerized systems. The tradition initiated by Dörner, on the other hand, is interested in the interplay of the cognitive, motivational, and social components of problem solving, and utilizes very complex computerized scenarios that contain up to 2,000 highly interconnected variables (e.g., Dörner, Kreuzig, Reither, & Stäudel's, 1983, Lohhausen project; Ringelband, Misiak, & Kluwe, 1990).

In summary, researchers' realization that problem-solving processes differ across knowledge domains and across levels of expertise and that, consequently, findings obtained in the laboratory cannot necessarily be generalized to problem-solving situations outside the laboratory, has during the past two decades, led to an emphasis on real world problem solving. This emphasis has been expressed quite differently in North America and Europe, however. Whereas North American research typically concentrates on studying problem solving in separate, natural knowledge domains, much of the European research focuses on novel, complex problems, and has been performed with computerized scenarios (see Funke, 1991, for an overview).

In essence, we argue that the current North American and European mainstream approaches to studying problem solving have adopted different definitions of problem solving. Much of the North American research compares the cognitive processes engaged in by experts and novices when faced with natural, knowledge-based tasks that constitute problems for novices and exercises for experts, and thus focuses primarily on learning. In contrast, much of the European work is conducted with complex tasks that are novel to all subjects. The emphasis here is on the mental steps underlying the solution process of novel and complex tasks.

An Integrated View

Following we offer our own definition of *CPS*, a definition that is firmly rooted in the European tradition and, in fact, incorporates many aspects of the definitions provided by the contributors to this volume (see previously discussed definitions). According to our definition,

> CPS occurs to overcome barriers between a given state and a desired goal state by means of behavioral and/or cognitive, multistep activities. The given state, goal state, and barriers between given state and goal state are complex, change dynamically during problem solving, and are intransparent. The exact properties of the given state, goal state, and barriers are unknown to the solver at the outset. CPS implies the efficient interaction between a solver and the situational requirements of the task, and involves a solver's cognitive, emotional, personal, and social abilities and knowledge.

Notice the differences between our definition and the definitions that feature prominent in the North American tradition. Anderson (1980, see beginning of this chapter), for the North American approach for example, defined *problem solving* as "any goal-directed sequence of cognitive operations" (p. 257), regardless of whether the task is novel or familiar to the solver, regardless of whether or not the task is complex, and regardless of whether or not a single barrier or multiple barriers exist between given state and goal state. Our definition, in contrast, constrains potential problems by requiring that they be (a) novel tasks that subjects are unfamiliar with, (b) complex, (c) dynamically changing over time, and (d) intransparent. In order to solve these problems, a solver has to be able to anticipate what will happen over time, and has to consider side effects of potential actions.

Also, note that according to our definition CPS is not simply an extension of simple problem solving (SPS), that is, problem solving involving relatively simple laboratory problems. CPS and SPS are qualitatively different. For example, whereas in SPS typically a single barrier needs to be overcome, in CPS a large number of barriers exists. Because there are multiple barriers, a single cognitive or behavioral activity may not be sufficient to reach the goal state. Rather, a well-planned, prioritized, set of cognitions and actions needs to be performed in order to get closer to the goal state.

In addition, note that in contrast to earlier, often implicit views, CPS is not viewed as deterministic in the sense that any problem-solving activity will always lead to the solution of a problem. Rather, CPS may lead to an approximate solution that may advance the solver but may not lead to actually solving the problem. For example, subjects performing the duties of the mayor of a computer-simulated town, may, even after some practice, still not be able to generate the best possible solution to a given problem. In fact, many, often computerized, tasks exist for which—due to the complex nonlinear relations among the task variables—the optimal solution is unknown. Of course, the absence of an optimal solution, while theoretically reasonable and even desirable, poses a problem to experimenters who want to determine the quality of subjects' performances, and to those who use microworlds for personnel selection purposes (see U. Funke, this volume).

Finally, because both the given state and goal state and also the barriers are intransparent in CPS, it is difficult for a solver to evaluate his or her progress toward problem solution. This makes it necessary for the solver to select and structure the interactions with the task such that information that is helpful for the evaluation of progress can be extracted.

Readers might want to keep our definition in mind when going through the following chapters. With a few exceptions (e.g., Krems, this volume), this definition or a somewhat modified version thereof, has been adopted by the contributors to this volume and by most of the European researchers in the area.

Summary

In summary, researchers adopt definitions that they perceive as useful, that is, that are consistent with their beliefs, knowledge, and theoretical goals. A definition can therefore be neither static nor commonly accepted. Rather, for any domain of research, a number of meaningful definitions coexist. In the area of problem-solving research, the current theoretical goals are quite different for North American and European researchers. The primary goal adopted by many North American researchers is to understand task performance and learning in natural knowledge domains. The primary goal adopted by many European researchers, in contrast, is to understand how people deal with complex, novel task situations. Because the theoretical goals differ for the two traditions, the definitions that have been adopted differ as well. Consequently, the two traditions are not concerned with the same phenomenon, and any comparison of research findings runs the risk of being meaningless.

A THEORETICAL FRAMEWORK
FOR COMPLEX PROBLEM SOLVING

In the previous two sections, we argued that the choice of a definition is affected by a researcher's theoretical goals, beliefs, and prior knowledge, and that a definition, once selected, affects how a phenomenon is empirically approached. A definition not only affects how a subject is studied empirically, however; it also affects which theoretical explanations of a phenomenon are acceptable. At a general level, this point is rather obvious. After all, one needs to explain what one studies. In addition, however, there are many, much more subtle, interactions between a definition and a theory. For example, if problem solving is defined in terms of cognitive, rather than neurophysiological, biological, or behavioral, processes, then it makes little sense to construct a theory of problem solving at a neurophysiological, biological, or behavioral level. The theoretical level must thus match the level adopted in the definition. In general, just as the choice of a definition is affected by theoretical goals, beliefs, and prior knowledge, so is the choice of an acceptable theoretical framework.

In the following, we present our thoughts on how a general theoretical framework for understanding problem solving that is based on our definition of CPS might look like. Our framework is based on the assumptions that, (a) our theoretical goal is to understand the interplay among cognitive, motivational, personal, and social factors when complex, novel, dynamic, intransparent tasks are solved, and, (b) the interplay among the various components can best be understood within an Information-Processing model. The framework is constrained, of course, by what is known already about CPS as it is defined above. Following, we therefore present a brief, nonexhaustive list of the main empirical phenomena that have been demonstrated in recent years, thereby summarizing many of the findings presented in this volume.

Internal Subject Factors

Experience. CPS appears to vary with the amount of experience an individual has in the task domain at hand (e.g., Krems, this volume). Experience affects the likelihood of successful problem solving, but more importantly, it affects which strategies are employed. It influences, for instance, whether or not a person experiments with a task; that is, whether or not the person exhaustively tests the hypotheses about task relations and tries to falsify the assumptions.

Cognitive Variables. There is considerable evidence that cognitive variables, such as background knowledge, monitoring and evaluation strategies, and cognitive style affect CPS. There is even evidence indicating that general intelligence, when measured appropriately, affects at least some aspects of CPS (e.g., Beckmann & Guthke, this volume). Also, it appears that at least under certain conditions, CPS performance and explicit task knowledge may be dissociable. That is, performance improvements can be found even in the absence of explicit knowledge about the task (e.g., Berry & Broadbent, this volume).

Noncognitive Variables. CPS appears to be enhanced by some noncognitive factors such as self-confidence, perseverance, motivation, and enjoyment. In general, both personality and social factors appear to influence CPS (e.g., Dörner & Wearing, this volume).

External Factors

Problem Structure. CPS appears to vary with the structure of the task including the semantics of the task, the complexity of the task, the transparency of the task, and so on (e.g., J. Funke, this volume).

Problem Context. The likelihood of successful CPS performance seems to vary with the semantic embeddedness of a task, that is, with whether or not the task is couched within a well-understood and familiar context (e.g., Huber, this volume).

Environmental Factors. Successful CPS performance is influenced by the environment within which a solver operates. This includes feedback and feedback delay, expectations, cooperation, peer pressure, and so on (e.g., Brehmer, this volume).

The Components of a Theory of CPS

These empirical findings have led us to construct a simple theoretical framework for understanding CPS that is depicted in Figure 1.1. The figure summarizes the basic components of our framework as well as the interrelations among the components. As can be seen, the framework contains three separate components: the problem solver, the task, and the environment.

Within the problem solver, we distinguish between static memory content and dynamic information processing. Memory is divided further into domain-general and domain-specific knowledge both of which affect CPS performance. Information processing includes the task strategies that are selected and the processes of task monitoring and progress evaluation. In addition, noncognitive problem-solver variables such as motivation and personality also factor into CPS performance.

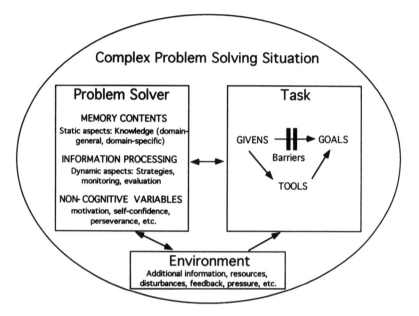

FIG. 1.1. CPS is viewed as the interaction between a problem solver and a task in the context of an environment. The figure shows only static aspects of the interaction. For additional information, see text.

The task itself is depicted in terms of the barriers that exist between a given state and a goal state (see our remarks on the gap definition). As explained previously, the barriers are assumed to be complex, dynamically changing, and intransparent; the transition from given to goal state is constraint by the problem solver's memory content and information processing, and by the tools that are available to the solver.

The environment includes the resources that are available for problem solving, as well as feedback, expectations, cooperation, peer pressure, disturbances, and so on. The environment affects both the problem solver and the task. It affects the problem solver by constraining the information processes that can be used and by influencing which knowledge is accessible. The environment affects the task by offering additional information, constraining which tools may be used, and so on. In addition, the environment can be changed actively by the problem solver but not by the task.

From this very simple view of CPS, it should become clear that two of the main questions that will need to be addressed by future research are as follows: Which components within the problem solver, task, and environment affect CPS in which way? How do the various components—the person, task, and environment—interact in affecting CPS performance? Clearly, much more research will need to be conducted before we can attempt to answer these questions.

SUMMARY

We argued that existing definitions of *problem solving* and *problem*, both explicit and implicit, differ widely. Some definitions focus on the interaction between task characteristics and observable behavior, other definitions focus on the interaction between task characteristics and nonobservable cognitions, whereas still other definitions focus on task characteristics alone. In addition, definitions differ in their category size and in how precise, or how fuzzy, their boundaries are.

We have made the distinction between a definition's purpose and its perceived usefulness. The purpose of a definition is to facilitate accurate communication. A definition is perceived as useful if meaningful generalizations can be drawn across the cases, or instances, subsumed by the definition. We have further argued that researchers adopt definitions that they perceive as useful, that is, that are consistent with their beliefs, knowledge, and theoretical goals. A definition can therefore be neither static nor commonly accepted. As an example, we stated that in the area of problem-solving research, the current theoretical goals are quite different for mainstream North American and European researchers. The primary goal adopted by many North American researchers is to understand task performance and learning in natural knowledge domains. The primary goal adopted by many European researchers, in contrast, is to understand how people deal with complex, novel task situations. Consequently, the definitions of problem solving adopted within the two approaches differ as well.

We have offered a definition of CPS that is consistent with the theoretical goal adopted by many of the European researchers, and, finally, have described our thoughts on how a theoretical framework of CPS that is based on this definition might look like.

In conclusion, we believe that research on CPS, despite its many shortcomings and despite the diverse approaches taken by North American and European researchers, carries the promise of a more realistic, real life approach to the psychology of action control within complex environments than has been offered in the past. This is a new and exciting area of research, and as the old saying goes, "Nothing is as promising as a beginning."

REFERENCES

Adam, C., & Tannery, P. (1908). *Oeuvres de Descartes (Vol. X)*. Paris: Léopold Cerf.
Amsel, E., Langer, R., & Loutzenhiser, L. (1991). Do lawyers reason differently from psychologists? A comparative design for studying expertise. In R. J. Sternberg & P. A. Frensch (Eds.), *Complex problem solving: Principles and mechanisms* (pp. 223–250). Hillsdale, NJ: Lawrence Erlbaum Associates.
Anderson, J. R. (1980). *Cognitive psychology and its implications*. New York: Freeman.
Anderson, J. R., Boyle, C. B., & Reiser, B. J. (1985). Intelligent tutoring systems. *Science, 228*, 456–462.

Anzai, K., & Simon, H. A. (1979). The theory of learning by doing. *Psychological Review, 86*, 124–140.

Bhaskar, R., & Simon, H. A. (1977). Problem solving in semantically rich domains: An example from engineering thermodynamics. *Cognitive Science, 1*, 193–215.

Broadbent, D. E. (1977). Levels, hierarchies, and the locus of control. *Quarterly Journal of Experimental Psychology, 29*, 181–201.

Bryson, M., Bereiter, C., Scardamalia, M., & Joram, E. (1991). Going beyond the problem as given: Problem solving in expert and novice writers. In R. J. Sternberg & P. A. Frensch (Eds.), *Complex problem solving: Principles and mechanisms* (pp. 61–84). Hillsdale, NJ: Lawrence Erlbaum Associates.

Carroll, L. (1935). *Through the looking glass and what Alice found there*. New York: The Limited Editions Club.

Chase, W. G., & Simon, H. A. (1973). Perception in chess. *Cognitive Psychology, 4*, 55–81.

Chi, M. T. H., Feltovich, P. J., & Glaser, R. (1981). Categorization and representation of physics problems by experts and novices. *Cognitive Science, 5*, 121–152.

Davis, G. A. (1973). *Psychology of problem solving: Theory and practice*. New York: Basic Books.

Davis, R. B. (1985). Solving the "three switch" problem: A case study. *Journal of Mathematical Behavior, 4*, 281–291.

Dörner, D. (1975). Wie Menschen eine Welt verbessern wollten [How people wanted to improve the world]. *Bild der Wissenschaft, 12*, 48–53.

Dörner, D. (1985). Verhalten, Denken und Emotionen [Behavior, thinking, and emotions]. In L. H. Eckensberger & E. D. Lantermann (Eds.), *Emotion und Reflexivität* (pp. 157–181). München, Germany: Urban & Schwarzenberg.

Dörner, D., Drewes, U., & Reither, F. (1975). Über das Problemlösen in sehr komplexen Realitätsbereichen [Problem solving in very complex areas]. In W. H. Tack (Ed.), *Bericht über den 29. Kongreß der DGfPs in Salzburg 1974* (Band 1, pp. 339–340). Göttingen, Germany: Hogrefe.

Dörner, D., & Reither, F. (1978). Über das Problemlösen in sehr komplexen Realitätsbereichen [Problem solving in very complex areas]. *Zeitschrift für Experimentelle und Angewandte Psychologie, 25*, 527–551.

Duncker, K. (1935). *Zur Psychologie des produktiven Denkens* [The psychology of productive thinking]. Berlin: Julius Springer.

Ewert, P. H., & Lambert, J. F. (1932). Part II: The effect of verbal instructions upon the formation of a concept. *Journal of General Psychology, 6*, 400–411.

Frensch, P. A., & Sternberg, R. J. (1991). Skill-related differences in game playing. In R. J. Sternberg & P. A. Frensch (Eds.), *Complex problem solving: Principles and mechanisms* (pp. 343–381). Hillsdale, NJ: Lawrence Erlbaum Associates.

Funke, J. (1991). Solving complex problems: Human identification and control of complex systems. In R. J. Sternberg & P. A. Frensch (Eds.), *Complex problem solving: Principles and mechanisms* (pp. 185–222). Hillsdale, NJ: Lawrence Erlbaum Associates.

Gerhardt, C. I. (1875–1890). *Die philosophischen Schriften von G. W. Leipniz* [The philosophical writings of G. W. Leibnitz] (Vol. I–VII). Berlin: Weidmannsche Buchhandlung.

Gödel, K. (1931). Über formal unentscheidbare Sätze der Principia Mathematica und verwandter Systeme I [Formally untractable problems of the Principia Mathematica and related systems]. *Monatshefte für Mathematik und Physik, 38*, 173–198.

Groner, M., Groner, R., & Bischof, W. F. (1983). Approaches to heuristics: A historical review. In R. Groner, M. Groner, & W. F. Bischof (Eds.), *Methods of heuristics* (pp. 1–18). Hillsdale, NJ: Lawrence Erlbaum Associates.

Hayes, J. (1980). *The complete problem solver*. Philadelphia: Franklin Institute Press.

Hegarty, M. (1991). Knowledge and processes in mechanical problem solving. In R. J. Sternberg & P. A. Frensch (Eds.), *Complex problem solving: Principles and mechanisms* (pp. 253–285). Hillsdale, NJ: Lawrence Erlbaum Associates.

Heppner, P. P., & Krauskopf, C. J. (1987). An information-processing approach to personal problem solving. *The Counseling Psychologist, 15*, 371–447.

Hunt, E. (1991). Some comments on the study of complexity. In R. J. Sternberg & P. A. Frensch (Eds.), *Complex problem solving: Principles and mechanisms* (pp. 383–395). Hillsdale, NJ: Lawrence Erlbaum Associates.

Kay, D. S. (1991). Computer interaction: Debugging the problems. In R. J. Sternberg & P. A. Frensch (Eds.), *Complex problem solving: Principles and mechanisms* (pp. 317–340). Hillsdale, NJ: Lawrence Erlbaum Associates.

Lesgold, A., & Lajoie, S. (1991). Complex problem solving in electronics. In R. J. Sternberg & P. A. Frensch (Eds.), *Complex problem solving: Principles and mechanisms* (pp. 287–316). Hillsdale, NJ: Lawrence Erlbaum Associates.

Mayer, R. E. (1992). *Thinking, problem solving, cognition* (2nd ed.). New York: Freeman.

Newell, A. (1983). The heuristics of George Polya and its relation to artificial intelligence. In R. Groner, M. Groner, & W. F. Bischof (Eds.), *Methods of heuristics* (pp. 195–244). Hillsdale, NJ: Lawrence Erlbaum Associates.

Newell, A., Shaw, J. C., & Simon, H. A. (1958). Elements of a theory of human problem solving. *Psychological Review, 65*, 151–166.

Newell, A., & Simon, H. A. (1972). *Human problem solving.* Englewood Cliffs, NJ: Prentice-Hall.

Polya, G. (1945). *How to solve it.* Princeton, NJ: Princeton University Press.

Ringelband, O. J., Misiak, C., & Kluwe, R. H. (1990). Mental models and strategies in the control of a complex system. In D. Ackermann & M. J. Tauber (Eds.), *Mental models and human-computer interaction* (Vol. 1, pp. 151–164). Amsterdam: Elsevier Science.

Sheerer, M. (1963). Problem solving. *Scientific American, 208*, 118–128.

Skinner, B. F. (1966). An operant analysis of problem solving. In B. Kleinmuntz (Ed.), *Problem solving: Research, method, and theory* (pp. 225–257). New York: Wiley.

Smith, M. U. (1991). A view from biology. In M. U. Smith (Ed.), *Toward a unified theory of problem solving. Views from the content domains* (pp. 1–20). Hillsdale, NJ: Lawrence Erlbaum Associates.

Sokol, S. M., & McCloskey, M. (1991). Cognitive mechanisms in calculation. In R. J. Sternberg & P. A. Frensch (Eds.), *Complex problem solving: Principles and mechanisms* (pp. 85–116). Hillsdale, NJ: Lawrence Erlbaum Associates.

Stanovich, K. E., & Cunningham, A. E. (1991). Reading as constrained reasoning. In R. J. Sternberg & P. A. Frensch (Eds.), *Complex problem solving: Principles and mechanisms* (pp. 3–60). Hillsdale, NJ: Lawrence Erlbaum Associates.

Sternberg, R. J., & Frensch, P. A. (Eds.). (1991). *Complex problem solving: Principles and mechanisms.* Hillsdale, NJ: Lawrence Erlbaum Associates.

VanLehn, K. (1989). Problem solving and cognitive skill acquisition. In M. I. Posner (Ed.), *Foundations of cognitive science* (pp. 527–579). Cambridge, MA: MIT Press.

Voss, J. F., Wolfe, C. R., Lawrence, J. A., & Engle, R. A. (1991). From representation to decision: An analysis of problem solving in international relations. In R. J. Sternberg & P. A. Frensch (Eds.), *Complex problem solving: Principles and mechanisms* (pp. 119–158). Hillsdale, NJ: Lawrence Erlbaum Associates.

Wagner, R. K. (1991). Managerial problem solving. In R. J. Sternberg & P. A. Frensch (Eds.), *Complex problem solving: Principles and mechanisms* (pp. 159–183). Hillsdale, NJ: Lawrence Erlbaum Associates.

Webster's New Twentieth Century Dictionary (2nd ed.). (1979). New York: Simon & Schuster.

Wheatley, G. H. (1984). Problem solving in school mathematics. (MEPS Technical Report No. 84.01). West Lafayette, IN: Purdue University, School Mathematics and Science Center.

Woods, D. T., Crow, C. M., Hoffman, T. W., & Wright, J. D. (1985). Challenges to teaching problem solving skills. *Chem 13 News, 155*, 1–12. Waterloo, Ontario, Canada: University of Waterloo.

CHAPTER TWO

Basic Topics and Approaches to the Study of Complex Problem Solving

Axel Buchner
University of Trier, Germany

INTRODUCTION

Basic research in the area of complex problem solving (henceforth CPS) has been criticized repeatedly for its lack of a theoretical foundation (Funke, 1986, 1991a). As will become apparent, this state of affairs has changed little. There is still a long way to go before a level of theoretical resolution is achieved that is comparable to that of the related areas of learning and memory research. This chapter describes and evaluates important basic research approaches to the study of CPS. Besides being strongly biased toward basic research, the discussion is naturally confined to topics not covered in detail in other chapters.

What follows is divided into four sections. Quite conventionally, a bit of history will make up the first section of the chapter. The historical perspective is useful in sketching what could be considered major trends in CPS research, the discussion of which will be spiced with a number of the area's most aggravating methodological problems. Second, approaches will be presented that try to pin down what CPS is by relating it to constructs traditionally used to describe interindividual differences. Some of this research will be called *deficit oriented*, mostly because of some researchers' conviction that subjects who fail can tell us more than those who succeed. In contrast, the third section will introduce *competence oriented* approaches that focus on determinants of successful learning and control. These approaches typically base their theorizing on formal analyses to the task environments. The final section will try to name and characterize interesting future directions of research in the area.

HISTORICAL AND METHODOLOGICAL ASPECTS

As has been pointed out in the first chapter, research on problem solving— particularly in the German-speaking countries—dates back to the very early days of Experimental Psychology. Basic research that looks at how people interact with complex dynamic task environments did not become possible, however, until new technological advances enabled the simulation of complex systems in laboratories. While this was a necessary precondition for this new line of problem-solving research, the force behind it arose largely from two other, independent sources. One was a sincere discontent with the limitations of the theoretical concepts present at the time which did not seem to be able to explain how people control "buildings, equipment, manpower and consumable supplies" (Broadbent, 1977, p. 192). The second source was a dissatisfaction with a *one-sidedness* of tasks (see Dörner & Reither, 1978, p. 527) used in typical laboratory studies on problem solving such as chess or the disk problem (Ewert & Lambert, 1932; later the problem was referred to as the *Tower of Hanoi*). Such problems were criticized for being too simple, fully transparent, and static, whereas real-world economical, political, and technological problem situations were said to be complex, intransparent, and dynamic. Thus, controlling dynamic scenarios such as simulated economies, cities, and factories would seem to bring real world problems into the laboratory (Dörner, 1981). It is probably not a mere coincidence that such statements emerged at about the same time as Neisser

(1976) published his influential plea asking for ecologically more valid studies in Cognitive Psychology.

However, as should become evident in the reminder of this chapter, although both approaches appear to have been motivated similarly, there are fundamental differences between them in terms of methodology, research strategy, and theoretical development, to name just a few. For instance, Broadbent (1977), in illustrating this point, described a study in which subjects controlled a simple city TRANSPORTATION SYSTEM that was based on two simultaneous linear equations. The number of individuals per bus and the available parking space could be manipulated by altering the time interval between buses entering the city and by altering the parking fees. Broadbent emphasized that the system was deliberately kept simple and mathematically well-defined "to allow an analysis of psychological processes" (p. 192).

The other end of the continuum is occupied by the often-cited LOHHAUSEN study (Dörner, Kreuzig, Reither, & Stäudel, 1983; see also Dörner, 1981, 1987). In this study, subjects were asked to control a small town (named LOHHAUSEN) by manipulating, for instance, the working conditions, leisure time activities, taxes, the housing policy and the like. Overall, the LOHHAUSEN computer simulation comprised more than 2,000 highly interconnected variables, far too many for subjects to digest even within the span of 8 two-hour experimental sessions.[1] The goal for subjects governing LOHHAUSEN was deliberately kept vague. They were simply told to make sure the town would prosper in the future. Each subject interacted with the system indirectly by telling the experimenter which measures to take. The experimenter would then make the appropriate inputs. Also, subjects had to acquire the information they felt to be important by asking questions of the experimenters who, in turn, tried to answer at the level of aggregation of the questions. In sum, the LOHHAUSEN study combined a number of features believed to be relevant in real-life political and economic decision making.

To return to Broadbent (1977), his focus was on the striking disparity between his subjects' satisfactory control performance on the one side and the lack of subjects' ability to answer questions about the system they had learned to control on the other. The fundamental question was which overall cognitive architecture would be capable of explaining such findings. In subsequent studies, Broadbent and Berry and their coworkers were able to pin down a number of factors that appear to influence the development of either control performance or verbalizable knowledge or both (e.g., Berry,

---

[1]While LOHHAUSEN certainly represents the "tip of the iceberg," the naturalistic task environments used in the *systems thinking* program (Dörner, 1983a) generally tend to be quite large and complex with many interconnected variables—typically about 10–60 (see Funke, 1988, 1991b, for a review and brief characterization of these systems).

1993; Berry & Broadbent, 1984, 1987, 1988; Broadbent, 1989; Broadbent, FitzGerald, & Broadbent, 1986; Hayes & Broadbent, 1988; this important research program is described in detail by Berry & Broadbent, this volume).

In contrast, Dörner and his coworkers (Dörner, 1979, 1981; Dörner, Kreuzig, Reither, & Stäudel, 1983; Dörner & Reither, 1978) as well as a number of other researchers committed to the so-called *systems thinking* program (Dörner, 1983a) primarily looked at *interindividual differences* in the control of simulated systems, with a particular focus on subjects' *deficits*. The reason for the focus on deficits was that "certain tendencies in behavior are more apparent with 'failures' than with 'normal' or with 'good' subjects" (Dörner, 1981, p. 165; translation by the author). Poor control was hypothesized to be due, for instance, to people's disregard of dynamic trends, their inability to understand the concept of exponential growth (but see Gediga, Schöttke, & Tücke, 1983), or their reasoning in causal chains as opposed to causal nets. Dangerous situations were hypothesized to provoke "cognitive emergency reactions" in which subjects reacted fast and without consideration of the circumstances (see Dörner, 1981, p. 167).

Also, it appeared that control performance could not be predicted by traditional tests of intelligence, at least not under conditions of "intransparent" system presentation (Putz-Osterloh, 1981; Putz-Osterloh & Lüer, 1981). This surprising finding became one of the most publicly emphasized, but also most controversial, pieces of evidence in the area. For instance, one debate that has not yet come to an end is whether or not nonsignificant correlations between test intelligence scores and control performance are simply artifacts brought on by poor and unreliable measures of control performance (Dörner & Kreuzig, 1983; Funke, 1983; Putz-Osterloh, 1983a; Schaub, 1990; Strohschneider, 1986; for a comprehensive discussion of this issue see Beckmann & Guthke, this volume). In the same vein, it was argued that how people come to be able to control complex dynamic systems is a field of research that cannot be tackled with established theories, nor with the methodology currently available, but requires completely new theories and research methods.

However attractive this approach may seem, there are a number of problems that come with using simulated scenarios constructed to mimic some aspect of reality (more or less adequately). As Broadbent (1977) has noted, in order to allow for an analysis of psychological processes, the task environment subjects interact with must not be too complex. For instance, it is difficult, if not impossible, to compare different naturalistic scenarios because their formal properties are largely unknown (Funke, 1984). As a consequence, it is difficult, if not impossible, to compare the results of experiments employing such scenarios and, hence, it is not surprising that the findings in the area appear rather inconsistent (Funke, 1984; Hübner, 1989). A related point is that it is very difficult to manipulate isolated properties of unsystematically constructed naturalistic scenarios (Brehmer, Leplat, & Rasmussen, 1991)—an essential for experimental research.

Also, systems designed primarily to mimic some aspect of reality often do not have a unique target state. Some researchers regard this as a desirable feature because it seems to make the simulation correspond even more closely to real life (Dörner, Kreuzig, Reither, & Stäudel, 1983). However, the obvious drawback is that if there is no performance goal, then it becomes extremely difficult to derive a reasonable dependent measure for subjects' performance. Simply picking out a number of system variables that are felt to be "essential for the maintenance of the system" (Dörner, Kreuzig, Reither, & Stäudel, 1983, p. 156; translation by the author) may be frequent practice, but it is hardly satisfactory, particularly when it is done post-hoc. Further, with naturalistic and formally intractable systems it is usually impossible to specify an optimal intervention or a sequence of interventions given the current state of the system because the problem space is unknown. This, of course, implies that one has no rational criterion for assessing the quality of an individual's performance. Hence, the differences in performance among several subjects cannot be evaluated either.

The list of serious problems one gets into with naturalistic scenarios as task environments is far from complete (see Funke, 1986, and Hübner, 1989, for more details), but it may suffice to illustrate that there appears to be a trade-off between the face validity of a task environment and the methodological standards of investigations employing it. Also, it is of course debatable whether or not *any* simulation can approximate reality at all (see Dörner, 1981, p. 165). For instance, real-life decisions about complex dynamic task environments typically stretch over time, whereas laboratory studies take a few hours at the most. In addition, political and economical decisions are usually not made solipsistically but rather are made within a social context. The question then becomes, why should one use naturalistic systems at all?

This question has stimulated a number of researchers to reject the idea of approximating reality with simulated systems in the laboratory as their primary goal. Instead, they began to search for ways to design systems that are formally tractable while still being dynamic and complex (Buchner & Funke, 1993; Funke, 1986, 1990, 1992b; Funke & Buchner, 1992; Hübner, 1987, 1988, 1989; Kluwe, Misiak, & Haider, 1989; Ringelband, Misiak, & Kluwe, 1990; Thalmaier, 1979). As will be discussed later, these systems not only have a unique performance goal but also offer the means to determine an optimal intervention given an arbitrary system state. These systems are also open to experimental manipulation and control because the systems' properties are well-known. Naturally then, this line of research is characterized by attempts to study cognitive processes by systematically varying the properties of the task environments. While simply manipulating aspects of the task environment would, of course, not yield anything except a few statistically significant results (Eyferth, Schömann, & Widwoski, 1986), the systematic variation and control of system properties both helps to detect effects that are unique to a specific task, and it serves to estimate the impact of these properties on processes of knowledge acquisition and knowledge application.

At this point, it is interesting to note that, within the *systems thinking* tradition, a few naturalistic scenarios have become quite popular and are typically referred to by their proper names as if they constituted experimental paradigms in their own rights. A short list of examples includes MORO (Putz-Osterloh, 1985, 1987; Putz-Osterloh & Lemme, 1987; Roth, Meyer, & Lampe, 1991; Strohschneider, 1986, 1991; Stäudel, 1987), FIRE (Brehmer, 1987, this volume; Brehmer & Allard, 1991; Dörner & Pfeifer, 1992; Schoppek, 1991), and the TAILORSHOP (Funke, 1983; Hörmann & Thomas, 1989; Hussy, 1991; Lüer, Hübner, & Lass, 1985; Putz-Osterloh, 1981, 1983b, 1987; Putz-Osterloh & Lemme, 1987; Putz-Osterloh & Lüer, 1981; Süß, Kersting, & Oberauer, 1991).[2] This development most likely is a consequence of the fact that naturalistic scenarios are formally intractable systems with largely unknown properties such that they do not lend themselves to experimental manipulations. Needless to say, simply using a task with largely unknown properties over and over again is not a solution to the problem.

The availability of formal tools to describe the dynamic task environments with sufficient precision provided a first basis for theorizing about how system knowledge could be represented in memory. For instance, Funke (1985, 1986) has suggested a class of dynamic tasks based on linear equation systems. The relations among the variables of these systems can be described by deterministic multivariate autoregressive processes. Consequently, Funke (1985, 1986) hypothesized that a subject exploring and later controlling a dynamic task environment that is based on linear equation systems, gradually constructs a causal model of the task. In a certain sequence, information is added to the model corresponding to the autoregressive processes' parameters (such as the direction and the relative strength of the interconnection between two variables).

The idea of taking the formal model of a task as a starting point for theorizing about its mental representation is perhaps best illustrated by analogy to the role of formal logic in research on deductive reasoning. While early hypotheses discussed in the psychology of reasoning rested on the

---

[2]MORO is a developing country scenario in which subjects can influence the living conditions of a ficticious nomadic tribe. FIRE is a fire fighting scenario in which fire fighting units must be deployed so as to minimize the impact of fires that emerge unpredictably at various locations of an imaginary terrain. This scenario—with a different semantic embedding—was first used in military contexts. Finally, subjects managing the TAILORSHOP must run a simplistic small company by purchasing raw materials, hiring and firing workers, and the like. Again, these scenarios have been described in detail by Funke (1986, 1988, 1992b).

premise that human inferencing was to be seen in close analogy to formal logic (Beneke, 1833/1877), it appears that the systematic deviations from this premise were particularly interesting cases for both empirical research and theorizing (e.g., Wason & Johnson-Laird, 1972). Very similarly, formal system characteristics, for instance those of linear equation systems, can be used as a starting point for theorizing about the representation of such systems in memory.

To summarize, research on human performance when interacting with complex dynamic systems has been coarsely divided into two different main streams. One approach has been to use naturalistic scenarios in order to bring everyday problems into the laboratory, and to try to identify interindividual differences in how subjects control a dynamic system. In contrast, the other approach has been to use formally well-defined systems with known properties and to systematically manipulate features of the task environment to test assumptions about how people acquire and use knowledge in interacting with these tasks. Each approach appeals to a different part of the research community.

Of course, the distinction between the two lines of research is not quite as clear-cut as has been portrayed here. For instance, researchers employing naturalistic scenarios do in fact manipulate *some* features of their tasks— features that do not require any knowledge of formal system properties such as the semantic context of the system (Hesse, 1982a) or the degree to which the system variables' interrelations are made transparent to subjects (Putz-Osterloh & Lüer, 1981). Nevertheless, the bisection appears useful in that it captures the general trends in the field. With this in mind, it is now appropriate to go into more detail and look at some of the major empirical and theoretical developments in the area.

THE SEARCH FOR INDIVIDUAL DIFFERENCES

A number of diverse constructs have been used as determinants of interindividual differences in system control performance. Among them, we find constructs that are known to have a psychometric background, such as test intelligence or motivation. In addition, a number of concepts have been coined rather ad hoc to describe *phenomenologically* what distinguishes good from poor system controllers. As mentioned previously, poor controllers have been said to be unable to understand the concept of exponential growth, to reason in causal chains rather than in causal nets, and to exhibit a tendency towards "intellectual emergency reactions" (see Dörner, 1981, p. 167). It is important to keep these two major classes of concepts separated because the former, but not the latter, are psychometrically founded as of yet. This, of course, must not be understood as a prejudice about the theoretical value of constructs from the one or the other class.

Intelligence, Learning Potential, and Motivation

One of the most startling results of early research on how people controlled dynamic systems was the lack of a correlation between subjects' intellectual abilities as assessed by Raven's (1965) Advanced Progressive Matrices or other standard tests of intelligence, and control performance—at least not when the problem was intransparent, as many real-life problems were said to be (Dörner, 1979; Putz-Osterloh, 1981; Putz-Osterloh & Lüer, 1981). These findings seemed rather plausible at the time, given the pertinent dissatisfaction with *static* and *artificial* standard tests of intelligence combined with the idea that naturalistic scenarios would somehow be more ecologically valid. This may help to explain, among other things, the popularity of control tasks in personnel selection (see U. Funke, this volume) despite warnings of experts in the field against this practice (Kluwe, Schilde, Fischer, & Oellerer, 1991). However, the patterns of correlations between measures of test intelligence and measures of control performance in subsequent studies have been much less clear, and their interpretation is subject of an ongoing debate (for details see Beckmann & Guthke, this volume). For a theory of how people control dynamic systems, however, the most promising way seems to go beyond simply correlating global test intelligence scores with control performance measures. Rather, it seems more interesting to try to single out components of intellectual ability that contribute to control performance under different experimental conditions. In other words, a purely *psychometric* approach is probably not sufficient if anything of theoretical relevance is to be gained.

Consider, for instance, the study by Hussy (1989) in which several variants of a relatively simple dynamic system were employed. Subjects' task was to control a LUNAR LANDER—its speed, heat, fuel resources, and height above the moon surface—and bring it to ground safely. The nonlinear problem is mathematically tractable (Thalmaier, 1979). The average deviation of a subject's intervention from what would be the optimal input served as performance measure. As in a number of studies before, Hussy (1989) manipulated how transparent the problem was for subjects. In the transparent condition, numerical information was provided about the effects of different slow-down maneuvers, and subjects received feedback about some of the system states. This information was not available in the intransparent condition due to "inoperative gauges." All subjects' intellectual abilities were assessed using scales from the Berlin Intelligence Structure Model (Jäger, 1982). According to this model, *operative factors* such as speed of processing, memory, or processing capacity with respect to verbal, figural, and numerical information processing must be distinguished. Among other things, Hussy (1989) found processing capacity to be the single most predictive operative factor, regardless of the experimental condition. However, in the intransparent condition, figural memory, but not verbal or numerical memory, predicted control performance. This finding fits the assumption that intransparent systems place particularly high demands on subjects' ability to generate and maintain mental models of the task for successful control.

Hörmann and Thomas (1989) used the same tasks to measure intelligence, but their subjects controlled the TAILORSHOP, a 24-variable scenario intended to simulate a small company that subjects were asked to run for 12 fictitious months. Hörmann and Thomas's results differed from those of Hussy (1989) in that control performance—the amount of capital accumulated over the 12 months—correlated with indicators of intelligence only under the transparent presentation condition. The authors also assessed subjects' system knowledge in terms of how many relations between variables subjects were able to reproduce correctly after the control trials. Hörmann and Thomas (1989) argue that this measure, in contrast to the control performance index, reflects how well subjects understood, and learned about, the complexity of the entire system. System knowledge correlated highest with the processing capacity operative factor. In the intransparent condition, the memory factor correlated with performance. The latter findings parallel those of Hussy (1989; see also Süß et al., 1991), but it should be kept in mind that the systems used appear to differ greatly (although we have no means to analyze exactly *how* they differ). Another problem is that the two studies rely on different dependent measures (in fact, the amount of capital accumulated in running the TAILORSHOP is a rather arbitrary, idiosyncratic measure of performance). Nevertheless, both studies seem promising for a future theory in that they combine a component-oriented view of what constitutes intelligence with theoretically meaningful experimental manipulations of system properties. In other words, studies on the relation between intelligence and the control of dynamic systems seem interesting to the degree to which they can contribute to answering the question which cognitive faculty is demanded by which property of the task.

A very recent development is to relate not static intelligence but rather subjects' learning potential to performance on dynamic control tasks (Guthke, 1993a; for details see Beckmann & Guthke, this volume). Both types of tasks seem to involve learning from feedback about success and failure which is not true for traditional tests of intelligence (Guthke, 1993b). Beckmann (in press) has provided interesting evidence pertaining to this presumption. He investigated the relation between both control performance and system knowledge on the one side, and learning potential performance on the other. Subjects interacted with a dynamic scenario based on linear equation systems. The same underlying system was either presented as an abstract MACHINE with three different dials as input variables and three gauges as output variables, or as a concrete CHERRYTREE with water supply, light, and warmth to be regulated, and the number of cherries, leaves, and insects on the tree as output variables. As it turned out, subjects learned nothing when interacting with the CHERRYTREE, and there was no relation between control performance and either of two learning potential tests. Presumably, the semantic context provided by the CHERRYTREE labels prevented subjects from acquiring new information. Rather, they maintained their inadequate prior knowledge. In contrast, however, subjects showed significant learning when interacting with the structurally identical MACHINE system, and there were indeed substantial correlations between learning about the system and performance on both learning potential tests. These results validate Guthke's (1993b) assumptions and show that it is rather promising to further explore what is or is not shared in terms of cognitive processes between interacting with complex dynamic tasks and the construct of learning potential.

Focusing on *nonintellectual* aspects of problem solving, Hesse, Spies, and Lüer (1983) investigated the influence of motivational factors on how well subjects controlled the spread of an epidemic in a small town. These authors based their study on a state-trait concept of motivation. The trait component—success versus failure orientation—was assessed by a questionnaire, while the state component was manipulated experimentally by describing the disease as rather, or not very disastrous; one group of subjects was told to fight smallpox, the other group fought influenza. The underlying system was identical for both groups. The smallpox, but not the influenza group, was assumed to show high degrees of *personal involvement.* A rather complex combination of the values of several system variables served as performance criterion. The results were rather clear; subjects in the smallpox group showed more personal involvement, took more time, and were better at controlling the spread of the disease than subjects in the influenza group. In addition, better performance for the smallpox problem was observed for subjects classified as success oriented. More detailed analyses with respect to the state component of motivation revealed, among other things, that highly involved subjects showed more signs of self-reflective and analytical cognitive activity which resulted in a better understanding of the system and a selection of more effective measures to control the spread of the diseases. Also, the trait-component of motivation resulted in better performance primarily because success-oriented, but not failure-oriented subjects *sustained* their initial levels of self-reflective activities.

This study is interesting not only because it helps to integrate problem-solving research with other research areas, but also because the authors took a step toward analyzing in more detail how relatively stable and relatively transient aspects of motivation influence the way people attempt to understand and control a dynamic system.

A number of other personality traits have been related to control performance with varying success. For instance, self-confidence and a questionnaire of *cognitive control* were found to correlate substantially with a summary performance score in the LOHHAUSEN task (Dörner, Kreuzig, Reither, & Stäudel, 1983; Kreuzig, 1981). One major problem is, however, that these assessments have taken place *after* the control task. Funke (1986) was able to show that post hoc correlations between control performance and the questionnaire of *cognitive control* were much larger than a priori correlations, suggesting that the questionnaire was capturing people's memory of having been successful or unsuccessful at the task rather than predicting success. In addition, the fact that subjects governing Lohhausen had to interact with the experimenter to retrieve system information and to make system interventions, may account for the role of self-confidence in control performance in this particular task.

Certain features of spoken language (e.g., use of words classified as *dogmatic* such as *all, always,* or *must*) were also related to poor control performance (Roth, 1985, 1987). Unfortunately, these results could not be replicated (Roth et al., 1991), and the theoretical connection between control performance and linguistic features remains unclear. Finally, eye movement patterns have also been found to covary with control performance. Lüer, Hübner, and Lass (1985) compared the best and worst subjects in their sample and found that less successful subjects showed unsystematic strategies of collecting information from the display.

Experts Versus Novices

Another typical approach to analyze how a task is performed is to look at what distinguishes experts from novices. Reither (1981) found that, in line with assumptions about differences between good and poor controllers (Dörner, 1981), novices were more likely to reason in causal chains as opposed to causal nets, and also more likely to ignore side effects when interacting with a scenario simulating "the climatic, ecological, and ethnic conditions of a region similar to Upper Volta in West Africa" (Reither, 1981, p. 126; translation by the author). Experts were economic aid professionals with 6 to 8 years of experience in Third World countries, and novices were postgraduates who were just about to start an economic aid career.

Putz-Osterloh (1987) compared seven economics faculty with a sample of 30 "unselected" students on their interactions with, first, the *economic* scenario TAILORSHOP and, later, the Third World *ecological* scenario MORO. Dependent measures were derived from subjects' control performances and from thinking aloud protocols. For both systems, Putz-Osterloh found that the experts were better than the student sample with respect to knowledge acquisition and verbalized intervention strategies. In contrast, experts' control performance was better at the economical scenario TAILORSHOP than at the ecological scenario MORO. In particular, when controlling the TAILORSHOP, experts, but not novices, were able to take into account *conflicting goals* such as simultaneously having to increase the company's revenues and the workers' wages. This was interpreted to show that experts have an advantage over novices because they can use their domain-specific knowledge to control the economic system, whereas their generalizable heuristic knowledge about how to operate complex systems shows up in better system knowledge and more adequately verbalized strategies in both systems. A replication of the previous study (Putz-Osterloh & Lemme, 1987) compared 24 graduate students in business administration who served as experts to 28 students from non-business areas. This time, experts were better at controlling both MORO and the TAILORSHOP. However, both groups of subjects were indistinguishable with respect to strategic knowledge.

Unfortunately, the pattern of results of these few studies on expert-novice differences is inconsistent and, so far, relatively uninformative for a theory of CPS. Future investigations should place more emphasis on defining and assessing in greater detail what knowledge and skills experts have that novices don't (see Funke, 1992b). Ideally, these differences should be explicated a priori on the basis of thorough task analyses and the cognitive processes the tasks involve, and not by simply observing how *apparent* experts perform at tasks that semantically appeal to the experts' professional designation. This, of course, is useful only if one believes that expertise in controlling complex dynamic systems is more than just the conditioned application of "grandmother's know-how" (Dörner & Schölkopf, 1991)

Self-Reflection, Heuristic Competence, and the Need to Gain Control: The Regulation of Actions

It seems highly plausible that self-reflection should be helpful in controlling complex dynamic systems. In particular, attempts to cope with critical situations of a system should both stimulate and benefit from self-reflective activities (Dörner & Schölkopf, 1991). Indeed, post-hoc analyses of subjects' verbalizations when interacting with complex dynamic systems have indicated that there might be a difference between *good* and *poor* controllers with respect to self-reflective activities (Dörner, 1981; Dörner, Kreuzig, Reither, & Stäudel, 1983; Reither, 1979). As we know from the study by Hesse et al. (1983), highly motivated subjects show more signs of self-reflection, and success-oriented subjects sustain their initial levels of self-reflective activities relative to failure-oriented subjects. Also, when the *matching familiar figures* test is used to distinguish between self-reflective subjects (more hits, longer latencies) and impulsive subjects (fewer hits, shorter latencies), better control of the LUNAR LANDER is observed with those classified as being self-reflective (Hussy & Granzow, 1987).

In addition, it has been shown that experimentally induced self-reflection is effective in improving performance on items taken from a standard test of intelligence (Hesse, 1982b). Putz-Osterloh (1983b) attempted to test empirically whether induced self-reflection also increases control performance when interacting with the TAILORSHOP. After subjects had made their interventions, they were to answer a number of questions (adapted from Hesse, 1982b) pertaining to their past interventions and to the possibilities to improve their interaction with the system. These manipulations had no effect on control performance. In a subsequent study, Putz-Osterloh (1985) investigated whether in the previous experiment the focus of subjects' self-reflection could have been too *general* to yield results that could be turned quickly into concrete interventions. One group of subjects practiced *specific* self-reflection while working on a training problem. Typical self-reflection questions were "Do I have a precise goal?" or "Do I have enough information?" Subsequently, subjects controlled the MORO system. In addition to control performance, system knowledge was assessed by recording the number of variables and their interrelations as they surfaced in subjects' think aloud protocols. Again, the group that had practiced self-reflection did not perform better at controlling the system nor at verbalizing system knowledge than the group with no self-reflective practice. Thus, induced self-reflection—with both rather general and relatively concrete foci—does not seem to have an influence on control performance. In the light of the present evidence, earlier conclusions based on correlational results that self-reflection is instrumental in improving learning about, and control of, complex dynamic systems, have to be interpreted with caution. As of yet, there is no evidence for a *causal* role of self-reflection in controlling complex systems.

Another trait-like concept that has been assumed to play a role in system control is subjects' so-called *heuristic competence* (Dörner, 1982; Dörner, Kreuzig, Reither, & Stäudel, 1983; Dörner, Reither, & Stäudel, 1983). Heuristic competence has been defined as "the confidence of a person in his or her abilities to cope successfully with novel situations" (Stäudel, 1988, p. 137; translation by the author). Heuristic competence is assumed to be relatively stable and to change only in the long run through accumulated experiences with novel problems. The construct is conceptually related to the *locus of control* (Rotter, 1966) and *self-efficacy* (Bandura, 1977) constructs. Indeed, the need to gain and maintain control is thought to be the *primary motive* that underlies subjects' interactions with complex dynamic systems (Brehmer, 1989; Dörner, 1983b; Dörner, Kreuzig, Reither, & Stäudel, 1983). A questionnaire has been developed that measures the construct of *heuristic competence* (Stäudel, 1988).

Currently, there is some evidence linking high heuristic competence to successful control of the MORO system (Stäudel, 1987), but there is also other evidence of no relation between heuristic competence as assessed by Stäudel's (1988) heuristic competence questionnaire and control performance with a relatively simple "cold-storage depot" (Reichert & Dörner, 1988).

Beyond the more *traditional* personality traits, *poor controllers*, that is, subjects who fail to gain control over a complex and intransparent task, are assumed to be distinguishable from *good controllers* by the typical errors they make (Dörner, Schaub, Stäudel, & Strohschneider, 1988). Over the years, quite a few of these errors have been extracted from observations and described in a number of studies conducted in Dörner's laboratory (Dörner, 1981, 1983b; Dörner & Pfeifer, 1992; Dörner & Reither, 1978; Reichert & Dörner, 1988). These errors are said to demonstrate, better than anything else, how cognition, emotion, and motivation interact in system control tasks. As an illustrative example, consider the feeling of loosing control over the system which may result in a "cognitive emergency reaction" (Dörner, 1981), a state in which subjects (a) reduce their self-reflective activities, (b) increase their tendency to react quickly, (c) entertain more and more reductive and rigid hypotheses about what is going on in the system to be controlled, and, (d) formulate increasingly global and abstract goals. As this example shows, errors may occur at four different stages: (a) in the area of self-organization, (b) when making decisions, (c) when framing hypotheses, and (d) when defining action goals.

Based on an analysis of poor controllers, Dörner et al. (1988) have presented an *action regulation* model of how the tendencies to commit errors such as the "cognitive emergency reaction" may develop. Even more, the model is designed to serve as a "general structure for the explanation of human behavior in complex dynamic systems" (p. 217; translation by the author). The model is based on a memory structure composed of interconnected sensory, motivational, and motor components for storing information about facts, needs, and actions, respectively. At the heart of the model, and central for the control of actions, are *intentions*. Intentions are *ephemeral* units consisting of *temporarily structured* information from memory. Each intention is assumed to comprise information about initial and final states, the past history of the system, the importance of the intention, its *temporal perspective* (i.e., the beginning and end of actions associated with the intention), the intention's *success probability*, and the competence to act according to the intention. Further, the model has four *information processing units*. One unit *generates intentions* from information available about the systems' needs and the current environment. Another unit *selects intentions* from information about the situation and the intentions currently active in some sort of intention working memory (combining the weighted importance of an intention with its associated success probability much like an expectancy-value model would predict). A third unit *promotes intentions*, either by activating automated action sequences or by initiating controlled planning activities. The final unit *perceives the environment in light of the currently active intentions*, delivering information about the space-time coordination of the system. Figure 2.1 graphically depicts the information processing units (in rectangles), together with the data structures (in ovals) they operate on.

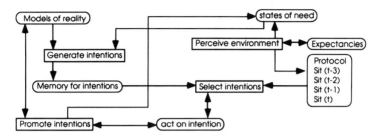

FIG. 2.1. Graphical illustration of the basic components of Dörner's model of action regulation. Information processing units are represented as rectangles and the data structures they operate on are represented as ovals (Dörner et al., 1988; see text for details).

As mentioned previously, this conceptual framework can be used to describe errors typical for poor controllers. For instance, if the intentions selected for processing change repeatedly, then the unit responsible for promoting intentions is under time pressure and works less well. In turn, the system's competence is reduced, a new intention (designed to find the causes for the failure) is added to the intentions working memory and competes with other *active* intentions. In addition, the weights of all active intentions have to be adjusted. Thus, the selection unit will change the intentions to be processed even more often, resulting in even worse processing of the intentions, and the associated states of need accumulate. At the end of the vicious circle we may find a "cognitive emergency reaction."

The model is designed to be implemented as a computer simulation (see Dörner & Wearing, this volume) and as such has a number of advantages over more vague earlier formulations (e.g., Dörner, 1982). Nevertheless, Funke (1992b) has criticized the model for being too weak to provide testable predictions, and also for presenting as causal hypotheses what are simply a priori truths to the competent language user (e.g., the importance of an intention is said to increase if the underlying state of need increases, see Dörner et al., 1988, p. 222). More precision is perhaps achieved easiest by incorporating in greater detail the theories the model capitalizes on in its current state. For instance, the operation of the unit that selects intentions might be specified according to existing expectancy-value theories (e.g., Feather, 1982). In addition, the concept of competence implied by the representation of each intention could be specified by incorporating assumptions from self-efficacy theory (e.g., Bandura, 1977).

However, it is granted that not all aspects of the theory can be open for empirical tests, and some tests of the action regulation model might indeed be possible. For instance, according to the model, higher competence should result in better overall performance but, as mentioned above, the evidence for this assumption is contradictory (Reichert & Dörner, 1988; Stäudel, 1987).

It will be interesting to see which other testable predictions will be derived from the model and submitted to empirical tests in the future.

Another noteworthy point about the model proposed by Dörner et al. (1988) is that, although it allows for the theoretical reconstruction of some typical errors of poor controllers, other errors identified in earlier research as *primary* by the same group of researchers (Dörner, 1981; Dörner, Kreuzig, Reither, & Stäudel, 1983) have been left out. Examples of such primary errors include subjects' inability to take into account side effects (i.e., subjects have been said to be reasoning in causal chains rather than in causal nets), or their lack of understanding of exponential trends. In the present model of action regulation, the focus appears to have shifted from looking at *why* subjects fail in terms of the cognitive processes involved to what happens *during the process* of failing.

The obvious alternative is, of course, to take a closer look at how subjects *learn* about a system and analyze what it takes to arrive at *successful control.* The approaches described in the rest of this chapter take this perspective and shall thus be referred to as *competence-oriented.* As will become clear, a competence-oriented perspective quite naturally leads not only to different research questions, but also to a different sort of model. The interest is primarily in the forms of learning, knowledge representation, and knowledge use when subjects interact with complex dynamic systems, and the focus is on the impact of the task's properties on these cognitive processes.

APPROACHES BASED ON FORMAL TASK ANALYSES

In order to determine the influence of task properties on learning and memory, one must be able to manipulate the task environment systematically. This, in turn, requires that the relevant task properties can be pinned down formally. The straightforward way to accomplish this goal is to search for an established formalism that can be used to describe interesting task environments and see how far one can go with it.

Linear Equation Systems

Funke (1985, 1986, 1992a, 1992b) has developed a theory that combines, in one homogeneous framework, three essential aspects of research on how people interact with complex dynamic systems: the formal description of the task environment, assumptions about learning and knowledge representation, and the diagnostic methods to assess what has been learned.

As a formalism for describing dynamic task environments, Funke suggests the theory of multivariate autoregressive processes, AR_k, where k is the degree of temporal dependency between the input of an exogenous system variable and its effect on an endogenous variable.[3] Bypassing the formal details, the approach is best described by giving an example. In one of Funke's typical task environments, the so-called SINUS scenario, inputs at three exogenous variables have effects on three endogenous variables of the system. Like most of Funke's systems, this scenario is time discrete and does not change states autonomously, that is, the system waits until the subject has made all inputs. The system is *abstract* in the sense that the labels of the exogenous and endogenous variables have no meanings in order to minimize the influence of prior knowledge (the approach is also applicable to semantically rich domains such as ecological systems, see e.g., Funke, 1985). Figure 2.2 presents the system in graphical form, and the simultaneous difference equations governing the system behavior are given in (1).

$$y_{1,t+1} = 1.0 * y_{1,t} + 10.0 * x_{1,t}$$
$$y_{2,t+1} = 1.0 * y_{2,t} + 0.2 * y_3,t + 3.0 * x_{3,t}$$
$$y_{3,t+1} = 0.9 * y_{3,t} + 2.0 * x_2,t + 0.5 * x_{3,t} \tag{1}$$

where $y_{i,t+1}$ represents the state of an endogenous variable i at time $t+1$, $y_{i,t}$ represents the state of an endogenous variable i at time t, and $x_{i,t}$ represents the state of an exogenous variable i at time t.

The SINUS scenario is only one instance of an infinitely large class of scenarios that are based on simultaneous difference equations. Actually, a software shell exists to generate new scenarios following this formalism. The precision and simplicity of the formalism makes it very easy to manipulate particular features of the task environment such as time delays, variable connectivity, et cetera. Also, goal states can be defined precisely, and for any current system state, it is possible to specify an optimal intervention. From a methodological point of view, these are major advantages over naturalistic scenarios (see also Kluwe et al., 1989; Ringelband et al., 1990).

Funke developed a theory of how people learn and represent what they have learned when interacting with systems of this sort. Basically, subjects are assumed to built a causal model of the task, to which the input and output variables and then the parameters of the AR_k-processes describing the system behavior are added in a certain sequence. Hypotheses about the relations between exogenous and endogenous variables are built in the order of their numerical strengths in the system, provided the user manipulates the particular x_i-y_j-relation by making an input at the exogenous vari-

---

[3]Hübner (1989) has argued that mathematical system theory may be a more adequate formalism to derive system properties. However, Funke's approach is preferred here because it implies both a representational theory and a method for constructing rational diagnostic procedures.

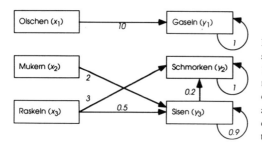

FIG. 2.2. Causal structure of the standard SINUS system (Funke, 1992b). Numbers next to the arrows represent the weights of the influence. Left of the figure: three variables that can be manipulated independently; Right, three variables that have to be controlled.

able. Relations with time-delays (i.e., $k \geq 2$) are built up later and more slowly. Relations open to direct manipulations (i.e., x_i-y_j-relations) are included before indirect relations (i.e., y_i-y_j-relations which result in *side-effects* for any direct influence on y_i). Providing a semantic context has the effect of adding parameters to the model before learning starts which means that some relations may not have to be explored. Relations set a priori are resistant to learning which is why providing a semantic context has detrimental effects if it induces false parameters. Finally, forgetting is also assumed to occur.

Hypotheses about relations are built up from data about current and memorized system states and interventions. According to Funke (1991b, 1992b), hypotheses about system relations can be represented in terms of the following quadruple:

$$H := \langle V_1, \ V_2, \ R, \ C \rangle \tag{2}$$

where V_1 and V_2 are the variables between which a relation R is assumed with confidence C. R comprises all forms of relations a subject may know, including qualitative information, quantitative information, and time delays. C is obviously conceived of in close analogy to the idea of the subject operating as an intuitive scientist.

Finally, Funke and his coworkers have also developed the diagnostic instruments suitable for assessing subjects' task-relevant knowledge in their paradigm (Funke, 1992a, 1992b; Müller, 1993). They distinguish between knowledge relevant to control performance and structural knowledge, a rather straightforward and common distinction (De Kleer & Brown, 1983; Kluwe & Haider, 1990).[4] Control performance, *CP*, is assessed as the distance of the endogenous variables to their goal states. More precisely, control performance is measured by

---

[4]This distinction appears similar, but is not identical to the distinction made by Berry and Broadbent and their coworkers (Berry & Broadbent, 1984, 1987, 1988; Broadbent et al., 1986; Hayes & Broadbent, 1988). For instance, Funke does not make any assumptions about the location of subjects' knowledge along the explicit-implicit continuum that is central to the work of Berry and Broadbent (see Berry & Broadbent, this volume).

$$CP = \frac{\sum_{i=1}^{n_y} \sum_{t=1}^{n_T} \ln |y_{ij} - g_i|}{n_y * n_T} \tag{3}$$

where n_y is the number of endogenous variables, n_T is the number of trials the system has to be controlled, g_i is the goal value for the endogenous variable i, and y_{it} is the empirical value of variable i at time t. The logarithmic transformation in assessing control performance reduces the influence of extreme deviations.

In order to assess subjects' structural knowledge, the *causal diagram analysis* was developed. Essentially, subjects receive a diagram similar to the one depicted in Figure 2.2. They are asked to fill in the relations they assume to be present in the system. Subjects may do this at one of three different levels of precision. They may simply state that a relation between two variables is present, they may add the relation's direction, or they may specify the relation's numerical value. A summary score is then computed from this information indicating subjects' structural knowledge.

Of course, other methods are possible to assess different aspects of subjects' knowledge about the task. For instance, Müller (1993) has explored the usefulness of reaction time analyses in a yes/no recognition task adapted for the paradigm. However, the advantage of the structural diagram analysis lies in the close relation between representational theory and diagnostic procedure. It is obvious that indices for control performance and structural knowledge can be dissociated. For instance, subjects may build up an *initial action base* (Kluwe & Haider, 1990) when first interacting with the system which may be too fragile and vague to be picked up by the structural diagram analysis. Also, even formally inadequate and fragmentary subjective models of the system structure may lead to considerable control performance (Ringelband et al., 1990). Haider (1992) has pointed out that such a constellation may look like a dissociation between *explicit* and *implicit* system knowledge. However, for his tasks, Funke assumed that subjects first built up structural knowledge which is then turned into successful control performance.

A number of experiments have been stimulated by the theory, examining how properties of the task environment affect the acquisition of structural knowledge and control performance. In these experiments, subjects typically explore the system for a number of trials before they are asked to control it. For instance, the basic SINUS system was manipulated to have either no, one, or two y_i-y_j-relations that result in side effects. Structural knowledge should become worse as a function of the number of y_i-y_j-relations present in the system, and control performance should be a function of structural knowledge. A path-analytic evaluation confirmed this prediction. A similar result was not found for y_i-y_j-relations (i.e., the effect of one variable at time

t on its state at time $t+1$ resulting in autonomous *growth* or *decline*). Structural knowledge and control performance did not depend on whether no, one, or two y_i-y_j-relations were present (Funke, 1992a, 1992b). Higher degrees of "connectivity" (more x_i-y_j-relations to be included into the model) resulted in both lower control performance and less structural knowledge (Funke, 1985).

If the semantic context of a scenario activates prior knowledge, some parameters are added to the subjects' model of the task before learning starts. This may have beneficial and detrimental effects on learning, depending on whether the actual system structure corresponds to subjects' pre-exploration model of the task or not. Funke (1992a, 1992b) has developed a simple eight variable *ecological* linear equation system according to recommendations provided by environmental experts. In a pilot study, 32 subjects were asked to draw causal diagrams of the system without having interacted with it. Each relation implemented in the scenario was assumed by at least 72% of the pilot subjects, confirming that the system corresponded to subjects' knowledge about the domain. In the subsequent experiment, half of the subjects explored and later controlled this system, while the other half interacted with a system in which the sign of two (out of five) x_i-y_j-relations had been changed. This relatively small change resulted in substantial decrements in both control performance and structural knowledge, showing that activating prior knowledge can effectively impair learning by exploration (see also Beckmann, in press).

If the effects of subjects' inputs are delayed (i.e., x_i-y_j-relations represent AR_2 rather than AR_1 processes), structural knowledge also suffers (Funke, 1985). Similar results have been reported by Brehmer and Allard (1991) and by Dörner and Preussler (1990). Dörner and Preussler (1990) confronted subjects with a relatively simple predator-prey system and asked them to adjust the predator variable so as to keep the prey population at a certain level. The authors manipulated a number of independent variables, but the one manipulation that impaired performance most was feedback delay. Brehmer and Allard (1991) used a variant of the FIRE FIGHTING scenario (see Footnote 2). This system is naturalistic in that it tries to model how a "fire chief" would make decisions about the deployment of fire fighting units. Nevertheless, Brehmer and Allard (1991) agree that in order to be useful for experimental research, certain features of the task must be open for experimental manipulations. Therefore, they developed a simulation system that allows to manipulate six different features of the scenario. In a first exploratory study, the authors varied two of these features, feedback delay and task complexity. Feedback about the fire fighting units' activities was either delayed by one or two time units or it was not delayed. In the low complexity condition, all units were equally effective whereas in the high complexity condition, some units were twice as effective as others. While the complexity manipulation had little effect, the feedback delay clearly impaired subjects' control performance. However, it is unclear whether subjects did not detect the delay or whether they were unable to include the delay into their model of the task.

Funke and Müller (1988) hypothesized that active intervention should be an important factor in learning to control a system. They manipulated whether subjects could actively control the SINUS system or simply observe the effects of interventions, and whether or not subjects were required to make predictions about the next system state after each intervention. Observers were yoked subjects in that each of them attended to the interventions and system states produced by an active control subject. In a final phase, all subjects had to control the system. As expected, active control resulted in better control performance, but making predictions had an unexpected negative effect on structural knowledge.

Berry (1991), using the SUGAR FACTORY scenario (Berry & Broadbent, 1984) further explored the role of active intervention. She found that, for instance, neither making decisions about the next intervention nor typing inputs according to another person's decisions alone had a positive effect on subsequent control performance relative to normal interaction with the system. Also, Hübner (1987) found that learning from an example how to control a technical system was drastically more efficient after some experience of active control. Thus, it appears plausible that both the process of generating an intervention from a given state and a desired next state and the experience of the contingency between one's intervention and the next system state are necessary for efficient initial learning. However, motivational effects may help to explain differences in performance: As we know from the study by Hesse et al. (1983) discussed earlier, personal involvement accounts for considerable differences in control performance. It might therefore be argued that active and uninfluenced interaction with the system simply creates higher personal involvement which then, in turn, plays a mediating role by stimulating other processes necessary for successful control.

To summarize, variations in task properties have noticeable influences on people's knowledge acquisition while interacting with dynamic systems. One of the advantages of Funke's approach is that it allows for the systematic variation of well-known task properties. In addition, the approach includes a theory of what and how people learn when exploring dynamic systems, and it includes rational methods for assessing this knowledge. The combination of these three aspects in one homogeneous framework contributes to the fruitfulness of this line of research.

Of course, the approach also has its limitations. First, the price of the formal lucidity of the task environments is the limited set of task properties that are available for manipulation. Although exponential behavior can be simulated with linear equation systems (one simply sets the weight of a

y_i-y_i-relation to a value larger or smaller than one for exponential growth or decline, respectively), other interesting behaviors such as sinusoidal or s-shaped trends and ramp-like or step-like developments are beyond the limits set by the formal basis. Second, and related to the first point, few if any real-world systems will have the exact properties of linear equation systems. The framework therefore does not have the ecological validity that appeared so important in the development of this research area. Nevertheless, real-world systems can at least be approximated (as in Funke's ecological scenarios) which is, after all, what naturalistic simulation systems do, too. Third, by its very nature, the framework places a heavy emphasis on task properties as determinants of human learning to control a system. This is, of course, a problem only if it leads to the neglect of other relevant variables. Funke (1992b) was aware of this possible shortcoming, and has suggested a taxonomy for further theorizing that includes not only task variables but also person variables (cognitive, emotional, and motivational states and traits) and properties of the situation (how the system is presented physically, and what the instructions define as the task to be performed).

Finite State Automata

A framework that shares some of the basic principles with the linear equation systems approach makes use of elementary concepts of the theory of finite state automata (see Buchner & Funke, 1993; Funke & Buchner, 1992 for details). Again, the theory serves as a tool for formally describing the dynamic task environment, it is used as a starting point for hypothesizing about how such systems are represented mentally, and it allows to derive rational methods for assessing these representations. First, as before, it will be necessary to introduce some of the basic concepts used in the approach. Then assumptions about learning and knowledge representation will be presented, and finally the diagnostic methods to assess what has been learned will be discussed.

A deterministic finite state automaton is defined by a finite set of input signals, a finite set of output signals, a finite set of states, and two mapping functions. To illustrate, input signals of a technical device could be buttons and dial positions that can be selected as input at a certain point in time. Output signals are all possible display settings. It is assumed that the system works on the basis of a discrete time scale. At each point in time, the automaton is in a certain state in which it receives one *input signal* (e.g., on a video recorder, the "fast forward" button is pressed). The system then moves to the *next state* which is determined by the *transition function* δ (e.g., the video recorder starts to wind the video tape). Subsequently, the device emits exactly one *output signal* which is determined by the *result function* λ as a consequence of the current state and the input signal (e.g., the "fast forward" arrows on the video recorder's front display are high-lighted). As with the linear equation systems approach, a software shell exists to generate arbitrary scenarios following this formalism.

As a concrete example, consider the SUGAR FACTORY as used by Berry and Broadbent (1984, this volume) and by others (Marescaux, Luc, & Karnas, 1989; McGeorge & Burton, 1989; Stanley, Mathews, Buss, & Kotler-Cope, 1989) to investigate different modi of learning while interacting with a dynamic task environment. The system operates according to a simple equation which states that the sugar output at time $t+1$, S_{t+1}, is determined by the most recent sugar output S_t and the present input I_t, the number of workers employed by the subject:

$$S_{t+1} = 2 * I_t - S_t \qquad (4)$$

where $1 \leq I \leq 12$ and $1 \leq S \leq 12$. The values of I are multiplied by 100 and the values of S are multiplied by 1,000 to represent the number of workers and the sugar output in tons, respectively, at time t. (In addition, a random component is usually added such that on two-third of the trials, the system changes, at time t, to a state that is one unit above or below the correct state according to the system equation. I ignore this random component here.)

A convenient way to describe a finite state automaton is by a state transition matrix. In its cells, the matrix contains the automaton's state at time $t+1$ (S_{t+1}, the next sugar output) given a specific state at time t (S_t, the current sugar output) and a specific input signal at time t (I_t, the number of workers employed). In each column, it contains the *function* of an input signal, whereas the rows reflect possible next states given a certain current state. The SUGAR FACTORY can easily be described in such terms of a state transition matrix (for more details, see Buchner, Funke, & Berry, in press).

As with the linear equation systems framework, the formal descriptions of automata provide not only the background for precise descriptions of task properties such as system complexity (McCabe, 1976), but they also serve as a starting point for hypothesizing about how people might learn to control automata and how what is learned might be represented. It is assumed that users' knowledge about a system can be described in terms of those parts of the transition matrix that are represented in memory and available for guiding system interventions. This is called the person's individual transition matrix (ITM) which may, of course, deviate from the automaton's transition matrix.

When confronted with a previously unknown automaton, learning must begin at the level of individual state transitions, composed of a previous state, an intervention, and a next state. A person's experiences of these transitions while exploring the automaton constitute the *entries* for the ITM.

At that level, a simple associative learning process is assumed to operate on states, interventions, and next states experienced by the exploring subject.

As learning proceeds, people will shift from using knowledge about individual state transitions to clustering state transitions. First, *routines* may be developed to get a system reliably from one particular state to a distant state. This can be referred to as the formation of *horizontal chunks* of state transitions. For example, the state transition sequence S_t-I_t-S_{t+1}-I_{t+1}-S_{t+2}-I_{t+2}-S_{t+3} may be reduced to the form S_t-$[I_t$-I_{t+1}-$I_{t+2}]$-S_{t+3}, where the interventions necessary to get from state S_t to S_{t+3} form one single component of a compound state transition and the user no longer needs to attend to the intermediate output signals (Anderson, 1981; Frensch, 1991; MacKay, 1982). Second, state transitions can be combined across a specific intervention or a specific state, given the intervention or the state can be identified as the source of a specific form of invariance. This process can be referred to as the formation of *vertical chunks* of state transitions. An example could be an intervention to change the mode of operation of a device (in the most simple case an on/off switch).

The formal descriptions of finite state automata also serve as tools for developing rational methods to assess system and control knowledge. For instance, state transitions consist of a given system state at time t (S_t), an intervention at time t (I_t), and a next system state at time $t+1$ (S_{t+1}). These elements can be used to generate *cued recall tasks* to assess what has been retained about a system by presenting two of the elements as cues for the third one (requiring predictive, interpolative, and retrognostic judgments if the missing element is S_{t+1}, I_t, and S_t, respectively). In all these tasks, the basic idea is to take *samples* from the ITM.

One can also expose subjects to entire state transitions that are either possible or impossible for a given device, and measure the speed and accuracy of the verification judgment. For instance, Buchner and Funke (1993) presented sequences of state transitions taken from an explored automaton for verification. If the second of two state transitions was a transition that, in the chronology of system events, had occurred after the first transition, reaction times were faster than when the second transition had actually occurred first, or was unrelated to the first one.

Further, a criterion for optimal control performance which is lacking for most naturalistic scenarios is readily available within the finite state automata approach. Given a present state of a discrete system and an arbitrarily defined goal state, it is always possible to specify whether there exists a sequence of interventions to reach the goal state and, if so, how many and which steps constitute an optimal sequence of interventions (i.e., a sequence involving a minimal number of steps). Subjects' exploration behavior (i.e., the way they approach the knowledge acquisition task) may be an interesting basis for additional dependent variables. A readily available indicator of exploration behavior is the number of different state transitions that are explored relative to all states in the state transition matrix of the system. The more different state transitions subjects explore, the more they should learn about the system. In a recent study (Buchner et al., in press), it has been shown that this may be one reason for negative correlations between control performance and so-called verbalizable knowledge (Berry & Broadbent, 1984). Note that "good controllers" reach the target state more frequently and, thus, experience a smaller area of the system's state transition matrix than *poor controllers*. On the other hand, verbalizable knowledge was assessed by items which probed subjects for the next system state given an old work force value, a current state of the system, and a new intervention. These items can be conceived of as samples from the state transition matrix. Consequently, good controllers who know less about the system's state transition matrix should be worse at these items, resulting in a negative correlation between control performance and verbalizable knowledge.

The associative learning mechanism assumed to be important in early learning about a new system has also been under examination. The basic idea has been that if an associative learning mechanism is at work, then one should be able to observe transfer interference similar to that known from the paired associative learning paradigm (Martin, 1965). After initially interacting with a *source automaton* (a simplified radio with a built-in alarm device), several groups of subjects tried to control different *target automata*. The state transition matrices underlying the target automata were identical for all groups but were completely different from that of the source automaton. However, the target automata differed with respect to the labeling of their input and output signals. For instance, in one condition, these labels were entirely new, whereas in a different condition, the original labels had been preserved. The latter case corresponds to the A-B, A-Br situation in paired associate learning (stimuli and responses from the first list are preserved in the transfer list but they are repaired) which is known to produce considerable negative transfer. In contrast, the former case corresponds to the A-B, C-D situation in which a completely new list is learned. Indeed, knowledge of state transitions, as assessed with predictive cued recall items, was worst for the "new automaton, old labels" condition, and was best for the "new automaton, new labels" condition.

Indirect measures have also been used to assess system knowledge (Buchner, 1993). In one experiment, subjects interacted with an automaton that was constructed such that it "understood" sentences generated by the finite state grammar used in typical implicit learning experiments (Reber, Kassin, Lewis, & Cantor, 1980). One group of subjects memorized sequences of inputs while another group made predictions about the next output signal. Output signals were patterns of 5 black squares in a 5×5 grid. In a subsequent phase, subjects were again instructed to make sequences of inputs. This time, an output signal was occasionally masked after a very brief display interval which previously had been adjusted for each subject's perceptual threshold. Subjects were asked to indicate which of a number of possible output signals they believed to have seen. The output signal actually presented was either the correct signal given the previous system state and the required intervention, or an incorrect signal. Both groups of subjects were better at identifying the output signal if it was correct than if it was incorrect. Moreover, when the output signal was incorrect, subjects did not choose the signal that would have been correct at that position in the sequence more often than would have been expected under conditions of guessing. This latter finding indicates that subjects indeed treated the test as an indirect test.

In recent experiments (Müller, Funke, & Buchner, 1994), the focus has shifted from singular associations to chunking processes. Subjects were trained on twelve element input sequences that were arranged on a structured display such that the first four and the final four elements of the sequence each took place in a different display structure. It was hypothesized that the display structure would induce a clustering of the elements into two *horizontal chunks*. In a transfer phase, subjects learned new input sequences in which four elements of the original sequence were retained. These four elements could either be the final *chunk*, or adjacent elements from both chunks, or four disconnected elements. As predicted, the chunk structure transferred and subjects in the first condition made significantly less errors than subjects in the other two conditions.

Finally, the finite state approach has also been fruitful in applied settings. Funke and Gerdes (1993) analyzed the standard manual of a popular video recorder brand. They asked whether the information contained in the manual was appropriate for building up an adequate ITM of the device. A typical inadequacy was, for instance, a lack of descriptions of output signals (essential for diagnosing what state the device is in). On the basis of this analysis, the authors developed an improved version of the manual designed to facilitate learning how to operate the video recorder. Subjects were asked to perform a number of *timer programming* tasks (i.e., they programmed the video recorder such that a certain TV show would be automatically tape-recorded). Subjects trying to program the video recorder with the old manual needed 27 minutes to perform the tasks as opposed to only 18 minutes for subjects who had received the improved version. The improved manual also resulted in higher accuracy scores. In addition, subjects in the improved manual group were significantly better at responding to interpolative cued recall items (given S_t and S_{t+1}, which input I_t is appropriate?).

This latter example demonstrates that the finite state automata framework can be useful not only for basic research on how people interact with complex dynamic systems, but also for questions of applied psychology. However, the major drawback of the finite state approach is that it becomes impracticable with large-scale systems (although some of the concepts developed within the approach seem transferable to larger systems). Nevertheless, many technical systems we deal with in everyday life are adequately described within the formalism provided by finite state automata theory. Examples include, besides video recorders, computer programs, TV sets, digital wrist watches, banking machines, and so on. Thus, the first point to be made here is that, in drawing upon a well-developed formalism for constructing dynamic task environments, one does not automatically loose ecological validity. One can have it both, ecologically valid task environments and the methodological advantages of well-defined task properties. In fact, the successful research of Funke and Gerdes (1993) shows this empirically rather than simply appealing to the ideal of ecological validity by constructing tasks that look natural.

The second point is that, contrary to widespread assumptions, learning to control complex dynamic tasks might not be fundamentally different from learning and memory as investigated in more traditional research paradigms. Rather, it appears that fundamental cognitive processes as investigated in traditional learning and memory research are also involved in people's interactions with dynamic task environments. Of course, it would be grossly inadequate to claim that there is nothing more involved in controlling a technical device than there is in memorizing lists of paired words. However, at a certain level, the two tasks seem to involve similar learning processes. This suggests that, besides emphasizing the uniqueness and novelty of the dynamic task environments paradigm (Dörner, Kreuzig, Reither, & Stäudel, 1983; Dörner & Reither, 1978), it might also be useful to consider the potential contributions of established theories of learning and memory for a theory of how people successfully perform in complex dynamic tasks.

CONCLUDING REMARKS AND FUTURE PERSPECTIVES

In this chapter, I have tried to provide an overview of the major lines of basic research on how people interact with complex dynamic tasks. Two different ways to approach the topic have been described. On one side, some researchers favor *naturalistic* scenarios as tasks, and they search explanatory constructs based on interindividual differences. On the other side, some researchers exhibit a strong preference for *well-defined* task environments and a focus on knowledge acquisition processes modulated by features of the tasks. Recent developments in basic research on how people control complex systems point to at least three different directions.

First, those interested in interindividual differences in CPS now try to move beyond the *psychometric* approach of simply correlating state or trait variables with ad hoc measures of control performance. Also, it is realized that much can be gained if the task environments used to assess control performance provide rational performance measures and are open to experimental manipulation. Beckmann's (in press) work on the relation between learning potential tests and system control is a good example of the progress already made in this area.

Second, some researchers involved in the *systems thinking* program moved towards action theory. They believe that cognitive, motivational, and emotional processes should not be analyzed separately if one wants to get a complete and realistic picture of how people come to control complex dynamic systems. One problem here is that the inclusion of theoretical terms from action theory such as intention (conceptually an action constituent requiring a deliberately acting person) into a (mechanistic) cognitive framework characterized by information processing units and knowledge structures as in Dörner et al. (1988) will result in the mixing of incompatible theoretical languages. On the surface, one finds semantically queer theoretical formulations (e.g., a processing unit is said to be *responsible* for generating intentions, see Dörner et al., 1988, p. 223), but more serious is that both precision and testability of such a theory will suffer. Another point is that, because there is no such thing as an unique action theory, one should make explicit the underlying perspective (Brandtstädter, 1985) to help clarify which theoretical relations are empirical and which are simply analytical.

A third approach is to search for interesting frameworks to adequately describe the formal basis of the task environment, to hypothesize about the systems' mental representation, and to derive rational measures of control performance and system knowledge. This approach is limited to the types of systems that can be formalized within a particular framework, and it does not take into account noncognitive processes that may be involved in controlling complex systems (although it is of course granted that such processes may play important roles). One of the more problematic aspects here is that focusing on formalizeable task properties, one tends to neglect subjects' prior knowledge. In fact, a number of studies using formally well-described systems have sometimes tried deliberately to exclude the influence of prior knowledge by avoiding meaningful labels of input and output variables (Buchner & Funke, 1993; Funke, 1992b). This *Ebbinghaus approach* to controlling dynamic task environments obviously has its merits in terms of rigorous experimental control, but it also has its limitations, and we do not necessarily have to go back to Bartlett (1932) to see those. Very likely, subjects virtually never control a real-world dynamic task without recourse to some sort of prior knowledge. According to Funke (1992a), the development here should be to focus more on the *interaction* of person, situation, and system influences, rather than on the *main effects* alone. This would include an explicit consideration and assessment of subjects' prior knowledge that is relevant to the simulation's domain. In addition, on the person side, Funke demands that the deficits in diagnosing *heuristic* knowledge be overcome.

Future research will also have to turn to questions that are currently ignored. For instance, the importance of real-time decisions for human system control has been pointed out repeatedly (e.g., Brehmer, 1989, this volume; Brehmer & Allard, 1991), but basic research has largely ignored this variable. Note that decisions can be real-time in a dual sense. First, subjects may have to plan and execute interventions under time pressure. This can be investigated with any of the available dynamic task environments by simply requiring the control task to be completed within a certain temporal limit (e.g., Dörner & Preussler, 1990). Reduced performance should result because the mental processes involved would terminate earlier than under normal circumstances. Second, the system subjects interact with may change autonomously as a function of time. Here, the time pressure is not set externally but is inherent in the task. In addition, subjects must deal with a special type of state change, namely autonomous state changes that are presumably quite different from the ones initiated by subjects' self-generated interventions. We know from the research of Funke and Müller (1988) and of Berry (1991) that learning is severely impaired when both the decision and the active intervention components are missing—which is what characterizes autonomous state changes.

The FIRE task used, for instance, by Brehmer and Allard (1991), is a major exception to the rule that virtually all scenarios employed so far—even the most complex and naturalistic ones—do not require real-time decisions under autonomous state change conditions. Here, we have a fundamental difference to applied research on process control (Bisseret, Figeac, & Falzon, 1988; Stríženec, 1980; Van Daele & De Keyser, 1991) where most complex systems people interact with require decisions in real time. Both the linear equation systems approach and the finite state automata framework can be adapted to incorporate the temporal dimension. For instance, in a finite state automaton one could simply add a separate column to the transition matrix analogous to a new input signal. This new column would contain, for each state, as parameters both the next system state S_{t+1} and the length of the time interval after which the specified state transition will occur, provided the user did not select a different intervention before the end of the time interval.

Another aspect currently ignored, but relevant from an *ecological* point of view is that professionals frequently cooperate with others in process control and decision making. Thus, as we learn more about the cognitive processes involved in an individual's interactions with complex dynamic systems, basic research should also move towards investigating process control embedded in group processes (Schmidt, 1991; Wærn, 1992). A related real-world area is the question of whether skills relevant for successful system control can be taught effectively (e.g., Sonntag & Schaber, 1988). For instance, if one of the primary errors people make when interacting with complex systems really is to reason in causal chains as opposed to causal nets, then teaching how to analyze feedback structures might help to remedy the problem. It is rather ironic that, as with dynamic task environments as tools to select personnel, the real world is again ahead of basic cognitive research in recommending "network thinking" as a "new instrument for tomorrow's successful business executives" (Probst & Gomez, 1991, Foreword; translation by the author).

Finally, the chapter has concentrated on psychological approaches embedded in empirical work rather than on the numerous formal modeling attempts such as *task action grammars* that claim *ex cathedra* to represent user's mental models of a task (e.g., De Haan, Van der Veer, & Van Vliet, 1991). In their current states, these models specify, at most, what the expert user must know to perfectly operate a device such as a computer program (e.g., De Haan & Muradin, 1992). However, it might be useful to explore whether attempts of formal modeling can be utilized for cognitive theories in the future. To repeat the basic idea again, the methodological advantages to be gained from precise formal analyses of the task environments cannot be overestimated, and the question of ecological validity is orthogonal to the question of whether or not a particular scenario has a naturalistic look. However, as with finite state automata and linear equation systems, such formalisms are useful only to the degree to which they can be used to develop theories about knowledge acquisition and knowledge use in dynamic task environments, and to create rational measures for assessing knowledge and control performance. The idea is always to take the formal model of a task as a tool to stimulate theorizing about the task's mental representation, knowing that, beyond a certain point, it will be the deviations from this conceptualization that will turn out to be interesting. This is, of course, an old idea: "By pushing a precise but inadequate formulation to an unacceptable conclusion we can often expose the exact source of the inadequacy and, consequently, gain a deeper understanding" (Chomsky, 1957/1971, p. 5).

REFERENCES

Anderson, J. (Ed.). (1981). *Cognitive skills and their acquisition.* Hillsdale, NJ: Lawrence Erlbaum Associates.

Bandura, A. (1977). Self-efficacy: Toward a unifying theory of behavioral change. *Psychological Review, 84,* 191–215.

Bartlett, F. C. (1932). *Remembering: A study in experimental and social psychology.* London: Cambridge University Press.

Beckmann, J. F. (in press). *Lernen und komplexes Problemlösen. Ein Beitrag zur Validierung von Lerntests* [Learning and complex problem solving. A contribution to validate learning potential tests]. Bonn, Germany: Holos.

Beneke, E. (1877). *Lehrbuch der Psychologie als Naturwissenschaft* [Primer of psychology as a natural science] (4th ed.). Berlin: Ernst Siegfried Mittler und Sohn. (Original work published 1833)

Berry, D. C. (1991). The role of action in implicit learning. *The Quarterly Journal of Experimental Psychology, 43A*, 881–906.

Berry, D. C. (1993). Implicit learning: Reflections and prospects. In A. Baddeley & L. Weiskrantz (Eds.), *Attention, selection, awareness, and control: A tribute to Donald Broadbent* (pp. 246–260). Oxford: Oxford University Press.

Berry, D. C., & Broadbent, D. E. (1984). On the relationship between task performance and associated verbalizable knowledge. *The Quarterly Journal of Experimental Psychology, 36A*, 209–231.

Berry, D. C., & Broadbent, D. E. (1987). The combination of explicit and implicit learning processes in task control. *Psychological Research, 49*, 7–15.

Berry, D. C., & Broadbent, D. E. (1988). Interactive tasks and the implicit-explicit distinction. *British Journal of Psychology, 79*, 251–272.

Bisseret, A., Figeac, L. C., & Falzon, P. (1988). Modelisation de raisonnements opportunistes: L'activité des specialistes de regulation des carrefours a feux [Modeling of "opportunistic" reasoning: The activities of traffic-control experts at intersections during a fire]. *Psychologie Française, 33*, 161–169.

Brandtstädter, J. (1985). Emotion, Kognition, Handlung: Konzeptuelle Beziehungen [Emotion, Cognition, Action: Conceptual relations]. In L. H. Eckensberger & E.-D. Lantermann (Eds.), *Emotion und Reflexivität* (pp. 252–264). München, Germany: Urban & Schwarzenberg.

Brehmer, B. (1987). Development of mental models for decision in technological systems. In J. Rasmussen, K. Duncan, & J. Leplat (Eds.), *New technology and human error*. New York: Wiley.

Brehmer, B. (1989). Dynamic decision making. In A. P. Sage (Ed.), *Concise encyclopedia of information processing in systems and organizations* (pp. 144–149). New York: Pergamon.

Brehmer, B., & Allard, R. (1991). Dynamic decision making: The effects of task complexity and feedback delay. In J. Rasmussen, B. Brehmer, & J. Leplat (Eds.), *Distributed decision making: Cognitive models for cooperative work* (pp. 319–334). New York: Wiley.

Brehmer, B., Leplat, J., & Rasmussen, J. (1991). Use of simulation in the study of complex decision making. In J. Rasmussen, B. Brehmer, & J. Leplat (Eds.), *Distributed decision making: Cognitive models for cooperative work* (pp. 373–386). New York: Wiley.

Broadbent, D. E. (1977). Levels, hierarchies, and the locus of control. *The Quarterly Journal of Experimental Psychology, 29*, 181–201.

Broadbent, D. E. (1989). Lasting representations and temporary processes. In H. L. Roediger & F. I. M. Craik (Eds.), *Varieties of memory and consciousness. Essays in honor of Endel Tulving* (pp. 211–227). Hillsdale, NJ: Lawrence Erlbaum Associates.

Broadbent, D. E., FitzGerald, P., & Broadbent, M. H. P. (1986). Implicit and explicit knowledge in the control of complex systems. *British Journal of Psychology, 77*, 33–50.

Buchner, A. (1993). *Implizites Lernen: Probleme und Perspektiven* [Implicit learning: Problems and future perspectives]. Weinheim, Germany: Psychologie Verlags Union.

Buchner, A., & Funke, J. (1993). Finite-state automata: Dynamic task environments in problem-solving research. *The Quarterly Journal of Experimental Psychology, 46A*, 83–118.

Buchner, A., Funke, J., & Berry, D. C. (in press). Negative correlations between control performance and verbalizable knowledge: Indicators for implicit learning in process control tasks? *The Quarterly Journal of Experimental Psychology*.

Chomsky, N. (1971). *Syntactic structures* (9th ed.). The Hague: Mouton. (Original work published 1957)

De Haan, G., & Muradin, N. (1992). A case study on applying extended task-action grammar. *Zeitschrift für Psychologie, 200*, 135–156.

De Haan, G., Van der Veer, G. C., & Van Vliet, J. C. (1991). Formal modelling techniques in human-computer interaction [Special Issue: Cognitive ergonomics: Contributions from experimental psychology]. *Acta Psychologica, 78*, 27–67.

De Kleer, J., & Brown, J. S. (1983). Assumptions and ambiguities in mental models. In D. Gentner & A. L. Stevens (Eds.), *Mental models* (pp. 155–190). Hillsdale, NJ: Lawrence Erlbaum Associates.

Dörner, D. (1979). Kognitive Merkmale erfolgreicher und erfolgloser Problemlöser beim Umgang mit sehr komplexen Systemen [Cognitive properties of successful and unsuccessful problem solvers when interacting with very complex systems]. In H. Ueckert & D. Rhenius (Eds.), *Komplexe menschliche Informationsverarbeitung* (pp. 185–195). Bern, Switzerland: Hans Huber.

Dörner, D. (1981). Über die Schwierigkeiten menschlichen Umgangs mit Komplexität [On people's difficulty when dealing with complexity]. *Psychologische Rundschau, 32,* 163–179.

Dörner, D. (1982). Wie man viele Probleme zugleich löst—oder auch nicht [How to solve many problems simultaneously—or none at all]. *Sprache & Kognition, 1,* 55–66.

Dörner, D. (1983a). Das Projekt „Systemdenken" [The "Systems Thinking" project]. In C. Schneider (Ed.), *Forschung in der Bundesrepublik Deutschland. Beispiele, Kritik, Vorschläge* (pp. 189–201). Weinheim, Germany: Verlag Chemie.

Dörner, D. (1983b). Kognitive Prozesse und die Organisation des Handelns [Cognitive processes and the organization of actions]. In W. Hacker, W. Volpert, & M. von Cranach (Eds.), *Kognitive und motivationale Aspekte der Handlung* (pp. 26–37). Bern, Switzerland: Hans Huber.

Dörner, D. (1987). On the difficulties people have in dealing with complexity. In J. Rasmussen, K. Duncan, & J. Leplat (Eds.), *New technology and human error* (pp. 97–109). New York: Wiley.

Dörner, D., & Kreuzig, H. W. (1983). Problemlösefähigkeit und Intelligenz [Problem solving ability and intelligence]. *Psychologische Rundschau, 34,* 185–192.

Dörner, D., Kreuzig, H. W., Reither, F., & Stäudel, T. (1983). *Lohhausen. Vom Umgang mit Unbestimmtheit und Komplexität* [Lohhausen. On dealing with uncertainty and complexity]. Bern, Switzerland: Hans Huber.

Dörner, D., & Pfeifer, E. (1992). Strategisches Denken, strategische Fehler, Streß und Intelligenz [Strategic thinking, strategic errors, stress, and intelligence]. *Sprache & Kognition, 11,* 75–90.

Dörner, D., & Preussler, W. (1990). Die Kontrolle eines einfachen ökologischen Systems [Control of a simple ecological system]. *Sprache & Kognition, 9,* 205–217.

Dörner, D., & Reither, F. (1978). Über das Problemlösen in sehr komplexen Realitätsbereichen [On problem solving in very complex domains of reality]. *Zeitschrift für Experimentelle und Angewandte Psychologie, 25,* 527–551.

Dörner, D., Reither, F., & Stäudel, T. (1983). Emotion und problemlösendes Denken [Emotion and problem solving]. In H. Mandl & G. L. Huber (Eds.), *Emotion und Kognition* (pp. 61–64). München, Germany: Urban & Schwarzenberg.

Dörner, D., Schaub, H., Stäudel, T., & Strohschneider, S. (1988). Ein System zur Handlungsregulation oder—Die Interaktion von Emotion, Kognition und Motivation [A system for action regulation or—The interaction of emotion, cognition, and motivation]. *Sprache & Kognition, 7,* 217–232.

Dörner, D., & Schölkopf, J. (1991). Controlling complex systems; or, expertise as "grandmother's know-how." In K. A. Ericsson & J. Smith (Eds.), *Toward a general theory of expertise. Prospects and limits* (pp. 218–239). New York: Cambridge University Press.

Ewert, P. H., & Lambert, J. F. (1932). Part II: The effect of verbal instructions upon the formation of a concept. *Journal of General Psychology, 6,* 400–411.

Eyferth, K., Schömann, M., & Widwoski, D. (1986). Der Umgang von Psychologen mit Komplexität [On how psychologists deal with complexity]. *Sprache & Kognition, 5,* 11–26.

Feather, N. T. (Ed.). (1982). *Expectations and actions. Expectancy-value models in psychology.* Hillsdale, NJ: Lawrence Erlbaum Associates.

Frensch, P. A. (1991). Transfer of composed knowledge in a multi-step serial task. *Journal of Experimental Psychology: Learning, Memory, and Cognition, 17,* 997-1016.

Funke, J. (1983). Einige Bemerkungen zu Problemen der Problemlöseforschung oder: Ist Testintelligenz doch ein Prädiktor? [Some remarks on the problems of problem solving research or: Does test intelligence predict control performance?]. *Diagnostica, 29*, 283–302.

Funke, J. (1984). Diagnose der westdeutschen Problemlöseforschung in Form einiger Thesen [Assessment of West German problem solving research]. *Sprache & Kognition, 3*, 159–172.

Funke, J. (1985). Steuerung dynamischer Systeme durch Aufbau und Anwendung subjektiver Kausalmodelle [Control of dynamic systems by building up and using subjective causal models]. *Zeitschrift für Psychologie, 193*, 443–466.

Funke, J. (1986). *Komplexes Problemlösen. Bestandsaufnahme und Perspektiven* [Complex problem solving. Overview and perspectives]. Heidelberg, Germany: Springer.

Funke, J. (1988). Using simulation to study complex problem solving: A review of studies in the FRG. *Simulation & Games, 19*, 277–303.

Funke, J. (1990). Systemmerkmale als Determinanten des Umgangs mit dynamischen Systemen [System features as determinants of behavior in dynamic task environments]. *Sprache & Kognition, 9*, 143–154.

Funke, J. (1991a). Probleme komplexer Problemlöseforschung [Problems of complex problem solving research]. In R. Fisch & M. Boos (Eds.), *Vom Umgang mit Komplexität in Organisationen. Konzepte—Fallbeispiele—Strategien* (pp. 95–105). Konstanz, Germany: Universitätsverlag Konstanz.

Funke, J. (1991b). Solving complex problems: Exploration and control of complex systems. In R. J. Sternberg & P. A. Frensch (Eds.), *Complex problem solving: Mechanisms and processes* (pp. 185–222). Hillsdale, NJ: Lawrence Erlbaum Associates.

Funke, J. (1992a). Dealing with dynamic systems: Research strategy, diagnostic approach and experimental results. *German Journal of Psychology, 16*, 24–43.

Funke, J. (1992b). *Wissen über dynamische Systeme: Erwerb, Repräsentation und Anwendung* [Knowledge about dynamic systems: acquisition, representation, and use]. Berlin: Springer.

Funke, J., & Buchner, A. (1992). Finite Automaten als Instrumente für die Analyse von wissensgeleiteten Problemlöseprozessen: Vorstellung eines neuen Untersuchungsparadigmas [Finite-state automata as instruments for the analysis of problem solving processes: Introducing a new research paradigm]. *Sprache & Kognition, 11*, 27–37.

Funke, J., & Gerdes, H. (1993). Manuale für Videorecorder: Auswahl von Textinhalten unter Verwendung der Theorie endlicher Automaten [Manuals for video recorders: Selecting text on the basis of finite state automata theory]. *Zeitschrift für Arbeitswissenschaft, 47*, 44–49.

Funke, J., & Müller, H. (1988). Eingreifen und Prognostizieren als Determinanten von Systemidentifikation und Systemsteuerung [Active control and prediction as determinants of system identification and system control]. *Sprache & Kognition, 7*, 176–186.

Gediga, G., Schöttke, H., & Tücke, M. (1983). Problemlösen in einer komplexen Situation [Problem solving in a complex situation]. *Archiv für Psychologie, 135*, 325–339.

Guthke, J. (1993a). Current trends in theories and assessment of intelligence. In J. H. M. Hamers, K. Sijtsma, & A. J. J. M. Ruijssenars (Eds.), *Learning potential assessment* (pp. 13–18). Amsterdam: Swets & Zeilinger.

Guthke, J. (1993b). Developments in learning potential assessment. In J. H. M. Hamers, K. Sijtsma, & A. J. J. M. Ruijssenars (Eds.), *Learning potential assessment* (pp. 43–67). Amsterdam: Swets & Zeilinger.

Haider, H. (1992). Implizites Wissen und Lernen. Ein Artefakt? [Implicit knowledge and learning. An artifact?]. *Zeitschrift für Experimentelle und Angewandte Psychologie, 39*, 68–100.

Hayes, N. A., & Broadbent, D. E. (1988). Two modes of learning for interactive tasks. *Cognition, 28*, 249–276.

Hesse, F. W. (1982a). Effekte des semantischen Kontexts auf die Bearbeitung komplexer Probleme [Effects of semantic context on problem solving]. *Zeitschrift für Experimentelle und Angewandte Psychologie, 29*, 62–91.

Hesse, F. W. (1982b). Training-induced changes in problem solving. *Zeitschrift für Psychologie, 190*, 405–423.

Hesse, F. W., Spies, K., & Lüer, G. (1983). Einfluß motivationaler Faktoren auf das Problemlöseverhalten im Umgang mit komplexen Problemen [Influence of motivational factors on problem solving performance in interacting with complex problems]. *Zeitschrift für Experimentelle und Angewandte Psychologie, 30*, 400–424.

Hörmann, H. J., & Thomas, M. (1989). Zum Zusammenhang zwischen Intelligenz und komplexem Problemlösen [On the relation between intelligence and complex problem solving]. *Sprache & Kognition, 8*, 23–31.

Hübner, R. (1987). Eine naheliegende Fehleinschätzung des Zielabstandes bei der zeitoptimalen Regelung dynamischer Systeme [An obvious error in estimating the goal distance while performing time-optimal regulations of dynamic systems]. *Zeitschrift für Experimentelle und Angewandte Psychologie, 34*, 38–53.

Hübner, R. (1988). Die kognitive Regelung dynamischer Systeme und der Einfluß analoger versus digitaler Informationsdarbietung [Cognitive regulation of dynamic systems and the influence of analogue versus digital presentation of information]. *Zeitschrift für Psychologie, 196*, 161–170.

Hübner, R. (1989). Methoden zur Analyse und Konstruktion von Aufgaben zur kognitiven Steuerung dynamischer Systeme [Methods for the analysis and construction of dynamic system control tasks]. *Zeitschrift für Experimentelle und Angewandte Psychologie, 36*, 221–238.

Humphreys, M. S., Bain, J. D., & Pike, R. (1989). Different ways to cue a coherent system: A theory for episodic, semantic, and procedural tasks. *Psychological Review, 96*, 208–233.

Hussy, W. (1989). Intelligenz und komplexes Problemlösen [Intelligence and complex problem solving]. *Diagnostica, 35*, 1–16.

Hussy, W. (1991). Komplexes Problemlösen und Verarbeitungskapazität [Complex problem solving and processing capacity]. *Sprache & Kognition, 10*, 208–220.

Hussy, W., & Granzow, S. (1987). Komplexes Problemlösen, Gedächtnis und Verarbeitungsstil [Complex problem solving, memory, and processing style]. *Zeitschrift für Experimentelle und Angewandte Psychologie, 34*, 212–227.

Jäger, A. O. (1982). Mehrmodale Klassifikation von Intelligenzleistungen [Multimodal classification of intelligent performance]. *Diagnostica, 28*, 195–225.

Kluwe, R. H., & Haider, H. (1990). Modelle zur internen Repräsentation komplexer technischer Systeme [Models for the internal representation of complex technical systems]. *Sprache & Kognition, 9*, 173–192.

Kluwe, R. H., Misiak, C., & Haider, H. (1989). Erste Ergebnisse zu einem Modell der Steuerung eines komplexen Systems [First results pertaining to a model of human control of complex systems]. In D. Dörner & W. Michaelis (Eds.), *Idola fori et idola theatri. Festschrift aus Anlass der Emeritierung von Prof. Dr. phil. et Dr. med. Hermann Wegener.* Göttingen, Germany: Hogrefe.

Kluwe, R. H., Schilde, A., Fischer, C., & Oellerer, N. (1991). Problemlöseleistungen beim Umgang mit komplexen Systemen und Intelligenz [Problem solving performance when interacting with complex systems and intelligence]. *Diagnostica, 37*, 291–313.

Krems, J., & Bachmaier, M. (1991). Hypothesenbildung und Strategieauswahl in Abhängigkeit vom Expertisegrad. *Zeitschrift für Experimentelle und Angewandte Psychologie, 38*, 394–410.

Kreuzig, H. W. (1981). Über den Zugang zu komplexem Problemlösen mittels prozessorientierter kognitiver Persönlichkeitsmerkmale [Assessing complex problem solving via process-oriented personality traits]. *Zeitschrift für Experimentelle und Angewandte Psychologie, 28*, 294–308.

Lüer, G., Hübner, R., & Lass, U. (1985). Sequences of eye-movements in a problem solving situation. In R. Groner, G. McConkie, & C. Menz (Eds.), *Eye movements and human information processing* (pp. 299–307). Amsterdam: Elsevier Science Publishers.

MacKay, D. G. (1982). The problems of flexibility, fluency, and speed-accuracy in skilled behavior. *Psychological Review, 89*, 483–506.

Marescaux, P.-J., Luc, F., & Karnas, G. (1989). Modes d'apprentisage sélectif et non-sélectif et connaissances acquisés au controle d'un processus: Evaluation d'un modèle simulé [Selective and non-selective learning in process control: Evaluation of a simulation model]. *Cahiers de Psychologie Cognitive European, 9*, 239–264.

Martin, E. (1965). Transfer of verbal paired associates. *Psychological Review, 72*, 327–343.

McCabe, T. J. (1976). A complexity measure. *IEEE Transactions on Software Engineering, SE-2*, 308–320.

McGeorge, P., & Burton, A. M. (1989). The effects of concurrent verbalization on performance in a dynamic systems task. *British Journal of Psychology, 80*, 455–465.

Müller, B., Funke, J., & Buchner, A. (1994). Diskrete dynamische Systeme: Der Einfluß perzeptueller Merkmale auf Komposition und Transfer von Bediensequenzen [Discrete dynamic systems: The impact of perceptual markers on composition and transfer of operating sequences]. *Zeitschrift für Experimentelle und Angewandte Psychologie, 41*, 443–472.

Müller, H. (1993). *Komplexes Problemlösen: Reliabilität und Wissen* [Complex problem solving: Reliability and knowledge]. Bonn: Holos.

Neisser, U. (1976). *Cognition and reality. Principles and implications of Cognitive Psychology*. San Francisco: Freeman.

Probst, G. J. B., & Gomez, P. (Eds.). (1991). *Vernetztes Denken. Ganzheitliches Führen in der Praxis* [Network thinking. Wholistic leadership in applied contexts] (2nd ed.). Wiesbaden, Germany: Gabler.

Putz-Osterloh, W. (1981). Über die Beziehung zwischen Testintelligenz und Problemlöseerfolg [On the relationship between test intelligence and success in problem solving]. *Zeitschrift für Psychologie, 189*, 79–100.

Putz-Osterloh, W. (1983a). Kommentare zu dem Aufsatz von J. Funke: Einige Bemerkungen zu Problemen der Problemlöseforschung oder: Ist Testintelligenz doch ein Prädiktor? [Comment on J. Funke's paper: Some remarks on the problems of problem solving research or: Does test intelligence predict control performance?]. *Diagnostica, 29*, 303–309.

Putz-Osterloh, W. (1983b). Über Determinanten komplexer Problemlöseleistungen und Möglichkeiten zu ihrer Erfassung [On some processes determining the interaction with complex problems, and on the possibilities to assess these processes]. *Sprache & Kognition, 2*, 100–116.

Putz-Osterloh, W. (1985). Selbstreflexionen, Testintelligenz und interindividuelle Unterschiede bei der Bewältigung komplexer Probleme [Self-reflection, intelligence test scores, and interindividual differences in complex problem solving]. *Sprache & Kognition, 4*, 203–216.

Putz-Osterloh, W. (1987). Gibt es Experten für komplexe Probleme? [Are there experts for complex problems?]. *Zeitschrift für Psychologie, 195*, 63–84.

Putz-Osterloh, W., & Lemme, M. (1987). Knowledge and its intelligent application in problem solving. *The German Journal of Psychology, 11*, 286–303.

Putz-Osterloh, W., & Lüer, G. (1981). Über die Vorhersagbarkeit komplexer Problemlöseleistungen durch Ergebnisse in einem Intelligenztest [On whether results from a test of intelligence can predict problem solving performance]. *Zeitschrift für Experimentelle und Angewandte Psychologie, 28*, 309–334.

Raven, J. C. (1965). *Advanced progressive matrices. Sets I and II. Plan and use of the scale with a report of experimental work*. London: Lewis.

Reber, A. S., Kassin, S. M., Lewis, S., & Cantor, G. (1980). On the relationship between implicit and explicit modes in the learning of a complex rule structure. *Journal of Experimental Psychology: Human Learning and Memory, 6*, 492–502.

Reichert, U., & Dörner, D. (1988). Heurismen beim Umgang mit einem „einfachen" dynamischen System [Heuristics in controlling a "simple" dynamic system]. *Sprache & Kognition, 7*, 12–24.

Reither, F. (1979). Über die kognitive Organisation bei der Bewältigung von Krisensituationen [On the cognitive organization when coping with critical events]. In H. Ueckert & D. Rhenius (Eds.), *Komplexe menschliche Informationsverarbeitung* (pp. 210–222). Bern, Switzerland: Hans Huber.

Reither, F. (1981). About thinking and acting of experts in complex situations. *Simulation & Games, 12,* 125–140.

Ringelband, O. J., Misiak, C., & Kluwe, R. H. (1990). Mental models and strategies in the control of a complex system. In D. Ackermann & M. J. Tauber (Eds.), *Mental models and human computer interaction* (pp. 151–164). Amsterdam: Elsevier Science Publishers.

Roth, T. (1985). Sprachstatistisch objektivierbare Denkstilunterschiede zwischen "guten" und „schlechten" Bearbeitern komplexer Probleme [Statistically objectifiable differences in thought styles in the handling of complex problems]. *Sprache & Kognition, 4,* 178–191.

Roth, T. (1987). Erfolg bei der Bearbeitung komplexer Probleme und linguistische Merkmale des Lauten Denkens [Success in solving complex problems and linguistic characteristics of thinking aloud]. *Sprache & Kognition, 6,* 208–220.

Roth, T., Meyer, H. A., & Lampe, K. (1991). Sprachgebrauch, Informationsstrukturierung und Verhalten in einer komplexen Problemsituation [Language use, cognitive differentiation, and behavior in a complex decision task]. *Sprache & Kognition, 10,* 28–38.

Rotter, J. B. (1966). Generalized expectancies for internal versus external control of reinforcement. *Psychological Monographs, 80* (1, Whole No 609).

Schaub, H. (1990). Die Situationsspezifität des Problemlöseverhaltens [The situational specificity of problem solving behavior]. *Zeitschrift für Psychologie, 198,* 83–96.

Schmidt, K. (1991). Cooperative work: A conceptual framework. In J. Rasmussen, B. Brehmer, & J. Leplat (Eds.), *Distributed decision making: Cognitive models for cooperative work* (pp. 75–110). New York: Wiley.

Schoppek, W. (1991). Spiel und Wirklichkeit—Reliabilität und Validität von Verhaltensmustern in komplexen Situationen [Game and reality—Reliability and validity of behavior patterns in complex situations]. *Sprache & Kognition, 10,* 15–27.

Sonntag, K., & Schaper, N. (1988). Kognitives Training zur Bewältigung steuerungstechnischer Aufgabenstellungen [A cognitive training program for monitoring complex automated production processes]. *Zeitschrift fur Arbeits-und Organisationspsychologie, 32,* 128–138.

Stanley, W. B., Mathews, R. C., Buss, R. R., & Kotler-Cope, S. (1989). Insight without awareness: On the interaction between verbalization, instruction, and practice in a simulated process control task. *The Quarterly Journal of Experimental Psychology, 41A,* 553–577.

Stäudel, T. (1987). *Problemlösen, Emotionen und Kompetenz* [Problem solving, emotions, and competence]. Regensburg, Germany: Roderer.

Stäudel, T. (1988). Der Kompetenzfragebogen. Überprüfung eines Verfahrens zur Erfassung der Selbsteinschätzung der heuristischen Kompetenz, belastenden Emotionen und Verhaltenstendenzen beim Lösen komplexer Probleme [The competence questionnaire. Test of an instrument to assess self-perceived heuristic competence, onerous emotions, and action tendencies in solving complex problems]. *Diagnostica, 34,* 136–147.

Strížanec, M. (1980). Man and the technical system. *Studia Psychologica, 22,* 265–268.

Strohschneider, S. (1986). Zur Stabilität und Validität von Handeln in komplexen Realitätsbereichen [On the stability and validity of complex problem-solving behavior]. *Sprache & Kognition, 5,* 42–48.

Strohschneider, S. (1991). Problemlösen und Intelligenz: Über die Effekte der Konkretisierung komplexer Probleme [Problem solving and intelligence: The effects of problem concreteness]. *Diagnostica, 37,* 353–371.

Süß, H. M., Kersting, M., & Oberauer, K. (1991). Intelligenz und Wissen als Prädiktoren für Leistungen bei computersimulierten komplexen Problemen [Intelligence and knowledge as predictors of performance in solving complex computer-simulated problems]. *Diagnostica, 37,* 334–352.

Thalmaier, A. (1979). Zur kognitiven Bewältigung der optimalen Steuerung eines dynamischen Systems [Cognitive mastering of dynamic system control]. *Zeitschrift für Experimentelle und Angewandte Psychologie, 26,* 388–421.

Van Daele, A., & De Keyser, V. (1991). Distributed decision making and time in the control of continuous processes. In J. Rasmussen, B. Brehmer, & J. Leplat (Eds.), *Distributed decision making: Cognitive models for cooperative work* (pp. 261–273). New York: Wiley.

Wærn, Y. (1992). Modelling group problem solving. *Zeitschrift für Psychologie, 200,* 157–174.

Wason, P. C., & Johnson-Laird, P. N. (1972). *Psychology of reasoning: Structure and content.* Cambridge, MA: Harvard University Press.

CHAPTER THREE

Complex Problem Solving: Toward a (Computersimulated) Theory

Dietrich Dörner
University of Bamberg, Germany

Alex J. Wearing
University of Melbourne, Australia

INTRODUCTION

Suppose that you are given a street map of Lohhausen, a town of 6,000 people, as well as information about its finances, taxation system, principal industries, and other commercial activities, and its schools. Suppose you are then told that you have been elected mayor for a 10 year term, and given the goal of ensuring that the inhabitants feel satisfied, both with the town and their own lives. Furthermore, you are told that you can get the information which is normally available to a mayor by asking questions of the experimenter, because you are a subject in an experiment on complex problem solving (CPS) and decision making. You are also told that the experimenter will serve as your Municipal Officer and will carry out any planning tasks you require. You are then informed you can spend time planning, asking questions and deciding what to do, following which you must provide a list of the decisions which are to be carried out in order to achieve your goals. The experimenter will then feed these decisions to the computer on which the township is simulated, and in the next experimental session you will receive the results. You will again be able to ask questions and plan, before making another round of decisions.

This is an example of a task which challenges the ability of subjects to tackle problems in a complex, dynamic and uncertain system. In a long sequence of studies we investigated the behavior of subjects with respect to forms of planning and decision making and especially with respect to errors. We mostly used computer simulated scenarios to study behavior of human beings when they are confronted with the challenge of tackling problems in dynamic, uncertain and very complex systems. These tasks varied widely. In one of our studies, for instance, the experimental subjects had to govern a computer-simulated small town (LOHHAUSEN) as mayor for 10 years and to look after the welfare of the inhabitants (see Dörner, Kreuzig, Stäudel, & Reither, 1983). In another study (MORO) our subjects had to organize developmental aid to a small seminomadic tribe of the southern Sahara (Sahel) region (see Stäudel, 1987; Strohschneider, 1990). In a third series of studies (AIDS) we investigated how subjects and groups of subjects developed strategies to fight an AIDS epidemic in a town modelled on the former West Berlin (see Badke-Schaub, 1993). In another study, we examined the behavior of subjects confronted with the task of managing the control of the production, sales, investment, and advertising strategies of a textile factory (MANUTEX, see Schaub & Strohschneider, 1992). In yet another group of experiments we investigated the behavior of subjects confronted with the task of fire fighting in a Swedish forest (see Dörner & Pfeifer, 1990, 1992; this task was originally developed by Brehmer and his coworkers; see also Brehmer, this volume).

In what follows, we summarize the findings of these and other studies, draw out some general observations, and take the first steps in developing a theory to account for the empirical results.

THE DIFFICULTIES OF PLANNING
AND DECISION MAKING IN COMPLEX, DYNAMIC,
AND UNCERTAIN ENVIRONMENTS

What makes this kind of task difficult? There are six branches of difficulties we will deal with in this section.

Goals. First, often there are difficulties with the goals of such a task. Mostly, the goal is not clearly defined; for example, what might "people should be satisfied with both the town and their own lives" mean? Such global goals must be decomposed into subgoals. For instance, one might decompose overall satisfaction into "good labor conditions," "good wages," "good housing," "opportunities for varied entertainment," and so on (Headey, Glowacki, Holmstrom, & Wearing, 1985; Headey & Wearing, 1992). Even so, most of these goals need further specification. To anticipate our discussion, the processes required for this goal decomposition are *dependency analysis*, and *whole-part analysis*. Dependency analysis involves finding those factors which influence a particular variable, for example, satisfaction, whereas whole-part analysis involves finding an answer to the question, for example, "What are the different particular feelings which together constitute a general feeling of well being?" Even when goals in a complex situation are fairly well-defined, it is often necessary to think about goals which are superimposed on the goals one may strive for at any given time. For instance, it would be a reasonable goal in the MORO simulation to strive for an increase of the size of the cattle population. It is important, however, in the MORO situation to know why this is a reasonable goal because one may be confronted with a situation in which it becomes impossible to increase the size of the cattle population. In such a case it would be necessary to change the goal and for this purpose it is necessary to know that the goal, "increase of the cattle population," is a subgoal of the goal "ensure the subsistence of the Moros." This knowledge makes it easy to switch to the goal "improve the methods of millet cultivation." (This example may seem rather trivial; however, human subjects in concrete decision making situations have often difficulties in switching from one goal to another because it is unclear to them as to why they are pursuing a certain goal.) As a consequence of the global goal being decomposed into many subgoals, another difficulty arises. As time is always limited it is necessary, not only for one action to serve more than one goal, but also to order the priority of these goals. However, in planning actions that are directed toward the most important and most urgent goal, it is important not to neglect the other objectives because the variables in the system may interact with one another, and courses of action directed at reaching an apparently secondary goal may come to have a significant effect overall (e.g., MacKinnon & Wearing, 1980, 1983).

Mental Representation. A second bunch of difficulties arises because of the need to build up a mental representation of the system to be managed (e.g., Dodds, Lawrence, & Wearing, 1991; Putz-Osterloh & Lemme, 1987; Putz-Osterloh, Bott, & Houben, 1988; Sonenberg, Lawrence, & Zelcer, 1992). In reality and in our simulation games, the agent often does not know the network of variables that constitute a system. In this case, it would be necessary to collect information about the system at the given moment and about its development to form hypotheses about the inner structure of the system. For instance, it is extremely important in the MORO game to generate the hypothesis that deep-water wells may have an impact on the ground water level. Otherwise, one might be too careless in drilling wells and therefore cause a severe shortage of water in the long run. (Again this seems to be a rather trivial example for a hypothesis about the inner structure of a system; it can be shown, however, that subjects even have difficulties in constructing such simple relations between the variables of a system.) A mental representation is necessary in order to estimate the direct and immediate as well as the side and the long range effects of the decisions. Of particular importance in building up this representation is a priori knowledge. In managing LOHHAUSEN, schemata about how administration and commerce function and the pattern of material and energy flows in ecological and economic systems are relevant. Such schemata can be used to guide hypothesis building by analogy transfer because they indicate where information is needed, and suggest the questions that must be asked to get at that information. A person with an abstract representation of the structure of a township will easily reach questions like "Is there a theater?" or "Is there a municipal library?" or "What is the situation with regard to effluent purification?" A priori knowledge about the structure of one system may be a great help in constructing a mental representation of another system; on the other hand it could be extremely misleading as a particular reality may not necessarily exhibit that kind of structure we have in mind. LOHHAUSEN and the township we are living in, might not be identical. Hamburg is not Melbourne, although both are large and Dörfleins is not Weetulta, although both are smaller!

Predicting the Future. If one has enough information about a system's structure and its state at the given moment, it makes sense to predict the future development of the system. In contrast to traditional tasks for investigating thinking in the psychological lab (e.g., Tower of Hanoi) our systems have their dynamics built-in, and, therefore, exhibit autonomous development (see Frensch & Funke, this volume). Therefore, it could be that it is not necessary to act at all to reach ones goals as the system's development produces the goal state independently. If, however, the system does not move autonomously in the desired direction, it is necessary to act, taking into account the autonomous developmental tendencies of the system. In any event, it is necessary to predict what will happen to the system.

Action Planning. When one knows the developmental tendencies of a system and the internal structure, it is necessary to plan actions. First, one has to find or prepare a goal-directed course of action (or several courses), and then one has to decide how to act. Planning (i.e., preparing a course of action) might be easy or difficult, depending on the structure of the domain of reality one has to cope with. Planning might be easy if there are not very many different actions available to influence the system's development, if these actions have no undesirable side or longterm effects, and if they can be implemented in a straightforward fashion. If, however, one has to tackle problems in a domain of reality where actions have a lot of side and longterm effects, if actions can only be implemented under certain conditions, and if actions are not deterministic but are stochastic (i.e., produce their outcomes not with certainty but with a more or less known probability), then planning could be extremely difficult and time consuming.

Monitoring the Effects. When a certain course of action has been chosen and implemented, it is necessary to monitor the effects. In complex systems this might not be a simple task, as there might exist considerable *dead-times*; that is, the time delay between the implementation of a certain course of action and its effect might be rather long. Therefore, monitoring the effects requires a lot of effort and a lot of analytical reasoning to separate the effects of one's actions from what is going on in the system.

Self-Monitoring. Last but not least, it is not only necessary to monitor the development of the system, but to monitor one's own strategies of information processing, for instance, the strategies for hypothesis formation, information collection, forecasting, planning, and decision making. One has to engage in self-reflection. To tackle problems in a very complex, dynamic domain of reality is not a one-shot job but a rather long-drawn activity. It may turn out that the strategies of information processing one has at one's disposal at the very beginning are suboptimal and need improvement. Hence, there is a *meta* difficulty, namely thinking about when and how to do what. As a mayor of LOHHAUSEN, one must organize the allocation of one's cognitive resources. We previously mentioned the necessity of ordering the priority of the goals, but this is only one aspect of self-organization. One must, for example, decide whether to go on with question asking (information seeking), or to stop in order to shift to the planning of actions, even though one's knowledge may still be incomplete. One must not only attend to and schedule different activities but also manage one's control system. One's methods of self-organization may be inadequate, making it necessary to deal with and improve them. (Because time is limited, however, it may sometimes be better to continue with concrete problem-solving activities.) Management of affect might be necessary (e.g., Omodei & Wearing, 1991) in order to continue to be effective because time pressure, combined with a restricted knowledge of the system, may lead to worry and helplessness (Janis & Mann, 1977; White, Wearing, & Hill, in press). It may become necessary to deal first with these feelings in order to remain able to act effectively. These difficulties are found not only with complex dynamic tasks, but are likely to be particularly important in these cases because the role of control processes is more important.

Figure 3.1 shows the process of action regulation in a complex system, subdivided into different tasks (see also Dörner, 1989). In the flow diagram of Figure 3.1, we listed the different processes in a sequence that is normally sound. But neither will these different phases of action regulation always show up in the behavior of subjects, nor is this sequence always sound. It might, for instance, be reasonable to go back from hypothesis formation to goal elaboration, as in the course of information collection and hypothesis formation, or it might turn out to be necessary to elaborate on new goals, to change existing goals, or to switch from one goal to another.

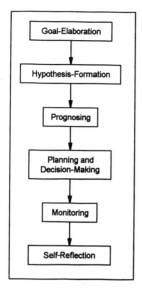

FIG. 3.1. Phases of action regulation.

THEORETICAL ACCOUNTS
OF COMPLEX PROBLEM SOLVING

The purpose of using complex dynamic tasks as experimental environments or microworlds (Brehmer, 1992; Brehmer & Dörner 1993; Funke, 1985, 1986) is to support the construction of a *theory*, which could explain CPS behavior. This seems necessary to explain more complex forms of behavior in everyday life. The normal decision-making situation in everyday life, unfortunately, is not as pure as the decision making setting in the psychological lab (see Pitz & Sachs, 1984). Not only cognitive processes, but a lot of emotional and motivational factors play a role. Normally the decision-situation in normal life exhibits a lot of intransparency with regard to the situation, the consequences of action, and the prerequisites of a decision. Until now psychological research tried to avoid the dirtiness of everyday life by cleaning, and therefore denaturalizing, such situations. The use of complex computersimulated tasks should revert this tendency.

Why not use traditional experimental designs? As we have seen, the behavior of subjects in LOHHAUSEN-like tasks can be decomposed into several distinct processes. Why not study these single processes of planning, building up a mental representation of a problem situation, decision making, self organization, asking questions, et cetera in isolation? Science, after all, proceeds by decoupling systems and studying them separated from their normal environments. Such studies of isolated variables have been (and are) fruitful, but in some cases it may turn out that the interaction between them is lost (e.g., Brehmer, 1974; Dörner, 1989). To gain an understanding of how planning behavior influences information gathering, how the necessities of a particular planning task shape information gathering, and how information gathering in turn shapes further planning, a complex experimental setting such as the one described previously is helpful, even necessary, in addition to the normal experimental procedure.

Microworld tasks are unusual in psychological research although their use in experimental research on problem solving and decision making is increasing (Brehmer, 1992; Brehmer & Dörner, 1993; Funke, 1988, 1991, this volume; Dörner, 1989; Omodei & Wearing, 1991, 1993). We assume, however, that situations exhibiting complexity and dynamic change are far more common than problems generally used in traditional psychological research on thinking and problem solving. As a result, the problem solving literature in psychology offers little theoretical guidance, although there are a few exceptions (Dörner, 1989; Epstein, 1980; Kuhl, 1985; Scheier & Carver, 1988).

When we turn to research traditions outside psychology, we find two theoretical approaches. The first is what could be called the rational-mathematical approach, and is best exemplified in the management sciences and the rational policy literature. Essentially, it involves a rigorous analysis of a problem situation in a way that allows it to be modeled mathematically so that optimization procedure can be applied. The second approach is rooted in political science, and usually involves detailed analysis of particular cases and drawing of general propositions from these cases. Examples are the work of Braybrooke and Lindblom (1963) on incremental decision making, and Allison's (1971) work on the Cuban missile crisis of 1962. None of these studies, however, submits the tasks to experimental analysis. The primary purpose of this chapter is not to review in detail the work of others, but to present the outline of a theory, along with some empirical evidence, concerned with organizing action in complex environments.

SOME EMPIRICAL RESULTS

In the following, we present some empirical results concerning the behavior of subjects when facing CPS tasks. We present results from different studies that are either typical for human behavior in complex situations, as similar results can be observed again and again, or are remarkable, as similar behavior tendencies may lead or have led to severe consequences in reality. Therefore, one has to take such tendencies of behavior into account when confronting subjects with complex tasks.

Goal Elaboration

It is rather common for subjects in situations with ill-defined goals to not at all invest much time and effort in the elaboration of goals. In the MORO game, for instance, experienced executives of German and Swiss manufacturing and service organizations used 31 minutes, on average, to complete the initial orientation phase, whereas the corresponding average time for students has been about 16 minutes (Schaub & Strohschneider, 1992). It is clear that for the experienced managers, the phase of initial orientation and goal elaboration is much more important than it is for the students. The managers invest nearly one quarter of the time period that is at their disposal for orientation and goal elaboration, whereas the students exhibit a stronger tendency to just begin. Later, the executives exhibit on average, a neatly planned and well organized behavior, whereas the students tend to muddle through (for details of expertise research see Shanteau, 1988).

Another commonly observed mistake with goal elaboration is a lack of attention to the balancing of contradictory goals. In a complex system, it is quite normal that different goals cannot be met in the same situation. It is, for instance, almost impossible to find a place for a factory with good traffic connections, cheap land, and a rich reservoir of skilled workers who are prepared to work hard and feel satisfied, even with low salaries. Normally one has to reduce one's level of aspiration for one or more of the different goals. Nonbalancing seems to be especially common when one of the subgoals is already met and is no longer salient as a goal to strive for. If the population of a suburban area asks for better traffic connections to the city, they will normally disregard the side effects of an improvement of the traffic situation, namely the disappearance of business and cultural life in the suburban area.

Information Collection and Hypothesis Formation

Rather frequently in information collection, *channeling errors* can be observed that result from a preformed image of reality. The subject is not prepared to look at the whole range of information but only at the narrow part which she or he, according to her or his image of the system, considers important (Baron, in press, refers to this as *myside-bias*). It is true that one necessarily has to confine information collection to the part of a system that is important. Typically, however, one does not know a priori which part of the system is the most important part at any given time, and often the importance changes with changing goals. It would be a mistake not to look aside and to assume that the image one has about the reality is automatically the correct one.

One can find the contrary tendency, too. Sometimes, subjects encapsulate in information collection. As they feel uncertain and not ready to act, they try to get more information as a basis for decision making. Bewildered by the new facets of the problem provided by new information, they decide still more information is necessary. The new information convinces them even more that the information at their disposal is not sufficient, and so on ad infinitum.

Especially when acting is necessary and urgent, the task of building hypotheses about an unknown piece of reality is a complicated one. It is much easier to stick to the image one has and to renounce hypothesis formation. But this works only if one gives up information collection. When one seeks new information, it is quite likely that the new information may raise some nagging suspicions about the hypotheses one has about the reality. If it becomes necessary to take a second look at reality, one may only look at those parts that provide noncontradictory information and enhance one's image of the reality. Thus, *dogmatic entrenchment* will result, and the individual will stick to his preformed hypothesis of the reality. This tendency will become even stronger if the individual gets the vague feeling that there might be something wrong with her or his hypotheses.

If such a development leading to dogmatic entrenchment is avoided and if an individual, under conditions of complexity and time pressure, begins to build hypotheses about the inner structure of the reality that he or she has to

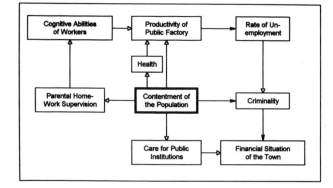

FIG. 3.2. Reductive hypothesis with one central variable: an example from
the LOHHAUSEN study. Solid arrows: positive relations (the more ... the
more); open arrows: negative relations (the more ... the less ...).

cope with, then it is highly probable that *reductive hypothesis formation* will
result. Figure 3.2 exhibits what is meant by reductive hypothesis formation.

Everything in the reality is reduced to one central variable. In the hypothesis system of Figure 3.2, this central variable is the contentment of the
population. The hypothesis was generated by an individual who had participated in the LOHHAUSEN study. Such reductive hypotheses have a lot
of advantages; first, they are easy to handle and to grasp; second, they
provide clear information about how to act; and third, every single piece
of such a hypothesis might be true. This means that it is in no way simple
to falsify such a hypothesis. One may believe in it and this provides security.
Indeed, the only flaw of such a reductive hypothesis might be that it is
incomplete. The incompleteness of such a reductive hypothesis, however,
has the severe consequence that an agent only considers such actions that
in her or his opinion have an impact on the central variable. Thus, wrong
plans (because they are too narrow) will result.

It is quite interesting for a theory of CPS that there seem to be striking
differences in the orientation and information intake behavior of successful
and unsuccessful subjects.

Figures 3.3 and 3.4 show the relative frequencies of transitions between
different forms of question asking, decision making (D), and information
phases (I) provided by the experimenter.

General orientation (GO) means questions as "Is there a theater in the
town?" or "Are there bank houses?"

Special orientation (SO) means questions like "What is the percentage
of income tax?" or "What is the cash-balance of the town?"

Exploration (EX) means questions like "How would more salary for the
workers influence the production rate of the municipal factory?" or "What
would the consequences of general rise of the taxation rates be?"

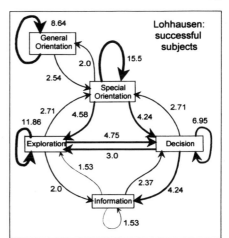

FIG. 3.3. Transitions (percentages) between different forms of information-processing in the LOHHAUSEN task: successful subjects.

It is clearly visible that the successful and unsuccessful subjects differ. Relative to the unsuccessful subjects the successful have fewer GO–GO, GO–SO, SO–GO and SO–SO transitions, but more SO–EX and EX–SO, EX–D and D–EX, D–I and I–D, EX–I and D–D. Unsuccessful subjects tend to move more within and between GO and SO, whereas the successful subjects move much more readily from state to state. In addition the successful subjects tend to *lump* their decisions (DD% = 6.95), indicating that they are employing a higher order strategy (DD% = 4.62 for the unsuccessful subjects).

Forecasting

For man it is not easy to handle time (e.g., Brehmer, 1990, 1992; Dörner & Preussler, 1990; Reichert & Dörner, 1988; Sterman, 1989). We live in the present, and the past disappears behind veils and is not at our disposal

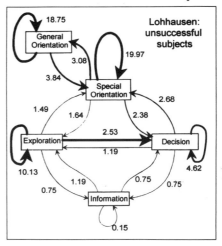

FIG. 3.4. Transitions (percentages) between different forms of information-processing in the LOHHAUSEN task: unsuccessful subjects.

anymore. Therefore, it is very difficult for us to build a good image of what is going on over time. We have difficulties in understanding the characteristics of developments simply because we forget so much. Therefore, the images we form about developments are often too simple. Linear extrapolation in one or the other form is rather common. "Last year we had 7,900 cases of AIDS, now we have 8,100, therefore we will have about 8,300 cases next year." Such forecasting may be quite successful in normal life for the prediction of events from one hour to the next or from one day to the next, but it fails with longterm developments. That is, the cognitive mechanism which proves to be quite appropriate in daily life is mostly inappropriate for the orientation in time over longer periods. Linear forecasting does not only occur with respect to future developments but to the acceleration of developments, too. If a development seems to be dangerous, for instance, one will often encounter a tendency to assume a constant or even growing acceleration rate. Such acceleration rates, however, can hardly be observed in natural processes. A growth process will normally exhaust its resources and therefore acceleration rates will shrink over the course of time.

In 1987, we asked 57 students to predict the development of the AIDS epidemic in Western Germany. Now, six years later (early 1993), we can check the validity of the students' predictions. Figure 3.5 shows the results of the study. A cluster analysis yielded four groups of subjects: Group E (14 subjects) used the method of linear extrapolation. Groups A and B (23 subjects) grossly overestimated the development, using the assumption that the acceleration rates would remain constant or grow linearly. Only the members of group C (13 subjects), formed an hypothesis about the development that was close to reality. An analysis of the commentaries made by our experimental subjects revealed that the members of group A and B were more alarmed by the danger of the AIDS epidemic than were the members

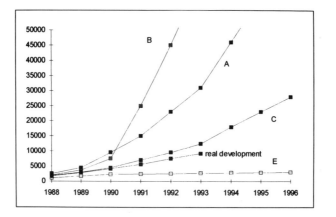

FIG. 3.5. Prognoses of the AIDS-epidemics in Germany.

of group E. This result shows that the subjects' choice of a prognosis model was triggered by their feelings or emotional states.

Predictions will be especially difficult when developments are not monotonic, but exhibit more or less sudden changes. Figure 3.6 shows data from Dörner and Preussler (1990, see also Dörner, 1989, p. 217) where experimental subjects had the task of predicting the development of a predator-prey system consisting of a sheep (prey) and a wolf (predator) population. In this task it was clearly visible to the experimental subjects that the predator population was growing, influencing the size of the prey population. Therefore, it should have been evident that after some time the predators would run into difficulties with foraging and would suffer from the decrease of the prey population. But this was not the prediction of the experimental subjects. They first underpredicted the growth of the wolf population, and then, with very few exceptions, were not able to predict the inversion of the predator population caused by the decrease of the prey population. On the contrary, they predicted for the inversion year an even higher rate of growth of the wolf population (see prediction for year 8).

We surmise from this result that subjects might have extreme difficulties in predicting developments that are governed by the laws of a deterministic chaos. Such developments, however, seem not to be infrequent in ecological, economical, and political contexts, yet we do not know of experiments that have used the task of predicting chaotic developments.

Planning and Decision Making

Planning means to create new courses of action by combining pieces which the planner finds in his memory model of the world. With complex systems, the main planning mistake seems to be to disregard side and longterm effects which nearly every action will have. As we have already explained, one can almost never do isolated things in complex systems. For example, the administration of a town wanted to strive for more greenery in the city. Thus, a decision was made that trees older than 10 years could not be felled without a special permit by the town authorities. What happened? Not an

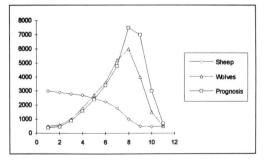

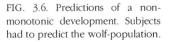

FIG. 3.6. Predictions of a non-monotonic development. Subjects had to predict the wolf-population.

increase in the number of trees in the town, as one might expect, but rather a decrease, as all owners of private gardens, faced with the prospect of not being masters of their own land any longer, felled a lot of trees that came close to the 10-year threshold that they were not absolutely certain they would like to live with for the next 20 years.

Another example for an undesired side effect, and one of the main causes for the Chernobyl disaster, was the decision by the operating team to increase the flow of water through the primary circuit to enlarge the cooling capacity of the reactor (see Reason, 1987). They disregarded, however, that this decision caused the program of the reactor to withdraw the graphite rods which served as a brake for uncontrolled reactions. The reason for this programming was that normally a decrease in steam pressure should be counterbalanced by an increase in the number of reactions. In this case, however, this was not the desired goal. The withdrawal of the graphite rods did not result in an increase of safety, but rather in a decrease.

When a planner confronts the challenge of taking into account side and longterm effects of her or his actions, she or he will run the risk of being caught in a vicious cycle of planning. Attempts to take into account all the side and longterm effects will result in more planning and information collecting about how to avoid the undesirable outcomes. It is not unusual that this will lead to the discovery of even more undesirable outcomes which deserve still more planning and information collection.

It is not uncommon to find that the process of planning is guided not by the goal which should be achieved but by the salience of the effects of one's actions. Thus, in an industrial enterprise facing the situation of a dramatic decrease in sales, the reason for the decrease was not analyzed. Instead, the firm began to restructure the whole organizational structure. This did not change anything with respect to the sales situation but gave the general managers the feeling they were doing something (see Janis & Mann, 1977).

To be able to do something gives a good feeling in a difficult situation and therefore, the goal of demonstrating one's ability to act might replace the original goal. In one of our experiments with the fire game we had two groups of subjects (Dörner & Pfeifer, 1990, 1992). One group of subjects had to solve the problems of this game under conditions of stress, induced by an unforeseeable loud noise. The other group worked without noise. The two groups differed with respect to their decisions. Subjects in the stress group preferred the *patrol command* (16% of all commands for the stress group versus 4% for the nonstress group) instead of the *goal-command*. The patrol command caused a lot of *action* on the screen; patrolling the fire-fighting units showed a lot of rather senseless motions, consuming a lot of fuel, whereas with the goal command the units moved in a straightforward fashion toward their respective goals. For the subjects under stress, the patrol command seemed to be a means of competence demonstration; these commands caused more salient effects than the goal commands.

All these different forms of planning and decision making may often appear in combinations. A subject may first feel uncomfortable with a complex situation and may begin with very careful planning. This, however, may generate a still greater nagging feeling, as planning and information collection uncovers the complexity and difficulty of the situation. The increased uncomfortable feelings may produce a sudden outburst of *actionism* which is directed not toward the goal to be achieved but toward a demonstration of competence.

Looking at subjects who are successful in a complex task and comparing their behavior with the behavior of subjects who are not successful, one finds differences in decision making behavior in terms of the number of intentions in relation to the number of decisions. Typically, with the successful individuals, one decision serves to meet several goals and one goal has connections with a number of different decisions. For instance, the goal of improving the financial state of the township of LOHHAUSEN was combined with the goal of stopping immigration in a decision that implemented an elaborate taxation system with heavy tax rates for immigrants. The goal, to stop immigration, was set up with the purpose of improving the housing situation, or at least to prevent it from getting worse.

Thus, we found a goal decision structure for our successful subjects where the goals formed a hierarchy such that macro goals were divided into several subgoals and the demands of several goals were met by one set of decisions. With unsuccessful subjects, the goals and decisions remained relatively unrelated to each other.

Similar results were found by Streufert (1984) for the decision making behavior of successful industrial managers. For instance, he found that a successful manager combines decisions about the person's situation with decisions about the financial situation and about product development, whereas less successful managers, as with our unsuccessful subjects, tend to make decisions that serve to complete just one intention. It is clear that such *concerted* decisions are more effective than isolated decisions.

A related result is that successful subjects tended to *lump* their decisions at the end of an experimental session whereas unsuccessful subjects distributed their decisions nearly uniformly over the whole time period (Schaub & Strohschneider, 1992). This result is clearly related to the *concerted* decision making behavior of the successful subjects.

Rather common for unsuccessful subjects is *thematic vagabonding*. This means a behavior of jumping from one topic of planning and decision making to another, when difficulties arise. Instead of trying to overcome these difficulties the subject turns to an other problem (and normally there are problems in abundance in complex systems). But this new field of occupation is left again in the moment when the subject has to face difficulties with this new problem. Then the subject changes to a third problem and so on, until the subject comes to rest with a problem which may be quite unimportant but is easy to solve.

A decision serves the purpose of approaching or reaching a goal, but in a complex system it is never quite clear whether a certain decision has really the intended effects. To adapt the decision-making behavior to the circumstances and conditions of a particular situation, it is necessary to check or monitor the effects of a decision.

Monitoring the Effects of One's Actions

Decisions in a complex situation often have long *dead times*. Successes or failures are not immediately visible but show up only after days, months, or even years. Feedback delay makes the control of the appropriateness of one's actions difficult. Rather often, the noncohesion of decision and effect will lead to an abandonment of monitoring the effects of one's actions. Monitoring is simply forgotten.

Additionally however, one can find conditions which strengthen the tendency to forget the monitoring of effects. Figure 3.7 shows one result of a MORO-type experiment (Reither, 1985). It shows the extent of effect monitoring of the experimental subjects in the first, second, third, and fourth 5-year period of the simulation (actually, the 5-years period lasted about 30 minutes each). It is clear that the experimental subjects did not monitor the effects of their actions to a great extent. More than 50% of the effects remained uncontrolled. But one can see a sharp decrease of even this low percentage after the 10th year. This decrease is due to a crisis introduced by the experimenter after the 10th year, namely an aggressive action from a country.

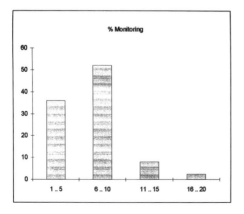

FIG. 3.7. Monitoring-rate of the effects of actions.

This unexpected event (which was not very dangerous, by the way) caused a nearly total neglect of monitoring. A *ballistic* form of action resulted; the actions were just fired like cannon balls, and similar to the flight of cannon balls; the course of the effects of the actions was not monitored and hence could not be corrected.

Reither also found that the variation of the *dosage* of decision making increased after the introduction of a crisis. (The term dosage here refers to the magnitude of a policy measure, e.g., the amount of increase in taxation or arms production.) That is, the control processes became much less finely tuned to the situation.

A further result of the Reither study concerns the discrepancies of the decision making behavior of the subjects from their respective value systems. The ratings were made after the experiment, and the subjects assessed their decision, not in their original form, but *depersonalized* so that they appeared to be the decisions of another person. On a 9-point scale, the discrepancies between values and decision making increased from 1.5 to about 7 after the introduction of the crisis. With its introduction, the value system of the subjects lost nearly completely their function as a regulatory system for planning actions. The experimental subjects exhibited, an immoral shift; their decisions were no longer in accordance with their system of values.

Self-Reflection

Human thinking and planning may be guided by certain rules but these rules are not inevitable laws. Humans are able to think about their thinking strategies and this renders thinking flexible. When confronted with the problems of a complex system, it is advisable to think about one's thinking. As we have shown in the preceding, a number of commonly used strategies of thinking and planning are quite inappropriate to meet the challenges of complex systems.

However, phases of spontaneous self-reflections are nearly absent in human thinking (see Dörner, 1974, p. 174). If one, however, induces self-reflection, then one can improve the capabilities of problem solving considerably (e.g., Hesse, 1982; Reither, 1979; Tisdale, 1994).

The abandonment of phases of self-reflection is often caused by the tendency to avoid doubts about the appropriateness of one's thinking abilities. Self-criticism implies the recognition of the mistakes one has made, and this may mean a loss of the feeling of competence. A high feeling of competence, however, is just what seems to be extremely needed in complex problem situations. Without such a feeling, one would not dare to tackle the problems of such a situation. And this may be the reason for abandoning self-reflection.

The abandonment of self-reflections means, however, that one will be caught in a vicious cycle of incompetence. Error-prone thinking tendencies are not detected; therefore, a lot of errors will result and actions will not have the desired effects. The ineffectiveness of one's actions, however, endangers the feeling of competence. Therefore, one tries to avoid the confrontation with the errors, which in turn blocks reflections about the reasons of the mistakes.

Stability of Performance

We have considered a large number of behavioral patterns of subjects. The question arises as to whether these patterns are dependent on relatively stable traits of personality or whether they are simply a function of the situation. Both dependencies and their interactions might exist, and they might have interactive relations with some general rules of information processing in human beings. Two studies were undertaken that exposed the same subjects twice or more to complex environments, and compared the behavioral patterns in the different situations.

In the first of these studies (Kühle & Badke, 1986), subjects were given four nondynamic complex political problems. One of these problems was the Louis XVI problem. The subjects received a transcription of the situation faced by Louis XVI in the year 1787 when the French government was faced with the collapse of the financial system of the state and a reformation of the taxation system had to take place. This meant imposing some financial sacrifices on the French nobility and the Church. (The plan was rejected, by the way, and was, one of the reasons for the French revolution.)

The subjects were given a simplified (but still complex) description of the situation and had to give elaborate proposals for their decision. In order not to evoke any knowledge about the actual event on the part of subjects, the situation was set in China before the time of Christ.

The other three situations were similar, difficult, political problems—one, for instance, represented the situation of the German Social Democratic party on the eve of the threatened collapse of the Western Front in 1918, when it was asked to take over governmental power in Germany. Again we transferred the situation, this time to the Italy of the 12th century.

The decision proposals of the subjects were rated by two independent judges, primarily on whether the proposals dealt with the central aspects of the respective problem. The intercorrelations of the judges were high, about 0.8, so we combined the two judgments to get for every subject on every problem one *elaboration index* as a measure of the quality of the proposals. The different elaboration indices correlated significantly with each other from 0.4 to 0.7.

One half year later, about half of the original subjects had to manage the MORO task (Stäudel, 1987) which concerns the situation of a nomadic tribe in the Sahel zone in Africa. The subjects had to cope with this dynamic, computer-simulated task, and we compared the effectiveness of our subjects with the summed elaboration indices of the four political problems. Again, we found a correlation of about 0.6 between the sum of the elaboration indices of the political problems and the effectiveness of the behavior in the MORO situation. These results support the hypothesis that some factors must be common to these different situations.

To shed some light on which personal characteristics might be involved in such a complex problem situation, Strohschneider (1986) exposed the same subjects twice (within an interval of 6 to 8 weeks) to the MORO task to determine whether microaspects of behavior were correlated in both situations. These results show a high level of consistency across the two tasks.

TOWARD A THEORY OF COMPLEX PROBLEM SOLVING

Previously we described several different patterns of behavior partly related to task success and failure. What kind of production systems explain these different patterns of behavior? How is the connection between such a production system and personality parameters related to success and failure? (It has not been very successful to reduce achievement in complex problems to test intelligence; see Putz-Osterloh, 1981; Putz-Osterloh & Lüer, 1981.) What would a theory look like that explains all those general tendencies and single mistakes and errors presented in the foregoing paragraphs?

Such a theory must integrate not only hypotheses about the pure cognitive functions of the human mind but must take into account hypotheses about motivational and emotional processes and the impact on processes of thinking and reasoning. What might a theory of CPS look like? In the following we will try to develop some ideas about factors and processes which should be taken into consideration as components of such a theory.

In Figure 3.8 a rough outline of the components of such a theory is exhibited. On the left side one can see the general flow of information processing is exhibited. Goals (maybe preliminary goals) form the raw material for *intention generation* which generally means an elaboration of the goals into more precise goals, goal-sub-goal-hierarchies, et cetera. This process is determined by the subjects view of the structure of reality and of his knowledge of the present state of the reality. The process of intention generation produces a memory structure, which we call *intention memory*. *Intention memory* is the input for *intention selection*. Intention selection determines which of the intentions in intention memory should be the object of the higher cognitive processes called *intention handling* in Figure 3.8. It is dependent of the subjects' view of his or her competence for tackling the problem, his or her view about the importance of the problem in the context of all the other problems and of his or her view of the urgency of the

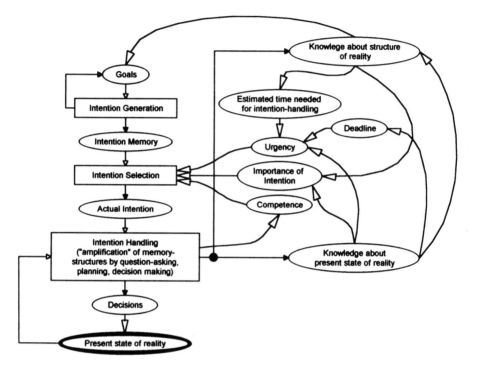

FIG. 3.8. The general shape of a theory on CPS. Read filled arrows as: "produce," "alter"; small unfilled arrows as: "is material for . . . "; large unfilled arrows as: "determines."

problem, which again is dependent on the knowledge of deadtimes and the estimation of the time, needed to solve the respective problem.

Intention handling means to look to the given state of the reality, to ask questions about this state and to enlarge ones knowledge about the general strucure of reality. (What are the variables the system *reality* consists of and how are they interconnected?) This process of an *amplification* of the knowledge structure is to a high degree a process of self-questioning by using one's own conceptual structures. On the basis of this knowledge decisions are made or further planning processes are launched.

In the following we describe some of the components and of the relations of this theory in greater detail.

- We describe the part of the theory concerning intention selection, which from our point of view is of primary importance to explain much of the dynamics of the observable behavior of our subjects.
- We will describe a theory about the central part of intention handling, namely the forms of memory search and memory usage in CPS. This

part of the theory is of great importance to explain, why our subjects ask which questions when and why they come to which decisions. More than by the traditional planning procedures (of the GPS-type for instance) our subjects come to a decision by elaborating their image of the system they have to cope with and their image of the momentarily given situation. We will consider the possible form of such an *amplification-procedure*.

- It seems necessary to look to some general conditions of human cognition and therefore we would like to draw the attention of the reader to some rather general factors which are of importance for action regulation in complex environments and which penetrate all the processes of goal-elaboration, of intention selection and of intention handling.

Intention Regulation

In our eyes the whole process of coping with a complex problem can be seen as a process of intention regulation. It is characteristic of our problems that they are polytelic. This means that our subjects have multiple goals. In the LOHHAUSEN game for instance an individual has to care for the education system of the town, has to have an eye on the cash balance of the municipal factory, has to think about the supply of residences and so on. All the problems demand a solution as soon as possible, but for human beings it is impossible to think consciously about more than one problem at the same time. That means that in a multi-problem situation it is necessary to organise a time-sharing process. The individual must decide when, and what time, and with which problems he or she should be occupied.

How is such a time-sharing process organized? To answer this question we have developed a theory of an *intention memory* together with a theory of *intention regulation*. In Figure 3.9 we exhibit one element of the intention memory.

At every moment there normally exist a lot of intentions for a problem solver. These intentions can form hierarchies according to their instrumentality. That is, there might exist subintentions for the main intention to care for a better supply of residences in the LOHHAUSEN game. Every intention has, at any given moment, a certain *strength*. The strength of an intention is the tendency to take over the control about higher mental functions. The strength of an intention is dependent on the importance of the underlying problem, the urgency, and the subjective feeling of competence. Roughly, the formula for the strength of an intention is:

$$\text{Strength} = \text{competence} * (\text{importance} + \text{urgency}).$$

(We will not consider the details of the mathematics underlying the actual computation of the strength. There is, for instance, an expectancy-value-

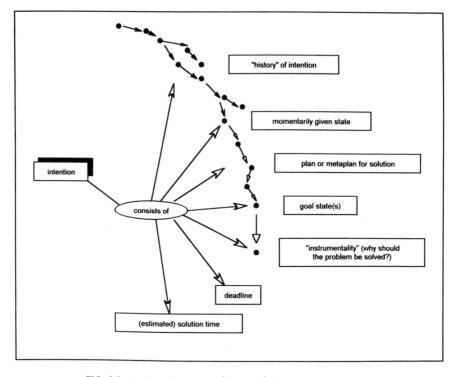

FIG. 3.9. An intention as an element of the intention memory.

component within this formula with competence representing expectancy of success and importance representing value; see Atkinson & Birch, 1978.)

In every moment, there is a competition of the different intentions, and the intention with the greatest strength wins and takes over control. As the parameters entering the computation of the strength of an intention are not at all stable within the process of tackling a complex problem, the strengths of the different intentions can vary considerably. If, for instance, a subject has chosen an intention for execution, it may be the case that within a short time the subject notices that the problem is much more difficult than expected. This experience will lower the (subjective) competence and the strength of the actual intention accordingly. This might result in another intention popping up and gaining access to the higher mental controls. If, again, the subject notices that this problem is also much more difficult than expected, *thematic vagabonding* might result and the subject might end up solving a problem that is not important at all, but is easy to solve.

The actual competence is dependent on the heuristic competence of an individual and on his or her *epistemic* competence. *Heuristic competence* is the confidence that an individual has about his or her abilities to find any missing operators, by thinking, reasoning, asking questions, et cetera.

Epistemic competence concerns the confidence of an individual that he or she already knows how to fulfill the requirements of a certain task.

Both forms of competence may vary during problem solving and in that way influence the strength of an intention. Intention selection consists of choosing that intention which at that particular time has the greatest strength. Although this is a quite simple theory, it explains why subjects sometimes hold on to their intentions until they are ready and why sometimes the intentions, which are just carried out, change quite rapidly.

Heuristic competence seems to be essential for the change of intentions. If heuristic competence is high, actual competence remains relatively stable whatever the fate of the epistemic competencies. If heuristic competence is low, however, epistemic competence plays an important role in determining the level of actual competence. Epistemic competence can easily be proved wrong. If one believes one knows how to raise the productivity of a plant, one can easily observe, by regulating success or failure, whether this belief is true or false. If the actual competence depends mainly on epistemic competence, failure will lower the actual competence drastically.

General Recursive Analytic-Synthetic Constellation Amplification

Previously we considered the *mechanics of intention* regulation as a competition of intentions. The intentions fight for access to the higher mental controls. In this paragraph, we look at the process of intention handling. We will try to get an idea of what it means that an intention has access to the higher mental controls. We consider the sequence of cognitive processes intended to achieve a system of operation designed to reach a goal.

There exist different levels of such processes: First, most subjects try to solve the actual problem just by activating an appropriate plan which exists already in their memory. This level is simple. If a plan exists, it will be carried out. If such a plan is not at hand (as it mostly will be the case), the next cognitive process will be some kind of planning. Other writers (e.g., Newell & Simon, 1972) have presented ideas about the possible forms of such planning processes but those theories seem to be incomplete. They center around acitivities of the composition of single pieces of operations to form long chains or networks (plans). With such experimental paradigms as the Tower of Hanoi or Missionaries and Cannibals planning activities of this form might indeed describe human behavior adequately, but for CPS they do not seem to be of great importance. For us *amplification-processes* of memory structures seem to be much more essential. Such *amplifications* serve several purposes: they produce new hypotheses about the structure of reality and they often lead directly to decisions (mostly without any planning activities). Planning activities of the traditional form could (but must not) follow such amplification-processes.

Decision making mostly should be preceded (and *is* mostly preceded) by processes that amplify the information about the facts and structures which are needed as raw material for planning. Such an amplification process can take different forms. It typically consists of a sequence of self questioning and asking questions from the environment.

Figure 3.10 exhibits an example of a theory that is concerned with how subjects pattern their question asking behavior. It is a hypothesis about the form of a GRASCAM (General Recursive Analytic Synthetic Constellation Amplification) process. A GRASCAM process is generally directed toward an enrichment and differentiation of the mental representation of a certain environment. The specific GRASCAM process of a subject can be identified in the pattern of questions a subject asks, "What is the state of the task?" or "How could I influence that state?" or "What will be the consequences of a certain event?" or "What is the normal context of a certain event . . . ?" and so on.

There are four levels of analysis within the system in Figure 3.10. The first one is the analysis of parts, the second one is the analysis of superordinates ("What is an X?"), the third one is the analysis of subordinates ("What other Xs

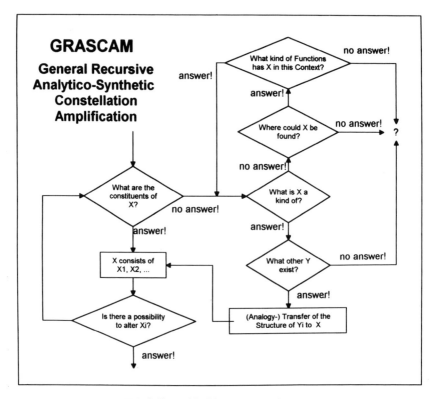

FIG. 3.10. A GRASCAM process. See text.

exist?"), and the last one is the analysis of the context of the unknown X. These levels of analysis correspond to the conceptual relations which Klix (1988, 1992) calls *relations concerning attributes* and *relations concerning events.* (The system in Figure 3.10 should not be taken as final. It is a starting point for a theory about how people perform memory searches and/or ask questions when they have to cope with a topic that is unclear to them.)

Let us look at an example of a concrete GRASCAM-process. Imagine that a subject has difficulties with the productivity of the municipal factory of LOHHAUSEN which produces watches. Thus, the subject asks him or herself or the environment, "What are the constituents of watch-manufacturing?" If the subject does not know or does not get an answer, the next step will be to ask for a superordinate of watch manufacturing. This could result in the judgment, "Watch manufacturing is a production process!" The next question would be, "Are there other types of production processes that I know?" The answer could be, "Well, I produce my own cigarettes! For this purpose, I need raw material, namely tobacco, paper, and a little bit of saliva. Additionally, some skill is needed, a little bit of experience, and a little bit of energy! Well then, what kind of skill and experience is needed for watch manufacturing, how much energy, and what kind of raw materials?"

This is a rather primitive sequence of questions, but it puts the subject into the position of getting a coarse idea about the process of watch-manufacturing and of asking the right questions. (If the question about the superordinate for watch manufacturing could not be answered, then the next step would have been to ask for the situation where watch manufacturing takes place. The study of the context of this production process could yield information about this kind of a production process.)

The main task in coping with a problem in our experiments is to build up a network of causal relations. A GRASCAM process will result in just such a network. Figure 3.11 demonstrates an elaborated network of causal and consists of relations. It is the product of a subject trying to get a better understanding of "How to influence the well being of the inhabitants of LOHHAUSEN." First, the subject asked (herself or the external world), "What does well-being consist of?" If she gets an answer to this question, she would investigate how one could influence the parts of this item. This could be successful or not. If it were not successful, the system would continue with this part of the original X as a new X and start the process again.

The network of Figure 3.11 seems to provide a rather good basis for planning and decision making. Why does such a memory structure help in constructing a network of causal relationships? Let us consider an example, the concept "decay." In a semantic network, this concept might look like the representation in Figure 3.12.

Besides the concept *decay*, we have two other general and abstract concepts, namely, *structure* and *object.* If someone possesses the concept of

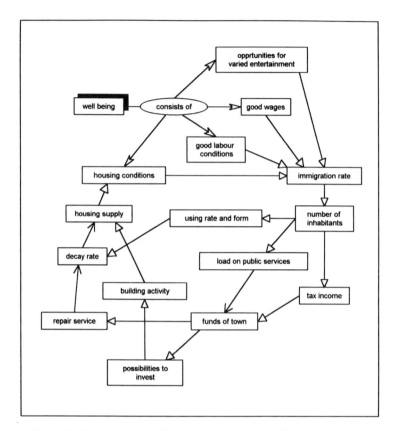

FIG. 3.11. Elaborated network of causal relations. Solid arrows: positive relations (the more ... the more, the less ... the less); open arrows: negative relations (the less ... the more, and vice versa).

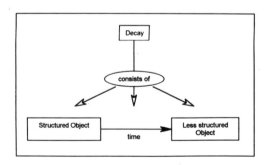

FIG. 3.12. Mental representation of the concept of decay.

decay in this form he or she will recognize a house as a structural object, and will therefore have available the idea that, over time, houses deteriorate and that this deterioration over time reduces the supply of residences. From that, the idea could arise that *one* measure to secure the supply of houses is to have a good repair and maintenance system.

This sounds quite trivial once it is explained but many people do not have such ideas spontaneously. Typically, our poorer subjects reiterate that they have no idea what to do. This appears to be indeed the case because they are not able to recognize things and events as special instances of an abstract concept. Therefore, things and events remain isolated for them, and they have no idea how to cope with them.

Figure 3.13 exhibits an unelaborated network. A subject with such a model of the town will arrive at a decision as well, but it will be a simple decision not connected to other aspects of the system. The subject will not exhibit a *concerted* decision making behavior, whereas a subject with the network of Figure 3.11 will.

The assumption that some subjects are able to construct a differentiated network of assumptions about the system, whereas other subjects only build up simple, straightforward networks, explains many of the empirical differences. It explains:

- The.differences in the number of decisions because an elaborated network will lead to more decisions.

- The differences in the coordination of decision making behavior, as a differentiated network will lead to more coordination.

- The larger number of GO (general orientation) questions for the unsuccessful subjects. They need information about the context because they are not able to answer the whole-part or the concrete-abstract questions of the GRASCAM process.

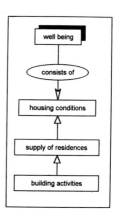

FIG. 3.13. An unelaborated network.

- The larger number of questions for the unsuccessful subjects because they need generally more information from external sources and cannot answer the questions of a GRASCAM-process for themselves.

- The thematic vagabonding behavior of the unsuccessful subjects because they run out of information early when coping with a problem.

- Why unsuccessful subjects feel bewildered and confused from the very beginning of an experiment.

What are the reasons why some people are able to construct relatively elaborate networks while others are not? One hypothesis is that some people have a memory structure that is broader with respect to concrete experiences and deeper with respect to abstract concepts.

Why is it that some subjects' memory structures are broad with respect to concreteness and deep with respect of abstractness? It may be that the positive feedback loop shown in Figure 3.14 plays an essential role in explaining the differences in certain personality traits with our subjects.

With heuristic competence, an individual is more willing to tackle risky, uncertain, unknown, and novel environments. Such environments produce many new experiences which normally do not fit into the cognitive system of the individual. That is, they produce cognitive dissonance. Cognitive dissonance is a challenge for the system of cognitive processes, the challenge being to remove this dissonance. Contradictions and dissonance can only be resolved by introducing abstract concepts that mediate between contradictory concrete experiences. Therefore, cognitive dissonance produces abstract concepts.

Abstract concepts, in turn, strengthen the heuristic competencies of an individual. High heuristic competence encourages one to tackle uncertain and novel environments. This brings novel experiences that often contradict

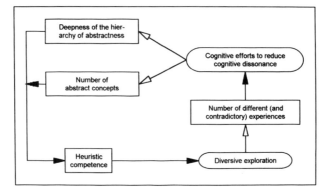

FIG. 3.14. Heuristic competence and the hierarchy of abstract concepts. Filled arrows should be read as "enhances," unfilled arrows as "produce."

the existing cognitive systems. We find here a positive feedback loop such that heuristic competence enhances itself!

Other hypotheses about the differences between successful and unsuccessful subjects in constructing complex networks are conceivable (see Putz-Osterloh, 1983, 1987). One is that the ability of a subject to translate verbal information into images could be important. What is the meaning, for instance, of "the inhabitants' well being" in the LOHHAUSEN study? To understand that, the concrete image of a normal housewife's day or the day of an inhabitant of an old people's home could be helpful. Through concrete imagery one can grasp the components of an abstract concept such as *well being.*

To be able to develop concrete images for a verbal (hence abstract) description of something, it is necessary, though not sufficient, to have a good representation of a causal network. One must often be able to connect concrete with abstract concepts. For example, understand rust as a product of an oxidation process might help in working out how to fight rust.

The whole process of intention handling is often enough triggered by what one generally calls *emotion.* One special and important form of such an influence is what we call emergency reaction of the cognitive system. For this reaction the feeling of competence is especially important. Assumptions about the "emergency reaction of the cognitive system" explain how success and failure in problem solving influence the form of thinking by triggering the emotional change in an individual. Roughly it has the form shown in Figure 3.15.

If the actual competence sinks below a certain limit, an emergency reaction of the cognitive system is triggered. For the subject this means that he or she gets into a negative emotional state, characterized by feelings of anger, often rage, or sometimes helplessness. This state of an emergency reaction changes the characteristics of thinking and planning. In general thinking switches over to a high readiness to react. The subject tries to get rid of problems as quickly as possible even if there is no direct time pressure. He or she does not think about the problems but quickly makes decisions

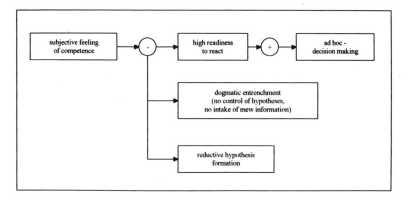

FIG. 3.15. Emergency reaction of the cognitive system.

which will be approximate, simple, and not well elaborated. Self-regulation activities are abandoned because they take too much time. For the same reason the intake of information is reduced to a minimum. The subject encloses—or better—entrenches himself or herself into assumptions and hypotheses which become a dogmatic system that cannot be disproved (e.g., Janis & Mann, 1977).

Four Determinants of Behavior

The processes of intention regulation, amplification and planning activities depend on certain conditions. They are triggered by motivations, emotions, and by the special shape of the memory systems of the individual. We believe that a lot of the deficiencies of human thinking and planning in the face of problems in very complex realities (the deficiencies of goal elaboration, forecasting, planning, decision making, effect monitoring, and so on) are mainly due to four reasons:

- the restricted capacity of human conscious thinking.
- the tendency of humans to guard their feeling of competence and efficacy.
- the weight of the *actual problem.*
- forgetting.

We discuss the role of these factors in human thinking and planning in complex realities. They play an important role in triggering information processing when coping with very complex problems.

The Role of the Restricted Capacity of Human Conscious Think-ing. Human beings constitute a wonderful system for monitoring and controlling extremely complex actions if these actions are highly routinized. Driving a car in the chaos of urban traffic is really a remarkable achievement. Not at all remarkable is the ability of man to divide, say, 371.68 by 4.57. She or he needs minutes for this calculation and her or his calculator would kill itself laughing if it could observe the low speed and the awkwardness of this operation. Human conscious thinking is not able to cope with more than a few pieces of information over a limited span of time. This enforces economical tendencies. Intuitively, man tries to use the limited resource of *conscious thinking* as economically as possible. This directly causes a lot of error tendencies such as reductive hypothesis formation, linear extrapolation, and reluctance in wasting energy in monitoring the effects of one's behavior.

The Role of the Feeling of Competence. To have the feeling of being able to act effectively is extremely important. We assume that man is highly motivated to guard this feeling against falsification. Jeopardizing this feeling of competence by a feedback of the ineffectiveness of one's actions may have different effects. One effect might be that one tries to acquire what is missing, that is, to learn how to cope with the problem. If the ability to acquire the missing capabilities is considered to be low (this is likely to be an implicit estimation), there will be a strong tendency to overlook the signals of incompetence or to fight related feelings by a demonstration of competence through actions which have an immediate and salient effect. From such tendencies, *ballistic* actions or overdoses will result.

The Role of the Weight of the Actual Motive. In complex, dynamic systems it is not enough to take care of the present and to solve the problems that show themselves at any given moment. One has to plan for the future and prevent unfavorable developments. But anticipated problems under otherwise comparable conditions never have the weight of actual problems and often a small, but actual problem draws much more attention than a development that will produce much bigger problems. For a smoker, the immediate satisfaction of smoking a cigarette will most easily overcome the concern of one's future health. The strong power of the actual motive is a primitive, but nevertheless an important, source of faulty planning and behavior. People have a strong tendency to think and act in terms of the present. Human beings have a high discount rate as the story of Jacob and Esau reminds us.

The Role of Forgetting. Humans are beings of the present; future and past exist for them only in shadowy outlines. Once it becomes past, the present loses most of its colors and contours. This hinders the process of developing a clear and correct image of the characteristics of a development. Especially slow motions in time are frequently be overlooked and hence cause surprises at a later time. Even when a development is noticed, forgetting tends to cause the production of a coarse and simple image of its characteristics. This results in the tendency to prognose linear developments. This tendency is strengthened by the fact that linear prognoses for short durations tend to be fairly accurate.

How to Test a Computer-Simulated Theory of Action Regulation

It is conceivable although difficult to cast all these assumptions about processes, memory structures, and their determinants into a theory of information processes and data structures, although work on the problem has begun

(Dörner, Schaub, Stäudel, & Strohschneider, 1988). The question, however, may be raised as to how one might test such a theory.

One cannot expect that the protocols of the simulation could be used as exact prognoses of the behavior of one single subject. There are a lot of parameters influencing the mode of operation of computersimulation of such a theory and one cannot hope to be able to measure all these parameters exactly for one human subject. As minor variations of the parameters may cause large differences in behavior it is questionable whether the very exact prediction of behavior of the (computersimulated) theory is of any value as it cannot be tested whether these predictions are right or not.

One way out of this difficulty is to compare *populations* of the predictions of the theory with populations of subjects behavior. But then one loses one of the strengths of such a theory, namely the exactness of the prediction, as one compares means. Even if the predictions of the theory are *right*, that is, do not deviate significantly from the means of the forms of behavior of the real subjects, the predictions might be trivial ("more time pressure, more *emergency reactions* of the cognitive system").

Another way of testing such a theory, and the only one which preserves the exactness of the predictions, is to *reconstruct* the behavior of single subjects by using the theory. That means that one should try to choose the parameters for the computer simulation in such a way that the computer reproduces the behavior of this subject (see Kluwe, this volume). In this way one cannot prove that the theory is the only possible form of an explanation of the subject's behavior, but it is shown that the theory is a *possible* explanation for the behavior. This process of reconstruction of individual forms of behavior could be repeated a lot of times. And if it turns out always that it is possible to reconstruct the individual subject's behavior (even extreme forms of behavior) only by changing the parameters, it becomes more and more improbable that all these reconstruction processes succeeded by chance.

CONCLUSION

To investigate CPS and to cast the observations of subjects behavior in very complex, uncertain, and dynamic environments into a theory of action regulation has only become possible when complex computing facilities made it possible to simulate such environments and to observe the behavior of human subjects carefully in the lab of the psychological experimenter. For us it seems to be a big chance to combine exactness of observation and exactness in the formulation of theories with the validity of the results for everyday life. Too long psychology tried to escape the challenge to explain *normal* behavior in *normal* behavioral settings by decomposing its topics into laboratory settings, the results of which could not be generalized for everyday life.

Empirical research and theorizing about CPS might be a way out of the dilemma of either to be lost in the *deep blue sea* of single case research and gloomy *hermeneutic meditation* about the reasons and causes of the decisions and actions of political, economical, or military leaders on the one hand, and the *narrow straits* of classical experimental research about decision making and planning (Brehmer & Dörner, 1993) on the other, where a lot of interesting phenomena simply do not show up.

REFERENCES

Allison, G. T. (1971). *Essence of decision: Explaining the Cuban missile crisis.* Boston, MA: Little, Brown.

Atkinson, J. W., & Birch, D. (1978). *Introduction to motivation* (2nd ed.). New York: Van Nostrand.

Badke-Schaub, P. (1993). *Gruppen und komplexe Probleme: Strategien von Kleingruppen bei der Bearbeitung einer simulierten Aids-Ausbreitung* [Groups and complex problems: Strategies of small groups working with a simulated Aids epidemic]. Frankfurt, Germany: Peter Lang.

Baron, J. (in press). Why teach thinking? *Journal of Applied Psychology.*

Braybrooke, D., & Lindblom, C. F. (1963). *A strategy of decision.* New York: The Free Press.

Brehmer, B. (1974). Hypotheses about relations between scaled variables in the learning of probabilistic inference tasks. *Organizational Behaviour and Human Performance, 11,* 1–27.

Brehmer, B. (1990). Strategies in real-time, dynamic decision making. In R. Hogarth (Ed.), *Insights in decision making. A tribute to Hillel J. Einhorn* (pp. 262–279). Chicago, IL: University of Chicago Press.

Brehmer, B. (1992). Dynamic decision making: Human control of complex systems. *Acta Psychologica, 81,* 211–241.

Brehmer, B., & Dörner, D. (1993). Experiments with computer-simulated microworlds: Escaping both the narrow straits of the laboratory and the deep blue sea of the field study. *Computers in Human Behavior, 9,* 171–184.

Dodds, A. E., Lawrence. J. A., & Wearing, A. J. (1991). What makes nursing satisfying: A comparison of college students' and registered nurses' views. *Journal of Advanced Nursing, 16,* 741–753.

Dörner, D. (1974). *Die kognitive Organisation beim Problemlösen* [The cognitive organization during problem solving]. Bern, Switzerland: Hans Huber.

Dörner, D. (1989). *Die Logik des Mißlingens* [The logic of failure]. Reinbek bei Hamburg, Germany: Rowohlt.

Dörner, D., Kreuzig, H. W., Reither, F., & Stäudel, T. (Eds.). (1983). *Lohhausen. Vom Umgang mit Unbestimmtheit und Komplexität* [Lohhausen. On dealing with uncertainty and complexity]. Bern, Switzerland: Hans Huber.

Dörner, D., & Pfeifer, E. (1990). Strategisches Denken und Stress [Strategic thinking and stress]. *Zeitschrift für Psychologie (Supplement), 11,* 71–83.

Dörner, D., & Pfeifer, E. (1992). Strategisches Denken, strategische Fehler, Streß und Intelligenz [Strategic thinking, strategic errors, stress, and intelligence]. *Sprache & Kognition, 11,* 75–90.

Dörner, D., & Preussler, W. (1990). Die Kontrolle eines einfachen ökologischen Systems [Control of a simple ecological system]. *Sprache & Kognition, 9,* 205–217.

Dörner, D., Schaub, H., Stäudel, T., & Strohschneider, S. (1988). Ein System zur Handlungsregulation oder—Die Interaktion von Emotion, Kognition und Motivation [A system for action regulation or—The interaction of emotion, cognition, and motivation]. *Sprache & Kognition, 7*, 217–239.

Epstein, S. (1980). The stability of behavior. II. Implications for psychological research. *American Psychologist, 35*, 790–806.

Funke, J. (1985). Problemlösen in komplexen, computersimulierten Realitätsbereichen [Problem solving in complex computersimulated domains of reality]. *Sprache & Kognition, 4*, 113–129.

Funke, J. (1986). *Komplexes Problemlösen. Bestandsaufnahme und Perspektiven* [Complex problem solving. Overview and perspectives]. Heidelberg, Germany: Springer.

Funke, J. (1988). Using simulation to study complex problem solving: A review of studies in the FRG. *Simulation & Games, 19*, 277–303.

Funke, J. (1991). Solving complex problems: Human identification and control of complex systems. In R. J. Sternberg & P. A. Frensch (Eds.), *Complex problem solving: Principles and mechanisms* (pp. 185–222). Hillsdale, NJ: Lawrence Erlbaum Associates.

Headey, B. W., & Wearing, A. J. (1992). *Understanding happiness: A theory of subjective well-being.* Melbourne, Australia: Longman Cheshire.

Headey, B. W., Glowacki, T., Holmstrom, E. L., & Wearing, A. J. (1985). Modelling change in perceived quality of life. *Social Indicator Research, 17*, 267–298.

Hesse, F. W. (1982). Training-induced changes in problem-solving. *Zeitschrift für Psychologie, 190*, 405–423.

Janis, I. L., & Mann, L. (1977). *Decision making.* Sydney, Australia: MacMillan.

Klix, F. (1988). On the role of knowledge in sentence comprehension. *Zeitschrift für Psychologie, 196*, 113–128.

Klix, F. (1992). *Die Natur des Verstandes* [The nature of reason]. Göttingen, Germany: Hogrefe.

Kuhl, J. (1985). Volitional mediators of cognition-behavior consistency: Self-regulatory processes and action versus state orientation. In J. Kuhl & J. Beckmann (Eds.), *Action control: From cognition to behavior* (pp. 101–128). New York: Springer.

Kühle, H.-J., & Badke, P. (1986). Die Entwicklung von Lösungsvorstellungen in komplexen Problemsituationen und die Gedächtnisstruktur [The development of solutions in complex problem situations and their relation to memory structure]. *Sprache & Kognition, 5*, 95–105.

MacKinnon, A. J., & Wearing, A. J. (1980). Complexity and decision making. *Behavioral Science, 25*, 285–296.

MacKinnon, A. J., & Wearing, A. J. (1983). Decision making in dynamic environment. In P. B. Stigum & F. Wenstop (Eds.), *Foundations of utility and risk theory with applications* (pp. 399–422). Dordrecht, The Netherlands: D. Reidel.

Newell, A., & Simon, H. A. (1972). *Human problem solving.* Englewood Cliffs, NJ: Prentice-Hall.

Omodei, M. M., & Wearing, A. J. (1991). *Cognitive commitment and affect in real time dynamic decision making tasks.* Paper presented to the thirteenth Research Conference on Subjective Probability, Utility, and Decision Making. Fribourg, Switzerland.

Omodei, M. M., & Wearing, A. J. (1993). *The Fire Space Chief. User manual.* Melbourne, Australia: University of Melbourne.

Pitz, G. F., & Sachs, N. J. (1984). Judgement and decision: Theory and application. *Annual Review of Psychology, 35*, 139–163.

Putz-Osterloh, W. (1981). Über die Beziehung zwischen Testintelligenz und Problemlöseerfolg [On the relationship between test intelligence and success in problem solving]. *Zeitschrift für Psychologie, 189*, 79–100.

Putz-Osterloh, W. (1983). Über Determinanten komplexer Problemlöseleistungen und Möglichkeiten ihrer Erfassung [On some processes determining the interaction with complex problems, and on the possibilities to assess these processes]. *Sprache & Kognition, 2*, 100–116.

Putz-Osterloh, W. (1987). Gibt es Experten für komplexe Probleme? [Are there experts for complex problems?]. *Zeitschrift für Psychologie, 195,* 63–84.

Putz-Osterloh, W., Bott, B., & Houben, I. (1988). Beeinflußt Wissen über ein realitätsnahes System dessen Steuerung? [Knowledge acquisition and improvement in system control]. *Sprache & Kognition, 7,* 240–251.

Putz-Osterloh, W., & Lemme, M. (1987). Knowledge and its intelligent application to problem solving. *German Journal of Psychology, 11,* 286–303.

Putz-Osterloh, W., & Lüer, G. (1981). Über die Vorhersagbarkeit komplexer Problemlöseleistungen durch Ergebnisse in einem Intelligenztest [On whether results from a test of intelligence can predict problem solving performance]. *Zeitschrift für Experimentelle und Angewandte Psychologie, 28,* 309–334.

Reason, J. T. (1987). The Chernobyl errors. *Bulletin of the British Psychological Society, 40,* 201–206.

Reichert, U., & Dörner, D. (1988). Heurismen beim Umgang mit einem "einfachen" dynamischen System [Heuristics of coping with a "simple" dynamic system]. *Sprache & Kognition, 7,* 12–24.

Reither, F. (1979). *Über die Selbstreflexion beim Problemlösen* [On self-reflection during problem solving]. Unpublished doctoral dissertation, FB 06 Psychologie der Universität Giessen, Germany.

Reither, F. (1985). Wertorientierung in komplexen Entscheidungssituationen [The role of values in complex decision situations]. *Sprache & Kognition, 4,* 21–27.

Schaub, H., & Strohschneider, S. (1992). Die Auswirkungen unterschiedlicher Problemlöseerfahrung auf den Umgang mit einem unbekannten komplexen Problem [Effects of different experiences with problems on how to deal with an unknown complex problem]. *Zeitschrift für Arbeits- und Organisationspsychologie, 36,* 117–126.

Scheier, M. F., & Carver, C. S. (1988). A model of behavioral self-regulation: Translating intention into action. In L. Berkowitz (Ed.), *Advances in experimental social psychology* (Vol. 21, pp. 303–346). New York: Academic Press.

Shanteau, J. (1988). Psychological characteristics and strategies of expert decision makers. *Acta Psychologica, 68,* 203–215.

Sonenberg, E. A., Lawrence, J. A., & Zelcer, J. (1992). Modeling disturbance management in anaesthesia: A preliminary report. *Artificial Intelligence in Medicine, 1,* 447–461.

Stäudel, T. (1987). *Problemlösen, Emotionen und Kompetenz* [Problem solving, emotions, and competence]. Regensburg, Germany: Roderer.

Sterman, J. D. (1989). Misperception of feedback in dynamic decision making. *Organizational Behavior and Human Decision Processes, 43,* 301–335.

Streufert, S. (1984). The dilemma of excellence: How strategic decision-making can kill you. *International Management, 4,* 36–40.

Strohschneider, S. (1986). Zur Stabilität und Validität von Handeln in komplexen Realitätsbereichen [On the stability and validity of complex problem-solving behavior]. *Sprache & Kognition, 5,* 42–48.

Strohschneider, S. (1990). *Wissenserwerb und Handlungsregulation* [Knowledge acquisition and action regulation]. Wiesbaden, Germany: Deutscher Universitäts Verlag.

Tisdale, T. (1994). *Bewußtsein, Selbstreflexion und Denken: der Versuch einer Integration* [A trial to integrate consciousness, self-reflection, and thinking]. Unpublished doctoral dissertation, Fakultät für Pädagogik, Philosophie, Psychologie der Universität Bamberg, Germany.

White, V. M., Wearing, A. J., & Hill, D. (in press). The conflict model of decision making and being screened for cervical cancer. *Journal of Behavioral Decision Making.*

PART TWO

GENERAL TOPICS
IN THE STUDY OF
COMPLEX PROBLEM SOLVING

CHAPTER FOUR

Feedback Delays in Complex Dynamic Decision Tasks

Berndt Brehmer

University of Uppsala, Sweden

INTRODUCTION

A recent book on *naturalistic decision making* (Klein, Orasanu, Calderwood, & Zsambok, 1993) notes that the kind of decision tasks that people meet in real life often differ from those that are used in traditional laboratory studies in decision making. Thus, laboratory tasks are usually static tasks, modelled on lotteries. They give the subjects unlimited time to choose among a set of alternatives described in terms of their outcomes and the probabilities that these outcomes will ensue, but the decision maker cannot in any way affect the outcome after the choice has been made. In contrast, many decision tasks outside the laboratory are dynamic, requiring the decision maker to choose a course of action under considerable time pressure, and the outcome is critically dependent on the decision maker's actions. Examples of such tasks are fighting a forest fire, managing a patient in intensive care, fighting a battle, and managing a company, to name a few, dramatic examples.

This chapter is concerned with people's ability to cope with such dynamic tasks in the laboratory. Following Brehmer and Allard (1991), dynamic tasks have three characteristics:

- They require a series of interdependent decisions.
- The state of the task changes, both autonomously and as a consequence of the decision maker's actions.
- The decisions have to be made in real time.

An example will, perhaps, make their nature clearer. Consider a fire chief faced with the task of fighting forest fires. He receives information about fires from a spotter plane. On the basis of this information, he sends out his fire fighting units (FFUs) to the fire(s). The units report back to him about their locations and activities. From this information and additional information from the spotter plane, he makes new decisions about where to send his FFUs until the fires have been extinguished. This task (a computer simulation of which will be used in the experiments to be reported in the following) has all of the characteristics of a dynamic task previously mentioned. Thus, a series of interdependent decisions is required: if the fire chief sends his FFUs to one location, this will obviously constrain his future decisions. The state of the fire changes both autonomously as a consequence of the strength and direction of the wind, and because of the fire chief's actions. Finally, the decisions must be made in real time, that is, they must be made when changes in the fire situation require them rather when than the fire chief feels ready to make them.

In such tasks, the problems facing the decision maker are as much a creation of his own decisions as of the environmental processes that he seeks to control. In short, the task and the decision maker are parts in the same feedback loop.

To function effectively in such an environment, the decision maker must be able to distinguish between those aspects of the state of the task that are caused by his or her actions and those that are caused by the environment. The feedback delays that are an inescapable feature of dynamic tasks often makes this difficult. Because of such delays the current state of the problem is the result of actions that were taken some time ago, rather than by the most recent actions. The results of the current actions will appear some time in the future. Therefore, it is no easy matter to assign changes in the environment to the appropriate decisions.

The central role of feedback delays becomes clear when we remember that the fundamental problem for the decision maker in a dynamic task is

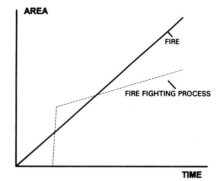

FIG. 4.1. The fire fighting task described as the problem of using one process, the fire fighting activity, to control another process, the fire.

to find a way of using one process to control another (Brehmer & Allard, 1991). Figure 4.1 illustrates this for the FIRE FIGHTING TASK. In the simple case of a fire in a uniform forest environment, the size of the burning area increases linearly with time and the rate at which it spreads depends on the nature of the forest and the strength of the wind. The effect of the fire fighting process also increases linearly with time; each FFU will be able to cover a constant forest area with water (or whatever extinction agent that is used) per unit time.

A time-area diagram such as that in Figure 4.1 illustrates both the temporal nature of the task and the strategic choices open to the fire chief. Note first, that although the fire is effective from time zero, the fire fighting process is only effective after some period of time. That is, there is what control engineers call *dead time*, a form of delay caused by the fact that it takes time for the FFUs to get ready and to reach the fire. Note that the appropriate strategy is different before the fire fighting function has crossed the fire function and after it has done so.

Before it has crossed the fire function, it is possible to extinguish the fire by a direct attack, for the fire fighting units are able to cover at least the same area as the fire covers. After the fire fighting function has crossed the fire function, this is no longer possible. In this case, the fire chief can only try to stop the fire from spreading, and then wait until so much of the fire has burned itself out that he or she can usefully fight what is left.[1] Diagrams of the kind shown in Figure 4.1 can be constructed for all spatio-temporal decision tasks, and they will show what the decision maker's strategic options are.

---

[1]In principle, there is also another option, that of dividing the fire into smaller fires by sending the FFUs into the fire, and then fighting these smaller islands. This may not be practicable in a real fire fighting, however. These three options, direct attack, encirclement, and dividing a large fire into smaller fires that can then be fought with the available resources seem to be the only possibilities that are open in any spatio-temporal problem that involves using one process to fight another, be it a fire fighting problem or a tactical military problem.

The Complex Nature of Feedback Delays
and the Models That They Require

When there are feedback delays, the information available at the moment of decision is not the information that the decision maker needs for the decision. However, the exact relation between the available information and the needed information depends on the form of delay.

Feedback delays may originate in different parts of the feedback loop. In fire fighting, for example, there may be delays in the FFU's response to commands, in their execution of the commands, and in their reports about the results of their actions. The first kind of delays is usually called *dead time* and it refers to the time required for the fire chief's commands to start taking effect (cf. Figure 4.1). The second represents the *time constant* of the system, that is, the time required for the control action to change the state of the system. The third corresponds to the usual form of feedback delay in psychological experiments, that is, a delay in the transmission of information about results, usually in the form of a delay in reinforcement. Here we will call this kind of delay *information delay.*

To control a task with delays, the decision maker needs a model of the task that allows him to infer the information that he or she needs. The demands on this model vary with the nature of the delay. When there is dead time and when the task involves significant time constants, the decisions will not take effect until some time after they have been made. This means that the situation may well be very different when the decision takes effect than when it was made. To compensate for this the decision maker needs a predictive model that can tell him what decision is needed some time before the information required for it is available. This makes a very stringent demand on the decision maker's model: it must enable the decision maker to predict the future state of the system that he seeks to control.

Such demands are often difficult to meet. Therefore, it is usually impossible to achieve perfect control in systems that have dead time, a problem well known to control engineers.

On the other hand, in tasks with information delays, the problem is that the information available at the time of decision pertains to some past state of the system. To control the system under such circumstances the decision maker needs a model that allows him to predict the actual state of the system from the information that is available.

If the decision maker does not develop the model required to master the problems caused by the feedback delays, he will never achieve control over the task. All of his decisions will be aimed at correcting past mistakes, and the system is likely to go into oscillation, a problem that is not unknown in complex systems controlled by human decision makers. The fact that feedback delays cannot be avoided in dynamic tasks and the consequences of not mastering them, creates the central problem of how people cope with feedback delays. This problem is central in the study of dynamic decision making, and thus for our understanding of how people cope with the tasks described by Klein et al. (1993) as typical of decision making outside the laboratory.

EFFECTS OF FEEDBACK DELAYS IN COMPLEX TASKS

In an earlier study in this series Brehmer and Allard (1991) investigated the effects of feedback delays in dynamic decision making using a simulated FIRE FIGHTING TASK (following is a full description of their experimental task). The delays were due to slow reporting by the FFUs about their location and actions, that is, the delay was a form of information delay. The results showed that such delays had disastrous effects upon the subjects' performance: In the delay condition there was essentially no learning, and thus no adaptation to the task. This was not expected, for although the subjects in the experiment were not informed about the possibility that there could be delays, they nevertheless had all the information they needed to infer not only that there were delays in the system, but also the nature of these delays.

Feedback delay is of course not a new variable in psychological research. However, most studies have been concerned with its effects in simple motor tasks (see, e.g., Bilodeau, 1966, for a review). In cognitive tasks such as concept learning or decision making, the effects have proved to be complex; for some tasks, the effects are negative, for others they are positive, and for still other tasks, there are no effects at all (Annett, 1969). In many studies the effects of feedback delays are confounded with those of other factors, such as the intertrial interval, and the interval between the feedback and the next response (Bilodeau, 1966). When the effects of such factors have been controlled for, the effects of feedback delays tend to disappear (Annett, 1969). There is, however, one kind of task for which effects of feedback delays are uniformly negative. This is when the subjects have to respond to a new stimulus before they receive feedback from the previous trial (see Lorge & Thorndike, 1935, for a classical demonstration). Dynamic tasks, such as Brehmer and Allard's FIRE FIGHTING simulation is similar to the Lorge and Thorndike task in that many decisions intervene between a decision and the feedback relevant to that decision. It is therefore not surprising that we find negative effects of feedback delays in this and other dynamic tasks.

Such negative effects were also found by Sterman (1989a, 1989b) who investigated the effects of feedback factors, including delays, using business games. He summarized his results in what he called the "misperception of feedback (MOF) hypothesis." According to this hypothesis, decision makers simply ignore all but the most obvious aspects of the feedback structure of a decision task.

Negative effects of feedback delays have also been obtained in studies of dynamic decision making in the German tradition of *complex problem solving* (the relation between dynamic decision tasks and the problem solving tasks used in the German tradition of *Komplexes Problemlösen* is discussed in Brehmer, 1992, and Brehmer & Dörner, 1993). Thus, Reichert and Dörner (1988), who examined individual differences in the manual control of a computer simulated cold storage facility, found that most of their subjects drove the simulation into oscillation in the same manner as had earlier been demonstrated in manual control tasks with delays by Crossman and Cooke (1974; see Moray, Lootstein, & Pajak, 1986, for a replication, using a computer simulated version of the original Crossman & Cooke task), and others. The oscillation results from the fact that the subjects, expecting a response from the system and not obtaining it when they expect it due to the delays in the system, will give new and usually stronger input signals to the system, causing it to overshoot the target. The subject will then try to correct for this overshooting, with the same disastrous result, causing a need for a new correction, and so on. Finally, Dörner and Preussler (1990), using a simulated ECOSYSTEM with one control variable and one controlled variable (which in turn affected two other variables), found negative effects of both information delays and dead time. Dörner and Preussler also found that when there was both slow reports and dead time, performance was about as good as when there were no delays at all. The generality of the latter finding is, however, uncertain. In an as yet unpublished study, we could not replicate this result with our FIRE FIGHTING TASK. On the other hand, Funke (1985) found no effects of delays on subjects' ability to control a simulated gardening task in which they had to control three variables by manipulating the settings of three control variables.

The simulations used in the German experiments on complex problem solving (CPS) differed from that used by Brehmer and Allard in that they were event-driven simulations. That is, the progress of the simulation stopped after the results of the subject's decisions had been computed and waited for a new decision. Brehmer and Allard's simulation was clock driven, so its progress did not stop and wait for the subjects to make their input. In event-driven simulations, it may well be more difficult to distinguish between dead time, time constants and information delays since nothing is observed between decisions; the simulation goes directly from one state to the next state without showing the actual process that leads from one state to the next. It is therefore not clear that one can always assign a delay to its place in the feedback loop. The possible differences between a clock driven and an event-driven simulation will be addressed as follows in Experiment III.

The explanation for the difference in results between Funke (1985) on the one hand, and those of Reichert and Dörner (1987) and of Dörner and

Preussler (1990), on the other, is not clear. It may be due to the fact that the delays employed in the latter two studies were greater than in the former study. The extent to which a feedback delay will affect performance negatively does, of course, not depend on the duration of the delay as such. A delay will have significant negative effects only if the delay is long in relation to the time required for a decision to take effect. It is possible that the difference in results is due to such factors; it is not quite clear what the relevant relations were in these experiments.

The following presents four experiments that aim at clarifying the effects of feedback delays in dynamic tasks. The first experiment is an attempt to test one of the possible explanations for the negative effects of feedback delays in Brehmer and Allard's (1991) original experiment, namely, that the subjects did not detect that there were delays. The aim of Experiment II is to ascertain whether feedback delays are simply ignored, or if they have effects on the subjects' strategies. The third experiment compares the effects of two kinds of delays, dead time and information delays, using both a clock driven and an event driven form of the same simulation. The final experiment examines the effects of feedback delays when subjects have been informed of the presence and nature of the delays.

Experiment I: Effects of Feedback Delay With Informed Subjects

One possible explanation for the negative effects of information delays in Brehmer and Allard's (1991) original experiment is that the subjects did not detect there were feedback delays despite the fact they had all the information that they needed to infer them. Experiment I was designed to test this hypotheses.

Experimental Task

The experiment was conducted with the same FIRE FIGHTING simulation as that used by Brehmer and Allard (1991). It requires the subjects to assume the role of a fire chief charged with the task of fighting forest fires. They receive information on a computer screen about fires and their location from a *spotter plane*. On the basis of this information, they may issue commands to their fire fighting units, commands that are then carried out by the units. The units report continuously to the subject about their activities and locations. The subjects can use this information to issue new commands until the fire has been extinguished (see the following for details). The simulation is an interactive FORTRAN program that allows the subjects to interact with the simulation in real time. In this experiment the simulation was implemented on a PDP 11/40 computer equipped with a GT-40 monochromatic display, a LA 36 DECWRITER keyboard/printer, and two RK11-01 disc drives with 1.2 megabyte discs.

The subject sat in front of the display with a keyboard to issue commands. On the screen there was a map in the form of a grid with 16×16 squares, each of which was coded in terms of a letter (A–P) and a number (1–16). Active fire was represented as pluses. Minuses denoted fire that had been extinguished or burned out. The subjects were told that this information came from a spotter plane. They could not influence this plane, for example, they could not ask it to go to a certain location and find out what is happening. This was not necessary, as the spotter plane always reported on the status of the whole area displayed on the map. However, the spotter plane reported only about fire. Information about the location of the FFUs and their activities came from the FFUs themselves.

Each FFU was represented by a number between 1 and 8, and the position of this number on the map indicated the position last reported by the FFU. In the middle of the map four squares were outlined with heavy lines. These four squares represented the base where the fire chief (the subject) was supposedly located. Directly below the map a weather report provided information about the general weather conditions; for example, *sunny*, the direction of the prevailing wind (shown by an arrow to avoid possible confusion from misinterpretation of verbal descriptions of wind direction), and about the time when the weather report was issued.

To the left of the map there were four displays. The top display showed the command that had just been typed by the subject. The second display showed the simulation time, and the third display the status reports from the FFUs. The first column in the latter display showed the reported status, which could be *ACT* (active, i.e., the unit is fighting fire), *PAS* (passive, i.e., the FFU is not doing anything, perhaps because it has put out the fire in its area), *FWA* (the FFU is on its way under centralized control, i.e., it is not allowed to fight fire until it reaches its destination and it must ignore the fires that it encounters en route to its destination) or *FWB* (the FFU is on its way under decentralized control, i.e., it is allowed to fight fires that it encounters en route to its destination). When under decentralized control, the FFU scans the eight cells surrounding its current position, and it could start fighting fire in any of them. When there was fire in more than one of the eight surrounding cells it chose the cell that lay in the direction of the location to which it had been ordered to go. After having reached its destination, the FFU reverted to FWA mode, and would remain in that location until it had received a new command. In this FWA mode, the unit would start fighting fire when the fire reached the cell in which it the FFU was located. The second column showed the reported position of the FFU, and the third column the destination to which the FFU had been ordered to go. The fourth column showed the time when the FFU reported. The bottom display was a list of the last command given to each of the eight FFUs.

The subjects sent their eight FFUs to different locations by means of either the FWA or FWB command previously described. A command included information about the mode of control, that is, FWA or FWB, the name of the unit (a number between 1 and 8), and a map reference, for example, *K11*, indicating the destination. The information on the screen was updated every 20 seconds. A 20 second time interval is called a *time unit.*

In the instructions the subject was given two goals: to protect the base, and to put out the fire(s) as soon as possible, with the obvious priority ordering. A trial ended when the fire(s) had been extinguished, or when the fire had reached the base.

A fire always started in one of the *high risk areas* C3, C14, N3, or N14, and spread in the direction of the prevailing wind. The first fire started at *t* = 5 time units, that is, after 100 seconds. Ten time units later, a second fire started in one of the other high risk areas. At the same time the direction of the wind changed, so that it now blew in the direction from the second fire towards the base. If the subject did nothing about this second fire it would reach the base at *t* = 60 time units. Thus, the second fire was always the most dangerous one in this experiment. The FFUs moved at the rate of one square per time unit. The eight FFUs were equally effective, and each FFU required five time units (100 sec) to extinguish the fire in a square.

Design

The factor that varied in the experiment was information delay. There were two experimental conditions. In the no delay condition, all FFUs reported back to the subjects about their position and activities without delay. In the delay condition, half of the FFUs reported with a delay of one time unit (20 sec), and the other four with a delay of two time units (40 sec). Subjects in both conditions were informed there might be delays, and that these delays might be located either in the *command* system, that is, the FFUs might be slow in responding to commands, or in the *report* system, that is, the FFUs might be slow in reporting about their activities and positions. In both conditions the subjects received six trials. Thus, the design of the experiment followed a 2 (delay conditions) by 6 (trials) factorial design with repeated measures on the second factor. Sixteen undergraduate students were paid to serve as subjects.

Procedure

The subjects were informed about the general nature of the task, their goals and the possibility of delays. They were allowed to familiarize themselves with the display and the commands and to practice the commands on the keyboard for 20 minutes. After completion of the sixth trial they were asked to indicate whether they had discovered any delays in the command or the report system, and if they had discovered such delays, which units had longer delays.

Each trial required about 20 minutes, and the subjects came to the experiment on two days, completing three trials each day.

Results

The simulation program stores everything that happens on a trial, and from this information it is possible to construct a number of dependent variables. In the present experiment, five variables were analyzed. The first two of these show the extent to which the subjects were able to meet the two goals, and the next three how they used their resources.

The Subjects' Ability to Meet the Goals

Base Losses. The percentage of trials ending with the fire reaching the base shows the extent to which the subjects were able to meet their first goal of protecting the base. In the no delay condition, 17% of the trials ended in loss of the base, while in the delay condition, 58% ended in this way, X^2 (1) = 12.36, $p < .001$.

Area Lost to Fire. The percentage of squares lost to fire at the end of a trial shows the extent to which the subjects were able to meet their second goal, that of putting out the fires as quickly as possible. Figure 4.2 shows that subjects in the no delay condition improved over trials but those in the delay condition did not. The main effects of delay, F (1, 14) = 37.17, $p < .001$, and trials, F (5, 70) = 17.34, $p < .001$, as well as the delay by trials interaction, F (5, 70) = 6.05, $p < .001$, were significant, and post hoc tests using Scheffé's procedure, confirmed the interpretation above.

Both indices of goal attainment tell the same story: Feedback delays had a negative effect on performance. To explain these effects, we turn to an examination of how the subjects used their resources.

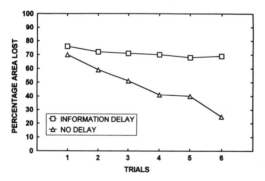

FIG. 4.2. Percentage area lost to fire as a function of delay in Experiment I.

How the Subjects Used Their Resources

Resource Allocation. The proportion of FFUs ordered to go to a given fire 5 time units after that fire has started shows the extent to which the subjects were able to cope with the time constants of the fire fighting task. A significant main effect of trials, $F(5, 70) = 7.78$, $p < .001$, demonstrated that the subjects learned to respond faster and more massively over trials, that is, they learned to deploy more and more FFUs during the first 5 seconds after a fire had started. They deployed more resources in the no delay condition than in the delay condition, $F(1, 14) = 24.41$, $p < .001$, and allocated more resources to the first fire than to the second fire, $F(1, 14) = 33.12$, $p < .001$.

The results for resource allocation show, first, that the subjects failed to redeploy their resources from the first to the second, more dangerous, fire. This explains why many trials ended in loss of the base. Second, the results show that the subjects deployed fewer FFUs in the delay condition than in the no delay condition. This explains why their performance in the delay condition was worse with respect to both measures. That there was no interaction between delay and the fire factor shows that the subjects' redeployment was equally deficient in both delay conditions. Third, the results show that the subjects learned to cope with the time constants of the task caused by the fact that it takes time for the FFUs to reach the fire. Even though the fire may be small when the subject first sends out his FFUs, it will be considerably larger when they reach it. It is therefore necessary to send out many units; the more rapidly these units are sent out, the fewer units will be needed to extinguish the fire, and the more FFUs can be kept in reserve for new fires. However, the subjects obviously managed to adapt to the demands of the fire fighting task less well in the delay condition. To understand this we need to examine the next measure, waiting times.

Waiting Times. The waiting time is the time a FFU is kept inactive after having carried out a command, for example, to go to a given location and/or after it has put out fire in its location.

Waiting times decreased over trials, $F(5, 70) = 7.27$, $p < .001$. They were longer in the delay condition than in the no delay condition, $F(1, 14) = 18.49$, $p < .001$. The mean waiting time for the FFUs with a 2 unit delay was 5.54 time units, compared to 3.17 time units in the no delay condition. The difference is 2.17, which closely corresponds to the magnitude of the delay. For the units with a delay of one time unit the mean waiting time was 4.56, that is, the difference compared to the no delay condition was 1.39 time units, again close to the actual delay.

These results show that the subjects did not compensate for the information delays. This leads the subjects to underestimate the number of FFUs they have available to them in the delay condition and explains why they failed to send out as many FFUs as quickly in this condition as they did in the no delay condition.

Decentralization. The proportion of FWB commands decreased from 41% in the first trial to 17% in the last, $F(5, 70) = 4.77$, $p < .001$. There was no significant effect of delay upon the percentage of FWB commands.

Subjects' Interpretation of the Delays

All eight subjects in the delay condition indicated that they had discovered there were delays. In the no-delay condition, only two subjects reported there were delays. The difference is significant ($p < .01$, Fisher's exact probability test). All subjects agreed that the delays were located in the command system, that is, they believed that the FFUs were slow in responding to the commands, rather than slow in reporting. There was no correlation between the subjects' judgments of delay and the actual magnitude of the delay (r_{pbis} = −.03, df = 56).

Discussion

The results of this experiment show that informing the subjects about the possibility of delays does not eliminate the negative effects of delay observed in earlier studies on dynamic decision making by Brehmer and Allard (1991), Dörner and Preussler (1990), Reichert and Dörner (1987), and Sterman (1989a, 1989b). Indeed, the results indicate that this information had no effect whatsoever: The subjects' performance in this experiment is virtually identical to that in the earlier Brehmer and Allard (1991) experiment.

In interpreting this result it is important to remember that the delays were in no way hidden from the subjects. Not only had they been alerted to the fact that there could be delays, there were also three sources of information that they could use to infer the delays and their nature. First, when there were delays the report time shown in the report display always lagged behind current time with a lag equal to the delay time. Second, there was a lag equal to the delay time between the moment when a command was given and the moment when information about the unit's response to that command was shown on the screen. Third, there was an clear conflict between some of the reports from the spotter plane and those from the FFUs. Thus, the FFUs would at times report fighting fire in an area where the spotter plane reported that the fire had already been put out. Thus, both the fact that there were delays and the nature of the delays could readily be inferred by someone who inspected the evidence to look for delays.

It is also important to remember that report delays of the kind introduced in this experiment is a form of delay for which it is, at least in principle, possible to compensate. To do so the subjects need to learn the duration of the delay and how long it takes for the FFUs to carry out the commands and then adjust their commands accordingly. That is, the subjects must learn to give their commands before the FFUs report that they have carried out their current tasks.

All subjects in the delay condition reported having detected that there were delays. However, all of them misidentified their nature and saw the delays as being caused by dead time, rather than slow reports. This shows that the subjects cannot have used all of the information that was available to them to infer the nature of the delays. Instead, the results suggest that the subjects only used the second piece of information described previously, that is, the fact that the results of a command would not appear immediately on the screen. Although this information tells the subject that there are delays, it gives no information about the nature of the delays; both dead time and information delay will show up in the same manner, namely, as a lag between a command and its result. Why the subjects chose the dead time interpretation rather than the report delay interpretation when they had been given both alternatives is not clear from the present results. However, the fact that they did suggests an explanation for why the subjects did not choose an appropriate strategy for coping with the delays: If they did not entertain the hypothesis that the delays were due to slow reporting, the subjects could, of course, not realize they could compensate for the delays by ordering a FFU to go to some other location before it reported having completed its current activity.

These results, then, suggest that the subjects restricted their attention to the map display. There are at least two possible explanations for this. First, it may be that the situation is so complex, and the time pressure so great, that the subjects are unable to keep track of all of the information that is available. Second, it may be that the static numerical information in the displays is less compatible with the subjects' task than the dynamic, analogue representation in the map. Other forms of displays may be necessary to help the subjects pay attention to the dynamic information. The question of how the dynamic properties of a system, such as its delays, should be represented to an operator remains one of the most important questions in research on human control of complex dynamic systems.

A third possibility, that subjects would have been unable to compensate for delays if they had useful information about the delays, seems unlikely. Open loop control as such is obviously not beyond the capacity of human controllers in dynamic systems, as shown in studies on human operators in manual control tasks (see, e.g., Crossman & Cooke, 1974). Indeed, even in the present experiment, there is evidence of open loop control for one kind of delays: the time constants that are caused by the fact that it takes time for the FFUs to move to a fire. Thus, the results on resource allocation show that subjects quickly found the appropriate open loop strategy of responding massively and rapidly to compensate for this delay caused by the time constants of the task. The important difference between the delays caused by slow reporting and those caused by the time constants seems to be that while the former have to be inferred the latter can be *seen* to happen (Brehmer, 1990).

In conclusion, the present experiment confirms earlier results on the effects of feedback delays on performance in dynamic tasks. The results also add to the generality of the earlier results in showing that the negative effects of delays are also obtained when the subjects have been alerted to the possibility of delays. However, because the subjects misinterpreted the nature of the delays, the results do not tell us whether subjects are able to compensate for delays or not. In Experiment IV, which investigates the effects of delays when subjects have been informed about the nature of the delays in the task, we will return to this problem.

Experiment II: Effects of Feedback Delay on Strategies

The results of Experiment I, like those of other experiments on feedback delays in complex systems, suggest that the subjects simply ignore the delays and employ exactly the same strategy when there are no feedback delays. The negative effects of the delays then come about because the strategy is less effective when there are delays. However, Experiment I does not give any direct information about the actual strategies of the subjects. They only show the results of these strategies on the performance. Experiment II was designed to give some information on the strategies themselves and how they are affected by feedback delays. It does that by examining the relative weights that subjects give to the two goals that they have in the simulation: to protect the base and to extinguish fire as quickly as possible.

In the experiment, two control groups performed under the same conditions of delay or no delay, respectively, throughout the experiment. Two experimental groups performed first under conditions of delay or no delay. They were then switched to the opposite condition. That is, subjects who first performed under conditions of delay were switched to a no delay condition, and vice versa.

On the hypothesis that the subjects' strategies are the same under conditions of delay and no delay, we expect that the experimental groups will perform in the same manner as their respective control groups with respect to both goals, that is, base losses and area lost.

Design

The experiment used the same fire fighting simulation as Experiment I. It was conducted in two stages, a learning stage and a transfer stage. The factor varied in the experiment was feedback delay, and the delay condition was the same as in Experiment I. The subjects in all four conditions performed eight trials of the same kind as those in Experiment I.

In the two control conditions, subjects performed under the same delay or no delay conditions throughout the experiment. For the two experimental groups, conditions changed after the 6th trial. In the delay-no delay condition, the delays were eliminated so that the FFUs in this condition now reported without delay. In the no delay–delay condition, delays were introduced after the 6th trial so that the FFUs now reported with a delay of 1.5 time units on the average (4 FFUs reported with a delay of 2 time units and 4 with a delay of 1 unit). The subjects were not informed that there would be delays, and the subjects in the experimental conditions were not informed of the change in the delays between trials 6 and 7.

The general procedure was the same as that in Experiment I. The subjects came to the experiment on two different days and performed four trials each day. Each trial required about 20 minutes. Thirty-two undergraduate students were paid to serve as subjects. They were randomly divided into four groups with the restriction that there should be eight subjects in each group.

Results

The performance measures were the same as those in Experiment I. Here, we concentrate on the results of the shift. The results before the shift were the same as in earlier experiments. There were no significant differences between groups sharing the same delay conditions before the shift. Subjects in the delay conditions lost more bases and more forest. They had longer waiting times than those in the no delay condition, but there was no difference with respect to the proportion of FWB commands. To test the hypothesis about the effects of feedback delays on the subjects' strategies, we now compare the mean performance in the last two trials before the shift with that for the two trials after the shift.

Base Losses. Performance after the shift was similar to that before the shift for the subjects in the no delay conditions: No trials end in base loss, regardless of whether the subjects had performed under conditions of delay or no delay before the shift. When there were delays after the shift, on the other hand, subjects who performed with delay before the shift performed considerably better than those who performed without delay (19% base losses compared to 44%).

Area Lost. Figure 4.3 shows that performance in the condition where a delay is introduced after the shift deteriorates to about the same level as that in the condition where the subjects have been performing with delays throughout the experiment.

The decrease in performance is significant, $F(3, 28) = 35.00$, $p < .01$, but the difference in performance between the two delay conditions after the shift is not. In the condition where the delay is removed, performance

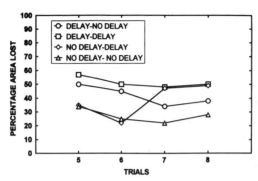

FIG. 4.3. Percentage area lost to fire before and after the shift in Experiment II.

improves after the shift, $F(3, 28) = 11.61$, $p < .05$, but not quite to the same level as that in the condition where the subjects have been performing without delays throughout the experiment. The difference in performance between the two groups is significant after the shift.

Waiting Times. After the shift, waiting times increased in the condition where delays were introduced while in the condition where delays were removed, waiting times went down. The changes are significant, $F(3, 28) = 31.51$, $p < .01$, and $F(3, 28) = 41.10$, $p < .01$, for the no delay–delay and delay–no delay conditions, respectively. After the shift, delay conditions differed significantly from no delay conditions, but there was no significant difference between the two conditions without delay after the shift, and no significant difference between the two conditions with delays after the shift.

In the last two trials before the shift, the mean difference in waiting times between the delay and no delay conditions were 2.3 time units, a value close, but not exactly equal, to the actual delay of 1.5 time units. Introduction of delays in the no delay–delay condition, raised the waiting time 1.6 time units. Eliminating the delays in the delay–no delay condition decreased waiting times 2 units. These results are generally consistent with those of Experiment I and suggest that subjects did not compensate for the delays in any of the experimental conditions with delays.

FWB Commands. The shift did not result in any change in the proportion of FWB commands. The average level of FWB was low in both conditions (about 25%) and did not change significantly over trials or with the shift.

Discussion

The results of Experiment II show that subjects do not employ the same strategies under conditions of delay and no delay: For the no delay–delay experimental group, performance deteriorated to the level of that in the delay–delay control group with respect to area lost to fire, but for the base loss measure it deteriorated to a level that was far worse than that in the control group. For the delay-no delay experimental group, the results were opposite to those for the no delay–delay control group. Thus after the shift, subjects in this group performed at the same level as those in the no delay–no delay condition with respect to the base loss measure. With respect to area lost, however, the subjects in the experimental group did not reach the same level of performance as the subjects in the no delay control group. These results suggest that the subjects learn to give a higher weight to the goal of protecting the base when there are delays than when there are no delays, presumably because this goal is harder to attain when there are feedback delays. The results with respect to waiting times show that this is not simply a matter of using the FFUs more effectively; the waiting time results show that subjects ignore delays in both conditions. Therefore, the greater success of the subjects who practiced in the no delay condition must be due to the fact that they learned to use relatively more of their FFUs to protect the base. (Absolutely, they still use fewer since they use fewer FFUs overall.) As a consequence, they had less resources for achieving their second goal, that of preserving the forest, and they were less effective than the subjects in the no delay condition with respect to this goal. In short, these results suggest that delays make subjects concentrate on the most important goal.

This concentration on protecting the base could be due to the fact that the feedback is less ambiguous with respect to the goal of preserving the base than with respect to that of extinguishing fire as quickly as possible. When the subjects lose the base, there is little doubt that they performed worse than they could have done, but when they lose 20% more forest than is necessary, it may be less obvious that they could have done better. This is because the subjects probably do not have any precise idea about the minimum possible loss of forest in the experiment. Indeed, they cannot have any precise idea about this, because there is no normative theory for this task that can tell them what it is possible to achieve. The outcomes with respect to area lost to fire are therefore likely to have less effect on their strategy than base losses do.

These results, then, point to a new factor in dynamic decision making: the greater ambiguity of feedback with respect to some of the goals. It stems from the fact that there is no normative theory for fire fighting as it is represented in the experiment that allows us to calculate the minimum loss of forest. This does not limit the generality of the fire fighting task. Normative theories generally cannot be developed for real time dynamic tasks (Rapoport, 1975). We should therefore expect to find differential ambiguity of feedback with respect to different goals in most real world dynamic tasks, and we would expect that the decision makers in such tasks would be more responsive to those aspects for which there is unambiguous feedback. Studies in our laboratory are currently directed at this problem. These studies examine the effects of an unambiguous form of feedback: explicit costs for using the fire fighting resources. Our first results suggest that the introduction of costs have negative effects on the other performance measures (Brehmer, Lövborg, & Winman, 1992), presumably because this explicit form of feedback attracts too much attention. This is consistent with the results of Experiment II.

Experiment III: Effects of Feedback Delay and Type of Simulation

Experiments I and II were concerned with two of the kinds of delays mentioned in the introduction: *time constants* and *information delays*. Experiment III was designed to investigate the effects of the third kind: *dead time*. Specifically, the experiment compares the effects of dead time and information delays. The reader will recall that the subjects in Experiment I interpreted the information delays in that experiment as dead time, and that their misinterpretation may well have been one of the reasons for why they failed to compensate for the delays. This makes it interesting to compare the subject's handling of dead time with their handling of information delays. In addition, Experiment III addresses the problem of simulation type. As noted in the introduction, simulations of dynamic systems can be designed as clock driven simulations (the type of simulation used in Experiments I and II) or event driven simulations (the type of simulation used in most of the German work on CPS). In the former kind of simulation, the progress is controlled by the computer's internal clock, so it is independent of the subject's actions; it does not stop and wait for the subject to think as, for example, simulations like MORO (Dörner, Stäudel, & Strohschneider, 1986) do. In the latter kind of simulation, the state of the system is presented to the subject who then makes his or her decisions. The decisions are input, and the simulation program computes the new state, presents it to the subject and waits for new input. In Experiment III, an event driven version of the FIRE FIGHTING simulation was used in addition to the ordinary clock driven version. In the former version, the simulation progressed time unit by time unit, and it stopped after the effects of the subject's input had been computed and presented. The subject could then use as much time as he or she wanted to make the decisions, which were put in, and the next state computed.

Design

The factors varied in the experiment were the type of feedback delay and the type of simulation. The feedback delay factor had three levels; no delay, information delays, and dead time. The delay was set to 2 time units in both delay conditions. Thus, in the information delay condition the FFUs reported about their activities and positions with a delay of 2 time units (40 sec) but they responded to commands without delay. In the dead time condition, the FFUs responded to a command only after two time units had elapsed, but they reported about their positions and activities without delay. The simulation factor had two levels; clock driven versus event driven simulation. In all six conditions, subjects went through six trials. Thus the design of the experiment followed a 3 (levels of feedback delay: no delay vs. information delay vs. dead time) by 2 (kinds of simulations: event driven vs. clock driven simulation) by 6 trials factorial design with repeated measures on the third factor. Forty-eight undergraduate students were paid to take part in the experiment.

Simulation

The experiment used the FIRE FIGHTING simulation described previously although it was run on an Apollo Dn580 work station instead of the PDP system used in the earlier experiments. There were three differences between this version of the FIRE FIGHTING simulation and that used in the earlier experiments. First, the color graphics capability of the Apollo system was used, although in a very limited way: fire was shown in red, rather than in green as in the earlier experiments. Second, a possibility of planning ahead was introduced by substituting the possibility of giving a series of two commands in sequence to a unit for the choice between FWA and FWB commands. Thus, the subjects could command each unit to first go to one location, then to another when it had put out fire in the first location. This gave the subjects a possibility to compensate for delays. If they used these kind of commands, they need not wait for the unit to report that it carried out a command to give it a new command. Third, an administrative time limit of 20 minutes was introduced for each trial. That is, if the subjects had not managed to extinguish the fire after 20 minutes, the trial was ended. This time limit was chosen on the basis of the results from the earlier experiments that indicated a trial usually took about 20 minutes. In all other respects, the experiment followed the same procedure as that in the earlier experiments, except for the differences noted in the design section concerning type of simulation.

Results

The Effects of Type of Simulation. The same dependent measures as those used in earlier experiments were used in this experiment. However, since only a small percentage of trials ended in loss of the base, this measure was not analyzed here. The low frequency of trials ending with a base loss was probably due to the time limit on the trials because of which the fire usually did not have had time to reach the base. For all measures analyzed in this experiment there were significant main effects of type of simulation, but this factor did not interact with any of the other factors (except in one case noted as follows). The subjects performed about 25% better with the event driven simulation than with the clock driven simulation. There were no interactions. That is, the subjects did not learn faster, nor did they respond differently to feedback delays in the event driven simulation. Thus, we may feel confident that the effects of feedback delays are not due to the kind of simulation used.

The Effects of Feedback Delays

Area Lost to Fire.   The analysis of variance yielded main effects of trials, $F(5, 210) = 21.8$, $p < .01$, and delays, $F(2, 42) = 25.7$, $p < .01$, but there were no interactions.

Figure 4.4 shows the effects of feedback delays over trials. As can be seen from this figure, subjects performed best when there were no delays and worst when there was dead time. Subjects having information delays fell in between these extremes. Compared to the results from earlier experiments in this series, the relative area lost to fire is smaller. In part, this is due to the fact that the results in Figure 4.4 have been averaged over the two types of simulation conditions, but this is only part of the explanation. It also turned out that most subjects failed to extinguish the fire during the 20 minute trial; only 35% of the trials in the no delay condition, 25% in the information delay condition, and 0% of the trials in the dead time condition ended with the subject having extinguished the fire, $X^2 (2) = 32.5$, $p < .01$. Therefore, most trials ended with the fire still raging and before the subjects had the possibility to lose as much forest as in Experiments I and II where a trial ended when the subjects had extinguished the fire or lost the base. The effect is obviously more pronounced for the delay conditions, where fewer trials ended with extinction of the fire. Thus, the results in Figure 4.4 cannot be directly compared to those of Experiments I and II, and the differences among the three feedback delay conditions are clearly underestimated because of the time limit. Therefore, we should not be too concerned

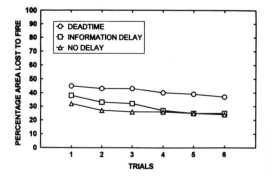

FIG. 4.4. Percentage area lost to fire as a function of type of delay and trials in Experiment III.

about the result that the information delay group ends up at the same level of performance as the no delay group. This is most likely an artifact of the time limit. Instead, the important result is that the information delay group looses more forest overall than the no delay group, but less than the dead time group, as is also supported by the fact that there was no interaction between trials and type of delay.

Waiting Time. The results for waiting time paralleled those for area lost to fire with significant effects of feedback delays, $F(2, 42) = 24.5$, $p < .01$, and trials, $F(5, 210) = 14.80$, $p < .01$. In addition, there was a significant interaction between delays and trials, $F(10/210) = 3.50$, $p < .01$, due to the fact that the differences among conditions decreased somewhat over trials. The subjects left the FFUs inactive for longer periods of time when there were delays than when there were no delays, and longer in the dead time condition than in the information delay condition.

The results in this experiment parallel those of Experiments I and II in that waiting times for the information delay group are longer than those of the no delay group. However, although the difference in the first trials comes close to the actual delay of two time units, suggesting that as subjects ignore the delays, the difference decreases somewhat over trials.

Waiting times were longest in the dead time condition. This cannot be explained in the same way as long waiting times in the information delay conditions. In the dead time conditions, the units are available when they have carried out a command, so the subjects can see what resources are available just as in the no delay condition.

Resource Allocation. As in earlier experiments, subjects allocated more resources to the first fire than to the second, $F(1, 42) = 170.87$, $p < .01$. This was true in all conditions, the fire factor did not interact with any of the other factors except trials, $F(5, 210) = 12.68$, $p < .01$. This interaction was due to a diminishing difference in allocation to the two fires over trials; allocation to the first fire decreased and the allocation to the second increased. The change was small for both kinds of fire, however, and the subjects were far from allocating most resources to the most dangerous fire even at the end of the experiment. This agrees with earlier results.

Also replicating earlier results, the subjects sent out fewer FFUs during the first 5 time units after a fire had started when there were feedback delays than when there were no delays. They sent out fewer units in the dead time condition than in the no delay condition, $F(2, 42) = 13.3$, $p < .01$, see Figure 4.5.

It is easy to understand why subjects sent out fewer FFUs in the dead time condition than in the other conditions. In this condition, where it will take some time for the FFUs to react to a command, the fire will spread

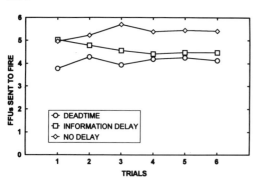

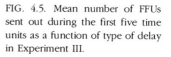

FIG. 4.5. Mean number of FFUs sent out during the first five time units as a function of type of delay in Experiment III.

more from the moment when a decision is made to that when the FFUs are in place than in the other conditions. Thus, if the subjects do not compensate for delays, the difference in the size of the fire when the decision is made and when it takes effect is greater in the dead time condition than in the other conditions of the experiment. It is therefore not surprising that the subjects send out relatively fewer units in the dead time condition than in the other conditions. The longer waiting times in the dead time condition are probably an effect of this too: if the subjects use fewer FFUs each unit will have to wait longer for a new decision on the average. The subjects in the information delay conditions also send out too few units, but this is presumably because they were not aware of all units that they actually had at their disposal. If they ignored the delays, they waited for a unit to report having carried out its command and did not know that the unit is available two time units earlier than it reports. Therefore, they often underestimated the number of FFUs that they could send to a fire.

Use of Planning Commands. The number of planning commands increased slightly over trials as shown by a significant main effect of trials, F $(5, 210) = 11.70$, $p < .01$, suggesting that the subjects found that these commands were useful as they gained experience with the task. There was also a trials by type of simulation interaction, $F (5, 210) = 2.33$, $p < .05$. Subjects in the event driven simulation used more planning commands than those in the clock driven simulation, but the difference in planning commands decreased over trials.

Discussion

The first result from this experiment is that the subjects perform at a lower level when facing a task with dead time than a task with no delays or a task with information delays. The reason for this lower level of performance is easy to find: it is due to the fact that they send out fewer FFUs to a new fire than the subjects in the other conditions. As explained previously, this is exactly what is to be expected if the subjects ignore the delays.

The effects of delays were the same both in the clock driven and the event driven version of the simulation. The subjects' performance was, however, better in the event driven version. The most likely explanation is that the subjects suffered less time pressure in the event driven version, and that they therefore could make better decisions. This interpretation is supported by the results of an as yet unpublished experiment which showed that decreasing time pressure in the clock driven version by increasing the time interval between updates had the same effect on performance as the introduction of an event driven simulation in this experiment. This suggests that if there is a difference between a clock driven simulation and an event driven one, it is quantitative, rather than a qualitative.

In the present experiment, the subjects were given a possibility to compensate for information delays by means of planning commands that allowed them to give a series of two commands in a row to a FFU. The subjects used these commands to a high degree, especially in the delay conditions. Their success in using them is uncertain, however. The only difference between the results of this experiment and those of earlier experiments is that the difference in waiting times between the no delay and the information delay group is somewhat smaller in this experiment. This is what should be expected if the subjects used the planning commands effectively. However, in a recent experiment designed to evaluate the effects of planning commands directly under conditions of information delay and no delay, we found no effects on performance of the possibility to use planning commands. Therefore, any conclusions about the effectiveness of these planning commands remains uncertain.

Experiment IV: Effects of Feedback Delay With Alerted and Informed Subjects

One possible explanation for the result in Experiment I that subjects did not compensate for delays is that they misinterpreted their nature: they saw them as dead time delays rather than information delays. In the present experiment, we examine how subjects cope with both dead time delays and information delays when they not only have been alerted to the possibility of delays, but informed of their nature as well.

Design

Two factors were varied in the experiment: type of delay and whether or not the subjects were informed of the delays. Each factor had two levels; those for the type of delay factor were dead time versus information delay; those for the information factor were information about delays and their nature versus no information about delays. In all four conditions, the subjects went through 6 trials. The design was thus a 2 (levels of delay) by 2 (information) by 6 (trials) factorial design with repeated measures on the third factor. Thirty-two undergraduate students were paid to serve as subjects.

Procedure

The simulation and procedure was the same as that in Experiment III.

Results

As in Experiment III, very few trials ended prematurely due to loss of the base, so this measure is not analyzed here.

Proportion of Trials When the Subjects Extinguished the Fire. Table 4.1 shows the percentage of trials when the subjects managed to extinguish the fire. As can be seen from the table, the subjects generally do not manage to extinguish the fire, only in the condition with information about information delays do we find any substantial number of trials during which the subjects managed to extinguish the fire. The differences are significant, X^2 (1) = 6.11, $p < .05$.

Area Lost to Fire. There was no effect of instructions (F < 1). Subjects in the dead time condition lost more forest than those in the report delay condition, $F(1, 28) = 15.13$, $p < 01$, and there was a general decrease over trials, $F(5, 105) = 36.60$, $p < .01$. These effects replicate those of Experiment III for this measure.

Resource Allocation. The results with respect to resource allocation also replicate those of the earlier experiments in showing that the subjects allocated more FFUs to the first than to the second fire, $F(1, 28) = 50.78$, $p < .01$, that their allocation increased significantly over trials, $F(5, 140) = 3.23$, $p < .01$, and more so for the first fire than for the second as confirmed by a significant fire by trials interaction, $F(5, 140) = 3.23$, $p < .01$.

There were no main effects of delay or information, but there was a significant delay by information interaction, $F(1, 28) = 30.65$, $p < .01$. The interaction was due to the fact that whereas the subjects deployed more resources in the information delay condition than in the dead time condition

TABLE 4.1
Percentage of Trials That End by the Subjects
Having Extinguished the Fires

	Information Delays	Dead Time
Information about delays	8	2
No information about delays	29	0

when they were not informed of the delays (2.15 vs. 1.03 for the mean number of FFUs sent out during the first 5 time units in the information delay and dead time condition, respectively), the reverse was true when they were informed of the delays (1.07 vs. 2.31 for the information delay and dead time condition, respectively). The reason for this interaction is not clear.

Waiting Times. For waiting times, there were no main effects of type of delay or information about delays, nor any interactions involving this factor. The only significant effect was that of blocks, indicating a general decrease in waiting times over trials, $F(5, 140) = 4.76$, $p < .01$.

Use of Planning Commands. There was no main effect of type of delay or information about delays (F < 1), only the main effect of trials, F $(5, 140) = 8.37$, $p < .01$, and the type of information by trials interaction, F $(5, 140) = 3.38$, $p < .01$, were significant. The interaction is due to the fact that the percentage of planning commands increased over trials in both conditions, but more so in the conditions where the subjects had been given information about the delays. This suggests that the subjects realized that the planning commands could be useful when they were told that there were delays. If they did, they were, however, apparently unable to translate this insight into effective decisions, for there were no differences in performance between the two information conditions.

Discussion

The results of Experiment IV show that information about the nature of the delays in the task does not improve the subjects' performance. This suggests that the problem decision makers have with delays is not simply a matter of misperceiving them as Sterman's (1989a, 1989b) MOF hypothesis suggests. That misperception occurs is confirmed by the results of Experiment I which showed that although the subjects were able to detect delays, they nevertheless misattributed these delays to dead time rather than information delays. The misperception hypothesis cannot, however, explain the results of the present experiment. They show that essentially the same effects of delays are obtained when the subjects are informed of the nature of the delays as when they must find the delays themselves. This suggests that the subjects also have problems in finding a way of compensating for the delays. That is, they do not develop the kind of model that they would need to compensate. This interpretation is also supported by the fact that although the subjects try to compensate for the delays by using more planning commands when they are informed of the delays, their performance does not improve as a consequence.

While these results suggest that the effects of feedback delays cannot be attributed to misperception of these delays only, they should not be taken as a disconfirmation of Sterman's MOF hypothesis. That hypothesis covers not only the effects of delays, but also the effects of what is usually called side effects (which are, of course, also due to feedback processes), a problem not directly studied in these experiments.

GENERAL CONCLUSIONS

The results of all four experiments agree in showing strong negative effects of feedback delays in dynamic decision making. In this, they agree with earlier results reviewed in the introduction.

The negative effects of delays cannot be explained by assuming that the subjects do not detect that there are delays, at least when they have been alerted to the possibility that there may be delays. We still lack an experiment where the subjects have been questioned about possible delays when they have not been forewarned that there may be delays. Such an experiment may well show that subjects also have problems detecting delays.

Sterman's (1989a, 1989b) MOF hypothesis receives some support from these results in that we find that the subjects in Experiment I mistakenly attributed the delays in that experiment to dead time rather than information delays. The generality of this finding remains uncertain, however. It may have been due to the particular displays used in the experiment, and with other forms of displays, subjects may interpret delays differently.

The results of Experiment IV show that subjects also have problems in compensating for delays when they know that there are delays and what the nature of these delays are. This suggests that misperception is not a complete explanation and that the subjects also have problems developing the kinds of models that are needed for compensation. The negative effects of delays only hold for the delays that have to be inferred. When the delays can be seen to happen, as is the case for the delays due to the time constants in these experiments, subjects compensate for them by means of a strategy of massive and rapid response to a fire. This suggests that it may be easier to develop the mental models that are needed for compensation for events that can be seen than for events that cannot be seen. This supports Johnson-Laird's (1983) suggestion that mental models have their origin in perception, and it raises the problem of how delays should be represented for the subjects to be able to develop adequate models. This is an important problem for applied research directed at improving people's control of dynamic systems. It also points to the important theoretical problem of trying to understand how people use different forms of information to develop mental models for dynamic systems, a question that has not yet been addressed upon in research on mental models.

A general finding in these experiments is that the subjects fail to redeploy their resources when a new fire starts. The explanation for this result is not clear. One possibility is that it is an attentional problem: the subjects concentrate so much on the task they are performing, that is, fighting the first fire, that they simply fail to detect the second fire until after some time. Another possibility is that the subjects misjudge the danger that the second fire presents, and think that they can leave it until they have finished the first fire, that is, their model of the fire process is not good enough to serve as an adequate guide for their resource deployment. To answer these questions we need a more detailed picture of the subjects' mental models of the fires, as well as measures of how the subjects allocate their attention in the FIRE FIGHTING TASK.

The main conclusion from these experiments, then, is that we now understand the nature of the problem of feedback delays better. There are, however, still quite a number of unchartered areas to explore for future experiments. But at least we now know where these areas are.

ACKNOWLEDGMENTS

This study was supported by grants from the National Swedish Defense Research Institute and the Swedish Council for Research in the Humanities and the Social Sciences. The author thanks Robert Allard, Anders Jansson, Iordanis Kavathatzopoulos, and Jan Kuylenstierna for their assistence in the experimental work.

REFERENCES

Annett, J. (1969). *Feedback and human behavior.* Harmondsworth, Great Britain: Penguin.

Bilodeau, I. M. D. (1966). Information feedback. In E. A. Bilodeau (Ed.), *Acquisition of skill* (pp. 255–296). New York: Academic Press.

Brehmer, B. (1990). Strategies in real-time, dynamic decision making. In R. Hogarth (Ed.), *Insights in decision making.* Chicago, IL: University of Chicago Press.

Brehmer, B. (1992). Dynamic decision making: Human control of complex systems. *Acta Psychologica, 81,* 211–241.

Brehmer, B., & Allard, R. (1991). Real-time, dynamic decision making: The effects of complexity and feedback delays. In J. Rasmussen, B. Brehmer, & J. Leplat (Eds.), *Distributed decision making: Cognitive models of cooperative work.* New York: Wiley.

Brehmer, B., & Dörner, D. (1993). Experiments with computer simulated microworlds. Escaping both the narrow straits of the laboratory and the deep blue sea of the field study. *Computers in Human Behavior, 9,* 171–184.

Brehmer, B., Lövborg, L., & Winman, A. (1992). Cost information in a dynamic decision task. In B. Brehmer (Ed.), *Separate papers of the MOHAWC project.* Roskilde, Denmark: Risø National Laboratory.

Crossman, E. R. F. W., & Cooke, J. E. (1974). Manual control of slow response systems. In E. Edwards & F. P. Lees (Eds.), *The human factor in process control*. London: Taylor & Francis.

Dörner, D., & Preussler, W. (1990). Die Kontrolle eines einfachen ökologischen Systems [Control of a simple ecological system]. *Sprache & Kognition, 9*, 208–217.

Dörner, D., Stäudel, T., & Strohschneider, S. (1986). *MORO. Programmdokumentation* [Description of MORO software]. Bamberg University, Lehrstuhl Psychologie II: Memorandum XX.

Funke, J. (1985). Steuerung dynamischer Systeme durch Aufbau und Anwendung subjektiver Kausalmodelle [Control of dynamic systems by building up and using subjective causal models]. *Zeitschrift für Psychologie, 193*, 435–457.

Johnson-Laird, P. N. (1983). *Mental models*. New York: Cambridge University Press.

Klein, G. A., Orasanu, J., Calderwood, R., & Zsambok, C. E. (Eds.). (1993). *Decision making in action: Models and methods*. Norwood, NJ: Ablex.

Lorge, I., & Thorndike, E. L. (1935). The influence of delay in the aftereffect of a connection. *Journal of Experimental Psychology, 18*, 917–921.

Moray, N., Lootstein, P., & Pajak, J. (1986). Acquisition of process control skills. *IEEE Transactions on Systems, Man, and Cybernetics, SMC-16*, 497–504.

Rapoport, A. (1975). Research paradigms for the study of dynamic decision behavior. In I. D. Wendt & C. Vlek (Eds.), *Utility, probability, and human decision making*. Dordrecht: Reidel.

Reichert, U., & Dörner, D. (1987). Heurismen beim Umgang mit einem einfachen dynamischen System [Heuristics of coping with a "simple" dynamic system]. *Sprache & Kognition, 7*, 12–24.

Sterman, J. D. (1989a). Modeling managerial behavior: Misperceptions of feedback in a dynamic decision making experiment. *Management Science, 35*, 321–339.

Sterman, J. D. (1989b). Misperceptions of feedback in dynamic decision making. *Organizational Behavior and Human Decision Processes, 43*, 301–335.

Implicit Learning in the Control of Complex Systems

Dianne C. Berry
University of Reading, Reading, England

Donald E. Broadbent
University of Oxford, Oxford, England

Unfortunately Donald Broadbent died suddenly while this chapter was in the final stages of preparation. It is not only a personal loss but also a loss to the field of implicit learning. He will be sadly missed.

INTRODUCTION

Over the past 15 years a growing number of studies has demonstrated some form of dissociation between people's ability to control complex systems and their associated verbalizable knowledge. These findings have often been interpreted as providing evidence for implicit as opposed to explicit learning. Implicit learning has been characterized as a process whereby a person learns about the structure of a fairly complex stimulus environment, without necessarily intending to do so, and in such a way that the resulting knowledge is difficult to express (Berry, 1994; Berry & Dienes, 1993). In contrast, explicit learning often involves deliberate attempts to solve problems and test hypotheses, and people are usually aware of much of the knowledge that they have acquired. Whereas most of this volume is concerned with explicit learning, we now focus on implicit learning in the control of complex systems.

Early studies in this area made fairly strong claims about the nature and extent of the dissociation between control performance and verbalizable knowledge. More recent studies, however, provide evidence suggesting that the dissociation may not be as great as was originally thought. We review both the earlier and the more recent evidence, primarily focusing on evidence that has come from studies employing the use of secondary tasks. We describe how early attempts to outline a possible mechanism for implicit learning were influenced by results from secondary task studies, and report a number of new findings with these tasks, suggesting the need for a revised account. Such an account is put forward in the final section.

EARLY STUDIES

Two studies in the mid-1980s seem to provide fairly strong evidence for a dissociation between people's ability to control complex systems and their associated verbalizable knowledge (Berry & Broadbent, 1984; Broadbent, FitzGerald, & Broadbent, 1986). Both studies examine the differential effects of task experience and verbal instruction on control performance and question answering.

Berry and Broadbent (1984) used the SUGAR PRODUCTION and PERSON INTERACTION TASKS which required people to reach and maintain specified target values of an output variable by varying a single input variable. In the case of sugar production, subjects took on the role of manager of a simple SUGAR PRODUCTION FACTORY and were required to reach and maintain specified levels of sugar output by varying the number of workers employed. In the case of PERSON INTERACTION, subjects were required to interact with a *computer person*. The communication was based on a fixed set of adjectives describing various degrees of intimacy of personal interaction. Subjects were told to shift the behavior of the person to the Very Friendly level and to attempt to maintain it at that level. The tasks were mathematically identical. The equation relating sugar output to workforce was the same as that relating the computer person's responses to those of the subject. The nature of the equation was such that there was not a unique output associated with any one input. In the case of sugar production, for example, the resulting sugar output depended on the previous sugar output as well as the new workforce figure. This made it more likely that subjects would exercise continuous control, rather than being able to hit the target by chance and then remain there simply by typing in the same input value. Following experience with the task, subjects were required to complete written questionnaires which asked about the relationships within the system. Typically, they were given a series of input and output values and were asked to predict the next output value (e.g., sugar output) given a new input value (e.g., workforce).

The results were very similar for the SUGAR PRODUCTION and PERSON INTERACTION TASKS. In both cases, practice significantly improved the ability to control these tasks but had no effect on the ability to answer post task written questions. Subjects who had received 60 trials of practice were *on target* on an average of 80% of the final five trials. Despite this relatively high level of performance, their post task questionnaire scores were no higher than those of subjects who had received either 30 trials of practice or no experience with the task at all. (In each case, performance levels on the questionnaire were around 15%.) In contrast, detailed verbal instructions on how to reach and maintain the target value significantly improved the ability to answer questions but had no effect on control performance. In addition to these differential effects, there was also no evidence for a positive association between task performance and question answering. Indeed, across three experiments, individuals who were better at controlling the task were significantly worse at answering the questions. We concluded therefore that these tasks might, at least under certain conditions, be performed in some implicit manner.

Broadbent, FitzGerald, and Broadbent (1986) came to a similar conclusion using a task based on a CITY TRANSPORT SYSTEM. In this task, people were required to control the number of passengers using the buses and the number of empty car parking spaces by varying the time interval between buses and the car parking fee. Broadbent et al. found that subjects improved in their ability to control the task with practice, but that there was not a corresponding increase in the number of correct answers to verbal questions about the system. They also found that verbal explanation had no effect on task performance (although in this case, the verbal explanation simply consisted of presenting the written questionnaire with the correct answers filled in), and that there was no correlation between control performance and question answering.

One criticism of the Berry and Broadbent (1984) and Broadbent et al. (1986) studies, however, is that the particular questions used in the post task questionnaires may not have been appropriate to the particular ideas of the people learning to control the systems. That is, subjects might have had knowledge that was relevant to controlling the tasks, but that knowledge was not assessed by the questions. Berry (1984, 1991), however, used a range of question types and still found evidence for a dissociation. For example, the original questionnaire presented people with a series of input and output values and asked them to predict the new state of the output variable given a new input value. Berry also worded questions such that subjects were again given a series of input and output values, but were asked which input value would be needed to bring the output value to target. Although this is more in line with what is required while controlling the task, performance was not better on these *estimated input questions.*

Furthermore, Stanley et al. (1989) asked people to practice either the SUGAR PRODUCTION or the PERSON INTERACTION TASK and then to explain verbally to somebody else how to control it. Although in this case people could choose their own words, subjects' own performance improved before they could tell somebody else how to succeed. Individual learning curves associated with the tasks showed sudden improvements in performance that were not accompanied by a similar increase in verbalizable knowledge. Stanley et al. (1989) suggested that there is a considerable difference between the amount of time it takes to acquire verbalizable knowledge and knowledge used to perform the control tasks. Subjects tend to become quite skilled in controlling the tasks long before there is much gain in verbalizable knowledge.

SUBSEQUENT QUALIFICATIONS

It was not the case, however, that performance and verbalizable knowledge were totally separable in the Stanley et al. (1989) study. Although a dissociation occurred at moderate levels of practice, it was found that highly experienced subjects were able to give verbal statements that helped novices to perform more successfully (although this was only true after 570 trials of practice). Stanley et al. (1989) suggested that people draw on two separate but interacting knowledge structures to perform these tasks. One knowledge structure is based on memory for past experiences (close analogies), and the other is based on one's current mental model of the task. Implicit sets of competing rules that control response selection are derived from both sources of knowledge. They suggested that dissociations between task performance and verbalizing occur because memory based processing tends to have more control over response selection because of its greater specificity, whereas a mental model tends to be the preferred mode for verbal reporting because of its greater accessibility.

McGeorge and Burton (1989) also used a talk-back method (getting subjects to provide instructions for the next subject) to elicit verbalizable knowledge after performance on the SUGAR PRODUCTION TASK. Rather than presenting the elicited instructions to subsequent subjects, however, they used them to develop computer simulations of subjects' control performance. Comparisons were made between simulated performance and observed performance. Using this method, McGeorge and Burton (1989) found that about one-third of their subjects reported heuristics that resulted in simulated performances that were either equivalent to, or better than, observed performance. Hence, after 90 trials of practice, some subjects were able to produce accurate verbal statements. McGeorge and Burton (1989) suggested that this may reflect the initial stages of development of a mental model.

Marescaux, Luc, and Karnas (1989), again using the SUGAR PRODUCTION TASK, demonstrated that subjects know more about situations that they have personally experienced. Their experiment was set up such that subjects interacted with the SUGAR PRODUCTION TASK for two sets of 30 trials, and then answered a number of post task questions (or situations). The questions were matched closely to the task in that they required subjects to estimate how many workers would be needed to reach target in different situations, and that they were presented on the computer so subjects saw just what they might have seen on the full task. An example situation was "if you had just employed 400 workers and if the sugar production was then 8,000 tons, what should you do next to bring the sugar production to target?" The questions varied along two basic dimensions. First, the target sugar output was either the same or different to that experienced while controlling the task. Second, the minihistory given to subjects at the start of each question was either taken from their own immediately preceding interaction, or was taken from a hypothetical interaction.

The results showed superior questionnaire performance when subjects had to reach the same target as they experienced while interacting with the task, and when the minihistories were taken from their own past experience. Subjects did not perform as well when faced with new random situations, a result which conceptually replicates Berry's (1984, 1991) findings with the estimated input questions. The key factor seemed to be that subjects were tested on specific situations which they themselves had experienced while interacting with the task. They did not seem to have learned anything that could be used in other novel situations.

Part of the motivation behind Marescaux et al.'s (1989) study was to see whether there was any evidence that subjects were responding according to a look up table; that is, whether they linked specific responses to specific situations (Broadbent et al., 1986). In line with this assumption, they found when subjects were shown situations in which they had previously been correct, the subjects' responses matched their previous responses 57% of the time. Marescaux et al. (1989) called this the *concordance* measure. However, Dienes and Fahey (1993) have recently argued that the Marescaux et al. (1989) study provides only suggestive evidence for a look up table because the authors did not compare their concordance measure with the concordance for incorrect situations, or with the baseline concordance that would be expected if subjects were not sensitive to the situation at all.

Dienes and Fahey (1993) repeated the Marescaux et al. (1989) study but included these extra measures. They found subjects performed best in old situations in which they previously had been successful (they were still at chance on new situations), and that subjects were consistent in responding to a situation in which they previously had been correct. This consistency was greater than a chance baseline. There was also some evidence that consistency for correct situations was greater than that for incorrect situations. Dienes and Fahey (1993) also extended the Marescaux et al. (1989) study by looking at whether performance on the situations task was dependent on subjects' ability to recognize previously seen situations as old. Interestingly, they found that there was no relation between correct responses on the old correct situations and subjects' ability to recognize them as old. This suggests that any look up table would not be based on explicit memory, and that Marescaux et al.'s (1989) situations task might be better viewed as tapping implicit rather than explicit knowledge.

Finally, Sanderson (1989) reported associations between performance and verbalizable knowledge under certain conditions, using Broadbent et al.'s TRANSPORT TASK. She suggested that the combination of high levels of practice with a larger solution space (in this case produced by requiring decimal precision as opposed to integer values) are particularly important in bringing out positive associations. She also stressed the weakness of assessing verbalizable knowledge solely by means of post task questionnaire (as was done in studies by Berry & Broadbent, 1984, and Broadbent et al., 1986). Instead, she advocated use of a mental models analysis technique in which subjects' question answers are compared with those that would be produced by a number of different mental models. She suggested that such a mental models analysis makes it clear that verbal knowledge can show a distinct change before it is reflected in raw questionnaire score.

Taken together, the studies by Stanley et al. (1989), McGeorge and Burton (1989), Marescaux et al. (1989), Dienes and Fahey (1993), and Sanderson (1989) suggest that the dissociation between task performance and associated verbalizable knowledge may not be as complete as was at first thought. People appear to develop some explicit knowledge as a result of task experience. The evidence seems to indicate, however, that increases in explicit knowledge occur *after* improvements in task performance, and that implicit knowledge may be largely limited to knowledge of specific personally-experienced situations.

The view that explicit knowledge develops as a result of extensive practice received support from a study with amnesic patients by Squire and Frambach (1990). They examined whether amnesics could learn to control the SUGAR PRODUCTION TASK at the same level as normal subjects. They found that amnesic patients performed just as well as the normal controls in an initial training session, but performed significantly worse in a second session. Squire and Frambach suggested this is because by the second session, the normal subjects were starting to build up explicit knowledge which could be used to improve performance still further. The amnesics, in contrast, were not able to do this.

CONDITIONS AND MODES OF LEARNING

Rather than simply demonstrating or denying dissociations, a more interesting approach has been to look at conditions that give rise to either implicit or explicit learning. Berry and Broadbent (1987, 1988) found that the salience of the relationship between the input and output variables is a particularly important factor in this respect. In the case of the SUGAR PRODUCTION and PERSON INTERACTION TASKS used by Berry and Broadbent (1984) and Stanley et al. (1989), the underlying relationship was relatively nonobvious or nonsalient. Following on from studies in the area of artificial grammar learning (e.g., Reber, 1976; Reber, Kassin, Lewis, & Cantor, 1980) Berry and Broadbent reasoned that if the underlying relationship was made more salient, performance and verbalizable knowledge might be positively associated. We devised a pair of PERSON INTERACTION TASKS to empirically test this suggestion. In both cases, each control action by the person produced an output from the system that depended only on that input and simply added a constant to it. In the salient case, the output appeared immediately, whereas in the nonsalient case it appeared only after the next input (that is, there was a lag). The results showed that in the case of the salient task, post task questionnaire scores were high and positively associated with control performance, whereas in the case of the nonsalient version, post task questionnaire scores were low and uncorrelated with control performance.

We also looked at the differential effects of presenting subjects with an explicit search instruction (see also Reber, 1976; Reber et al., 1980) on performance on the salient and nonsalient PERSON TASKS. The nature of the instruction was such that subjects were told that the computer person's responses were determined by the subjects' responses and that it might help them control the person better if they tried to work out exactly how the computer's responses were related to their own. It was found that for subjects interacting with the salient PERSON TASK, the search instruction had a significant beneficial effect on subsequent control performance compared with that of control subjects. In contrast, the reverse effect was found for subjects interacting with the nonsalient PERSON TASK. In this case, the search instruction had a significant detrimental effect on subsequent control performance compared with that of control subjects.

On the basis of this study, we distinguished between two different possible modes of learning in complex situations where people have to acquire knowledge about the relationships between a number of variables without necessarily knowing in advance what the key variables are. The first mode was described as an implicit or unselective one in which a person encountering a complex task may observe the variables unselectively and may attempt to store all of the contingencies between them. The contingencies could be represented as a set of procedures or as some form of look up table. In either case, a particular set of circumstances would give rise to a particular response. An alternative mode of learning was described as a selective or explicit one in which a few key variables are selected and only the contingencies between these key variables are observed. Provided that the correct variables are selected, this will be a fast and effective method of learning that is also likely to result in a form of knowledge that can be made explicit because of the relatively small number of relationships involved. However, if the task involves many irrelevant variables and the wrong variables are selected for examination, this mode of learning will do badly compared with the unselective mode.

More recent studies have provided additional evidence for this distinction between implicit and explicit learning modes. Berry (1991), for example, found that experience of watching another person interacting with the salient PERSON CONTROL TASK had a beneficial effect on subsequent control performance with the same task, whereas the experience of watching another person interacting with a nonsalient PERSON CONTROL TASK (either the 1984 or 1988 relationship) had no significant effect on subsequent control performance. Subjects had to interact with the nonsalient tasks directly in order for learning to occur. Similarly, Dienes and Fahey (1993) examined performance on their situations task (see previous section) following experience of interacting with either the salient or nonsalient PERSON CONTROL TASK. They found that following interacting with the nonsalient task, subjects' knowledge was limited to situations they had previously seen (in line with the findings for the SUGAR PRODUCTION TASK). However, in the case of the salient task, subjects were able to respond correctly to new situations. Dienes and Fahey (1993) suggested that subjects might learn the salient task partly by a look up table and partly by acquiring general knowledge they could apply to any situation.

One difficulty with the previous conceptualization centers around the notion of salience. We defined salience as the probability that key variables in the task will be chosen if a person learns by the selective rather than the unselective mode. We suggested a number of ways in which this probability could be increased, such as by reducing the number of irrelevant factors in a situation, by making the key events act in accordance with general knowledge from outside the task, or by having the key events occur at the same time rather than at different times. Despite this, there is no independent means of defining salience in relation to particular tasks. The two PERSON TASKS, for example, differ in many ways, most notably in terms of task difficulty. Therefore, it could be differences in this, or some other factor, that leads to the pattern of results observed.

Another problem with the initial characterization is that a simple distinction between implicit and explicit learning modes could be considered extreme (Berry, 1994). It is probably more useful to think in terms of there being a number of different modes which fall along a continuum. These different learning modes, or styles, differ in the extent to which actions (or decisions) are driven by conscious beliefs. It also seems unlikely that each mode operates only in isolation. Rather, it seems that in any complex learning task, performance is likely to involve a subtle combination of implicit and explicit learning processes. Similarly, the knowledge gained as a result of interacting with a complex learning task is likely to involve both implicit and explicit aspects, rather than being solely one or the other. The particular balance will depend on both the experimental instructions and the salience (however this is defined) of the crucial variables (Berry & Broadbent, 1987).

THE PROBLEM OF MECHANISM

The studies reviewed show that implicit and explicit learning are affected by different variables. The next step is to identify a possible mechanism, or mechanisms, to account for these phenomena. A few years ago the evidence suggested a model that covered part of the facts, but now needs correction. The essential features were:

- Explicit and implicit learning were based on rather different knowledge bases. The first used restricted symbolic, often verbal, knowledge whereas the second used broader subsymbolic, often nonverbal, knowledge.
- Because of its selective and limited character, explicit learning was more likely to be disrupted by secondary tasks. Implicit learning on the other hand, was thought to be much more resistant to secondary tasks.

- The two forms of learning were seen as alternative, the presence of one tending to inhibit or replace the other.

The third feature was intended to explain that certain tasks are learned worse with explicit instructions than incidentally (Berry & Broadbent, 1988; Reber, 1976). The effect is not universal (Mathews et al., 1989; Reber et al., 1980), but could be explained by the suitability of the task for explicit learning; that is, its *salience*. The second feature, however, was derived from studies of secondary tasks, and it is in this field, that fresh data now exist. In the following, we shall look at this evidence.

THE MODEL IN NEED OF CORRECTION

A convenient statement of the older view is provided by Broadbent (1989), and this position will be restated before it is challenged. The paper rests heavily on a study with the PERSON CONTROL TASK by Hayes and Broadbent (1988) and a study with a different control task (the WHALE GAME) by Porter (1986, 1991).

The PERSON CONTROL TASK

In the Hayes and Broadbent (1988) study, subjects interacted with the salient and nonsalient PERSON CONTROL TASKS devised by Berry and Broadbent (1988). In addition, a random number generation task was performed as a secondary task. There was no evidence of a differential effect on original learning, or on the accuracy of performance of a previously learned task; but there was an effect when the input-output relationship was unexpectedly changed without warning while the secondary task continued. (Before the change, the system had given an output lower by a constant amount than the input, whereas after the change it gave an output higher than the input).

In two experiments, the *salient* task showed a larger deterioration after this reversal than did the *nonsalient* task. This interaction appeared to depend on the presence of the secondary task; in a third experiment without such a task, the salient task showed a smaller effect of reversal than the nonsalient. Thus, this study supports the notion of a special symbolic store for explicit memory; and therefore a greater resistance of implicit tasks to distracting activity.

The WHALE GAME

Additional evidence for the position adopted by Broadbent (1989) came from studies by Porter (1986, 1991) using a different control task. The WHALE GAME involved two tasks, both concerned with controlling a whale in the sea. One task was to eat plankton by swimming towards it and occupying the same location. The other task was to avoid being caught by Eskimo hunters, whose kayaks would pursue the whale and could only be avoided by placing the whale behind an iceberg. The pursuing kayak would then collide with the iceberg and sink.

The verbal statements of the subjects showed good verbal knowledge of the plankton task, but poor knowledge of the kayaks. In fact, many people had false perceptions of how best to avoid the kayaks, such that the strategies subjects reported verbally were negatively related to successful task performance. A number of secondary tasks were combined with the game, and the effects on the plankton task were universal; it deteriorated with an instruction to articulate continuously, with a task of generating a random series of digits, and with increasing verbal memory load (in the latter case only when instructions were to treat the plankton as more important than the kayaks). The first and last of these had no effect on kayaks at all, and random generation only did so at low levels of practice.

Thus, if kayaks and plankton are regarded as implicit and explicit respectively, these results favor the notion of a special symbolic store for explicit memory; and a much greater resistance of implicit memory to secondary tasks. For future reference, however, note that the secondary tasks were all verbal, and also note that people had false knowledge about kayaks rather than merely an absence of knowledge.

THE EVIDENCE REQUIRING A CHANGE IN THE THEORY

A number of more recent experiments, however, show these results hold only under certain conditions, which alters their interpretation. We now look at this more recent evidence.

The PERSON CONTROL TASK

There have been three attempted replications of the work of Hayes and Broadbent (1988); one gave the same result rather weakly, one failed completely to do so, and the third gave equivocal results suggesting individual differences. Therefore, the details of the experiments are of some interest.

Sanderson (1990, Experiment 2) provided the weakly supportive result; she repeated the design of Experiment 2 of Hayes and Broadbent (1988). In that design, original training took place with no secondary task, then the secondary task was introduced, and finally there was an unexpected reversal of the control relationship. In Sanderson's results, this reversal produced a deterioration in both salient and nonsalient tasks, but the size of the drop was (just) significantly larger in the salient task than in the other. It is worth noting that the secondary task was more demanding than random generation is; it was a *one back* memory task, in which each of a series of signals was to produce a response. The response was determined by the previous signal, not by the current one.

Green and Shanks (1993, Experiment 2B) used the design of Experiment 3 of Hayes and Broadbent (1988), in which both original training and reversal took place in the presence of a secondary task. (They had, however, an important difference in the instructions given to subjects, which we shall discuss later.) In their results, there was no significant difference at all between salient and nonsalient tasks in the size of the deterioration after the reversal. Numerically, any insignificant difference was in the wrong direction.[1]

The equivocal result is provided by Sanderson (1990, Experiment 1). That study, like her other one, used the design of Hayes and Broadbent (1988, Experiment 2), and also used the same random number generation task as the original study did. Although the average results did show a slightly greater deterioration on the salient task after the reversal, and Newman-Keuls tests assessed it as significant whereas the corresponding effect on the non-salient task was not, the overall interaction of phase and task was insignificant. Sanderson (1990) rightly therefore regards this as a failure to support Hayes and Broadbent (1988).

Explanations of the Discrepancies: Individual Differences

Unlike other authors, Sanderson (1990) analyzed the performance of her individual subjects and separated them into groups showing different strategies. This can be done by looking at two correlations; that of the person's decisions with their own past decisions, and that with the extent of the previous error on that trial. For example, in the original learning phase the subject's decisions are sometimes correlated with their own immediately previous decision, with no relation to the actual success achieved. Another possible pattern is that decisions made by the subject are inversely correlated with the last output from the system and unrelated to the previous decision. Thus, if the output is too high, the subject tends to pick a low input and vice versa.

A third pattern combines both the correlation with the previous decision and the influence of the success on the last trial. Thus, the subject keeps a

---

[1]They also (Experiment 1B) carried out a less strict replication in which reversal occurred following the first block of trials showing more than a criterion level of performance. Comparisons with this block are, of course, contaminated by regression to the mean, and are therefore suspect. In addition, the procedure meant that reversal occurred at much lower levels of practice than those used by Hayes and Broadbent (1988). Thus, attention should be concentrated on 2B as there are obvious explanations of 1B.

reasonably constant input, but modifies it depending on recent success. Finally, there is a strategy in which the subject no longer moves up and down to compensate for previous errors, but holds reasonably constant at a fixed level giving successful performance. The four strategies mentioned tend to occur in the order described; out of 16 people who showed one of these four strategies in phase 1 of the two experiments and a different one in phase 2, only one moved in the opposite direction. This is adaptive; the last strategy mentioned will give the highest level of success.

Sanderson (1990) also related the strategy to performance under reversal, though only for the salient task. She separated those showing the last, optimal, strategy from all the others; and in Experiment 1 showed a highly significant difference in the degree of deterioration after reversal. People using the optimum strategy showed no deterioration at all while the others gave a steeper one; the relevant interaction gave $p < 0.005$. Interestingly, this did not appear if subjects were separated by their verbal reports; it was necessary to use the objective criterion of performance. (Even the performance criterion did not show the effect in her Experiment 2, which showed an overall effect similar to that of Hayes and Broadbent.)

Clearly, the effect of reversal found on the salient task will depend on the proportion of subjects who have adopted the optimum strategy by the time of reversal. If there are many, reversal will have little effect; if there are few, it will have a large effect. In Sanderson's case, such subjects were fewer in the nonsalient case; she found none in that group in either experiment who achieved that strategy after the first practice block, whereas five of the salient subjects had done so. Thus, a possible explanation of the discrepancies is that they are due to sampling factors altering the proportion of people with various strategies.

A rather different explanation in terms of sampling has been suggested by Green and Shanks (1993). They noted that Hayes and Broadbent (1988) set no minimum level of performance for their subjects, and they suggested that the nonsalient group might therefore have included some subjects who had learned very little before the reversal of the relationship. Naturally, these subjects would not be hampered by the reversal, and might even show learning after it. This suggestion is a priori very plausible, but there are a number of details of all three experiments that seem to argue against it.

First, the suggestion is contradictory to the result of Sanderson already quoted. It was her best subjects, not her worst, who showed little decline after reversal.

Second, Green and Shanks (1993) themselves (whose main analysis was based only on subjects who had achieved a criterion by the end of practice) conducted an analysis including all subjects tested, however bad their performance before reversal. The result of Hayes and Broadbent (1988) was still not found. (Interestingly, they could obtain that result by eliminating *good* subjects from the nonsalient group, in partial agreement with the finding of Sanderson, 1990.[2])

Third, and most directly, the individual data of the second and third experiments of Hayes and Broadbent (1988) are available to us; and they show that this is not the explanation. The clearest evidence comes from Experiment 2, in which one can confine analysis to those subjects who achieved the Green and Shanks (1993) criterion of 6/10 on original learning. Comparison of performance before and after reversal is then independent of this selection, so no regression to the mean can occur; and the reversal has a more damaging effect on the salient group. In Experiment 3, the results on selected subjects are numerically in the same direction, the decline being nearly twice as large in the salient group; but the number of subjects passing the criterion is in this case too small for significance.

Thus, there must be some other feature of the Hayes and Broadbent (1988) experiment that was different from that of Green and Shanks (1993); such as a higher incidence of subjects in the latter experiment who used the optimal strategy.

Explanations: Prior Instructions

It was found by Berry and Broadbent (1988) that the exact wording of instructions is important in these tasks. The basic instruction is to explain to the subjects the options open to them, and the goal of securing *friendly* behavior from the computer person. With such instructions, subjects generate a variety of hypotheses about the task, derived from everyday life. Sanderson (1990) used similar nondirective instructions.

Berry and Broadbent (1988), however, showed that adding an extra phrase would markedly depress the nonsalient task and assist the salient task. The phrase was, "You do realize that Ellis's responses are determined by your responses. On the next set of trials it might help you control Ellis better if you try to work out how Ellis's responses are related to your own—try to crack the pattern." This, of course, would tend to reduce the use of everyday life hypotheses; real people rarely base friendship on one or even two reactions. The phrase was intended to induce explicit learning in the sense of Reber (1976), and the double dissociation in the results suggested that it did have some effect.

Unfortunately, Green and Shanks (1993) included such a phrase in their instructions to all subjects; it was "You can therefore control Ellis's attitude because every time that you change your attitude towards Ellis, Ellis's attitude

---

[2]They also appeal to the fact that the bad subjects before reversal showed less deterioration than the good ones; but this, of course, is again a case of regression to the mean. Selecting the best subjects at time 1, will always tend to show a relative drop to a later measurement at time 2.

will shift accordingly." This statement is true for the salient task, but, in its obvious sense, was false for the nonsalient task; in that group, people might change their attitude and see no change, or an inappropriate change, due to past action. It was this inappropriateness of the obvious hypothesis that made Berry and Broadbent's (1984) *explicit* instruction have its effect; a further verbal direction, telling the subject that a lag was involved, gave a large benefit to the nonsalient group.

Thus, the difference in instructions may explain why the results of Green and Shanks (1993) disagreed with those of Hayes and Broadbent (1988). It would not, however, explain the discrepancies within Sanderson's (1990) results. Yet, a difference of instruction is likely, as we have seen, to lead to a difference in strategy, depending on the correctness of the instructions. The two kinds of explanation may conceivably be the same. The question of instructions, however, raises the question of false and conflicting knowledge from past experience.

The WHALE GAME

Since the work of Porter (1986, 1991), a further group of experiments has been carried out on the same task by Thurber (1992). She replicated the basic effect of Porter; random generation had no effect on the kayak (possibly implicit) score, but caused the plankton (possibly explicit) score to deteriorate. In addition, she replaced random generation by a nonverbal task; foot reactions to the pitch of tones. This task impaired both kayaks and plankton.

Such a result destroys the argument that implicit tasks are immune to secondary tasks. These results also do not fit with the simple notion that the plankton task uses verbal resources and the kayaks nonverbal ones. That notion would in any case be implausible; most complex tasks involve many functions, and interference may occur at alternative sites. For instance, it is quite possible that the foot reactions of Thurber's (1992) nonverbal task may interfere with the manual ones of both kayaks and plankton. This argument itself, however, makes it puzzling that random generation leaves the kayaks task unaffected.

It may be relevant here that uninstructed subjects have false ideas about the kayak task, rather than simply an absence of knowledge. For instance, if the whale strikes an iceberg it destroys it, leaving fewer possible hiding places for the whale. When asked verbally, people think they should avoid icebergs; but objectively this is uncorrelated with success. There are too many icebergs for any important number to be lost during a run. One ought therefore not to worry about collisions.

Perhaps such false verbal ideas hamper performance, but are impaired by random generation. With this in mind, Thurber (1992) gave new subjects preliminary instructions that countered the false preconceptions. When she did this, it made no difference to the effects of the nonverbal secondary task: both plankton and kayaks were impaired by the tone task. However, random generation now impaired kayaks as well as plankton.

The false verbal preconception, therefore, was essential for Porter's (1986, 1991) result. It only matters, of course, for the effects on kayaks; plankton shows the same results regardless of instructions or the nature of the secondary task. In explaining the results of verbal secondary tasks on kayaks, we are uncertain on two questions: First we do not know whether the verbal secondary task impairs both verbal and nonverbal knowledge about kayaks, or whether it solely impairs verbal aspects of that task, and second we do not know whether performance on kayaks is always based on a constant mixture of verbal and nonverbal knowledge, or whether verbal instruction may cause it to shift to become purely verbal.

If the first answer is given to both questions, or if the second answer is given to both questions, then the experimental results can be explained. For the present purposes it does not matter which is true.

On the first pair of assumptions, the verbal secondary task impairs nonverbal knowledge of the kayaks. In the uninstructed case, this bad effect is canceled by the good effect of impairing the (false) verbal knowledge. Therefore, no overall impairment appears. In the instructed case, the knowledge being impaired is correct whether verbal or nonverbal; so an impairment appears.

On the second pair of assumptions, the disruption of verbal knowledge has no effect on uninstructed subjects because for them it was irrelevant to performance. In the instructed case, however, people rely more on verbal knowledge, which is in this case correct. Thus there will be an impairment.

It is clear that neither of these explanations requires the explicit and implicit strategies to be alternatives. The pattern of data found by Porter (1986, 1991) has now been explained without that assumption.

A REVISED SYNTHESIS

We believe that the current evidence is best explained by the following set of principles:

- Keeping the idea that some knowledge is symbolic (verbal) and some is subsymbolic (nonverbal). These broad categories of knowledge are most readily tested by different methods of measurement; questioning or measuring performance. They are also most readily acquired in different ways; verbal instruction and direct task experience being examples.

- Abandoning the idea that the symbolic system is uniquely vulnerable to secondary tasks. Each system is subject to interference from other tasks that will increase with overlap of the tasks in the usual way.

- Abandoning the idea that one system inhibits or is alternative to the other. The two forms of knowledge may develop independently.

- Adding the idea that each kind of knowledge may have initial biases from past situations, and that these may not agree. Pre-existing knowledge, and its degree of correctness, then become important.

These four principles explain the various results in the following ways.

In the PERSON CONTROL TASKS. The fact that there are inappropriate expectations may underlie the frequent dissociation between performance and verbal measures of knowledge. This suggestion has been made previously by Stanley et al. (1989) when reporting that the two measures show signs of learning at different stages of practice. The same experimental team had found distinctions between performance on the PERSON CONTROL TASK and the formally identical SUGAR PRODUCTION TASK. Expectations of persons are different from expectations of sugar factories. At least this is true in some populations; the two tasks had not been found to differ in the work of Berry and Broadbent (1984). Thus, it is plausible that practice will, in the absence of false assumptions, improve both verbal and non-verbal knowledge; when assumptions are false, the nonverbal may develop at a different speed from the verbal. That at least is true with the salient/nonsalient tasks of Berry and Broadbent (1988).

Successful performance after practice is based on different knowledge in salient and nonsalient tasks. If a secondary task is applied in either case, it may impair either form of knowledge. There is no particular reason (on the revised assumptions) for expecting the effects on original learning to be larger on salient rather than on nonsalient tasks. However, once a relationship has been learned, there will be preexisting knowledge of one type or of the other. The effect of any reversal in the relationship may therefore depend on the knowledge being used for the task. If the person is using relatively context-free rules, these may be less impaired. Thus, a person who has learned "When too low, move up" will continue to do so after a reversal and will do quite well. Conversely, one who has learned "Input value x and ignore the situation" will also continue to do so, but will do badly. It is most unlikely that anybody will be able to use a context dependent rule of the type "Remember last input to and output from the system; subtract first from second; input a value that much different from target." The exact effect of the secondary task will therefore depend on the strategy that the learning situation has induced.

*In the **WHALE GAME.*** For the plankton score, practice and prior experience cause an agreement between performance and verbal knowledge. Both verbal and nonverbal secondary tasks will interfere with performance. We do not know whether they do this through impact on the same mechanism or on different mechanisms. The effect is unaltered by previous instruction on the kayak task, since that has no effect on the knowledge used in the plankton task.

For the kayak task, however, untutored verbal knowledge is contradictory to the nonverbal knowledge gained by practice; therefore, performance may be satisfactory even when explicit statements about the task are wrong. That is, performance is adequately determined by nonverbal knowledge. When a nonverbal secondary task is present, it impairs the nonverbal aspects of the kayak performance. The effects of verbal tasks will be bad or neutral depending on the correctness of the verbal knowledge and also the extent to which that knowledge is emphasized by instructions.

SUMMARY

This chapter has reviewed evidence for the existence of implicit learning in relation to the control of complex systems. In particular, it has focused on evidence coming from studies employing the use of secondary tasks. It has shown how recent results from such studies have necessitated changes to earlier accounts of implicit learning. In line with this, a revised synthesis has been put forward. Further studies in the area are needed in order to assess the validity of this revised account.

It is interesting to note that parallel findings in other areas have also called for modifications to earlier accounts of implicit learning. Recent studies on artificial grammar learning (Dienes, Broadbent, & Dienes, 1991; Perruchet & Pacteau, 1990), sequence learning (Perruchet & Amorim, 1992), and even simple rule learning (Cock, Berry, & Gaffan, 1994) suggest that we need to be cautious when interpreting evidence in favor of implicit learning.

REFERENCES

Berry, D. C. (1984). *Implicit and explicit knowledge in the control of complex systems.* Unpublished doctoral thesis, University of Oxford, United Kingdom.

Berry, D. C. (1991). The role of action in implicit learning. *Quarterly Journal of Experimental Psychology, 43,* 881–906.

Berry, D. C. (1994). Implicit learning: Twenty-five years on. A Tutorial. In C. Umilta & M. Moscovitch (Eds.), *Attention and Performance XV* (pp. 755–782). Cambridge, MA: MIT Press.

Berry, D. C., & Broadbent, D. E. (1984). On the relationship between task performance and associated verbalisable knowledge. *Quarterly Journal of Experimental Psychology, 36,* 209–231.

Berry, D. C., & Broadbent, D. E. (1987). The combination of explicit and implicit learning processes. *Psychological Research, 49,* 7–15.

Berry, D. C., & Broadbent, D. E. (1988). Interactive tasks and the implicit-explicit distinction. *British Journal of Psychology, 79,* 251–272.

Berry, D. C., & Dienes, Z. (1993). *Implicit Learning: Theoretical and Empirical Issues.* Hove: Lawrence Erlbaum Associates.

Broadbent, D. E. (1989). Lasting representations and temporary processes. In H. L. Roediger & F. I. M. Craik (Eds.), *Varieties of Memory and Consciousness: Essays in honour of Endel Tulving* (pp. 211–227). Hillsdale, NJ: Lawrence Erlbaum Associates.

Broadbent, D. E., FitzGerald, P., & Broadbent, M. H. P. (1986). Implicit and explicit knowledge in the control of complex systems. *British Journal of Psychology, 77,* 33–50.

Cock, J., Berry, D. C., & Gaffan, E. A. (1994). New strings for old: The role of similarity processing in an incidental learning task. *Quarterly Journal of Experimental Psychology, 47,* 1015–1034.

Dienes, Z., Broadbent, D. E., & Berry, D. C. (1991). Implicit and explicit knowledge bases in artificial grammar learning. *Journal of Experimental Psychology: Learning, Memory, and Cognition, 17,* 875–887.

Dienes, Z., & Fahey, R. (1993). *The role of implicit memory in controlling a dynamic system.* Manuscript submitted for publication.

Green, R., & Shanks, D. (1993). On the existence of independent explicit and implicit learning systems. *Memory and Cognition, 21,* 304–317.

Hayes, N., & Broadbent, D. E. (1988). Two modes of learning for interactive tasks. *Cognition, 28,* 249–276.

Marescaux, P., Luc, F., & Karnas, G. (1989). Modes d'apprentissage selectif et nonselectif et connaissances acquises au control d'un processus: Evaluation d'un modele simule [Selective and non-selective learning in process control: Evaluation of a simulation model]. *Cahiers de Psychologie Cognitive, 9,* 239–264.

Mathews, R., Buss, R., Stanley, W., Blanchard-Fields, F., Cho, J., & Druhan, B. (1989). The role of implicit and explicit processes in learning from examples: A synergistic effect. *Journal of Experimental Psychology: Learning, Memory, and Cognition, 15,* 1083–1100.

McGeorge, P., & Burton, M. (1989). The effects of concurrent verbalisation on performance in a dynamic systems task. *British Journal of Psychology, 80,* 455–465.

Perruchet, P., & Amorin, M. (1992). Conscious knowledge and changes in performance in sequence learning: Evidence against dissociation. *Journal of Experimental Psychology: Learning, Memory, and Cognition, 18,* 785–800.

Perruchet, P., & Pacteau, C. (1990). Synthetic grammar learning: Implicit rule abstraction or explicit fragmentary knowledge. *Journal of Experimental Psychology: General, 119,* 264–275.

Porter, D. (1986). *A functional examination of intermediate cognitive processes.* Unpublished doctoral thesis, University of Oxford, United Kingdom.

Porter, D. (1991). Computer games and cognitive processes: Two tasks, two modes, or too much? *British Journal of Psychology, 82,* 343–358.

Reber, A. S. (1976). Implicit learning of synthetic languages: The role of instructional set. *Journal of Experimental Psychology: Human Learning and Memory, 2,* 88–94.

Reber, A. S., Kassin, S., Lewis, S., & Cantor, G. (1980). On the relationship between implicit and explicit modes in the learning of a complex rule structure. *Journal of Experimental Psychology: Human Learning and Memory, 6,* 492–502.

Sanderson, P. (1989). Verbalizable knowledge and skilled task performance: Associations, dissociations, and mental models. *Journal of Experimental Psychology: Learning, Memory, and Cognition, 15,* 729–747.

Sanderson, P. (1990). *Implicit and explicit control of a dynamic task: Empirical and conceptual issues.* EPRL Report 90-02, University of Illinois.

Squire, L., & Frambach, M. (1990). Cognitive skill learning in amnesia. *Psychobiology, 18,* 109–117.

Stanley, W. B., Mathews, R., Buss, R., & Kotler-Cope, S. (1989). Insight without awareness: On the interaction of verbalization, instruction and practice on a simulated process control task. *Quarterly Journal of Experimental Psychology, 41,* 553–577.

Thurber, B. (1992). *Aspects of implicit and explicit knowledge.* Unpublished master's thesis, University of Oxford, United Kingdom.

CHAPTER SIX

Complex Problem Solving
as Multistage Decision Making

Oswald Huber
University of Fribourg, Switzerland

INTRODUCTION

One of the central topics of decision theory are decisions made under uncertainty and risk. In these decision situations, the decision maker (DM) has to choose exactly one of two or more alternatives. For example, a DM has the choice to take (alternative 1), or not to take (alternative 2), a medicine prescribed for her illness. Each alternative has one or more consequences (outcomes). In the example, alternative 1 may have at least two consequences: The person's health may improve (outcome 11) and/or the person may suffer from severe alopecia as a side effect (outcome 12).

Whether or not a consequence occurs is not in the hands of the DM but depends on chance, nature, luck, etc. The probability of the various outcomes is more or less precisely known to the DM. An overview of decision making under uncertainty and risk is offered by Slovic, Lichtenstein, and Fischhoff (1988), for instance. Recent developments are described in Camerer and Weber (1992), and Payne, Bettman, Coupey, and Johnson (1993).

Decision making under uncertainty and risk is mainly studied with static or single stage decisions. Each decision is considered an isolated task; what was chosen in an earlier decision is irrelevant for the present decision.

In a multistage, or dynamic decision task, the DM has to make a *series* of decisions under risk and uncertainty. Here, the unit of analysis (e.g., Rapoport, 1975) is the series of decisions, not an isolated decision as in single stage decision making. This type of analysis rests on the assumption that in a series of several decisions, these decisions are interdependent.

A multistage decision task can be interpreted as an interaction between a DM and an open system (see, e.g., Mackinnon & Wearing, 1985). The DM's task is to optimize one or more variables (the *target variables*), or to attain satisfying values on the variables, by engaging in a series of decisions. In many everyday situations, a DM has to govern a system in such a way. Examples are an executive manager and the factory he or she is in charge of, and a person and her or his personal economical situation.

The interpretation of a multistage decision task as one in which the DM has to govern a system relates multistage decision making to complex problem solving (CPS). However, tasks typically used in multistage decision research are much less complex than those commonly employed in CPS research (see Frensch & Funke, this volume), as many examples described in this volume show. I shall discuss the advantages and disadvantages of this fact later.

In the first two sections, I describe the multistage investment task and the results of previous research with this task. In the third section, I summarize my own experiments with the investment task. The fourth section sketches a provisional model of the decision process in the multistage investment task. In the fifth section I describe expansions of the simple investment task, and in the last section, I discuss the multistage decision making approach in relation to CPS.

A SIMPLE MULTISTAGE INVESTMENT TASK

A simple multistage task has been used in numerous experiments. The task is described in Funk, Rapoport and Jones (1979), for example. In a multistage investment task, the DM starts with a specific amount of units (e.g., money). This is termed the capital c_0. There are two random events, W (win) and L (loss), respectively. The probabilities for events W and L, $p(W)$ (probability of winning) and $p(L)$ (probability of losing) are constant and are known to the DM, with $p(W) + p(L) = 1$. At the beginning of a trial i, the DM may put any proportion of the available capital c_{i-1} at stake. s_i is the stake in absolute units, $s\%_i$ is the percentual stake in trial i. If event L occurs, then the DM loses the stake s_i, (i.e., $c_i = c_{i-1} - s_i$). If event W takes place, then the DM receives the stake s_i plus a win $w * s_i$, where the winning factor w is a positive constant (i.e., $c_i = c_{i-1} + w * s_i$). The new capital c_i is the capital available at the beginning of the next trial, $i + 1$. The game is terminated when either $c_i = 0$ or $i = N$, where N is a number set in advance by the experimenter that is not necessarily known to the subject. An investment task of this format can be described formally as a multistage betting game, that is, a gamble that is played repeatedly (see, e.g., Funk et al., 1979).

Rapoport and Jones (1970) have derived the optimal strategy for playing this type of multistage betting game, a strategy that simultaneously maximizes capital and minimizes the bankruptcy probability. With the winning factor and the probabilities of winning and losing fixed, the optimal strategy is a constant percentage strategy. That is, the DM should invest a constant proportion of the current capital in each trial, independent of current capital size or previous wins and losses. If $p(W) > .5$, then the optimal percental stake $s\%_{opt}$ is defined as $s\%_{opt} = ((w * p(W)) - p(L)) / w$. If $p(W) < .5$, then $s\%_{opt} = 0$.

PREVIOUS FINDINGS WITH THE INVESTMENT TASK

The investment task described previously, and similar ones, have been investigated in several studies. Most of the following results are reported and summarized in Rapoport and Jones (1970) and in Funk et al. (1979). In these studies, several task variables were investigated, for example, the probabilities $p(W)$ and $p(L)$, the winning factor w, the amount of start capital c_0, and the number of trials. Results, however, are not necessarily comparable across studies because different studies employed different variations of the task. For example, in Funk et al. (1979), the DM had to divide the stake among two alternatives, whereas the subjects in Kleiter and Wimmer (1974) could increase the probability of winning in each trial by buying information. The generalizable results seem to be that DMs usually do not employ the constant percentage strategy described previously. Betting is affected, for example, by the size of the available capital, and by previous wins and losses. There is a consistent effect of current capital size: The higher the available capital, the lower the percental stake. In addition, a kind of gambler's fallacy effect can be observed: Subjects bet higher percental stakes after a sequence of losses than after a sequence of wins. Betting behavior seems not to change systematically over the course of an experiment as a function of the number of trials. Interestingly, there seem to be no stable results concerning variations of the winning factor w. In most studies, an increase in the probability of winning leads to higher percental stakes (e.g., Kleiter & Wimmer, 1970: MacCrimmon & Wehrung, 1986), but see Rapoport, Jones, and Kahan (1970).

Most of the research on multistage decision making was conducted in the 1960s and 1970s. Later, interest in the topic faded. One can only speculate about the reasons why this happened. I presume that the theoretical approach taken at the time may have overemphasized optimal strategies and traditional decision theory. Optimal strategies were based on decision models (mainly the Subjectively Expected Utility Model, see, for example, Slovic, Lichtenstein & Fischhoff, 1988) that were falsified as descriptive models of decision behavior during the same time period. For a review and discussion of the earlier work, see Rapoport (1975) and Kleiter (1975).

RESEARCH WITH THE INVESTMENT TASK

In this section, I present the main results of some experiments with the investment task that I have performed together with collaborators or that have been performed by my students. First, I describe the main task that we have employed.

The BREEDING LIZARDS TASK

In the BREEDING LIZARDS TASK, the abstract investment task is embedded into an *ecological* context. DMs are asked to increase the number of the Golddotted Whiptail Lizards, a species on the verge of extinction, by as much as possible. Subjects are instructed that the Golddotted Whiptail Lizards live in Northern Mexico. They are a very interesting species because they consist solely of females who reproduce by parthenogenesis. However, because they are very prone to environmental factors, they are already extinct in their natural habitat. Only a small number of lizards has survived in one zoological laboratory but, for reasons unknown, they are not capable of reproducing in the laboratory. The Golddotted Whiptail Lizards grow quite old (about 70 years), but if they do not reproduce, the species will become extinct. Recently, a good breeding place has been discovered. However, the place lies in an area with numerous small volcanos that emit gas clouds from time to time. Normally, the gas clouds are harmless for lizards but if a lizard breathes this gas while breeding, mother and offspring die. It is not possible to predict when gas clouds are emitted, only the probability for emission ($p(L)$) is known. Therefore, all lizards in the breeding place and all offspring are killed with probability $p(L)$, and breeding is successful with probability $p(W) = 1 - p(L)$. Because the alternative is extinction, the breeding place must be utilized if one wants to increase the number of lizards, despite the risk.

Subjects in this task have to decide for, say 20 breeding periods (trials), how many of the at the moment available lizards (*capital*) to put into the breeding area (*stake*). The rest (*capital–stake*) stays safe in the laboratory. If no gas cloud occurs (event W with probability $p(W)$), then each lizard gives life to n offspring (that is, $w = n$). The offspring are already fertile in the following breeding period. If a gas cloud is emitted (event L with probability $p(L)$), then all lizards in the breeding place are killed and no offspring are produced. The starting capital is c_0 lizards. Notice that the parthenogenesis of the Whiptail Lizards is in accordance with reality (Cole, 1984), but the other assertions made in the instructions are fictitious.

Description of Experiments

In Experiment 1 (Huber, 1994), the effects of the joint variation of the winning factor (return rate), the probability of winning, and the start capital were investigated in the BREEDING LIZARDS TASK. Forty subjects (nonstudents) participated in the experiment. Independent variables were, (a) the probability of winning $p(W)$ (successful breeding), (b) the winning factor w (number of offspring), and (c) the start capital c_0. There were two levels of $p(W)$, one-third and two-third, two levels of the winning factor w, 1 and 2, and two levels of start capital c_0, 20 and 100 lizards.

Experiment 2 (Huber, 1994) with 60 subjects (nonstudents) was designed to replicate the result of Experiment 1 concerning the variation of the winning factor with a bigger difference between the two winning factor conditions, and to test the effect of three different cover stories. Independent variables in this experiment were, (a) the winning factor w, (b) the probability of winning $p(W)$, and (c) the cover story. There were two levels of the winning factor w, 1 and 4, two levels of $p(W)$, one-third and two-third, and three cover stories, trees, business investment, and gamble.

Trees. Here, the subject had to breed resistant fir trees which were to be implanted in mountain areas endangered by avalanches. In the breeding area, the plants were threatened by acid rain. This task was conceptually very similar to the BREEDING LIZARDS TASK.

Business investment. In this task, the subject had to increase her or his capital (money) by investing it in a risky business venture at the stock exchange.

Gamble. Here, the task was to increase a score of points. The situation was described as a gambling task. This task was similar to the tasks used in the experiments summarized by Rapoport and Jones (1970) and Funk et al. (1979).

Experiment 3 examined whether decision behavior changes when subjects repeatedly perform the same task. In this experiment, the task was similar to the BREEDING LIZARDS TASK. Subjects had to breed couples of Ara parrots in a South American jungle. Couples of birds in the breeding places were endangered by disturbances caused by the local drug cartel.

The independent variable in Experiment 3 was game. Thirty nonstudents performed the task seven times. The probability of winning was $p(W) = 2/3$, the winning factor was $w = 1$, and the start capital $c_0 = 10$. The number of trials in each of the seven games was a random number varying between 12 and 18, with an average of 15.

Experiment 4 (Huber, Debeutz, Pratscher, & Quehenberger, 1990) investigated the influence of individual differences in perceived control on decision behavior. Forty subjects (nonstudents and students) worked on the BREEDING LIZARDS TASK. The experimentally manipulated independent variable was the probability of winning (one-half versus two-thirds); an additional independent subject variable was generalized locus of control (internal versus external).

Experiment 5 (Schmid, 1987) used a variation of the BREEDING LIZARDS TASK in which the loss was not caused by a random variable, but by a negative feedback loop. There were no volcanoes in the breeding area, but there were predators. Each of them devoured one lizard during a breeding period. The number of predators in a trial depended on the number of lizards put at stake in the previous trial. Therefore, by betting (very) low in one trial, the DM could reduce the number of predators in the next trial. The negative feedback loop was not known to the subjects at the beginning of the experiment, but its knowledge was crucial for optimizing the decisions. The 24 subjects were students of different areas. Also, a thinking aloud protocol was collected.

Decision Behavior

Typically, the main dependent variable used with this type of experiments is the stake s_i in trial i. Absolute stakes, however, are only comparable if the capital size in the respective trial is taken into account. Therefore, absolute stakes s_i were converted to percental stakes $s\%_i$ for the results described in the following. The percental stake $s\%_i$ specifies which percentage of the available capital c_{i-1} in trial i is put at stake, $s\%_i = s_i/c_{i-1}$.

Effect of Winning Probability

There was a clear effect of the probability of winning. In conditions with a higher probability of winning, mean percental stakes were higher. In all experiments where $p(W)$ was varied, the effect was significant, except in one case where it was marginally significant. Averaged over experiments, the mean percental stakes $s\%_i$ were .37 with $p(W) = 2/3$, .30 with $p(W) = 1/2$, and .25 with $p(W) = 1/3$. This result is in accordance with previous research using the multistage investment task. However, previous research usually used winning probabilities of .5 or higher. Therefore, it was interesting to see what our subjects did when the probability of winning was below .5. Even in the most unfavorable condition ($p(W) = 1/3$, $w = 1$), where the DMs should have bet a stake of zero, the mean stake $s\%_i$ was .16, and very few subjects bet zero.

Effect of Winning Factor

For experiments 1 and 2, we predicted that a higher winning factor w would *not* lead to higher percental stakes. This prediction is important because it is not consistent with previous studies. At first, the prediction is, in fact, quite implausible. One would expect DMs to increase their percental stakes when the conditions of the game become more favorable, corresponding to the higher percental stakes that are chosen when the probability of winning increases. The optimal strategy also prescribes a higher stake with a higher winning factor. On the other hand, a higher winning factor allows the DM to reduce the perceived risk because the same amount of win can now be gained with a much smaller stake. If one assumes that the perceived risk has a greater weight than the attempted win, then the prediction becomes more plausible.

The hypothesis was confirmed in both experiments. In fact, the mean percental stakes were lower in conditions with a higher winning factor. This finding can be explained by the effect of capital size (see next section). The crucial test is the first stake $s\%_1$ because the available capital is controlled by the experimenter in trial 1. There was no significant difference between the first stakes $s\%_1$ in the two winning factor conditions of Experiments 1 and 2.

The surprising effect that a higher winning factor does *not* lead to higher percental stakes seems to be quite reliable. The two experiments were performed with different cover stories by different experimenters in different countries. The four experimenters running Experiment 2 had no knowledge of the hypothesis concerning the non-effect of the winning factor. In fact, they expected an increase of stakes with the higher winning factor. Therefore, experimenter expectation cannot be responsible for this particular finding.

Effect of Capital Size

Previous research has shown that lower stakes are bet when the capital is higher. Usually, in these experiments, the effect of capital size has been investigated in one of two manners:

- The range of observed capital sizes was divided into a set of absolute capital classes that were independent of the capital a DM gained during the experiment. However, if subjects differ by much in their capital sizes, one has the choice of concentrating the analysis on a range common to most subjects, or of using a broader range and excluding a substantial number of subjects. Both solutions are, of course, quite unsatisfactory.

- For each DM, the range of his or her capital sizes was divided into, say, five categories (ranging from very high to very low). As a consequence, almost all subjects could be categorized within the same set of categories. If, however, the range of capital sizes differs by much among subjects, then the categories become quite meaningless, because the category *very high* may contain values between 30 and 35 for one subject, for instance, and values for more than 100,000 for another.

In our experiments there were great differences in capital size. For example, for one subject in Experiment 4 the maximum number of available lizards was 20, whereas another subject had 160,800 lizards in one trial (and lost them all). In Experiment 3, one subject completed the task with a capital of 2,775,280,000 fir trees, whereas others finished with less than the start capital.

Because of these large interindividual differences, none of the two methods to study the effect of capital size was deemed acceptable. Therefore, we investigated the effect of *relative* capital size instead of absolute size. The effect of relative capital size can be estimated for each subject individually, by computing the correlation $r(s\%_i, c_{i-1})$ between the percental stakes $s\%_i$ and the capital c_{i-1} available in trial i. The mean correlation averaged over all experiments was $r(s\%_i, c_{i-1}) = -.34$. In all cases, the correlation was negative. The negative correlation is in accordance with the assumptions and previous results.

The negative correlation between capital size and percental stakes can also explain local effects, for example, the effect of a decreasing percental stake in conditions with a higher winning factor. In conditions with a higher winning factor, DMs usually have more capital available. For example, in Experiment 1, the mean final capital was 30.75 in condition $w = 1$ and 432.5 in condition $w = 2$. In Experiment 2, it was 867.97 in condition $w = 1$ and 251,857.6 in condition $w = 4$. Because more capital leads to lower stakes, the decrease of percental stakes in the conditions with a higher winning factor is explained by the size of the current capital.

Learning Effects

Learning effects are changes in betting behavior either over the course of trials within one play of the gamble, or over repeated plays of the gamble. For the dependent variables used to detect learning effects, see Huber et al. (1990) or Huber (1994).

In Experiments 1 to 4, no learning effect within one play of the gamble could be discovered. In Experiment 5, betting behavior changed systematically when subjects discovered the negative feedback loop. This result is reported in greater detail below.

In Experiment 3, no learning effect over repeated plays of the gamble was observed. In Experiment 1, there was a small learning effect between gambles 1 and 2. Percental stakes in the second play of the game were smaller than in the first. This effect seems to have been due mainly to those subjects who bet a stake of 100% at least once and completed the gamble with a result lower than the start capital. These subjects seemed to learn that putting 100% of the capital at stake is dangerous.

History of Wins and Losses

In none of the experiments was a difference between the mean percental stakes after one win or one loss observed. An interesting question is whether percental stakes change systematically if the DM encounters not only one win or loss, but a *series* of consecutive wins or losses, respectively.

In order to investigate this question, the mean percental stakes for series of 1, 2, 3, and so on, consecutive wins and series of 1, 2, 3, and so on, consecutive losses, respectively, were computed for each subject. These means were submitted to a trend analysis. The slope b of the linear trend ($s\%_i = a + i * b$, with trials i as discrete units of time) of percental stakes in the series of consecutive wins and of consecutive losses was used as the dependent variable.

Percental stakes were nearly constant over series of wins (that is, $b \approx 0$), but were positive over series of losses (averaged over experiments, $b = 0.04$). Thus, in general, DMs *increase* the percental stakes when they experience a series of consecutive losses. This result can be interpreted as an instance of the *gambler's fallacy* (see, for example, Wagenaar, 1988). The gambler's fallacy leads people to believe that a positive event is due after a run of negative events, or, more generally, that a series of independent trials with a certain outcome will soon be followed by the opposite outcome. It is interesting to note that the gambler's fallacy occurs only in series of losses but not in series of wins, although the situations are formally identical.

This asymmetry between series of losses and series of wins rules out an explanation based on the negative correlation between the size of the available capital and the percental stake. It is clear that the size of the available capital *decreases* in a series of losses, but in a series of wins, the available capital increases, which should result in a corresponding reduction of percental stakes.

Effect of Different Problem Formulations

Experiment 2 tested explicitly whether different formulations of one and the same abstract problem lead to differences in decision behavior. In none of the dependent variables could a difference between the three cover stories be found.

Thus, the different cover stories create decision problems which constitute problem isomorphs in the sense of Hayes and Simon (1976), at least insofar as decision behavior is concerned. This offers the opportunity to select the cover story for an experiment that is the most interesting to subjects. Embedding the decision problem into some kind of ecological context, as is done in the BREEDING LIZARDS TASK, seems to establish an intrinsic challenge for almost all subjects such that no further payment of subjects is necessary.

Negative Feedback Loop

The variation of the investment task used in Experiment 5 (Schmid, 1987) differed from the basic version used in the other experiments in that an intransparency condition was introduced. In Experiment 5, there were no volcanoes in the breeding area killing the lizards, but there where predators. Each of the predators devoured one lizard during a breeding period. The number of predators in a trial depended on the number of lizards put at stake in the previous trial, because the amount of food (number of lizards) available to the predators determined the number of offspring the predators could rear. Therefore, by betting (very) low in one trial, the DM could reduce the number of predators in the next trial. The negative feedback loop was not known to subjects at the beginning (intransparency), but its knowledge was crucial for optimizing the decisions.

The main research question was how easy or difficult it was to discover the negative feedback loop, and in what respects DMs who detected the feedback loop (*detectors*) differed from those who did not (*nondetectors*). Each subject played the game three times.

In addition, in Experiment 5 we collected thinking-aloud protocols. The transcribed protocols were first broken down into semantic units. Then each semantic unit was assigned to one of the coding categories. This procedure is similar to the one described in Ericsson and Simon (1984). The following coding scheme was developed on the basis of protocols obtained with a pilot study.

Facts (*F*): A statement replicating presented information, for example, "Now I have 17 lizards."

Analysis (*A*): A statement inferring new information from available information, for example, "Now the increase is smaller than it was before."

Hypothesis (*H*): A statement concerning a hypothesis about the system, or a test of such a hypothesis. For example, "If I put many lizards into the breeding area, this will affect the number of predators only in later trials," or "Aha, this idea was wrong."

Planning (*P*): A statement involving a plan for future actions, for example, "Now I will put five lizards into the breeding area two more times." The number of future trials a plan covered was also registered.

Justified decision (*JD*): A statement containing the choice of a stake in connection with a justification, for example, "Now that we have few predators, we can put more than half of them into the breeding area."

Detection of the negative feedback loop (*DNFL*): The first statement indicating that the subject had detected the crucial negative feedback loop, for example, "I shall put none into the breeding area, in order to starve out the predators," or "I bet nothing for three consecutive times. Then the predators will be gone, and I can send all lizards into the breeding area."

Metacognition (*M*): A statement indicating a cognitive process at the metalevel of problem solving. These included self-reflections ("I proceed in a quite unsystematic manner"), self-evaluations, and formulations of problem solving goals ("I want to get information about the mortality").

Subjects who detected the negative feedback loop (code *DNFL*) in one of three sessions were classified as *detectors*, those who did not as *nondetectors*. Four of the 24 subjects detected the negative feedback loop during the first play of the game, four during the second play, and four during the third play. Thus, altogether, there were 12 detectors, and 12 nondetectors.

Obviously, detecting the feedback loop was quite difficult for the subjects. It had already become apparent during pilot testing that the feedback loop had to have a very distinct effect in order to be detected at all. Therefore, the function we selected relating the number of predators to the number of lizards put into the breeding area turned out to be not realistic, biologically speaking. For the same reason, the task was restricted to a feedback loop with a one period lag. As the results showed, even under these conditions only half of the subjects detected the negative feedback loop, and most of them not before the task had been repeated. For the problem of feedback delay in more complex tasks, see Brehmer (1992; this volume).

The optimal strategy in this variation of the BREEDING LIZARDS TASK seems to be to alternate one trial with a zero stake and two trials with a stake of 100%. This is a *feedforward* strategy in the sense of Brehmer (1992). A gamble should be started with two trials betting 100% because the initial number of predators is low. All the detector-subjects alternated low and high-stake trials, although they did not perform optimally. The mean length of a betting low sequence of trials was 1.90, the mean length of a betting high sequence 2.30. Of the eight detectors who began at least one new session after the detection of the negative feedback loop, seven started with a betting-high sequence with a mean length of 2.79. Three of the detectors attempted to optimize their strategy, and tested different lengths of betting low and betting high sequences. Three others tried out different, less optimal strategies later.

The total number of lizards bred in the three sessions (breeding success) was significantly correlated with the detection of the negative feedback loop, $r(23) = .43$. There are several reasons for the relatively small correlation. Some of the detectors discovered the negative feedback loop quite late, and therefore had only few trials left to breed lizards. Some detectors did not bet 100% and 0% but rather 80% and 10%, for instance, or tried out different strategies. On the other hand, one of the nondetectors was quite successful. This subject used a strategy resembling the optimal one for one and a half sessions. She alternated low and high stakes in odd and even trials, but without having detected the negative feedback loop. She abandoned this strategy at the beginning of the third session.

Detectors and nondetectors differed in a variety of verbal codes. Detectors analyzed the situation more frequently (A-statements), although this was true only for the first play of the gamble, not for later ones. Detectors also verbalized more statements involving the formulation and test of hypotheses about the system than nondetectors. This was true not only for statements concerning hypotheses in general, but also for statements concerning correct hypotheses. Detectors justified their decisions to a greater extent. Although detectors did not develop more plans of actions than did nondetectors, they generated more *long-term* plans (two or more future trials). Detectors also had more *M*-statements in the third session, indicating cognitive processes at a metalevel. There was no difference between detectors and nondetectors in the number of *F*-statements they verbalized. All these findings are in congruence with the results of research on CPS (e.g., Dörner, Kreuzig, Reither, & Stäudel, 1983; Putz-Osterloh, 1983; Schweiger, Anderson, & Locke, 1985; see also Eyferth, Schömann, & Widowski, 1986), if one equates detectors with good problem solvers and nondetectors with poor ones.

Although the verbal data revealed clear differences between detectors and nondetectors, the betting behaviors of the two groups (before the detectors had discovered the negative feedback loop) were quite similar. There were, however, a few exceptions.

The detectors' stakes had a higher variance than those of the non-detectors. This result can be interpreted in line with a corresponding result in Huber et al. (1990). Detectors appear to be more active in terms of acquiring information and using it actively to deal with a problem. In the present task, the information available concerned the variables of the system. Detectors took the current status of the relevant system variables more often into account than did the nondetectors. Because the value of the relevant variables could vary a lot from trial to trial, the resulting stakes could be very dissimilar. The bigger variance of the stakes of the detectors is also in accordance with a result reported by Schweiger et al. (1985) that seems to indicate that too much consistency in decision making is not efficient.

Nondetectors increased their stakes during a session ($b = 0.01$), whereas detectors decreased them ($b = -0.03$). Although betting cautiously is more optimal when the mental representation of a system is not adequate, the detectors did not breed more successfully *before* they had detected the negative feedback loop.

Most of the findings concerning behavioral data were in agreement with the results of previous research with investment tasks (Funk et al., 1979; Rapoport & Jones, 1970). Percental stake and available capital have a negative mean correlation, and percental stakes increase over a series of losses.

In this experiment, the combination of verbal and behavioral data was very fruitful and revealed a more complete picture than could have been obtained by either measure alone. Neglecting either behavioral data or verbal ones would have led to a biased view concerning the differences between good and poor decision makers.

Locus of Control

Experiment 4 investigated the influence of interindividual differences in perceived control on decision behavior in the BREEDING LIZARDS TASK. Because the investment task was new to the subjects, and we were interested in the DMs' general expectations, the concept of *generalized* locus of control was relevant. This concept was operationalized with the IPC-questionnaire of Krampen (1981), which is a German adaptation of Levenson's IPC-scales (Levenson, 1972). The IPC-scales consist of three subscales: The I-scale measures people's perceived degree of control over their own lives, the P-scale deals with powerful other persons, and the C-scale measures perception of chance control. In the BREEDING LIZARDS TASK, control over the target variable (capital) is divided between the DM and *chance*, therefore the C-scale was taken as the most appropriate measure of control. C-externals (abbreviated: *externals*) expect chance forces to be in control, whereas C-internals (abbreviated: *internals*) do not.

Internals differed from externals on various dependent variables. They bet higher mean percental stakes than the externals, especially in connection with a higher probability of winning (two-third vs. one-half), and higher maximum percental stakes. Betting behavior of internals was more flexible, which was reflected in the higher variance of percental stakes and the greater mean absolute difference between percental stakes on consecutive trials. In series of losses, internals increased their stakes drastically from trial to trial (mean $b = .11$), whereas the externals' stakes decreased (mean $b = -.02$). There was no difference between internals and externals in series of wins.

The results are a confirmation of the hypothesis that the internals are more active than externals in terms of acquiring information in a problem-solving task and using it actively to deal with a problem (see, e.g., Sandler, Reese, Spencer, & Harpin, 1983). In the investment task, the available information concerns the variables of the system, including the observed behavior of the system. Internal DMs more often take into account the current status of the relevant system variables. Because the values of these variables may vary much from trial to trial, the resulting stakes show a high variability.

The result that on some dependent variables, the difference between internals and externals was more pronounced in condition $p(W) = 2/3$ than in condition $p(W) = 1/2$, seems to indicate that the interaction between person variables and situation variables should also be taken into account.

The results summarized so far show perceived control to be a personality characteristic which has some predictive power for decision behavior in the investment task. Does it also predict the final breeding success? Interestingly, this is not the case. The mean final capital (number of lizards at the end of the experiment) did not differ between the internal-external groups. In the internal group, however, variability of final capital was very high: There were some large final capitals, but 40% of the internals finished with a capital of zero. In the external group, there were no final capitals as large as in the internal group, but there was only one external subject with a final zero score. Thus, although there were some subjects with outstanding results, the internals as a group did not perform better than the externals. One explanation for this is that internals sometimes grossly overestimate their proportion of control, leading them to make very risky decisions (betting a stake of 100%).

Measuring Performance Quality

In CPS tasks where the DM has to optimize one or more target variables of a system or to attain satisfying values on the variables, determining the degree of success is often difficult (e.g., Funke, 1986). In order to arrive at an overall measure of performance quality, it is necessary to combine performance indicators on various target variables.

Final Capital

In our investment task presented here, there is only one target variable, the capital. Therefore, *final capital* is a *natural* measure of performance quality. Three aspects have to be taken into account, however, when final capital is used.

First, the final capital value does not contain details about the process of decision making. For example, in a BREEDING LIZARDS TASK with very favorable conditions (e.g., $p(W) = 2/3$, $w = 2$) and a start capital of 20, a final capital of 50 is a rather poor result. However, this result may be achieved by betting extremely cautiously and suboptimally during the whole task, or by betting quite well over 24 trials and making the mistake of putting 99,950 lizards of 100,000 at stake at the very last trial. Both kinds of behavior can be observed in experiments.

Second, the final capital does not only depend on the decision behavior of the subject, but also on the specific sequence of wins and losses. In our Experiments 1–4, the sequences of wins and losses were generated by a random process for each subject individually. Therefore, with a fixed probability of winning, the created sequences of wins and losses may be quite different for different subjects (as predicted by a binomial distribution). As a consequence, it makes sense to compare mean final capitals of groups of subjects, but not of individual subjects. If one is interested in interindividual comparisons of final capitals, it is necessary to work with standardized series of wins and losses.

Third, if the final capital enables a comparison of groups—or with controlled series of wins and losses—individual DMs, it does not tell how good or poor the subjects perform *objectively*. If one is interested in that question, a comparison with some optimal strategy is indispensable.

Comparison of Actual and Optimal Percental Stakes

In order to evaluate the percental stake $s\%_i$ in a trial i, it can be compared to the optimal stake $s\%_{opt}$ as prescribed by some theory. An example is the optimal stake derived by Rapoport and Jones (1970; see previously discussed). Usually, in favorable conditions ($p(W) > .5$), the subjects' stakes are too low. Because DMs do not make use of higher winning factors (see above), this discrepancy is especially prominent when $w > 1$.

Observed stakes depart from the optimal ones also in very unfavorable conditions (e.g., $p(W) = 1/3$, $w = 1$), but here they are too high. People should bet zero, but they do not.

If one is interested in an overall measure of performance, a measure based on the discrepancies between the optimal and the observed stakes in the sequence of trials has to be defined as mean discrepancy or maximal discrepancy, for example.

If one wants to evaluate discrepancies between optimal stakes and those bet by subjects, the problem of the sensitivity/insensitivity of system behavior to such differences has to be taken into account also (see Rapoport, 1975). In many decision tasks, substantial deviations from optimal strategies often produce only small changes in the results.

Comparison of Final Capital
and Optimal Final Capital

The difference between final capital and optimal final capital can be defined as an overall measure of performance quality. The optimal final capital is the final capital a subject would have gathered if he or she had always bet the optimal stake $s\%_{opt}$. The optimal final capital can be computed for the specific sequence of wins and losses a subject has experienced. Usually, the observed final capitals are clearly smaller than the optimal final capitals because of the discrepancy between the real and the optimal stakes. However, there are always a few lucky subjects with a real final capital that is larger than the optimal one, especially under unfavorable conditions.

A MODEL OF THE DECISION PROCESS
IN THE MULTISTAGE INVESTMENT TASK

Despite the relatively large amount of research on multistage decision making during the 1960s and 1970s, no theory of decision making in the investment task has yet been developed that can account for all, or even the main, empirical findings. Furthermore, very little is known about the (cognitive) processes that are relevant in decision making with the multistage decision task. Therefore, I have recently attempted to develop a first sketchy model of the decision process in the investment task (Huber, 1990).

I assume that the following five subprocesses can be identified when a DM is confronted with the investment task. Several of these subprocesses may be simultaneously active.

Mental Representation of the System

At the beginning of his or her work on the task, the DM constructs a mental representation of the system to be controlled. This representation comprises the structure of the system (system variables and relations among them), its momentary state, and possibly a subset of its past states. If an appropriate mental representation is already available, it is activated. The representation is not stable, especially during the early phases of the interaction between the DM and the system, and may be updated, changed, adapted, and so forth.

Verbal data from Schmid (1987) support the hypothesis that a mental representation is constructed at the beginning of the interaction. For the first phase of his experiment, the multistage task was identical to the investment task described previously. Verbal items related to the representation of the system were uttered more often during the first half of trials than the second half, as were verbal items dealing with the mental representation at a metalevel (e.g., evaluating the representation). Verbal items indicating other subprocesses (e.g., concerning target goals) were equally frequent in both halves.

Information for the construction of the mental representation stems from both external and internal sources. External sources are the instructions and the observed behavior of the system; an internal source is the DM's knowledge about the problem domain (e.g., zoology, volcanoes, stock exchange).

The mental representation influences how the system is perceived, is crucial for the generation, evaluation, and adaptation of goals, and affects the choice of a stake. It is also the knowledge base for the generation of strategies, and permits *simulations* and anticipations.

The concept of perceived control is consistent with the assumption of a mental representation of the system. Perceived control can be interpreted as a subset of the DM's hypotheses about the system. Specific expectations may exist, for example, concerning the system's behavior at the next trial that are based on mental simulation and may have a high subjective probability of being correct.

Goals Concerning Target Variables

A goal prescribes which value or set of values the target variable(s) should reach. In the investment task, capital is the target variable. The first general goal is established in the instructions, namely to increase the capital by as much as possible. The DM may formulate subgoals or intermediate goals (e.g., to reach a specific amount of, say, 1.000 units of capital). If there are several goals, then a list of goals is formed. If necessary, priorities have to be established. The goal list may be changed during the decision process; new (sub)goals may be created, and others may be removed because they have been reached or cannot be attained any longer.

Strategies for Reaching Target-Variable Goals

A (betting) strategy is an explicit rule (conditional or not) for choosing a stake, for example, "If the probability of winning is smaller than .50, then bet very low," or "Bet zero for three times in a row in order to eliminate the predators, then send all lizards into the breeding area." A DM can maintain several strategies at the same time. A strategy is based on the mental representation of the system. It may also be learned directly (e.g., as advice from an experienced DM).

Choice of a Stake

This subprocess is necessarily activated in each trial. The choice of a stake may be influenced by a variety of variables and factors. A betting strategy may narrow down the range of stakes from which the DM chooses.

In the investment task, the DM cannot influence the probabilities of winning and losing, but can adjust the amount to be lost or to be won by the choice of the stake. The DM presumably tries to find a balance between two conflicting goals, (a) maximizing the win in the trial by putting 100% of the available capital c_{i-1} at stake, and (b) minimizing the risk by betting a stake of zero. According to the relative weights of these two goals, the DM selects a higher or a lower percental stake.

The relative weights of the two goals are determined by the perceived risk and by the size of the available capital c_{i-1}. Please note that the winning factor w does not influence any of these components. The lower the available capital c_{i-1}, the higher the relative weight of the goal to bet high stakes.

Perceived risk increases with the amount of possible loss (i.e., the stake s_i) and the subjective probability of losing. The higher the perceived risk, the higher the relative weight of the goal to bet low stakes. The view of risk as a function of the size of loss and the probability of losing is consistent with one of the common definitions of risk, see, for example, Vlek and Stallen (1981). The objective probabilities of winning and losing, $p(W)$ and $p(L)$, respectively, are stable throughout the experiment. For the subjective probabilities of winning and losing, the stable objective probabilities may be superimposed by local expectations. For example, a long series of losses may increase the subject's expectations of a win (gambler's fallacy). The DM is assumed to select a stake s_i that results in a tolerable perceived risk and, at the same time, in an acceptable win.

Planning and Control (Metaprocesses)

Metaprocesses are processes controlling a DM's dealing with the system. One type of control processes concerns the generation and evaluation of betting strategies. A strategy is a hypothesis that is evaluated and may turn out to be wrong. Other control processes involve process goals. Process goals are connected not with the target variable(s), but with the process. For example, a DM may formulate the goal to develop a betting strategy. To pursue a process goal, plans and strategies must be established. For example, the DM may plan to observe the behavior of the system for some trials, and then on the base of the observations work out a betting strategy.

INCREASING THE COMPLEXITY OF THE SIMPLE INVESTMENT TASK

Starting with a very simple task (i.e., the investment task), has the advantage that the task's complexity can be increased gradually, and that one has control about which aspects to make more complex. If there are several problem isomorphs of an investment task, one can select the cover story that is best suited to be expanded if one wants to model a more complex task. Thus, by making the simple task more complex, one can gradually make the investment task more similar to the tasks used in research on CPS.

The BREEDING LIZARDS TASK offers numerous possibilities for making it more complex. For example, we are completing two experiments at present in which two critical events (volcanoes and migrating lizard-eating birds) are introduced, rather than only one. The two events are introduced either simultaneously, or one after the other. The probabilities of the two events are varied separately and systematically.

In another experiment (Experiment 6), the lizards were endangered by the volcano but also by a specific deadly disease in the breeding area. The DM could vaccinate any proportion of animals put into the breeding area, which made them immune against the disease. However, for the vaccination of each five lizards, one lizard had to be sacrificed for the production of the serum. Thus, the DM had to decide how many lizards to put into the breeding area (all of which were endangered by the volcano), *and* how many of these to vaccinate (all animals not vaccinated were threatened by the disease). The probabilities for the eruption of the volcano and the outbreak of the disease were varied: one-sixth (volcano) and one-third (disease), respectively, in the *high-disease* condition, and one-third and one-sixth in the *high-volcano* condition. Twenty-seven nonstudents participated in this experiment.

Only a part of the data of Experiment 6 has been analyzed at present. In the *high-disease* condition, the mean percental total stake (vaccinated + nonvaccinated lizards) was .39; in the *high-volcano* condition it was .34, the difference was significant. The mean stakes were about as high as they were in the condition $p(W) = 2/3$ in the simple task version. There are two possible explanations for this result, (a) DMs do not combine the two probabilities, but, rather, select the maximum of the two, or (b) people combine the probabilities, but take into account the fact that the effect of the disease can be neutralized by vaccination. The second explanation could also account for the higher percental stakes in the *high-disease* condition because here, a greater part of the danger can be neutralized. Results from the experiments mentioned above (with volcanoes and migrating lizard-eating birds) should enable us to decide between the two explanations.

An important dependent variable in Experiment 6 was the proportion of vaccinated lizards $sv\%_i$ out of all lizards that were put into the breeding area ($sv\%_i = [number\ of\ vaccinated\ lizards\ in\ trial\ i]\ /\ s_i$). As predicted, the proportion of vaccinated lizards increased with the probability of the occurrence of the disease: $sv\%_i = .45$ in the *high-disease* condition, and .21 in the *high-volcano* condition.

Experiment 6 also investigated interindividual differences in perceived control (cf. Experiment 4). There was no difference in mean percental total stakes between the internal and external groups, but, as predicted, the groups showed different vaccinating behavior. In the *high-volcano* condition, both groups vaccinated a proportion of .21, whereas in the *high-disease* condition, $sv\%_i = .55$ for the internals and .31 for the externals. Here, too, the interaction between person variables and situation variables proved to be important.

DISCUSSION

Compared to the (frequently computer simulated) microworlds used in CPS research, the basic version of the investment task as described in the Introduction to this chapter is extremely simple. The other described versions and expansions of the task are only slightly more complicated. To cite some main differences between the investment task and complex problems (see Brehmer, 1992; Frensch & Funke, this volume; Funke, 1986; Omodei, 1993):

- The system to be governed in the investment task consists of very few variables, whereas, for example, Dörner's LOHHAUSEN (Dörner et al., 1983) comprises more than 2,000 variables.
- The DM makes a choice on one variable only (stake), whereas in complex problems there are many variables to act on.
- The system is explained in advance in all relevant details to the subject, there is no intransparency.
- The system does not change if the DM does nothing (bets a stake of zero), thus the system has no *Eigendynamic*.
- The system gives immediate feedback, there is no delay.
- Basic parameters of the system (e.g., winning factor w) do not change during the interaction.
- No real-time component is involved.

The use of relatively simple tasks in studies of multistage decision making and CPS has several advantages:

- The task is fully understood by the researcher.
- It is possible to formally derive an optimal strategy, either by analytical methods or by simulation (e.g., Schmid, 1987), and to compare the observed behavior with the optimal behavior.
- It is easier to formulate hypotheses about the effect of variations of system variables on behavior.
- The interaction between system factors, on the one hand, and individual and situation factors, on the other hand, can be investigated more easily (see Funke, 1992).

- The abstract task can be embedded into various contexts; it is therefore possible to test whether or not different task formulations constitute problem isomorphs.

- The simple task can gradually be made more complex. The effect of each factor increasing complexity can be tested. Thus, the different kinds of relations within a system (see Funke, 1992) can be studied more easily.

An open question is the generalizability of the results found with simple investment tasks. The investment task is a special type of problem with a moderate degree of complexity. Therefore, we cannot expect the behavior in this task to necessarily generalize to very complex tasks like LOHHAUSEN (Dörner et al., 1983) or to a real-time FIRE FIGHTING TASK (Brehmer, 1992; Omodei, 1993). However, it may very well be possible that a complex task in real life or in the laboratory contains one (or more) investment tasks as a subproblem. Behavior in such a subproblem should be predictable from results based on investigations with multistage decision tasks.

This consideration rests on the assumption that a complex problem can at least partially be decomposed into simpler independent subproblems. For example, detection of a negative feedback loop could be considered a subproblem that is independent from the problem of choosing an investment stake in the face of a probabilistic environment, or from the problem of constructing a decision strategy in a specific task. For a test of the decomposition assumption, we would need a satisfying and detailed taxonomy of problem types.

The concept of generalized perceived control turned out to have some predictive power for decision behavior. Maybe, this result is not as surprising as the fact that a simple test such as the IPC-test (Krampen, 1981; Levenson, 1972) enables predictions. As a next step, the connection between perceived control and perceived uncertainty and task-specific perceived control should be investigated. The concept of generalized perceived control could also be fruitful in CPS. Internals should be more active in terms of acquiring information in a CPS task, and in using it to actively construct a mental model of the system to be governed. Furthermore, generalized as well as specific perceived control are probably related to the concept of (general and task-specific) *heuristic competence* (Stäudel, 1987). For example, a higher degree of perceived control may be the result of having higher heuristic competence, or, internality may cause people to acquire more actively problem solving heuristics. Of course, perceived control may be erroneous.

Theories of multistage decision making also attempt to explain decision behavior as it is affected by the experimental variation of certain task variables, for example, the stake bet by a DM as a consequence of the probability of winning. This seems to be a rather neglected or sometimes explicitly excluded (see, e.g., Brehmer, 1992) theme in CPS theory. However, the experimental variation of task variables is necessary if one wants to investigate individual differences in problem solving and decision behavior, as our results show. Thus, research on multistage decision making complements research on CPS, and may help to bring together decision theory and CPS theory.

ACKNOWLEDGMENTS

The subjects in Experiment 1 were run by E. Achermann and K. Diethelm. Experiment 2 was performed by S. Danninger, H. Hagleitner, M. Höpflinger and H. Hutter at the University of Salzburg (Austria) under the supervision of the author. Experiment 3 was performed by A. Bravo, S. Frölicher and P. Schellenberg, and Experiment 6 by D. Achermann, P. Gründler and C. Maurer, all at the University of Fribourg under the supervision of the author. The statistical analyses for Experiments 1, 2, and 3 were done by Stefan Zysset, for Experiment 6 by Odilo Huber. I want to express my thanks to all of them.

REFERENCES

Brehmer, B. (1992). Dynamic decision making: Human control of complex systems. *Acta Psychologica, 81*, 211–241.

Camerer, C., & Weber, M. (1992). Recent developments in modeling preferences: Uncertainty and ambiguity. *Journal of Risk and Uncertainty, 5*, 325–370.

Cole, C. J. (1984). Unisexual lizards. *Scientific American, 250*, 84–90.

Dörner, D., Kreuzig, H. W., Reither, F., & Stäudel, T. (1983). *Lohhausen. Vom Umgang mit Unbestimmtheit und Komplexität* [Lohhausen. On dealing with uncertainty and complexity]. Bern, Switzerland: Hans Huber.

Ericsson, K. A., & Simon, H. A. (1984). *Protocol analysis: Verbal reports as data.* Cambridge, MA: MIT Press.

Eyferth, K., Schömann, M., & Widowski, D. (1986). Der Umgang von Psychologen mit Komplexität [On how psychologists deal with complexity]. *Sprache & Kognition, 5*, 11–26.

Funk, S. G., Rapoport, A., & Jones, L. V. (1979). Investing capital on safe and risky alternatives: An experimental study. *Journal of Experimental Psychology: General, 108*, 415–440.

Funke, J. (1986). *Komplexes Problemlösen—Bestandsaufnahme und Perspektiven* [Complex problem solving. Overview and perspectives]. Berlin: Springer.

Funke, J. (1992). Dealing with dynamic systems: Research strategy, diagnostic approach, and experimental results. *The German Journal of Psychology, 16*, 1, 24–43.

Hayes, J. R., & Simon, H. A. (1976). The understanding process: Problem isomorphs. *Cognitive Psychology, 8*, 165–190.

Huber, O. (1990). Cognitive processes in multistage decision making. In K. J. Gilhooly, M. Keane, R. H. Logie, & G. Erdos (Eds.), *Lines of thinking: Reflections on the psychology of thought. Vol. 1* (pp. 327–336). Chichester: Wiley.

Huber, O. (1994). Decision behavior in a multistage investment task. *Acta Psychologica, 85*, 139–154.

Huber, O., Debeutz, A., Pratscher, J., & Quehenberger, I. (1990). Perceived control in a multistage decision task. *Journal of Behavioral Decision Making, 3*, 123–136.

Kleiter, G. D. (1975). Optimal policies, degradation, and cognition. In D. Wendt & C. Vlek (Eds.), *Utility, probability, and human decision making* (pp. 370–376). Dordrecht, The Netherlands: Reidel.

Kleiter, G. D., & Wimmer, H. (1974). Information seeking in a multistage betting game. *Archiv für Psychologie, 126*, 213–230.

Krampen, G. (1981). *IPC-Fragebogen zu Kontrollüberzeugungen* [IPC-questionnaire on locus of control]. Göttingen, Germany: Hogrefe.

Levenson, H. (1972). Distinctions within the concept of internal-external control: Development of a new scale [Summary]. *Proceedings of the 80th Annual Convention of the American Psychological Association, 8*, 261–262.

MacCrimmon, K. R., & Wehrung, D. A. (1986). *Taking risks*. New York: The Free Press.

Mackinnon, A. J., & Wearing, A. J. (1985). Systems analysis and dynamic decision making. *Acta Psychologica, 58*, 159–172.

Omodei, M. (1993). *Fire Chief: A computer simulated real time dynamic decision making task*. Unpublished doctoral dissertation, University of Melbourne, Australia.

Payne, J. W., Bettman, J. R., Coupey, E., & Johnson, E. J. (1993). A constructive process view of decision making: Multiple strategies in judgment and choice. In O. Huber, J. Mumpower, J. Van der Pligt, & P. Koele (Eds.), *Current themes in psychological decision research* (pp. 107–141). Amsterdam: Elsevier Science Publishers.

Putz-Osterloh, W. (1983). Über Determinanten komplexer Problemlöseleistungen und Möglichkeiten zu ihrer Erfassung [On some processes determining the interaction with complex problems, and on the possibilities to assess these processes]. *Sprache & Kognition, 2*, 100–116.

Rapoport, A. (1975). Research paradigms for studying dynamic decision behavior. In D. Wendt & C. Vlek (Eds.), *Utility, probability, and human decision making* (pp. 349–369). Dordrecht, The Netherlands: Reidel.

Rapoport, A., & Jones, L. V. (1970). Gambling behavior in two-outcome multistage betting games. *Journal of Mathematical Psychology, 7*, 163–187.

Rapoport, A., Jones, L. V. & Kahan, J.P. (1970). Gambling behavior in multiple-choice betting games. *Journal of Mathematical Psychology, 7*, 12–36.

Sandler, I., Reese, F., Spencer, L., & Harpin, P. (1983). Person environment interaction and locus of control: Laboratory, therapy and classroom studies. In H. M. Lefcourt (Ed.), *Research with the locus of control construct, Vol. 2* (pp. XX–YY). New York: Academic Press.

Schmid, H. (1987). *Problemlöseprozesse in einer komplexen Problemsituation* [Problem solving processes in a complex problem solving situation]. Unpublished doctoral dissertation, University of Salzburg, Salzburg, Austria.

Schweiger, D. M., Anderson, C. R., & Locke, E. A. (1985). Complex decision making: A longitudinal study of process and performance. *Organizational Behavior and Human Decision Processes, 36*, 245–272.

Slovic, P., Lichtenstein, S., & Fischhoff, B. (1988). Decision making. In R. C. Atkinson, R. J. Herrnstein, G. Lindzey, & R. D. Luce (Eds.), *Stevens' Handbook of Experimental Psychology. Vol. 2: Learning and Cognition* (pp. 673–738). New York: Wiley.

Stäudel, T. (1987). *Problemlösen, Emotionen und Kompetenz* [Problem solving, emotions, and competence]. Regensburg, Germany: Roderer.

Vlek, C., & Stallen, J. P. (1981). Judging risks and benefits in the small and in the large. *Organizational Behavior and Human Performance, 28*, 235–271.

Wagenaar, W. A. (1988). *Paradoxes of gambling behaviour*. Hove, UK: Lawrence Erlbaum Associates.

PART THREE

THE DIFFERENTIAL APPROACH TO COMPLEX PROBLEM SOLVING

CHAPTER SEVEN

Complex Problem Solving, Intelligence, and Learning Ability

Jens F. Beckmann
Jürgen Guthke
University of Leipzig, Germany

INTRODUCTION

It is very common, even for psychologists, to assume that a person's intelligence is closely related to the person's ability to solve complex problems. The higher a person's intelligence, so the assumption, the better the person's problem-solving skills. Zero correlations between performances on traditional intelligence tests and on complex problem solving (henceforth CPS) tasks, therefore, are not only surprising, but highly counterintuitive. In the following, we briefly summarize the European research that has dealt with the relation between traditional measures of intelligence and problem solving skill, and analyze the variables that appear to moderate the relation between the two concepts. We argue that the relation between intelligence and CPS performance can be understood only if, (a) CPS tasks satisfy certain measurement requirements, and if, (b) traditional intelligence test scores are not considered optimal measures of intelligence. If both requirements are met, that is, if intelligence is measured as the capability to learn (see Sternberg, 1985), and CPS task environments meet strict methodological requirements, then positive associations between the two types of performances can be found. We argue that overcoming the theory deficit on the part of both CPS research and traditional intelligence test research is a necessary prerequisite for obtaining more differentiated and reliable answers concerning the relation between intelligence and CPS performance.

COMPLEX PROBLEM SOLVING AND INTELLIGENCE

Within the framework of CPS research, studies on the relation between the ability to control dynamic task environments (i.e., CPS tasks) and performance on intelligence tests have played a prominent role, especially in problem-solving research as it has been conducted in Germany during the last two decades (e.g., Dörner, 1979). For researchers focusing on understanding CPS, the assumption that successful problem solving performance requires intelligent behavior has been the main rationale underlying comparisons of subjects' performances when trying to control dynamic systems and when coping with the demands of intelligence tests. For those studying intelligence tests, the comparison has been founded on the a priori assumption that intelligence tests should capture something akin to an individual's general ability to solve problems (e.g., Sternberg, 1982). In both cases, research on the relation between the two concepts has served the purpose of determining the validity of the constructs involved, namely the ability to solve problems and to perform well on intelligence tests.

Empirical Research

The picture that emerges when one reviews the existing empirical evidence in favor of and against the link between CPS performance and intelligence is rather muddled. In some instances, substantial correlations are reported; in other studies, zero correlations are reported (for a review, see Kluwe, Schilde, Fischer, & Oellerer, 1991). These inconsistencies were, and still are, the starting points for rather heated debates. To get a more differentiated picture of the situation, consider Table 7.1. The table depicts the four logically possible outcomes of research on the relation between CPS and intelligence.

Cell 1 describes a situation where no relation between problem solving performance and intelligence is theoretically expected and, indeed, no such link is obtained empirically. The dominant theoretical claim advanced by researchers whose work is consistent with this situation is that no association exists between the two concepts because the ecological validity of the CPS paradigm (or its implementation) is greater than the ecological validity of intelligence tests. According to this line of reasoning, CPS tasks are more realistic tasks than are intelligence tests because many CPS tasks, such as computer-simulated scenarios, mirror everyday problems (such as governing a small town [Dörner, Kreuzig, Reither, & Stäudel, 1983]; running a textile factory [Putz-Osterloh, 1981]; working as a Peace Corps member [Strohschneider, 1986]; or being in charge of a fire brigade [Brehmer, 1987, this volume; Dörner & Pfeifer, 1993]). Thus, empirical studies that find no evidence for an association between the two concepts, support the assumption that traditional intelligence tests are out of touch with reality. This interpretation, in turn, has led to calls for a new assessment of intelligence that focuses on so-called operative intelligence (e.g., Dörner, 1986). Unlike static intelligence tests, *operative intelligence* tests are designed to measure more complex and hence ecologically more valid processes (e.g., Dörner & Kreuzig, 1983) that may be affected by noncognitive person characteristics (emotional reactions, assertive behavior, etc.).

Cell 2 of Table 7.1 describes a situation where an association between CPS performance and intelligence is theoretically expected, but is not obtained empirically. Typically, the failure to obtain empirical support is ex-

TABLE 7.1
Theoretical and Empirical Relations Between Test Intelligence and CPS

	As Expected	Contrary to What Was Expected
zero correlation	cell 1	cell 2
non-zero correlation	cell 3	cell 4

plained by referring to a lack of reliability and/or validity of the problem-solving tasks used (e.g., Amelang & Bartussek, 1990; Funke, 1984). The main brunt of the argument centers on the intuitive manner in which CPS tasks are often constructed, and on the frequently encountered *ad hoc* nature of the operationalization of problem-solving performance. Thus, an association between test intelligence and CPS performance is not obtained empirically because of shortcomings in the way CPS tasks are constructed and CPS performance is measured.

Cell 3 of Table 7.1 describes a situation where a relation between CPS performance and intelligence is theoretically expected and is also obtained empirically. Typically, empirical support is obtained when the intelligence construct is viewed in a more differentiated way than traditionally, or when the CPS task is similar to the intelligence testing situation. The latter situation is often realized when abstract systems are used that cannot be solved by simply applying prior knowledge and that have well-defined goals. If one reviews the results of studies focusing on specific subcomponents of intelligence, rather than on a global assessment of the intelligence construct, then the picture that emerges is quite consistent. In many studies, substantial correlations between factor K ("processing capacity" [Verarbeitungskapazität]) in the Berliner Intelligenz-Struktur-Test (BIS; Jäger, 1982) and CPS performance have been reported (e.g., Hörmann & Thomas, 1989; Hussy, 1992; Jäger, 1991; Süß, Kersting, & Oberauer, 1991). BIS processing capacity captures the ability to recognize relations and rules, and to form formal logical inferences (in figure series and number series tests, and in analogies, respectively), and is roughly comparable to Thurstone's reasoning factor.

Different aspects of intelligence appear to be related to different aspects of CPS performance. For instance, sometimes knowledge acquisition in a CPS environment is measured separately from knowledge application. Knowledge acquisition can be assessed by, among others, thinking aloud protocols, judgments about the truth of statements about the structure of a system, prognoses, retrognoses, and causal diagram analyses. Often, measures of knowledge acquisition correlate with intelligence test scores.

Cell 4 of Table 7.1 represents a situation where no link between CPS performance and intelligence is theoretically expected, but such a link is obtained empirically. Although theoretically possible, reports that would fit this situation are very rare, as one might expect.

Explanatory Concepts

As we have seen previously, both the theoretical expectations and the empirical evidence regarding a link between CPS performance and intelligence vary among those examining the issue. Why is it that researchers cannot agree on whether to theoretically expect a link between the two concepts?

And why is it that the empirical findings are not consistent? We have briefly touched on some of the reasons for the theoretical and empirical discrepancies already. In the following, we discuss more systematically potential moderator variables that may mediate the relation between intelligence and CPS performance.

Naturality. Many CPS environments are constructed with the explicit goal in mind that they represent a *natural* problem situation. What is considered natural and what is not, however, is frequently based on face validity. In our view, equating naturality with ecological validity, which is frequently done, is inappropriate. Often, ecological validity is simply viewed as a characteristic of the test situation. Rarely, if ever, is an attempt made to verify ecological validity empirically. The ecological validity of a CPS environment is thus postulated ex cathedra.

If one argues that the naturality of a task is primarily dependent upon surface characteristics, then the question may be raised of how many subjects actually run a textile factory or are Peace Corps members in real life. Fortunately, the chaotic control behavior so often observed when highly complex natural situations, simulated by computer, are dealt with, is seldom matched by ecological reality (the Czernobyl accident). Following Müller's (1993) line of reasoning, one may ask why artificial laboratory tasks or the use of abstract problems are not adequate means for obtaining answers to scientific questions. Or to put it differently: Why is the analysis of actual everyday behavior not enough if our goal is to understand CPS? In our view, CPS research should not be conducted as an alternative to artificial laboratory experiments, but should skillfully create experimental conditions such that scientific questions can be addressed. Laboratory problems should representatively reflect the depth structure of everyday problems but not necessarily their surface structure and their specific semantic embedding. In addition, as is required of intelligence tests and developmental tests, both theoretical and empirical evidence is needed to ensure that these problems are representative of the task demands of a particular subsample of everyday problems. If laboratory problems are generated along these lines, we believe, then they are indeed suited to answering scientific and diagnostic–practical questions. The CPS tasks commonly encountered in the literature, in contrast, are frequently selected at random.

Interaction Between Solver and Task. The fact that CPS performance in the well-known LOHHAUSEN study (Dörner et al., 1983) was related solely to extroversion and self-confidence (and not to intelligence) shows, among other things, that when subjects deal with complex problems, motivational and emotional factors may predict success to a greater extent than intellectual factors. We suspect that the LOHHAUSEN finding may have been due to the fact that subjects' interactions with the system were mediated by the experimenter. That is, in order to obtain information about the system, subjects had to ask the experimenter more or less intelligent questions. It is, of course, hardly surprising to find that in this interaction, subjects' self-confidence and extroversion play major roles. One might concur with Dörner (1986) in suggesting that successful coping with problems in everyday life calls for just those person characteristics that are not closely related to intelligence in the traditional sense of the word.

The question of interest, in the face of such confounding of cognitive and noncognitive explanatory variables, is how differentiating statements can be made about the individual variables' effects (e.g., in diagnosis and in interventions). We do not gain much by describing a person as a poor problem solver if we cannot specify which cognitive and noncognitive components are responsible for the person's failure. When the subjective components of a CPS situation are standardized through the use of direct subject–computer interactions, then CPS performance may indeed be predicted by intelligence.

Goal Definition. Existing research suggests that problem solving behavior under well-defined goals (e.g., reaching and maintaining a particular state of a system) is more easily compared to (test) intelligence than problem solving behavior under ill-defined goals (e.g., Strohschneider, 1991). For example, the goal to be pursued in the complex LOHHAUSEN system mentioned previously, was to ensure the well-being of a fictitious city in the near and distant future. At least part of the reason why such vague goal definitions are provided in the first place is that researchers are often interested in the process of goal formulation because successful management of real-world problems frequently requires a goal definition.

Tasks with well-defined goals establish a common standard for interindividual comparisons, and make the CPS situation more similar to the intelligence test situation. In order to be comparable to the intelligence test situation, however, the standard used to evaluate a subject's problem-solving performance must be transparent to the subject also. In other words, both the goal and the evaluation function must be laid down a priori, and must be clearly specified in the instructions subjects are given.

Semantic Embeddedness. Semantic embeddedness represents another variable that potentially mediates the relation between intelligence and problem solving performance. Depending upon the kind of semantic embedding of a complex problem, more or less comprehensive prior knowledge is activated. The problem solving process, in turn, may be different when prior knowledge is used relative to when it is not used (see Frensch & Funke, this volume). This, of course, does not say anything about the suitability of prior knowledge for successful problem management. Prior knowledge may stand in the way of, or may aid, successful problem solving. In general, we may assume that prior knowledge influences the problem solving process. Interindividual differences in prior knowledge can act to artificially reduce correlations between intelligence and problem solving performance or can even cause the correlations to vanish completely. On the other hand, controlling for the effects of prior knowledge, for example by using abstract complex problems that do not activate prior knowledge, or by using a procedure to assess prior knowledge, is likely to lead to substantial correlations with intellectual performance.

Transparency. Some researchers have argued that the greater the transparency of a CPS situation, the better it can be compared to the traditional intelligence test situation because of the greater resemblance between the two situations in terms of task requirements (Hörmann & Thomas, 1989; Hussy, 1989; Süß et al., 1991). However, the transparency problem at issue here seems to relate less to the transparency of problems than to the (confusing) nontransparency of the definition of the concept itself. In many studies, transparency, or more typically nontransparency (which is one of the features of complex problems described by Dörner et al., 1983), is defined in different ways. As a result, transparency is experimentally manipulated in different ways. For example, complex problems where the values of all inherent system variables are constantly displayed (that is, subjects do not need to actively search for this information), are sometimes called transparent. At other times, transparent may mean that subjects are shown diagrams that display the relations among all system variables (e.g., Putz-Osterloh & Lüer, 1981). With respect to the latter in particular, one may argue that the processes involved may be better described as exercise completion rather than problem solving (see Frensch & Funke, this volume). In any event, the results of many studies dealing with the transparency effect cannot be compared directly because transparency is defined differently in the different studies. Because of this problem, and because some studies have even reported substantial correlations between intelligence and performance on problems that lack transparency (e.g., Süß et al., 1991), we do not know at this time whether transparency has any effect on the relation between CPS performance and intelligence.

Comparability. A great number of quite heterogeneous instruments and definitions have been subsumed under the generic term *complex problem solving*. The inflation-like spawning of ever-new complex problems adds to the difficulty of structuring research findings. Progress reports testifying to this productivity have been issued by Funke (1986, 1991b, 1992a, 1992b). The ongoing boom is both a cause and an effect of the nature of the process of theory formulation deplored by, among others, Dörner (1992). Current theory formulation is perhaps best described in terms of a substitutive, rather than accumulative, or integrative, strategy of comparing individual studies and their theoretical foundations. In light of this strategy, it is difficult to argue against the dearth of theory in research on problem solving, to which many researchers have drawn attention (e.g., Buchner, this volume; Fillbrandt, 1992; Funke, 1992b). Developing a taxonomy of complex problems, as suggested by Funke (1990, 1991a) and Brehmer (1990), must be considered a first step toward the formulation of a problem solving theory. A taxonomy, perhaps based on the mathematical description of complex problems (e.g., Buchner, this volume; Buchner & Funke, 1993; Funke, 1993) ensures, on the one hand, comparability of various complex problems with one another, and, on the other hand, comparison to specific intelligence test items. An important aspect of such a taxonomy should be the assessment of the difficulty of problems.

Difficulty. Problem difficulty has also been discussed as a potential moderator variable mediating the relation between problem solving performance and intelligence (e.g., Hussy, 1985; Raaheim, 1978). Problem demands should neither be too high nor too low. Correlations between intelligence scores and CPS performance are expected to be highest with problems of average difficulty. This underlines anew the need for a theoretically founded taxonomy of problems because without a frame of reference one may only speculate about the difficulty of complex problems. Degree of familiarity is intimately related to problem difficulty. If, for example, the degree of familiarity is so high that the problem constitutes a task that can be solved simply by memory recall, then correlations with intelligence are likely to be low (Raaheim, 1990).

Task Requirements. Occasionally, even seasoned researchers argue that certain CPS situations are too complex to be of any use in experimental research. Clearly, a detailed task analysis is necessary before CPS performance can be related to intelligence. Often, the task demands of complex problems and those of intelligence tests differ widely. CPS tasks typically emphasize *processes*; decision-making and planning processes, the reduction and generation of information, processes that develop knowledge structures, or action control processes that are based on feedback and active information search. Traditional intelligence tests, by contrast, heavily emphasize the *results* of performance (Kluwe et al., 1991). These different objectives should lead researchers to expect moderate relations between intelligence scores and CPS performance. More substantive correlations between the two concepts can only be expected if one succeeds in operationalizing different aspects of the problem solving process (such as knowledge acquisition and knowledge application) that are more or less similar to the intelligence tests in terms of their task demands.

Multidimensionality. As previously indicated, a meaningful analysis of the relation between test intelligence and CPS performance must take into account the multidimensionality of both the intelligence and the CPS construct. However, existing attempts to translate this idea into action by using statistical, multivariate methods to analyze the relation are still hampered by the completely unsatisfactory degree of elaborateness of any theory of CPS (see also Buchner, this volume; Frensch & Funke, this volume). Wittmann and Matt (1986), for instance, point to the asymmetrical approach taken in the frequent correlational studies. In order to permit a truly fair comparison between the intelligence test situation and the CPS situation, the two situations must be symmetrical, that is, their parameters must be comparable. Thus, any comparison of global intelligence test scores with specific CPS performance parameters is highly questionable.

Reliability. We have already touched on the issue of the reliability (and ultimately validity) of the measures capturing problem solving performance. Clearly, any test of the relation between test intelligence and CPS performance does not lead anywhere if there are reasonable doubts concerning the reliability of the data on which the test is based (e.g., Funke, 1986; Tent, 1984). Estimating the reliability of a CPS measure is problematic with regard to at least two aspects. First, CPS sets in motion processes of knowledge acquisition that make a simple repetition of measurement less meaningful. Second, because of the lack of a taxonomy of problems, it is difficult to construct two exactly parallel complex task environments in order to obtain a reliability estimate by means of the equivalence method.

A rather interesting approach to this problem has recently been developed by Müller (1993). Müller used an abstract complex system that could be described in terms of a set of linear equations. The system consisted of two identical subsystems (a fact subjects did not realize). Subjects' performances could thus be compared on the two structurally identical subsystems. Müller obtained rather encouraging reliability estimates of .92 and .86 for two measures capturing subjects' quality of knowledge acquisition and of system control, respectively.

Validity. The correlation between intelligence test scores and measures of CPS performance may also be affected by a lack of internal and external validity of the CPS measures. The often reported lack of an association between test intelligence and CPS points, of course, to the need for divergent validation of CPS measures. However, there is also a need for convergent validation. That is, if CPS is not related to traditional intelligence, then what is it related to? Of course, validating (with either the convergent or the divergent objective in mind) one potentially invalid construct (CPS) with another potentially invalid construct (test intelligence) is, at the very least, highly questionable.

Summary

From the viewpoint of cognitive psychology, the theory deficit of both CPS and intelligence test research must be dealt with (e.g., Sternberg, 1982) if we want to move from unsatisfactory global correlations between intelligence test scores and CPS performance to a more differentiated analysis. We need to know more about exactly which cognitive processes are engaged in particular CPS situations and in the intelligence test situation in order to make specific predictions about the relation between CPS parameters and intelligence test scores. Consistent with what Sternberg demanded as early as 1982, future research should pay more attention to the constructs involved in information processing (e.g., working memory) than to the global ability constructs used in differential intelligence research.

In summary, in order to assess the relation between intelligence and CPS, a great number of factors (task and situation characteristics) must be taken into consideration. To arrive at a synthesis and to gain new insights, it is necessary to systematically vary individual task components both on the side of CPS and on the side of intelligence tests. However, as previously mentioned, at least some researchers claim that certain variables, such as knowledge acquisition (learning), for instance, cannot be examined in an intelligence test environment. We argue, in contrast, that these topics can be investigated within an intelligence-testing framework, and discuss just such an approach in the following section. The idea behind the so-called learning test concept is to construct intelligence tests such that learning becomes possible through feedback and prompts during test application.

LEARNING TESTS: ALTERNATIVES
TO CONVENTIONAL INTELLIGENCE TESTS

For more than two decades, our research group (Guthke, 1972, 1992) has been engaged in developing a new type of intelligence test, which we have labeled learning test. The main idea behind the learning test concept is that researchers record not only a subject's momentary performance in a one-time administration of a test procedure, as is done in the usual static intelligence test situation, but also the subject's responses to repeated, standardized questions that are built into the test. Through repeated measurements we are able to determine subjects' learning potentials. This, in turn, is helpful in distinguishing potentially educable mentally retarded and more severely retarded children, for instance, and, in general, in increasing the intelligence test's validity. Notice, by the way, the parallels between the reasons for developing learning tests and for introducing the CPS paradigm. In both cases, researchers were dissatisfied with the static diagnostic information yielded by intelligence tests.

History of Learning Tests

In the international literature, various terms have been used to denote the learning test concept. Apart from the word *Learning Test* (Lerntest), coined especially by the Leipzig research group (e.g., Guthke, 1972, 1977), the terms *Testing the Limits* (e.g., Hamers, Sijtsma, & Ruijssenaars, 1993; Schmidt, 1971;), *Dynamic Assessment* (Lidz, 1987; 1991), *Dynamic Testing* (e.g., Carlson & Wiedl, 1980), and *Interactive Assessment* (Haywood & Tzuriel, 1992) are used. Haywood and Tzuriel (1992), referring to the healthy diversity in this field, distinguish among a "Russian–German tradition, represented in the work of Vygotsky, and subsequently the German Lerntest movement, Swiss-Israeli tradition [based on Piaget and Rey] that has crossed both the Mediterranean and the Atlantic; an American–Canadian–Australian tradition that has strong roots in experimental psychology; [and] a Swiss–French tradition that displays both neo Piagetian and experimental roots" (p. 5). In describing the theoretical underpinning of the learning test concept, most authors refer to an idea by Vygotsky (1934/1964). He had demanded that, in developmental psychology and diagnostics, both the zone of present development and the zone of proximal development (see, for example, Minick, 1987) be identified.

Basic Concepts

In contrast to authors of intelligence tests, psychologists studying thinking have never identified thinking processes in the way the customary intelligence test does, that is, by simply testing subjects on their knowledge of the correct solution to a pool of items. Instead, these researchers have typically used a method where subjects have the opportunity to learn from test repetitions (the procedure adopted with the Tower of Hanoi; e.g., Klix & Lander, 1967), from feedback about the effects of their actions, and from prompts given during the problem solving process (e.g., Rubinstein, 1961). Learning psychologists point out that the best way to predict future learning is to use *learning samples* as predictors (e.g., Ferguson, 1954). All these suggestions, along with many others coming from the basic disciplines, have led to the learning test approach (Guthke, 1977).

Types of Learning Tests

As far as test items are concerned, learning tests emphasize conventional intelligence test items, on the one hand, and curriculum-specific or domain-specific items, on the other hand (see Hamers et al., 1993).

With reference to the time expenditure and learning test situation, one distinguishes between long-term learning tests and short-term learning tests. The *long-term learning test*, involving a pretest, a training phase, and a posttest, is the classical learning test. Items used in this type of test include the familiar items employed in traditional intelligence tests. Frequently, the Raven Matrices provide the material upon which long-term learning tests are based.

The *Reasoning Learning Test* (LTS; Guthke, Jäger, & Schmidt, 1983) is an example of a long-term learning test. After a pretest battery of items consisting of number series, figure series, and analogies has been administered, subjects undergo individual or group training involving programmed manuals that are designed to teach problem solving strategies. On a posttest, parallel items are used to examine the extent to which subjects improved their performance as a result of the training.

A main objection to the long-term learning test, raised especially by clinical practitioners, is that it takes too much time. Therefore, *short-term learning tests*, involving one test session only, have been developed over the past few years. In contrast to long-term tests, here the training phase is directly implemented into the test procedure.

Diagnostic Programs

In our view, the future of intelligence assessment lies in combining test construction and task and process analysis within the learning test concept (see Brown & French, 1978; Klix, 1983; Lidz, 1987; Sternberg, 1985). In this way, the procedural weaknesses and shortcomings of the theoretical foundation of traditional intelligence tests may be overcome. The so-called *Diagnostic Programs* can be considered a new kind of short-term learning potential test with a theory-guided item construction. The main features of these programs are:

- Content validity or description of the objective demand structure of individual items as emphasized by Brown and French (1978) and Klauer (1984). Unlike in classical test theory, what is determined here are not just the statistical indices of difficulty of the item pool, but also the cognitive operations needed to solve the items.
- Sequential structure of tests (progressing from simple to more demanding items).

- Systematic feedback and prompts to ensure that subjects cannot proceed to the next item until all preceding items have been solved (see Bloom's Mastery Learning; Bloom, 1968). In contrast to long-term learning test, in which the training phase is interposed between the pretest and the posttest, the learning is evoked directly during the testing.
- Determination of the course of the learning process.

A number of diagnostic programs have been developed during the past few years. Most have highly complicated branched ramification rules due to the fact that they tend to combine the learning potential test concept with an adaptive test strategy (Hornke, 1976; Weiss, 1985). The goal is to achieve a high degree of individualization of testing and training such that prompts and item order vary as a function of the type of errors made (e.g., Guthke et al., 1991).

TASK REQUIREMENTS IN COMPLEX PROBLEM SOLVING SITUATIONS AND IN LEARNING TESTS

Similarities

In our view, one of the most important commonalities between the learning test situation and the CPS situation is the emphasis on subjects' opportunity for learning. Learning may occur during the testing phase and may be due to feedback provided either by the experimenter or by the computer informing about the consequences or the adequacy of different potential interventions. The lack of feedback may be one main reason why traditional intelligence test scores and CPS performance often either are not correlated or are correlated to a low degree. Of course, even in a conventional intelligence test situation, there exist opportunities for learning, especially in the case of such homogenous tests as the Raven Test (Raven, 1965). However, there is much less implicit opportunity for learning in traditional intelligence test situations than is there in CPS and in learning test situations (Guthke, 1972). Furthermore, neither classical test theory nor more modern probabilistic test theory regard this as a desideratum. Suffice it to think of the demand that items should be stochastically independent.

In contrast to traditional intelligence tests, the call for items to be stochastically independent is deliberately abandoned for learning tests and for CPS research. (In CPS research, the individual trials, time units, or the relations among system variables that are to be identified, might be considered items in the widest sense of the word.) On the contrary, for these tasks it is desired that items build upon one another, as is the case in dynamic task environments, and in the Diagnostic Programs, for instance. This requirement is believed to increase item validity because everyday thinking also involves complex item structures rather than a collection of unrelated microproblems (as simulated by item pools in traditional intelligence tests).

In both the learning test and the CPS situation, subjects are much more active than they are in conventional intelligence tests. This is true especially for the long-term learning tests (see, for example, the *Reasoning Learning Test* developed by Guthke et al., 1983), where subjects are supposed to acquire heuristic strategies by working programmed textbooks during the training phase that help them to solve posttest items. Similarly, in CPS research subjects are frequently asked to acquire control-relevant system knowledge through active exploration before their control knowledge is assessed. It is conceivable, therefore, that both CPS and learning test performance are more heavily influenced by motivational and emotional factors than is performance on conventional intelligence tests (e.g., Dörner et al., 1983; Guthke & Lehwald, 1984). Short-term learning tests, which have a shorter knowledge acquisition phase than many complex tasks and long-term learning tests, are expected to be less dependent on motivation. In one of our own studies, however, we found that in adaptive computer learning tests, pupils who were inadequately motivated to acquire knowledge tended nevertheless to engage in uncontrolled trial and error behavior (often to a greater extent than in conventional intelligence tests) just to find out about the computer's response. Similar behavior has been observed in CPS research (so-called cognitive emergency reactions [Dörner et al., 1983]). Interestingly, we also found that, in short-term learning tests, it was possible to push impulsive but nonetheless adequately motivated children (i.e., children with minimal cerebral dysfunctions) to increasingly adopt a more reflective coping style after they had been exposed to negative feedback during the testing phase (Guthke & Löffler, 1983). The conclusion seems warranted that both CPS research and learning tests open up greater possibilities for investigating achievement and learning behavior than do conventional intelligence tests.

Differences

Learning tests are still more similar in a variety of points to traditional intelligence tests than they are to CPS tasks. For example, both learning tests and CPS tasks provide more prompts for learning than the conventional intelligence tests, but they usually differ in the amount of prompting. This is at least partially due to the fact that learning tests were originally designed for differential diagnosis in the below-average domain of intellectual functioning (e.g., Guthke, 1985), whereas in most cases only cognitively efficient subjects are asked to solve complex problems. For the latter, simple "correct versus wrong feedback" without detailed reasons concerning the quality of their responses is enough to produce learning gains. Poor and average performers, on the other hand, require more massive help. Therefore, in contrast to CPS tasks, feedback in learning tests is much more direct and more elaborate, in order to enable subjects to find the correct solutions as quickly as possible.

Dependent upon the type of problem and on how the problems are presented, CPS tasks involve quite different kinds of feedback as well. Generally, feedback is provided in less direct ways than in learning tests. Long-term learning tests have a training phase interspersed between the pretest and the posttest. In research on CPS, such extended phases for teaching heuristics or metacognitive strategies are used only in exceptional cases (e.g., Dörner et al., 1983).

In contrast to a typical CPS situation which is marked by a low degree of transparency, the goal in a learning test situation is always precisely defined. In addition, learning tests do not have a polytelic goal structure; the sole goal to be attained is the correct solution. As a rule, like traditional intelligence tests, learning tests consist of a number of items that are easy to separate (but are not stochastically independent); they do not, however, consist of only *one*, more or less complex, problem.

Summary

Despite the similarities between CPS tasks and learning tests, and irrespective of the operationalizations of the two constructs, a global perspective integrating the two constructs may not be possible at this time. What is needed first is experimental research that captures the relation between the two concepts in the presence or absence of potential mediator variables. The experimental study described briefly in the following section was conducted with this aim in mind (for a detailed description of the study, see Beckmann, in press).

AN EXPERIMENTAL STUDY ON THE ABILITY TO SOLVE COMPLEX PROBLEMS, THE ABILITY TO LEARN, AND INTELLIGENCE

This experiment was conducted to study the effects of semantic embeddedness and of prior knowledge on the relation between problem solving performance and test intelligence. Starting point for the experiment was the assumption that CPS performance would be significantly correlated with traditional intelligence scores, but only when the CPS situation was abstract, that is, when no prior knowledge existed that could aid in task performance. By contrast, the problem solving performance shown by subjects dealing with a semantically embedded dynamic system was expected to be correlated with traditional intelligence test scores to a much lower degree (hypothesis 1).

Another focus of the experiment was the relation between CPS performance and learning test performance. We expected that learning test performance would be a better predictor of knowledge *acquisition* in a CPS situation than would be traditional intelligence test performance (hypothesis 2), but that the two predictors would not differ in how well they predicted CPS task performance.

Methods

Instruments. We used two short-term learning tests that may both be characterized as Diagnostic Programs (see previously mentioned test). The tests were the Adaptive Figure Series Learning Test (ADAFI; Guthke, Räder, Caruso, & Schmidt, 1991) and the Adaptive Analogies Learning Test (ADANA; e.g., Stein, 1993). For measuring intelligence, we used components of conventional intelligence tests that tapped processing capacity ("Verarbeitungskapazität" [Jäger, 1982]). To allow a fair comparison of conventional intelligence tests and learning tests, two tests were chosen that did not differ in content. We employed the Analogies sub-test of the Amthauer Intelligenz-Strukturtest (IST; Amthauer, 1973) as the conventional counterpart of the ADANA, and the pretest of the LTS 3 (figure series; Guthke et al., 1983) that can be interpreted as a conventional test version of the ADAFI.

Subjects performed a computer-administered complex dynamic system. The construction of the system was based on work performed by Funke and his associates (e.g., Funke, 1993). The system consisted of three independent (exogenous) variables and three dependent (endogenous) variables. The states of the three endogenous variables varied as a function of their own previous values, and the values of the exogenous variables. The behavior of the system could be described in terms of a linear system of equations (first order autoregressive processes).

The system was a transparent, complex, interconnected dynamic system with multiple goals. The system was stable over time, deterministic, and without time delays, and was thus, like SINUS (e.g., Funke, 1991b), an ideal instrument for experimental manipulation of system attributes. The subjects' task was to first acquire knowledge about the structure of the system within 21 simulation cycles, and then to reach and to maintain a defined target state during the following seven simulation cycles.

Manipulation of System Attributes. We systematically varied the semantic embedding of the system, but held the overall system structure constant. That is, the two versions of the problem were described by the exact same system of linear equations. The semantic embedding was manipulated with the goal of varying the extent to which the system activated prior knowledge. To this end, two different cover stories were developed for the dynamic system. The semantically embedded version (S+) represented a CHERRY-TREE, together with the exogenous variables *light, water supply*, and *warmth*, and the endogenous variables *cherries, leaves*, and *beetles*. The abstract version (S−), which was not expected to activate prior knowledge, represented a fictitious MACHINE consisting of three control devices and three displays.

Dependent Measures. After each of their interventions, subjects were asked to describe their newly acquired knowledge about the structure of the system (dependency of the variables). Reports were made in the form of judgments about the existence respective nonexistence of relations among the system variables (causal diagrams). The judgments were aggregated into an index of sensitivity using a threshold model (cf. Snodgrass & Corwin, 1988). The index of sensitivity P_r (averaged over 21 exploration cycles), represented the measure of the quality of knowledge acquisition (KAC).

The quality of knowledge application (KAP) was measured by the Euclidean distance and averaged over seven control cycles between the actual control intervention performed by subjects and the optimal intervention that would have led to the desired goal state.

The measure for our short-term learning tests was based on the number of items completed and the number of prompts required. Both parameters were combined into a new measure, which we called *number of steps*. The average number of steps needed in the two learning tests represented the measure of learning ability (LT).

The average standard norm of the two intelligence tests was our measure of conventional intelligence (IT).

Subjects and Procedure. A total of 92 pupils (mean age = 14.4 years) performed the CPS task individually (first session). Subjects were randomly assigned to one of the two experimental conditions (52 subjects in condition S+, 40 subjects in condition S−). In the second session, the conventional intelligence tests were administered. The short-term learning tests were administered in sessions 3 and 4.

Results and Discussion

In order to test hypothesis 1, we calculated the Pearson correlation between problem-solving performance (here we distinguish between knowledge acquisition performance, and control performance, or knowledge application) and intelligence test performance separately for each of the two experimental groups (i.e., S+ and S–). The results are displayed in the first row of Table 7.2. Only knowledge application (KAP) in the abstract condition (S–), which was assumed not to activate prior knowledge, was reliably correlated with traditional test intelligence ($t(38) = 2.38$), all other correlations were not reliable. These findings support our assertions that the semantic embeddedness of a complex problem mediates the relation between traditional measures of intelligence and CPS performance.

The table also contains the results pertaining to the question of whether learning test performance is a better predictor of the quality of problem solving than conventional intelligence test performance (hypothesis 2). The second row of the table contains the Pearson correlations between knowledge acquisition (KAC), knowledge application (KAP), and learning test performance (LT), separately for the two semantic conditions (S+ and S–). In line with hypothesis 2, statistically significant differences (in the sense of a higher predictive power of the learning tests) were found only under abstract problem solving conditions. Thus, hypothesis 2 can be confirmed only for abstract systems that do not activate prior knowledge.

One may ask what may have been responsible for the nonreliable correlations between problem solving performance (especially with S+) and both intelligence test performance and learning test performance. Figure 7.1 displays the mean knowledge acquisition performance over the 21 exploration cycles in the two semantic conditions.

In the semantic embedding condition (S+), neither knowledge was acquired, nor could any previous knowledge be identified in the sample (P_r obtained prior to the first exploratory intervention was close to zero). However, knowledge acquisition did occur in the abstract condition (S–). In neither condition was relevant prior knowledge found. Thus, the argument that prior knowledge may have been responsible for the zero correlations between CPS performance and intelligence cannot be confirmed.

Surprisingly, however, the two samples did not differ with regard to KAP, $t(90) = 0.596$, $p > 0.05$. We interpret this finding as suggesting that it is

TABLE 7.2
Pearson Correlation Coefficients Between Conventional Intelligence
Test (IT) or Learning Test (LT) and Knowledge Acquisition (KAC)
or Knowledge Application (KAP) Under Semantic Embedded (S+)
and Abstract (S–) Conditions

	S+		S–	
	KAC	KAP	KAC	KAP
IT	.05	.09	.11	.36*
LT	.03	.03	.52*	.57*

Note. *$p \leq 0.05$.

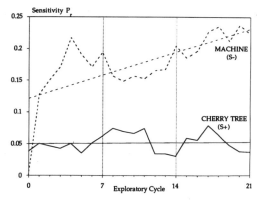

FIG. 7.1. Knowledge acquisition during the exploratory cycles for the two embeddedness conditions (straight lines represent regression lines).

possible to adequately control complex systems in the absence of explicitly acquired knowledge (Kluwe et al., 1991; see also Berry & Broadbent, this volume). We assume that the familiarity caused by the semantic context may have led the explorers of the system to develop *sham confidence* that interfered with knowledge acquisition. In our experiment, use of situationally unspecific heuristics (ad hoc control) led to similar knowledge application scores. The reliable Pearson correlation between knowledge acquisition (KAC) and knowledge application (KAP) with the abstract, dynamic MACHINE system, $r_{(KAC, KAP)} = .51$, shows that when at least some knowledge is acquired, then the amount of learning will be a major predictor of knowledge application. In other words, system control is not random. Recall that the two semantic CPS conditions differed exclusively with respect to the labeling of the variables in the dynamic system. The two samples were identical with regard to traditional intelligence and learning test performance. We interpret the different correlations with intelligence and learning test performance as pointing to differences in the determination of knowledge application under abstract conditions and under semantic embedding conditions.

CONCLUDING REMARKS

The relations found among the constructs of intellectual status, CPS performance, and learning ability are summarized in Figure 7.2. The figure represents, under problem solving conditions that do not activate prior knowledge, the overlap as well as the differences among the different constructs.

In the abstract condition, system knowledge was acquired, and the quality of knowledge application, that is, system control, depended on the quality of knowledge acquisition. Furthermore, a significant correlation between knowledge acquisition in CPS and performance on short-term learning tests

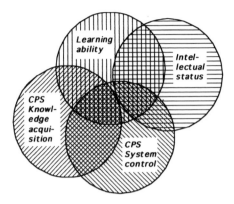

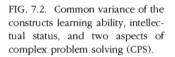

FIG. 7.2. Common variance of the constructs learning ability, intellectual status, and two aspects of complex problem solving (CPS).

was found. At least in the present experiment, this effect was independent of conventional measures of intelligence. Therefore, these two circles do not overlap in Figure 7.2.

In other words, if knowledge is acquired in a CPS situation, then the amount of knowledge acquired is more likely to be predicted by a subject's learning ability than by the subject's traditional intelligence score. For learning test researchers, the demonstration of a stronger association of the learning test versus the conventional intelligence test with knowledge acquisition in CPS is a major contribution toward the construct validation of the learning test. Many researchers concerned with problem solving would expect this result also, of course, because they proceed on the implicit assumption that in their scenarios learning processes are evoked to a greater extent than in the usual intelligence tests. On the other hand, knowledge application in CPS seems to be more strongly related to traditional intelligence than to knowledge acquisition. Therefore, there seems to be another possibility to account for the inconsistent evidence described at the beginning of this chapter. Thus, seemingly contradictory evidence (association versus zero correlations with intelligence test performances) may to a considerable extent depend on how the quality of problem solving is operationalized. If knowledge acquisition performance is measured, then no correlation with intelligence test performance scores should be expected. If, however, the measures focus on control performances, then at least when problem solving involves abstract, transparent tasks of average complexity with clearly defined goals, substantial correlations with intelligence performance are likely to be found.

In light of the findings reported here, the interpretations of zero correlations between problem-solving performance with semantically embedded systems and intellectual status appear in a different light. Zero correlations may simply be due to a lack of knowledge acquisition. Many studies do not perform an explicit assessment of knowledge acquisition. Whenever there is an assessment of knowledge acquisition and there is evidence of successful knowledge acquisition, then relations between knowledge application (that is, control performance) and intelligence test scores are reported (e.g., Süß et al., 1991). Of course, these claims call for more systematic testing.

ACKNOWLEDGMENTS

Preparation of this chapter was supported by a grant from the "Deutsche Forschungsgemeinschaft (DFG)" to the second author and to Joachim Funke (ref. no. Gu 297/2 and Fu 173/2).

REFERENCES

Amelang, M., & Bartussek, D. (1990). *Differentielle Psychologie und Persönlichkeitsforschung* (3., überarbeitete und erweiterte Auflage) [Differential psychology and research on personality]. Stuttgart, Germany: Kohlhammer.

Amthauer, R. (1973). *IST-70. Intelligenz-Struktur-Test* [Test of the structure of intelligence]. Göttingen, Germany: Hogrefe.

Beckmann, J. F. (in press). *Lernen und komplexes Problemlösen. Ein Beitrag zur Validierung von Lerntests* [Learning and complex problem solving. A contribution to validate learning potential tests]. Bonn, Germany: Holos.

Bloom, B. S. (1968). *Learning for mastery.* Los Angeles, CA: Center for Study and Evaluation of Instructional Programs.

Brehmer, B. (1987). Development of mental models for decision in technological systems. In J. Rasmussen, K. Duncan, & J. Leplat (Eds.), *New technology and human error* (pp. 111–120). Chichester, England: Wiley.

Brehmer, B. (1990). *Towards a taxonomy for microworlds* (Technical Report ESPRIT Basic Research Actions MOHAWC). Roskilde, Denmark: Riso National Laboratory.

Brown, A. L., & French, L. A. (1978). The zone of potential development: Implications for intelligence testing in the year 2000. *Intelligence, 3*, 155–277.

Buchner, A., & Funke, J. (1993). Finite-state automata: Dynamic task environments in problem-solving research. *The Quarterly Journal of Experimental Psychology, 46A*, 83–118.

Carlson, J. S., & Wiedl, K. H. (1980). Applications of a dynamic testing approach in intelligence assessment: Empirical results and theoretical formulations. *Zeitschrift für Differentielle und Diagnostische Psychologie, 1*, 303–318.

Dörner, D. (1979). Kognitive Merkmale erfolgreicher und erfolgloser Problemlöser beim Umgang mit sehr komplexen Systemen [Cognitive properties of successful and unsuccessful problem solvers when interacting with very complex systems]. In H. Ueckert & D. Rhenius (Eds.), *Komplexe menschliche Informationsverarbeitung* (pp. 185–196). Bern, Switzerland: Hans Huber.

Dörner, D. (1986). Diagnostik der operativen Intelligenz [Diagnosis of operative intelligence]. *Diagnostica, 32*, 290–308.

Dörner, D. (1992). Über die Philosophie der Verwendung von Mikrowelten oder "Computerszenarios" in der psychologischen Forschung [On the proper use of microworlds or "computer scenarios" in psychological research]. In H. Gundlach (Ed.), *Psychologische Forschung und Methode: Das Versprechen des Experiments. Festschrift für Werner Traxel* (pp. 53–87). Passau, Germany: Passavia-Universitäts-Verlag.

Dörner, D., & Kreuzig, H. W. (1983). Problemlösefähigkeit und Intelligenz [Problem solving ability and intelligence]. *Psychologische Rundschau, 34*, 185–192.

Dörner, D., Kreuzig, H. W., Reither, F., & Stäudel, T. (1983). Lohhausen. Vom Umgang mit Unbestimmtheit und Komplexität [Lohhausen. On dealing with uncertainty and complexity]. Bern, Switzerland: Hans Huber.

Dörner, D., & Pfeifer, E. (1993). Strategisches Denken, strategische Fehler, Streß und Intelligenz [Strategic thinking, strategic errors, stress, and intelligence]. *Sprache & Kognition, 11,* 75–90.

Ferguson, G. A. (1954). On transfer and the abilities of man. *Canadian Journal of Psychology, 8,* 95–113.

Fillbrandt, H. (1992). Zur Methode der Erforschung von Problemlöseprozessen [On the method of exploring problem solving processes]. *Zeitschrift für Psychologie, 200,* 3–18.

Funke, J. (1984). Diagnose der westdeutschen Problemlöseforschung in Form einiger Thesen [Assessment of West German problem solving research]. *Sprache & Kognition, 3,* 159–172.

Funke, J. (1986). *Komplexes Problemlösen. Bestandsaufnahme und Perspektiven* [Complex problem solving. Overview and perspectives]. Heidelberg, Germany: Springer.

Funke, J. (1990). Systemmerkmale als Determinanten des Umgangs mit dynamischen Systemen [System features as determinants of behavior in dynamic task environments]. *Sprache & Kognition, 9,* 143–153.

Funke, J. (1991a). Keine Struktur im (selbstverursachten) Chaos? Erwiderung zum Kommentar von Stefan Strohschneider [No structure in (self-induced) chaos? A reply to the comment by Stefan Strohschneider]. *Sprache & Kognition, 10,* 114–118.

Funke, J. (1991b). Solving complex problems: Exploration and control of complex systems. In R. J. Sternberg & P. A. Frensch (Eds.), *Complex problem solving: Principles and mechanisms* (pp. 185–222). Hillsdale, NJ: Lawrence Erlbaum Associates.

Funke, J. (1992a). Dealing with dynamic systems: Research strategy, diagnostic approach and experimental results. *The German Journal of Psychology, 16,* 24–43.

Funke, J. (1992b). *Wissen über dynamische Systeme: Erwerb, Repräsentation und Anwendung* [Knowledge about dynamic systems: Acquisition, representation, and use]. Heidelberg, Germany: Springer.

Funke, J. (1993). Microworlds based on linear equation systems: A new approach to complex problem solving and experimental results. In G. Strube & K. F. Wender (Eds.), *The cognitive psychology of knowledge* (pp. 313–330). Amsterdam: Elsevier Science Publishers.

Guthke, J. (1972). *Zur Diagnostik der intellektuellen Lernfähigkeit* [On the diagnosis of intellectual learning ability]. Berlin: Deutscher Verlag der Wissenschaften.

Guthke, J. (1977). *Zur Diagnostik der intellektuellen Lernfähigkeit* [On the diagnosis of intellectual learning ability]. Stuttgart, Germany: Klett.

Guthke, J. (1985). Ein neuer Ansatz für die rehabilitationspsychologisch orientierte Psychodiagnostik—das Lerntestkonzept als Alternative zum herkömmlichen Intelligenztest [A new approach in psychodiagnostics from the viewpoint of rehabilitation psychology—The learning test concept as an alternative to the conventional intelligence test]. In K. H. Wiedl (Ed.), *Rehabilitationspsychologie* (pp. 177–194). Stuttgart, Germany: Kohlhammer.

Guthke, J. (1992). Learning Tests—The concept, main research findings, problems, and trends. *Learning and Individual Differences, 4,* 137–152.

Guthke, J., Jäger, C., & Schmidt, I. (1983). *Lerntest "Schlußfolgerndes Denken" (LTS)* [Learning test "Reasoning"]. Berlin: Psychodiagnostisches Zentrum der Humboldt-Universität.

Guthke, J., & Lehwald, G. (1984). On component analysis of the intellectual learning tests. *Zeitschrift für Psychologie, 192,* 3–17.

Guthke, J., & Löffler, M. (1983). A diagnostic program (learning test) for the differential assessment of school failure in first grade pupils. In H. D. Rösler, J. P. Das, & I. Wald (Eds.), *Mental and language retardation* (pp. 41–50). Berlin: Deutscher Verlag der Wissenschaften.

Guthke, J., Räder, E., Caruso, M., & Schmidt, K.-D. (1991). Entwicklung eines adaptiven computergestützten Lerntests auf der Basis der strukturellen Informationstheorie [Development of an adaptive computer-based learning test based on structural information theory]. *Diagnostica, 37,* 1–28.

Hamers, J. H. M., Sijtsma, K., & Ruijssenaars, A. J. J. M. (Eds.). (1993). *Learning potential assessment*. Amsterdam: Swets & Zeitlinger.

Haywood, H. C., & Tzuriel, D. (Eds.). (1992). *Interactive assessment*. New York: Springer.

Hörmann, H.-J., & Thomas, M. (1989). Zum Zusammenhang zwischen Intelligenz und komplexem Problemlösen [On the relation between intelligence and complex problem solving]. *Sprache & Kognition, 8*, 23–31.

Hornke, L. F. (1976). *Grundlagen und Probleme antwortabhängiger Testverfahren* [Foundations and problems of response-related test procedures]. Frankfurt, Germany: Haag und Herchen.

Hussy, W. (1985). Komplexes Problemlösen—Eine Sackgasse? [Complex problem solving—A dead end?]. *Zeitschrift für Experimentelle und Angewandte Psychologie, 32*, 55–77.

Hussy, W. (1989). Intelligenz und komplexes Problemlösen [Intelligence and complex problem solving]. *Diagnostica, 35*, 1–16.

Hussy, W. (1992). *Denken und Problemlösen* [Thinking and problem solving]. Stuttgart, Germany: Kohlhammer.

Jäger, A. O. (1982). Mehrmodale Klassifikation von Intelligenztestleistungen. Experimentell kontrollierte Weiterentwicklung eines deskriptiven Intelligenzstrukturmodells [Multimodal classification of performance in intelligence tests]. *Diagnostica, 28*, 195–226.

Jäger, A. O. (1991). Beziehungen zwischen komplexem Problemlösen und Intelligenz—Eine Einleitung [Relations between complex problem solving and intelligence—An introduction]. *Diagnostica, 37*, 287–290.

Klauer, K. J. (1984). Kontentvalidität [Content validity]. *Diagnostica, 30*, 1–23.

Klix, F. (1983). Begabungsforschung—ein neuer Weg in der kognitiven Intelligenzdiagnostik? [Research on giftedness—a new avenue in cognitive intelligence assessment?]. *Zeitschrift für Psychologie, 191*, 360–387.

Klix, F., & Lander, J. (1967). Die Strukturanalyse von Denkprozessen als Mittel der Intelligenzdiagnostik [The structural analysis of thought processes as an instrument of intelligence assessment]. In F. Klix, W. Gutjahr, & J. Mehl (Eds.), *Intelligenzdiagnostik* (pp. 245–271). Berlin: Deutscher Verlag der Wissenschaften.

Kluwe, R. H., Schilde, A., Fischer, C., & Oellerer, N. (1991). Problemlöseleistungen beim Umgang mit komplexen Systemen und Intelligenz [Problem solving performance when interacting with complex systems and intelligence]. *Diagnostica, 37*, 291–313.

Lidz, C. S. (1987) (Ed.). *Dynamic assessment. An interactional approach to evaluating learning potential*. New York: Guilford Press.

Lidz, C. S. (1991). *Practitioner's guide to dynamic assessment*. New York: Guilford Press.

Minick, N. (1987). Implications of Vygotsky's theories for dynamic assessment. In C. S. Lidz (Ed.), *Dynamic assessment: An interactional approach to evaluating learning potential* (pp. 116–140). New York: Guilford Press.

Müller, H. (1993). *Komplexes Problemlösen: Reliabilität und Wissen* [Complex problem solving: Reliability and knowledge]. Bonn, Germany: Holos.

Putz-Osterloh, W. (1981). *Problemlöseprozesse und Intelligenztestleistung* [Problem solving processes and performance in intelligence tests]. Bern, Switzerland: Hans Huber.

Putz-Osterloh, W., & Lüer, G. (1981). Über die Vorhersagbarkeit komplexer Problemlöseleistungen durch Ergebnisse in einem Intelligenztest [On whether results from a test of intelligence can predict problem solving performance]. *Zeitschrift für Experimentelle und Angewandte Psychologie, 28*, 309–334.

Raaheim, K. (1978). *Problem solving and intelligence*. Bergen, Norway: Universitetsforlaget.

Raaheim, K. (1990). Intelligence and problem solving: Intelligent behavior in daily life. In D. Frey (Ed.), *Bericht über den 37. Kongreß der Deutschen Gesellschaft für Psychologie in Kiel. Vol. 2* (pp. 97–107). Göttingen, Germany: Hogrefe.

Raven, J. C. (1965). *Advanced progressive matrices. Sets I and II. Plan and use of the scale with a report of experimental work*. London: Lewis.

Rubinstein, S. L. (1961). *Das Denken und die Wege seiner Erforschung* [Thinking and ways to investigate it]. Berlin: Volk und Wissen.

Schmidt, L. R. (1971). Testing the Limits im Leistungsverhalten: Möglichkeiten und Grenzen [Testing the Limits in performance testing]. In E. Duhm (Ed.), *Praxis der klinischen Psychologie* (pp. 2–29). Göttingen, Germany: Hogrefe.

Snodgrass, J. G., & Corwin, J. (1988). Pragmatics of measuring recognition memory: Applications to dementia and amnesia. *Journal of Experimental Psychology: General, 117,* 34–50.

Stein, H. (1993). *Entwicklung eines fehlerorientiert adaptiven, computergestützten Lerntests mit verbalen Analogien* [Construction of a failure-adaptive, computer-assisted learning test with verbal analogies]. Unpublished doctoral dissertation, Universität Leipzig, Leipzig, Germany.

Sternberg, R. J. (1982). Reasoning, problem soving, and intelligence. In R. J. Sternberg (Ed.), *Handbook of human intelligence* (pp. 225–240). New York: Cambridge University Press.

Sternberg, R. J. (1985). *Beyond IQ. A triarchic theory of human intelligence.* New York: Cambridge University Press.

Strohschneider, S. (1986). Zur Stabilität und Validität von Handeln in komplexen Realitätsbereichen [On the stability and validity of action in complex domains of reality]. *Sprache & Kognition, 5,* 42–48.

Strohschneider, S. (1991). Problemlösen und Intelligenz: Über die Effekte der Konkretisierung komplexer Probleme [Problem solving and intelligence: The effects of problem concreteness]. *Diagnostica, 37,* 353–371.

Süß, H.-M., Kersting, M., & Oberauer, K. (1991). Intelligenz und Wissen als Prädiktoren für Leistungen bei computersimulierten komplexen Problemen [Intelligence and knowledge as predictors of performance in solving complex computer-simulated problems]. *Diagnostica, 37,* 334–352.

Tent, L. (1984). Intelligenz und Problemlösefähigkeit. Kommentar zu Dörner & Kreuzig [Intelligence and problem solving. Comment on Dörner & Kreuzig]. *Psychologische Rundschau, 35,* 152–153.

Vygotsky, L. S. (1964). *Denken und Sprechen* [Thinking and speaking]. Berlin: Akademie-Verlag (Original work published in Russian in 1934).

Weiss, D. J. (1985). Adaptive testing by computer. *Journal of Counseling and Clinical Psychology, 53,* 774–789.

Wittmann, W. W., & Matt, G. E. (1986). Aggregation und Symmetrie. Grundlage einer multivariaten Reliabilitäts- und Validitätstheorie, dargestellt am Beispiel der differentiellen Validität [Aggregation and symmetry. Foundations of a multivariate theory of reliability and validity, exemplified with the concept of differential validity]. *Diagnostica, 32,* 309–329.

CHAPTER EIGHT

Cognitive Flexibility and Complex Problem Solving

Josef F. Krems
University of Regensburg, Germany

INTRODUCTION

To behave effectively in a changing environment requires an information processing system that can easily adapt to new tasks and to new situations. This ability depends on the degree of flexibility of the system. A highly flexible system can adapt to a variety of new conditions, whereas an inflexible or rigid one is limited to a comparatively small set. At a very general

201

level, to be flexible one needs to acquire new skills and relevant knowledge very quickly in unknown situations as well as to transfer and adjust already available knowledge so that it meets the demands of the new situation. In a strict sense, it may be necessary to modify strategies and procedures in every problem-solving situation. By definition, to solve a problem, contrary to just performing a task, requires more than just bringing to bear prior acquired knowledge. In many cases, finding a solution requires changing the point of view, as in the candle problem (Duncker, 1935), changing mental representations, as in the mutilated checkerboard problem (see Anderson, 1990, p. 245), or changing strategies, for example, switching from a goal-driven to a more data-driven procedure.

I mainly address here how flexible behavior is related to the availability of domain knowledge. As a subclass of complex problems, I will primarily deal with abductive reasoning tasks, especially in the domains of clinical reasoning, trouble-shooting, and debugging.

COGNITIVE FLEXIBILITY, COMPLEX PROBLEM SOLVING, AND EXPERTISE

Cognitive Flexibility

Cognitive flexibility can be defined as a person's ability to adjust his or her problem solving as task demands are modified. Flexibility refers to the selection and/or modification of available problem solving techniques, methods, or strategies as a function of changes of the task or situation. As a result, task requirements and problem solving can be closely tuned which improves problem solving performance. There appear to be at least three task-dependent mechanisms that are important for flexible problem solving (see Krems, 1994). For each mechanism, it is important not only that the agent has choices but that he or she is able to make the right choices.

The first is multiple interpretations of data. A flexible problem solver is able to consider several alternative interpretations of a given situation. When the situation warrants a change, the problem solver is able to switch from one interpretation to another.

Second is modifying representations. A flexible problem solver chooses an appropriate representation for the task and current situation, for example, between a concrete or abstract representation, a functional or structural representation, or a principle-oriented or surface-oriented representation.

Third is modification of strategies. A flexible problem solver can change strategies to reflect changes in resources and task demands. These strategy changes might reflect resource usage, or the basic problem solving approach (e.g., from a more goal-oriented to a more data-oriented approach, from a top down to a bottom up, from an exploratory to a confirmatory strategy).

Psychological studies on flexibility versus rigidity, as with most topics of modern cognitive psychology, can be traced back to the Würzburg school and the Gestalt psychologists (see Hörmann, 1955, for a review of the early literature). Especially the work on sets (Einstellungen) and their perseverative effect showed that behavior cannot be explained just by the strength of associations. Selz (1913) claimed that productive thinking depends on the ability to transfer known problem solutions to methods that can be applied for deriving new insights.

Wertheimer (1925) introduced the concept of restructuring (Umzentrierung) or *structural reorganization* (1945, p. 73). Using examples from mathematics, he showed how modifying the point of view could affect one's ability to find problem solutions. Wertheimer emphasized that reorganization is not an arbitrary transition from one representation to another; rather, it stems from the functional requirements of the structure of the task. Duncker (1935) also analyzed functional fixedness and restructuring. In his theory, restructuring is the modification of the functional value (Funktionalwert) of elements of the givens in a problem situation. He discussed two hypotheses in order to explain the cause of the inability to restructure: the fixedness of the problem solver to the perceptual structure of the task and the rigidity of the knowledge representation. "The *poor* mathematician is not able to restructure so easily because his thought material is relatively inelastic, rigid, and therefore not sufficiently plastic to be reshaped" (Duncker, 1935/1945, p. 110). Functional fixedness may also result from expectations about the conventional way to find a solution based on training or recent experiences, called set or Einstellungs-effects. Luchins (1942) found that procedures that proved efficient in some situations also were used in situations in which much more adequate methods were available. One early definition of flexibility was based on subjects' ability to modify task-dependent sets (e.g., Süllwold, 1959). Luchins and Luchins (1959) also proposed psychometric procedures to assess a subjects' degree of mental flexibility. Other questionnaires or tests to assess cognitive or behavioral flexibility were developed by Cattell and Eber (1962), Amthauer (1973), and Bitterwolf (1992).

In factor analytic approaches, plasticity and restructuring were also extensively discussed as crucial components of human intelligent behavior. For example, *plasticity* in Meili's theory of intelligence (Meili, 1951) refers to people's ability to adapt to modifications in tasks. Also, Thurstone's (1944) concepts of *flexibility of closure* and *speed of closure* as parts of the primary mental abilities deal with the ease and speed in reinterpreting a set of data. In Guilford's (1959) theory, *cognitive flexibility* is considered a precondition of creative behavior. The definition of flexibility emphasizes the change of current beliefs and strategies of the problem solver. In Rozin's (1976) evolutionary theory of intelligence, flexibility is considered an essential feature of a highly developed species. Flexibility—together with proceduralization—

also plays a major role in Sternberg's (1988) concept of intelligence. According to Sternberg, intelligent thinking (i.e., the activation of intelligence in a problem solving context), is essentially bound to flexible information access. Yet it is still unclear whether flexibility should be considered a separate, genuine factor of intelligence (Sternberg, 1988) or whether flexibility depends on domain-specific knowledge as has been stated by Howe (1988).

In research on the psychology of personality, factor-analytic techniques were used to identify dimensions of cognitive control, which, taken together, may be called cognitive styles. Flexible versus constrained control or field-dependency versus field-independence were considered major factors (see Graumann, 1966, for a review).

Complex Problem Solving

A problem is called *complex* if both the goal state and the initial state are clearly defined, and if (a) there is no precise definition of the problem-space (i.e., a complete list of state attributes and their possible values is not available) and, (b) there is no precise definition of the operators that are available (i.e., what can be done).

Both (a) and (b) depend on *domain-specific features* (e.g., the context, the number and connectivity of relevant variables, the number of exceptions) and on the *level of expertise* (i.e., amount of knowledge about these domain-specific features) of the problem solver. For example, debugging computer programs can be considered a complex problem because the elements that belong to the problem space depend on situational variables that cannot be stated in the general problem definition, but that affect the solution process (e.g., type of hardware, specificity of debugging tools, *typical* bugs depending on the level of expertise of the program's author).

In general, complex problem solving (henceforth CPS) is viewed as more or less equivalent to problem solving in semantically rich domains or in knowledge-rich tasks (Simon, 1979). This is—at a knowledge level—equivalent to the standard definition of complex problems given by Funke (1991). Funke claims that problems are complex because of the intransparency, polytely, number and connectivity of variables, dynamic developments and/or time-delayed effects. From a knowledge-level point of view, these features lead to a situation in which the elements of the problem space and the applicable operators are unclear for a problem solver.

At a first glance, a high degree of flexibility seems to be required to solve a complex problem. One essential characteristic of complexity is the lack of a clear description of the problem space or the availability of general, task-independent algorithms. Therefore, in defining and finding *new* ways to solve a problem, cognitive flexibility seems to be a necessary ability. Schmuck (1992) found that in a microworld setting (FIRE FIGHTING) subjects with a high degree of strategic flexibility are better problem solvers. But in other studies (e.g., Dörner, 1986) no correlation could be detected between measures of general mental abilities like flexibility and the quality of subjects' problem solutions.

Expertise

Expertise refers to the domain-specific problem-solving abilities of a person. These consist of task and domain-related skills and knowledge that enable a problem solver to consistently reach an outstanding level of performance. In research on the nature of expertise, different answers have been found to the question of whether flexibility is more typical for experts or novices. One would—at first glance again—expect that flexibility should primarily be a characteristic of experts. They are able to use their knowledge in different situations for varying needs and can therefore cover a broader range of problems. In Spiro's cognitive flexibility theory (Spiro et al., 1991), a multifaceted knowledge representation which enhances transfer between different contexts is considered a crucial feature of expertise. Egan and Greeno (1973) found that experts' long-term knowledge is more accessible and therefore also more available for different purposes. In contrast, Frensch and Sternberg (1989, p. 164) claim: ". . . that inflexibility and expertise are inextricably linked." They summarize different findings from memory research that suggest that domain knowledge, especially in highly automated procedures, can produce inflexible behavior. In their own experiments, Frensch and Sternberg (1989) investigated the consequences of modifying surface versus structural features of a task. They found that highly trained subjects were more affected by structural modifications than were novices. Experts who had proceduralized their knowledge reacted less flexibly and were more affected by changes of the general principles that were necessary for solving the task. Also, Anzai and Yokoyama (1984) found that experts modify the mental representation of a task less often than intermediates do. Charness and Bieman-Copland (1992), on the other hand, reason that experts may develop multiple representations for a problem, allowing them to find a solution by operating at different levels of abstraction.

In summary, there are contradictory predictions and findings concerning whether domain knowledge, especially for highly automatized skills, leads to more flexible or to more rigid problem solving behavior. It appears that flexibility is domain dependent and perhaps even task dependent within a domain. In the following section I take a closer look at a specific domain and specific task, and will discuss some of my own experimental research on expertise and flexibility in diagnostic reasoning. The general goal of this ongoing research has been to enlarge the defining features of expertise in terms of characteristics of the cognitive system. Up until now, levels of expertise have been primarily distinguished by using external features like the number of years of experience and of job-related training, criteria that do not guarantee expertise by themselves although they normally correlate with the degree of expertise.

COGNITIVE FLEXIBILITY IN DIAGNOSTIC REASONING

The main goal of a diagnostic task is to find plausible categorizations or explanations for a set of observations. The process of diagnosis is normally referred to as abduction (Peng & Reggia, 1990). From an information processing point of view, abduction can be viewed as the sequential comprehension and integration of data into a single situation model that represents the currently best explanation of the data. Based on Funke's (1991) definition, abductive reasoning can be considered a subclass of CPS. The underlying situation is, by definition, *intransparent*: that is, only symptoms are available and causes have to be inferred. In addition, the connectivity pattern between causes and evidences (i.e., medical diagnosis) is normally highly complex. We assume that the development of expertise based on intensive training and practice includes the extension of the knowledge base as well as the construction of a knowledge organization that is adjusted to the specific needs and requirements of the most frequently encountered problem solving situations. Abductive reasoning is nonmonotonic, meaning that there is no general algorithm that guarantees truth-preserving conclusions. This also means that the best explanations have to be considered the most plausible *assumptions* that connect evidences and diagnostic categories. One feature of expertise, therefore, should be to take into account that conclusions might turn out wrong; one should be aware of exceptional cases, consider plausible differential diagnoses, and so on. Because of these characteristics of the domain, experts should be more flexible in modifying their current diagnostic assumptions.

In what follows, I report some experimental findings with regard to this general prediction. Notice that flexibility in modifying assumptions should also counteract the so-called confirmation bias. Experimental results relevant to this hypothesis are described. And, finally, in order to examine the generality of the findings across different domains, results from studies are presented that investigated troubleshooting and computer program debugging.

Flexibility in Hypothesis Modification

Efficient diagnostic reasoning in *semantically rich domains* is essentially constrained by the generation and examination of diagnostic hypotheses. Feltovich, Johnson, Moller, and Swanson (1984), Groen and Patel (1988), and others found no differences between novices and experts in the frequency and type of concepts employed in diagnostic problem solving in the medical domain, although differences were found in the substance and the quality of concepts.

We assume that at least some of the obtained differences between experts' and novices' solutions can be traced to the modification of hypotheses. By generating a larger number of assumptions during diagnostic reasoning, a larger number of alternatives can be inspected, thereby raising the probability of considering the correct element. The modification of hypotheses includes not only the exchange of elements within the set of hypotheses being considered but also their order with respect to the probability of correctness. Because of experienced problem solvers elaborate knowledge structures (cf. Glaser, 1989), wherein diagnostic categories are closely knit, be it by symptoms, cause, or form of treatment, experts can easily shift from one schema to another when interpreting data. They also rarely have the problem of overemphasizing the correlation within small sets of data, as suggested by Murphy and Wright (1984) as typical of early learning phases.

In general, an inverted u-shaped relation between the predictive value of symptoms and the flexibility in data interpretation might be expected. Flexibility is not to be expected if the prognostic value of data is comparatively high or low. In the former case, the findings are clearly defined with no need for alternative interpretations; in the latter case, the number of possibilities is too large for subjects to be able to come up with a reasonable diagnostic category. Because experts' knowledge contains highly connected elements, we expect that when confronted with fuzzy or ambiguous items they will consider multiple interpretations of the situation. Less experienced diagnosticians, due to a more rigid knowledge organization and processing strategy, will in contrast, tend to focus on single categories. Despite disconfirming some facts, novices' lack of knowledge of alternatives should force them to hold a single hypothesis longer than experts. These assumptions were confirmed in an experimental study (Krems & Prechtl, 1991). Participants in the experiment were 10 experienced diagnosticians (with an average age of 38; length of practical experience 10.3 years; with a maximum of 13 and a minimum of 5 years) and 10 diagnosticians who were new to the field. None of the beginners had more than one year of experience and all had completed the university degree in clinical psychology no more than a year prior to the study.

Two patient histories were used to describe a fictitious patient with various symptoms. In the first patient history (A), the highly diagnostic information was presented at the beginning; in the other history (B), it was presented at the end. Thus, in condition A the pertinent diagnostic category could be recognized after analyzing only a small amount of data at the beginning of the case. In the second condition, identification was possible only after receiving the last items.

The items of the patient history were presented to the subjects in succession. The subjects were asked to concurrently verbalize their thoughts and conclusions referring to diagnostic categories. Following the presentation of the last item, subjects had to give a summarizing diagnostic decision of the entire case. They also had to choose categories from a diagnostic list containing 40 items from the ICD (International Classification of Diseases, chapter V, Dilling, Mombour, & Schmidt, 1991). The 40 nosological categories, symptoms, and syndromes were classified in a 4-level hierarchy.

We found that the number of diagnostic hypotheses did not depend on the subjects' experience level, but did depend on the predictability of the symptoms. This was true only for the verbal protocols, however. In addition, novices and experts did not differ in the number of assumptions they checked after every item.

However, in their concluding diagnostic decision, experts generated a larger number of plausible explanations. The less experienced subjects tended to rely more rigorously on single diagnostic categories as a comprehensive conclusion of all patient symptoms.

In condition A with the predictive items at the beginning, experts and novices did not differ in the degree of specificity of their hypotheses. In contrast, in condition B with the unpredictive items at the beginning, experts generated hypotheses at a more specific hierarchy level than novices.

On average, in the first and middle phase of the process of diagnostic reasoning a greater number of hypotheses were generated. Again, we found no correlation between competence level and phase of hypothesis generation.

In summary, the main differences between experts and novices were found in the summarizing diagnostic decision. Experts consider a greater number of diagnoses than do novices. This can be interpreted as verification of the concept of cognitive flexibility. In general, we conclude that the limitations of the novices with regard to their final diagnostic decision cannot be traced to a higher certainty in their judgment, but is probably due to a categorical decision on their part to reject or accept the current hypothesis. With reference to the work of Feltovich et al. (1982) and Murphy and Wright (1984), it seems likely that novices knowledge is organized around textbook cases with few interconnections. Therefore, competing diagnoses cancel each other out. If more than one of these patterns are activated, novices, more than experts, tend to integrate subsequent information with the already established interpretation. If this fails, another hypothesis is selected. Novices consider alternative explanations but reject them by the time they make a conclusive decision. However, experts knowledge also contains information about overlapping areas. Therefore, it is easier for them to consider diagnostic categories which are treated as mutually exclusive categories for novices.

Confirmation Bias

If one can show that a subject seeks, weights, or remembers confirming information of hypotheses more than disconfirming information, than a confirmation bias can be stated (see Fiedler, 1983). Confirmation bias also refers to hypothesis-testing strategies that can lead to an unwarranted belief in a hypothesis (Klayman & Ha, 1987). The less flexible a person is in modifying diagnostic assumptions, the higher her or his chances for a confirmation bias. It could be shown that this bias is weakened if plausible alternatives are available or if the person can rely on problem solving experiences (Gadenne & Oswald, 1986). This leads one to assume that the confirmation bias may be reduced with increased domain knowledge. Using a medical domain, we investigated whether the confirmation bias depends on the degree of domain-knowledge, and if so, if this knowledge is task-dependent, domain-dependent, or both (Krems & Zierer, 1994).

Four groups of subjects (n = 32) with varying degrees of medical education and experience were recruited:

- 8 experts experienced (14.5 years of job experience) in internal medicine.
- 8 novices inexperienced (job experience: 2.6 years) in internal medicine.
- 8 experts experienced (job experience: 13.7 years) in neurology.
- 8 novices inexperienced (job experience: 4.7 years) in neurology.

The subjects had to diagnose medical cases from internal medicine. Therefore, the subjects in groups one and two were the high-domain knowledge experts for solving the problem and subjects in groups three and four the low-domain knowledge experts. Both cases consisted of symptoms, a preliminary diagnostic hypothesis, and a correct final diagnosis. Case A consisted of 27 symptoms (preliminary hypothesis: Asthma bronchiale, final diagnosis: heart failure). Case B consisted of 22 symptoms (preliminary hypothesis: Hepatitis; final diagnosis: obstruction due to Cholelithiasis). Every case contained symptoms, which, (a) supported the preliminary hypothesis (3 in case A, 3 in Case B); (b) supported both hypotheses (8 in case A, 10 in Case B); (c) supported the final hypothesis (7 in case A, 4 in Case B); (d) supported the final hypothesis strongly (9 in case A, 5 in Case B).

A preliminary diagnosis was provided and the subjects had to assess the symptoms according to the existing diagnosis or to an alternative diagnosis they could provide.

We found that subjects did not differ in the number of correct final diagnostic conclusions. Thus, even inexperienced low-domain knowledge subjects had enough domain knowledge to solve the experimental tasks.

As might be expected, high-domain knowledge experts developed more coherent pathophysiological explanations, and modified their diagnostic assumptions earlier. Figure 8.1 shows the average number of single symptoms that had to be given to the four groups of subjects before they switched from one hypothesis to another. An analysis of variance (ANOVA) showed significant effects only for the factor domain-knowledge, but not for the factor experience. It could also be shown that high-domain knowledge subjects' judgment remained more stable. Sequential models of categorical regression revealed that experts categorized symptoms that could have supported the preliminary or the alternative hypotheses as weakening the preliminary assumption. The pathophysiological explanations, developed as concluding summaries of the data, were categorized according to the degree of coherence. Log-linear analyses of the dependency structure of the factors (domain-knowledge, experience, and coherence) showed again that only the degree of domain-knowledge covaries with highly coherent explanations.

In summary, high-domain knowledge experts seem to have less of a confirmation bias than intermediates or novices. This difference does not appear to be caused by differences in amount of domain knowledge, but rather by a more case-based representation of the medical knowledge including counter-examples and exceptions (see also Boshuizen & Schmidt, 1992) on the part of the experts. A more flexible manner to modify and change diagnostic assumptions is therefore facilitated.

Abductive Reasoning in Trouble-Shooting

Previously we stated that flexibility in problem solving also encompasses the selection and application of solution strategies. This assumption was investigated in the context of automotive trouble-shooting (Krems & Bachmeier, 1991). A second goal of this study was to reexamine our previous conclusions in a domain that was outside medical diagnosis. We assumed that competence groups would differ in the number of generated hypotheses that relate nonspecific symptoms to causes (see Feltovich et al., 1984; Mehle, 1982). We also expected novices to be less flexible in the interpretation of

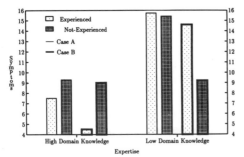

FIG. 8.1. Average number of inspected symptoms before the alternative diagnosis is considered. Data are from four groups of subjects with high- versus low-domain knowledge and with high versus low experience diagnosing medical cases.

data. After having selected a single diagnostic category, they would retain the assumption for a longer time than experts. Experts would be more flexible with their diagnostic assumptions and would be affected by a confirmation bias to a lesser degree than novices. We also expected differences in the breadth and depth of experts' and novices' search.

The experiment consisted of two phases. In the first phase, the subjects were asked to name all known causes for a certain defect. In the second phase, three malfunctions were displayed by means of a variant of the tab item technique (Glaser, Damrin, & Gardner, 1954). The subjects were presented with 91 cards grouped into six categories: electricity, ignition device, motor and motor control, fuel supply, voltage generator, and general data. The top of the cards contained information that could be asked for. The bottom of the cards contained the respective information. The cards were classified using a three-level hierarchy of specificity. The general task of the subjects was to find the cause of a malfunction by verifying their assumptions and getting specific information through inspecting the cards. The list of cards inspected allowed us to reconstruct subjects' diagnostic assumptions and their switching between categories and specificity levels.

Sixty subjects from the motor vehicle branch participated in the experiment. Dependent on qualification and degree of job experience, they were assigned to three groups of 20 subjects each.

The first group consisted of novices; trainees in the third year of education with no job experience (mean age = 18.15 years).

The second group was intermediates; employees with job experience of several years (mean age = 29.95 years; mean experience = 9 years, minimum = 2 years, maximum = 28 years).

The third group was experts; chief mechanics with job experience of several years and with advanced additional trainings (mean age = 31.5 years; mean experience = 11.1 years, minimum = 4 years, maximum = 35 years).

For the first phase of the experiment, a very nonspecific malfunction was selected: motor knocks when running idle. Many possible alternatives can explain the cause of this car trouble. For the presentation of symptoms by means of the tab item technique, three malfunctions were defined (poor performance in all areas; motor staggers when running idle; vehicle doesn't start).

For the nonspecific car malfunction, we found that job experience was inversely proportional to the number of assumptions that subjects considered as plausible causes. The expert group considered, on the average, 6.9 causes, the intermediates 9.0 and the novices 9.5. This difference was statistically not significant, however. However, the correlation between years of job experience and number of hypotheses was significant. We found that the number of card selections decreased with the competence level.

The number of requested data (i.e., the number of cards checked) can be interpreted as a measure of subjects' solution effort for solving the problem. This number decreased with the competence level. Experts showed a shorter search path to the correct solution.

The number of possible explanations for the malfunction in the experiment (first phase) and the number of cards selected (second phase) are commonly related to the competence dimension.

The search depth concerns the specificity of the hypotheses. Within the five categories, every card was constructed at one of three specificity levels. An example for the most global level is: defect in the fuel system. An example for the most specific level is: pilot jet contaminated. Experts more often selected cards from the most specific level; novices considered data from all three levels.

The search breadth—the number of categories from which information was requested—depended on the competence level. Experts' solutions possessed the smallest breadth.

We also investigated how many data were successively selected from one category before an alternative hypothesis was considered. If one uses, out of all selections, only those in which more than four cards from one category were inspected in succession, only 4 examples from the expert group, 23 from the intermediates, and 48 from the novices could be found. The mean length of selection sequences was 4.5 for the experts, 5.0 for the intermediates, and 5.5 for the novices. A low level of expertise is associated with a higher fixation on a selected category. Experts modify and change their hypotheses comparatively earlier (see Figure 8.2).

In accordance with Mehle's (1982) findings but contrary to the results from our first study, we found that experts verify hypotheses in a more limited search space. This result can be interpreted as evidence for a depth first search strategy in contrast to the breadth first strategy used by novices. When considering this finding in light of the limitation of the search space, one has to assume a tuning of the domain knowledge with mounting experience (Rumelhart & Norman, 1978). Confronted with very nonspecific symptoms, the expert's set of hypotheses is relatively small, thus allowing them to use a positive test strategy for their assumptions. When confronted with disconfirming data, the experts change assumptions earlier than novices do.

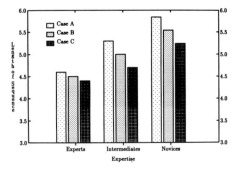

FIG. 8.2. Average number of inspected data before a diagnostic assumption is modified. Data are from three competence groups diagnosing faults (three cases) in a technical device.

Computer Program Debugging

Program debugging is an abductive task in which a problem solver attempts to find an explanation (e.g., a line of code) for certain symptoms (e.g., an error message). The task can be conceptualized as a goal-directed search through a computer program. Symptoms are error messages, differences between intended and observed program results, results from tests or mental evaluation of code segments, and so on. A goal state is reached if the debugger is able to explain why the expected result cannot be produced by the given program and when the incorrect code segment can be named.

Experimental studies suggest that experts do not generate better initial hypotheses than novices (Vessey, 1989), but are able to modify their error related assumptions in a much more flexible manner. Experts' strategies in this domain do not appear to be organized according to a hierarchical structure. A rigid, pattern like approach is more typical for beginners. An experts' way of proceeding in program analysis is based on *local* information combined with prototypical knowledge for hypothesis generation and for guiding the search in program texts (cf. Katz & Anderson, 1988). Adelson (1984) found that in the analysis of programs, experts focus on the algorithm or the goal (i.e., what a program does), whereas novices concentrate on the process (i.e., how a program works) or on surface features. Experts also identify and analyze significant and important code segments more quickly than nonexperts do (Mehmanesh & Krems, 1988). Generally, debugging success essentially depends on the availability, choice, and flexible modification of search strategies (see Gilmore, 1990).

SUMMARY AND CONCLUSIONS

Previously I addressed the general question of how flexibility in CPS is connected to expertise. A special class of problems was considered for which the definition of the problem space and of the operators depends on domain knowledge. The complexity of these problems depends on the amount of knowledge that can be brought to bear during problem solving. Therefore, one might expect both qualitative and quantitative aspects of CPS to be affected by expertise, the domain-specific knowledge and skills, of a problem solver. Expertise should also covary with cognitive flexibility, which refers to a person's ability to adjust available problem solving means to new situations. This general assumption was investigated for abductive reasoning problems. The experimental studies on flexibility in clinical reasoning, troubleshooting, and debugging showed concordant and discordant results: For example, in debugging, a more breadth first strategy, whereas in troubleshooting a more depth first strategy was observed for experts. In the medical domain, the number of diagnostic hypotheses did not depend on the level of expertise whereas these two variables were negatively correlated in the technical domain. These contradictions encourage a research strategy that clarifies the interaction between task and domain-specificities and problem-solving behavior. For example, in the technical domain, a reasonable approach to trouble-shooting is to make inferences from the developers' design-principles (e.g., functionality, performance, costs) to structural features of a device. This kind of reasoning is impossible in medical diagnostic reasoning.

The following results were consistently obtained for all the domains:

- Experts tend to modify their current diagnostic hypotheses more often during diagnostic reasoning than novices. This was shown in the first and second study.

- Experts tend to use a positive test strategy to a lesser degree. This conclusion is based on the study on troubleshooting and on the confirmation bias.

- The ability to flexibly change assumptions is likely based on case-based knowledge and does not appear to be a domain-general ability.

The empirical results also suggest that cognitive flexibility is positively correlated with expertise. Contrary to Frensch and Sternberg's (1989) view, I conclude that domain knowledge does not obstruct people in adapting and adjusting their problem solving abilities to new constraints. One reason for the apparent contradiction in findings might be that the subjects in Frensch and Sternberg's study had to solve problems in novel tasks in which they could not truly be considered experts. In our studies, however, the tasks remained *typical* for a domain. Another methodological explanation that holds true for most *contrastive* studies on the nature of expertise can also be stressed for our experiments: The number of subjects is comparatively small and differs between studies. Subjects who differ in their levels of expertise clearly do not only differ in years of training or job-related education but also in age, social status, et cetera. Results that are not based on confounding these variables will require long-term studies in which the development of domain and task related problem solving is investigated over at least a couple of years.

Another way to evaluate assumptions about the development of expertise in CPS is to use process models that are implemented as computer programs. I briefly summarize a general model of the acquisition of abductive skills and their flexible use (Johnson & Krems, 1993).

In general, a system is labeled flexible if it is able to adjust problem solving to a changing environment reacting in real time. The general question then is: what makes a model of solving abduction problems flexible? For a possible answer, two of the mechanisms mentioned in the introductory section of this chapter may be used as guidelines.

First is modification of strategies. An inflexible model will always use the same strategy and will always work on explaining data and refining hypotheses in the same sequence. In contrast, a flexible method might use several different techniques for arriving at an answer: data-driven rule out, causal reasoning, data-driven abstract hypothesis generation. A flexible technique could also interleave explaining data, refining existing hypotheses, ruling out hypotheses, and so on.

Second is multiple interpretation of data. Inflexible methods can only make use of a fixed set of knowledge (usually predetermined), which leads to a standard interpretation of data. Flexible techniques, however, make use of any available knowledge and the fact that knowledge dynamically determines, at run-time, the particular sequence of problem solving actions.

Our model is based on Abd-Soar (see Johnson & Smith, 1991). Abd-Soar adopts the theoretical commitments of Soar's problem space computational model (Newell, 1990) to provide dynamic, run-time composition of action sequences. Skill acquisition is based on the compilation of deliberate problem solving into recognition rules that can quickly produce the appropriate action for the problem instance being solved. In this model, abduction is viewed as the sequential comprehension and integration of data into a single situation model that represents the currently best explanation of the data. When new data becomes available, the situation model is first updated to include the new evidence. Next, the new data must be comprehended to determine what it implies about the situation. The result of comprehension is one or more possible explanations for the data. If one of the explanations is consistent with the rest of the situation model, it is added to the model and more data is gathered. When an explanation is inconsistent with the model, an anomaly has occurred and the model must be updated by either finding an alternative explanation for the new data or by altering an explanation for the old data.

An inflexible abductive system would sequence operators in a fixed way and implement each operator using a fixed strategy. A flexible system like Abd-Soar dynamically sequences the operators at run-time based on the task at hand and the knowledge available to solve that task. It also dynamically selects from among several alternative methods for implementing each operator. Abd-Soar does not rely on fixed criteria for selecting which data to explain or which hypothesis to use to explain data. These are all determined at run-time based on the available knowledge. When to refine an existing hypothesis, to modify a current explanation, or to collect more data is also determined at run-time. In general, this model gains flexibility in solving abduction problems by using task-dependent knowledge allowing at run-time—without predefined fixation—to adjust problem solving methods to task requirements.

ACKNOWLEDGMENTS

The chapter was completed during a half-year research visit at The Ohio State University, Laboratory of Knowledge-based Medical Systems at Columbus, Ohio. It was substantially improved by comments and suggestions from Todd Johnson and Jack Smith. Frank Ritter at Nottingham, England, and Till Pfeiffer at Regensburg, Germany, also made many insightful remarks.

REFERENCES

Adelson, B. (1984). When novices surpass experts: The difficulty of a task may increase with expertise. *Journal of Experimental Psychology: Learning, Memory, and Cognition, 10,* 483–495.

Amthauer, R. (1973). *Intelligenz-Struktur-Test I-S-T 70.* Göttingen, Germany: Hogrefe.

Anderson, J. R. (1990). *Cognitive psychology and its implications.* New York: Freeman.

Anzai, Y., & Yokoyama, T. (1984). Internal models in physics problem solving. *Cognition and Instruction, 1,* 397–450.

Bitterwolf, W. (1992). *Flexibilität des Handelns* [Flexibility of action]. Regensburg, Germany: Roderer.

Boshuizen, H. P. A., & Schmidt, H. G. (1992). On the role of biomedical knowledge in clinical reasoning by experts, intermediates, and novices. *Cognitive Science, 16,* 153–184.

Cattell, R. B., & Eber, H. W. (1962). *The sixteen personality factor questionnaire test.* Champaign, IL: Institute for Personality and Ability Testing.

Charness, N., & Bieman-Copland, S. (1992). The learning perspective: Adulthood. In R. J. Sternberg & C. A. Berg (Eds.), *Intellectual development* (pp. 301–327). New York: Cambridge University Press.

Dilling, H., Mombour, W., & Schmidt, M. H. (1991). *Internationale Klassifikation psychischer Störungen* [International classification of mental disorders]. Bern, Switzerland: Hans Huber.

Dörner, D. (1986). Diagnostik der operativen Intelligenz [Diagnosis of operative intelligence]. *Diagnostica, 3,* 290–308.

Duncker, K. (1935/1945). *Zur Psychologie des Problemlösens—On problem-solving.* Washington, DC: The American Psychological Association.

Egan, D. E., & Greeno, J. G. (1973). Acquiring cognitive structure by discovery and rule learning. *Journal of Educational Psychology, 64,* 85–97.

Elstein, A. S., Shulman, L. E., & Sprafka, S. A. (1978). *Medical problem solving: An analysis of clinical reasoning.* Cambridge, MA: Harvard University Press.

Feltovich, P. J., Johnson, P. E., Moller, J. H., & Swanson, D. B. (1984). LCS: The role and development of medical knowledge in diagnostic expertise. In W. J. Clancey & E. H. Shortliffe (Eds.), *Readings in medical artificial intelligence* (pp. 275–319). Reading, MA: Addison-Wesley.

Fiedler, K. (1983). Beruhen Bestätigungsfehler nur auf einem Bestätigungsfehler? Eine Replik auf Gadenne [Are confirmation biases due to confirmation biases? A reply to Gadenne]. *Psychologische Beiträge, 25,* 280–286.

Frensch, P. A., & Sternberg, R. J. (1989). Expertise and intelligent thinking: When is it worse to know better? In R. J. Sternberg (Ed.), *Advances in the psychology of human intelligence.* Vol. 5 (pp. 157–188). Hillsdale, NJ: Lawrence Erlbaum Associates.

Funke, J. (1991). Solving complex problems: Exploration and control of complex systems. In R. J. Sternberg & P. A. Frensch (Eds.), *Complex problem solving* (pp. 185–222). Hillsdale, NJ: Lawrence Erlbaum Associates.

Gadenne, V., & Oswald, M. (1986). Entstehung und Veränderung von Bestätigungstendenzen beim Testen von Hypothesen [Origin of and changes in confirmatory tendencies in hypothesis testing]. *Zeitschrift für Experimentelle und Angewandte Psychologie, 33,* 360–374.

Gilmore, D. J. (1990). Expert programming knowledge: A strategic approach. In J. M. Hoc, T. R. C. Green, R. Samurcay, & D. J. Gilmore (Eds.), *Psychology of programming* (pp. 223–234). London: Academic Press.

Glaser, R. (1989). Expertise and learning: How do we think about instructional processes now that we have discovered knowledge structures? In D. Klahr & K. Kotovsky (Eds.), *Complex information processing. The impact of Herbert A. Simon* (pp. 269–282). Hillsdale, NJ: Lawrence Erlbaum Associates.

Glaser, R., Damrin, D. E., & Gardner, F. M. (1954). The tab item: A technique for the measurement of proficiency in diagnostic problem-solving task. *Educational and Psychological Measurement, 14,* 283–293.

Graumann, C. F. (1966). Nichtsinnliche Bedingungen der Wahrnehmung [Non-sensual conditions of perception]. In W. Metzger (Ed.), *Handbuch der Psychologie Band I, 1. Halbband: Wahrnehmung und Erkennen* (pp. 1031–1096). Göttingen, Germany: Hogrefe.

Groen, G. J., & Patel, V. L. (1988). The relationship between comprehension and reasoning in medical expertise. In M. T. H. Chi & R. Glaser (Eds.), *The nature of expertise* (pp. 287–310). Hillsdale, NJ: Lawrence Erlbaum Associates.

Guilford, J. P. (1959). *Personality.* New York: McGraw-Hill.

Hörmann, H. (1955). Zum Problem der psychischen Starrheit (Rigidität) [On the problem of fixedness (rigidity)]. *Zeitschrift für Experimentelle und Angewandte Psychologie, 3,* 662–683.

Howe, M. J. A. (1988). Intelligence as an explanation. *British Journal of Psychology, 79,* 349–360.

Johnson, T. A., & Krems, J. (1993). *A proposed model of human abductive skill and its acquisition.* Columbus, OH: LKBSMS Technical Report 93-317-12.

Johnson, T. A., & Smith, J. W. (1991). A framework for opportunistic abductive strategies. In *Proceedings of the Thirteenth Annual Conference of the Cognitive Science Society* (pp. 760–764). Hillsdale, NJ: Lawrence Erlbaum Associates.

Katz, I. R., & Anderson, J. R. (1988). Debugging: An analysis of bug-location strategies. *Human-Computer Interaction, 3,* 351–399.

Klayman, J., & Ha, Y. (1987). Confirmation, disconfirmation, and information in hypothesis testing. *Psychological Review, 94,* 211–228.

Krems, J. (1994). *Wissensbasierte Urteilsbildung* [Knowledge-based diagnostic reasoning]. Bern, Switzerland: Hans Huber.

Krems, J., & Bachmaier, M. (1991). Hypothesenbildung und Strategieauswahl in Abhängigkeit vom Expertisegrad [Hypothesis formation and strategy selection dependent on level of expertise]. *Zeitschrift für Experimentelle und Angewandte Psychologie, 38,* 394–410.

Krems, J., & Prechtl, C. (1991). Urteilsbildung und Berufserfahrung: Eine experimentelle Untersuchung zur Generierung, Evaluation und Modifikation diagnostischer Hypothesen. [Judgment formation and professional experience: An experimental study on the generation, evaluation, and modification of diagnostic hypotheses]. *Zeitschrift für Experimentelle und Angewandte Psychologie, 38,* 248–263.

Krems, J. F., & Zierer, C. (1994). Sind Experten gegen kognitive Täuschungen gefeit? Zur Abhängigkeit des confirmation bias von Fachwissen [Can experts resist cognitive illusions? On the dependence of confirmation bias from expert knowledge]. *Zeitschrift für Experimentelle und Angewandte Psychologie, 41,* 98–115.

Luchins, A. S. (1942). Mechanization in problem solving. *Psychological Monographs, 54.*

Luchins, A. S., & Luchins, E. H. (1959). *Rigidity of behavior.* Eugene, OR: University of Oregon Press.

Mehle, T. (1982). Hypothesis generation in an automobile malfunction inference task. *Acta Psychologica, 52,* 87–106.

Meili, R. (1951). *Lehrbuch der psychologischen Diagnostik* [Psychodiagnostics]. Bern, Switzerland: Hans Huber.

Mehmanesh, H., & Krems, J. (1988). SHERLOCK.0—Kognitive Modellierung von Debuggingstrategien [SHERLOCK.0—Cognitive modelling of debugging strategies]. In W. Hoeppner (Ed.), *Künstliche Intelligenz* (pp. 216–225). Berlin: Springer.

Murphy, G. L., & Wright, J. C. (1984). Changes in conceptual structure with expertise: Differences between real-world experts and novices. *Journal of Experimental Psychology: Learning, Memory, and Cognition, 10,* 144–155.

Newell, A. (1990). *Unified theories of cognition.* Cambridge, MA: Harvard University Press.

Peng, Y., & Reggia, J. A. (1990). *Abductive inference models for diagnostic problem-solving.* New York: Springer.

Rozin, P. (1976). The evolution of intelligence and access to the cognitive unconscious. In J. M. Sprague & A. N. Epstein (Eds.), *Progress in psychobiology and physiological psychology* (pp. 245–280). New York: Academic Press.

Rumelhart, D. E., & Norman, D. A. (1978). Accretion, tuning, and restructuring: Three modes of learning. In J. W. Cotton & R. L. Klatzky (Eds.), *Semantic factors in cognition* (pp. 37–53). Hillsdale, NJ: Lawrence Erlbaum Associates.

Schmuck, P. (1992). Zum Zusammenhang zwischen der Effizienz exekutiver Kontrolle und dem mehrfachen Lösen eines komplexen Problems [Efficiency of executive control processes and behavior stability in repeated complex problem solving]. *Sprache & Kognition, 11,* 193–207.

Selz, O. (1913). Die Gesetze der produktiven Tätigkeit [The laws of productive activity]. *Archiv für die Gesamte Psychologie, 27,* 367–380.

Simon, H. A. (1979). Information processing models of cognition. *Annual Review of Psychology, 30,* 363–396.

Spiro, R. J., Feltovich, P. J., Jacobson, M. J., & Coulson, R. L. (1991). Cognitive flexibility, constructivism, and hypertext: Random access instruction for advanced knowledge acquisition in ill-structured domain. *Educational Technology, 31,* 24–33.

Sternberg, R. (1988). *The triarchic mind.* New York: Penguin.

Süllwold, F. (1959). Bedingungen und Gesetzmäßigkeiten des Problemlöseverhaltens [Conditions and regularities of problem solving]. In H. Thomae (Ed.), *Bericht über den 22. Kongre der Deutschen Gesellschaft für Psychologie in Heidelberg 1959* (pp. 96–115). Göttingen: Hogrefe.

Thurstone, L. L. (1944). *A factorial study of perception.* Chicago, IL: University of Chicago Press.

Vessey, I. (1989). Toward a theory of computer program bugs: An empirical test. *International Journal of Man-Machine Studies, 30,* 23–46.

Wertheimer, M. (1925). *Drei Abhandlungen zur Gestalttheorie* [Three studies on Gestalttheory]. Erlangen, Germany: Palm & Enke.

Wertheimer, M. (1945). *Productive thinking.* New York: Harper & Row.

CHAPTER NINE

Using Complex Problem Solving Tasks in Personnel Selection and Training

Uwe Funke
University of Hohenheim, Germany

INTRODUCTION

Computer-based complex problem solving (henceforth CPS) scenarios that simulate real-life tasks were originally introduced to increase the ecological validity of the tasks used in problem solving research. The perceived increase in ecological validity, in turn, made these scenarios attractive to researchers interested in practical applications of basic research such as personnel selection and training. The adoption of complex scenarios for the purposes of personnel selection and training was by no means a sudden and swift event, however. Rather, simulations of job-related tasks had been used for personnel selection purposes for some time already (e.g., work samples as parts of assessment center programs: J. Funke, 1993; Thornton & Cleveland, 1990), and equipment simulators had become quite common in personnel training (Hays & Singer, 1989; Howell & Cooke, 1989). The popularity of management games (Graf, 1992; Keys & Wolfe, 1990), from which CPS scenarios are not always easily distinguished (Leutner, in press; Strohschneider & Schaub, in press), and of system oriented management concepts (Ulrich & Probst, 1988) further added to the attraction of CPS scenarios for selection and training purposes.

Computer-based scenarios have become accepted tools of the trade partly because their introduction has been less resisted than other psychological methods by management and personnel. Two of the main reasons for the acceptance are the favorable conditions for cognitive regulation and task execution (e.g., continuous feedback and control over the task; Fruhner, Schuler, Funke, & Moser, 1991), and the motivating effects of playing simulations (Leutner, 1992).

This chapter is divided into two main sections. In the first section, I discuss how and under which circumstances CPS research and CPS scenarios can be used for the purpose of personnel *selection*. In the second section, I describe how CPS scenarios can be applied to personnel *training*.

COMPLEX PROBLEM SOLVING AND PERSONNEL SELECTION

CPS scenarios are used as diagnostic tools in personnel selection to predict job success. That is, a person's performance on a simulated complex dynamic system is used as a predictor of how well, or how poorly, the person will perform on the job. A personnel decision is thus based on a person's performance on a simulated system. CPS scenarios have been used to aid in the selection of personnel for management jobs (J. Funke & Rasche, 1992; Hasselmann, 1993; Putz-Osterloh, 1990), jobs in industrial research and development (R&D; U. Funke, 1992), and jobs requiring the operation of complex equipment (Bartram, 1987). In Germany alone, there are more than a dozen commercial suppliers of CPS scenarios.

Basic and Applied Research

CPS scenarios in personnel selection are not perfect examples of the two-stage model, according to which practical applications always follow basic research findings and theories. In any case, Schönpflug (1993) has generally questioned the adequacy of the two-stage model for the field of psychology, and has argued that stage one, basic research, may be helpful, but neither necessary nor satisfactory for stage two, the applied stage. Considering the different objectives and quality standards of basic and applied CPS researchers, it is common for the former to strive for an understanding of the process underlying CPS performance, and for the latter to concentrate on the outcome of CPS. In general, basic research on CPS is useful for applied settings only to the extent that basic research addresses applied questions, that is, to the extent that the two approaches share a common goal (Frensch & Funke, this volume).

At the present time our understanding of the basic processes underlying CPS performance is, however, nowhere close to satisfactory (J. Funke, 1992; Kluwe, Schilde, Fischer, & Oellerer, 1991). Most importantly from the perspective of personnel selection and training, we still lack a taxonomy according to which CPS scenarios can be classified with regard to their cognitive requirements (J. Funke, 1992). Such a taxonomy would allow not only for the construction of scenarios for a given set of requirements, but also for the comparison of different scenarios, potentially eliminating empirical inconsistencies that have been reported across studies. From the perspective of personnel selection and training, it is also unfortunate that basic research on individual differences in CPS has recently decreased in frequency (but see Dörner, 1986; Dörner, Kreuzig, Reither, & Stäudel, 1983). Even disputes concerning the proper research strategy (factorial experiments versus single case methods) continue (Dörner & Wearing, this volume; J. Funke, 1992, this volume; Kluwe, this volume; Strohschneider & Schaub, in press).

On the other hand, shortcomings of basic CPS research do not necessarily translate into shortcomings for applied research. It is possible, for example, that measurement instruments criticized within the realm of basic research (e.g., Eyferth, Schömann, & Widowski, 1986) can nevertheless be fruitfully employed to answer applied research questions. And the assumption that personnel selection with CPS scenarios would operate with an undetermined global trait *CPS ability* (Strohschneider & Schaub, in press), overlooks the fact that simulation measures are generally based on a sample approach (Wernimont & Campbell, 1966), and that measuring and predicting individual performance does not necessarily imply the use of unidimensional trait constructs.

Even when theoretical concepts and instruments borrowed from basic research can be applied toward personnel selection and training, they often need to be modified to fit a specific context and/or sample. It might be necessary, for instance, to modify task instructions in order to communicate clear and standardized goals to all participants, or to change a complex system such that it does not contain randomly changing variables, in order to avoid interindividual differences in the task that subjects are facing (U. Funke, 1991).

CPS Scenarios as Diagnostic Tools

In general, the measurement instruments used in personnel selection can be classified into trait-oriented and simulation-oriented instruments. Trait-oriented instruments, including the classical ability and personality tests, measure unidimensional constructs that have been deemed relevant in trait oriented job analyses. Simulation-oriented instruments include work samples, that is, tasks that simulate components of a job that have been identified as typical and important for job performance, but that do not demand job-specific knowledge that is available only to those who have performed the job previously. Compared to tests, work samples require a heterogeneous set of traits, they are typically more similar to the job tasks, and are more comprehensive, that is, they include demands of planning, evaluating, and adapting to dynamically changing conditions as are found in group discussions or role plays, for instance (U. Funke, 1993).

Many CPS scenarios claim to simulate *natural* real-life tasks (e.g., Dörner et al., 1983; Hasselmann, 1993). Four different positions appear to be taken by those constructing CPS scenarios with regard to the similarity between scenarios and real-life jobs. First, some researchers simply assume, based on characteristics of their scenarios, that the scenarios are similar to real jobs without bothering to analyze the job requirements (e.g., Dörner et al., 1983; Hasselmann, 1993; Putz-Osterloh, 1990; Schaub & Strohschneider, 1992). However, analyses of management jobs, for instance (see Borman & Brush, 1993 for an overview), have not always supported this assumption. In addition, Obermann (in press) notices that job characteristics are not always stable, and that managers for instance, reduce the complexity and dynamics of their job considerably by applying domain-specific knowledge (e.g., time management, delegation).

Second, some researchers construct their scenarios after using task inventories or behaviorally oriented job analyses to analyze job requirements (e.g., Schuler, Funke, Moser, & Donat, in press). Using this approach, Schuler et al., for instance, found that the validity of their scenario varied as a function of the complexity of the job requirements.

Third, some researchers try to construct domain-specific scenarios based on detailed expert interviews (e.g., Strauß, Hasselmann, & Hasselmann, 1993). This method is, however, affected by inconsistencies in the experts' statements and by the difficulty of translating the statements into system characteristics. Therefore, the exact relation between scenario and job characteristics is difficult to establish. In addition, these domain-specific scenarios make the selection of novice workers virtually impossible.

Finally, a systems-oriented approach (e.g., Kluwe, 1990) may also be used to capture the similarity between CPS scenarios and job characteristics. In theory, this approach comprises, (a) a fine-grained cognitive task-analysis of the job requirements based on systems theory, and, (b) the use of known relations between system characteristics and job requirements to construct scenarios with predetermined requirements. Although this approach has considerable appeal, it is not operational yet, as it requires considerable basic research to provide the methods for step (a) and information for step (b).

In summary, CPS scenarios are useful for personnel selection purposes, but only if the scenarios capture important job requirements. If they don't, then we cannot expect performance on the scenarios to predict job performance. Even if the scenarios do capture important job requirements, their predictive value is not guaranteed. At the very least, the measures assessing performance on a scenario must be both reliable and valid, and they must be consistent with those aspects of job performance that they are trying to predict. Next, I discuss which performance measures have generally been used to predict job success, and summarize the studies that report reliability and validity coefficients for performance measures.

Measuring Simulation Performance

The quality of performance on any CPS scenario can be measured in various ways. First, the quality of performance may be represented by some combination of the final scores on important system variables. Second, performance quality may be reflected by the knowledge that is available about the system's internal structure. And finally, performance quality may be represented by the strategy or the activities used to control the scenario (e.g., the pattern of different actions, of planning and decision making).

In order to allow comparisons of the predictive power of different scenarios, relative, rather than absolute measures of performance must be utilized. Such relative measures can be derived by computing the distance between the obtained and the optimal performance on the system (J. Funke, 1992; Hübner, 1989), for example. If an optimal solution cannot be determined for a system, then obtained scores can be compared to the system baseline (Strohschneider, 1986), to scores computed by mathematical optimization procedures, or to expert judgments (Bartram, 1987).

It is somewhat unfortunate that in most studies relevant for personnel selection, performance quality has been measured only in terms of the scores on system variables. Rarely have measures been used that capture the strategy or the activities in controlling a system. Such measures of the process of how a system is controlled, I believe, would be far more important for personnel selection, feedback, and training. It is difficult, however, to develop such measures because they assess information that is time and context dependent. The only halfway reasonable measure that captures the process of performance and is available today may be expert judgments based on observational or thinking aloud data or on automatically recorded actions by the programs (e.g., information requests, decisions, or analyses of results).

If subjects' scores are to be used for personnel selection purposes, then scenarios must be standardized because the tasks faced by different subjects must be comparable. Standardizing scenarios includes, for example, setting clear goals in order to avoid subjective redefinitions of the task. Most threats to the standardization of CPS scenarios are caused by the dynamics of the system. From a measurement point of view, this could impede the determination of useful scores (Kubinger, 1993). One problem of dynamics is that the subjects themselves inevitably change the difficulty of their task constellation as they move through the system in individual pathways (but see Streufert et al., 1988, for how to counteract this problem).

Measurement Quality

Clearly, CPS measures must be both reliable and valid if they are to be used to select the right person for a given job. Assessing the reliability and validity of the measures is thus essential. Next, I summarize the main empirical studies aimed at providing estimates of reliability and validity for CPS scenarios.

Reliability Studies

Test-Retest Reliability. One apparent difficulty of assessing the test-retest reliability of a scenario is the fact that subjects learn while they are controlling a system. Typically, system knowledge is low at the outset but increases throughout the simulation. Thus, comparing subjects' performance at the beginning with the performance sometime later will likely underestimate reliability. Conversely, comparing two performances when learning has reached a plateau, may lead to overestimation of reliability (Putz-Osterloh & Haupts, 1990; Schoppek, 1991).

Other variables that may affect test-retest reliability estimates are, for instance, unclear goals provided to the participants (Hasselmann, 1993), changes in the system variables or in the situational conditions (Süß, Oberauer, & Kersting, 1993), or systematic drop out of participants with lower cognitive abilities (Süß, Kersting, & Oberauer, 1991). In general, measures that are consistent with the logic underlying a scenario show higher test-retest reliabilities (e.g., J. Funke, 1983; Hasselmann, 1993; Süß et al., 1991). Typically, test-retest reliabilities range from the low .40s to the high .80s for different scenarios and different dependent measures. For the scenario TAILORSHOP, for example, the test-retest reliability appears to be about .70, a number approximated in four independent studies (J. Funke, 1983; Hasselmann, 1993; Süß et al., 1991, 1993).

Split-Half Reliability. Müller (in press) has proposed to determine the reliability of CPS measures through use of split-half estimates. Split-half reliabilities can be computed when a scenario consists of two structurally identical, unrelated subsystems, that are presented to participants as one integrated system. In this way, learning is held constant across subsystems. Müller obtained split-half reliabilities of .83 and .86 that far exceeded the test-retest reliabilities of .49 and .58. Unfortunately, the reliability of most of the existing scenarios cannot be determined by using Müller's approach because these systems do not contain structurally identical, independent subsystems.

Parallel-Test Reliability. Developing parallel forms of a CPS scenario is rather difficult because even slight changes in the surface characteristics of the task (e.g., cover story, design of the user interface) may affect performance (Kluwe et al., 1991). To measure the parallel-test reliability of the scenario DISKO, U. Funke (1992) constructed a parallel version by changing only the currency (deutschmark : francs = 1 : 3) and the name of the product manufactured. In order to keep learning effects constant, both scenarios were simultaneously presented to subjects in a multitasking environment. Participants had to manage the two simulations simultaneously, and were not told that the two systems were structurally identical. In fact, only one out of 14 participants noticed that the two scenarios were identical in terms of their system structures.

The parallel-test reliabilities for three different dependent variables were .83, .88, and .85, far exceeding the test-retest reliabilities of .53, .63, and .54, for the same dependent variables. Parallel-test reliabilities for other scenarios have ranged from .58 to .70 for the scenario FIRE (Putz-Osterloh, 1993) to an average of .72 for the scenarios WOODLINE COUNTY and SHAMBA (Streufert et al., 1988).

Validity Studies

Construct Validity. Researchers have frequently tried to establish the construct validity of their scenarios by correlating CPS performance with scores on cognitive tests, and, less frequently, with personality tests. Unfortunately, diverging results are frequent, and the situation is further complicated because scenarios, situational conditions, constructs, and operationalization differ widely among the studies. Kluwe et al. (1991) summarize the empirical results and they question the adequacy of this kind of construct validity research altogether, because it does not differentiate between structure-oriented and process-oriented research. Nevertheless, low correlations with cognitive ability measures are grounds for worry, as they stand in contrast to at least some meta-analytic results that demonstrate the validity of cognitive abilities tests in general (Hunter & Hunter, 1984; but see Funke, Krauß, Schuler, & Stapf, 1987).

Some researchers have proposed to use correlations among different measures of task performance as indicators of the internal validity for CPS scenarios (Putz-Osterloh, 1990). This approach appears highly questionable, however, because different measures capture different aspects of task performance. In addition, dissociations among different measures may be expected dependent on the level of instruction and of background knowledge (Kluwe & Haider, 1990). In general, correlations among different dependent measures tend to range from .30 to .50 (U. Funke, 1992; Putz-Osterloh, 1993; Schaub, 1990).

One way of demonstrating the content validity of scenarios is to compare experts, for example senior managers who presumably have acquired general problem solving skills (e.g., heuristic competence) during many years of experience, and novices, for example students, in terms of their performances on a scenario. The finding that experts perform better than novices in scenarios simulating domains that are unfamiliar to both groups indicates that the scenarios capture at least some components of general problem solving skills (Hasselmann, 1993; Putz-Osterloh & Lemme, 1987; Schaub & Strohschneider, 1992).

Criterion Validity. The criterion validity of the measures used to assess subjects' performance on a scenario, and ultimately to select the right subjects for a job, is critically important, and is a fundamental quality standard in personnel selection research and practice. Do CPS scenarios reliably predict the quality of job performance? And if they do, do they add anything above and beyond what is predicted by more commonly employed paper-and-pencil tests (e.g., IQ tests, ability tests)?

Criterion validities as high as .50 have been reported in the literature. Before the results of these studies are taken too serious, let me add, however, that most studies have employed rather small sample sizes (ranging from $n = 21$ to $n = 111$), and in addition, can be criticized for questionable job performance measures. Indeed, the measures of job performance used in most studies reported in the literature (Hasselmann, 1993; Obermann, 1991; Streufert et al., 1988) were not based on job analyses. Thus, the actual goals and demands of the jobs might not have been represented sufficiently. The global criteria used to measure job performance, such as job level and salary, or trait ratings, may not have captured the essence of job performance and may have been contaminated by third variables (Borman, 1991). For some of the criteria used, for example the "frequency of encountering complex problems," or ratings of performance potential, the relation to job performance can hardly be recognized.

Additional problems can be localized in the rating process of performance appraisal. Self ratings (e.g., Streufert et al., 1988) are biased, and differ systematically from supervisor ratings (Harris & Schaubroek, 1988). When human resource staff are used as raters (e.g., Hasselmann, 1993), the raters may be familiar with both the predictor scores of candidates as well as their performance level, thus contaminating predictor and criterion scores, resulting in artificial validity coefficients. When predictor scores are unknown to the raters of job performance to avoid any contamination of predictors and criteria, and when job specific behaviorally anchored supervisor ratings of job performance based on job analyses are used (e.g., U. Funke, 1992), then validity coefficients are typically found that range from the low .20s to the high .30s.

Further aspects of the criterion-related validity have yet to be considered. For example, we lack empirical studies that test how different types of scenarios, performance criteria, and job requirements affect validity. Furthermore, the importance of considering *specific job requirements* instead of general families of jobs, such as management jobs, has been pointed out recently. U. Funke (1992) sorted a sample of scientists and engineers working in different jobs in industrial research and development into two groups according to the level of cognitive skills their jobs required (see also Schuler et al., in press). The validity of the scenario DISKO was around .40 for the high skill level group, but was zero for the low skill level group.

In addition, tests of *incremental validity*, that is, a scenario's capability to predict job performance above and beyond the prediction achieved by standard methods, are essential in personnel selection programs, and have so far only been studied for job performance in solving complex research and development problems (U. Funke, 1992). In a hierarchical regression analysis that included cognitive and personality scales as well as work sample scores, performance on a scenario was the best predictor of job performance. *Fairness,* or more exactly, predictive bias, that is, group differences in validity or regression slopes, have also not been determined so far. Occasionally, lower mean performance of female participants in CPS scenarios has been reported (Badke-Schaub, 1987; Kreuzig & Schlotthauer, 1991), partly in combination with less computer experience of females (Süß, Beauducel, Kersting, & Oberauer, 1992).

Summary

In summary, the available reliability data for computer-based scenarios are below those of psychometric tests, especially of tests of intelligence. However, if one takes the technically unfavorable conditions for determining reliability estimates into account, then the results look rather promising. For example, other simulation-oriented selection methods, such as group discussions (Bass, 1954; Gatewood, Thornton, & Hennessey, 1990) and in-baskets (Schippman, Prien, & Katz, 1990), generally generate reliabilities lower than those reported for CPS scenarios. Improvements in the formal properties of CPS scenarios that are used in personnel selection could increase the reliability estimates even further.

The criterion validity coefficients reported previously have to be interpreted very cautiously, however. The relation between predictors and criteria remains unclear; the samples are too small. Additional validity studies are clearly needed, and specific aspects of validity, such as incremental validity and the redundancy of CPS results with traditional methods, should be considered. Nevertheless, the results that have been obtained so far are promising, especially when they are compared to the validity estimates obtained with other simulation-oriented methods such as in-baskets and group discussions (e.g., Robertson & Kandola, 1982).

COMPLEX PROBLEM SOLVING
AND PERSONNEL TRAINING

Personnel training in work organizations has until recently been dominated by training programs that were based on behavioral and social learning theories (Tannenbaum & Yukl, 1992). With recent technology-driven and organizational changes, technical and social tasks have become more and more complex, unpredictable, and poorly defined, and require more inferences and understanding, diagnostic judgment and decision making (Patrick, 1992) than ever. With the growing importance of these complex cognitive skills, more attention has been given to concepts of cognitive learning, instruction, and training (Howell & Cooke, 1989; Sonntag & Schaper, 1992).

Because CPS scenarios can simulate tasks with the specific characteristics mentioned previously, CPS-based training as a method of personnel training in work organizations has been advocated in psychology (Dörner, 1989; Leutner, in press; Strohschneider & Schaub, in press; Thornton & Cleveland, 1990), as well as in system-oriented management science (Ulrich & Probst, 1988). Among the specific advantages (Bakken, Gould, & Kim, 1992; Dörner, 1989; Graham, Morecroft, Senge, & Sterman, 1992; Leutner, in press) that CPS scenarios have are: (a) the opportunity for practice (e.g., learning by doing; experimenting without risks and costs), (b) augmented feedback (e.g., compressed time and space increases awareness of time-characteristics, system-dynamics, and side-effects; direct relation to own decisions is conducive to reflection), (c) an increased motivation (e.g., provoking challenge and curiosity), and (d) an adaptability to training objectives (e.g., variation of complexity; combination with tutoring methods).

Training Needs and Training Objectives

Is there any need for job training that can be accomplished with CPS scenarios? If so, are the needs specific or general? Better performance and more effective general cognitive strategies of experts (e.g., managers with several years of experience) compared to novices on CPS scenarios that neither group is familiar with (Putz-Osterloh & Lemme, 1987; Schaub & Strohschneider, 1992), is often taken as evidence for general training needs (Dörner, 1989) that could potentially be addressed by CPS scenarios. Low performance on artificial CPS scenarios (Dörner et al., 1983), even for experts in the real jobs (Senge & Sterman, 1992), on the other hand, is interpreted as implying that training should be specific, that is, tailored toward very specific job requirements, rather than general. Because CPS scenarios are, however, never exact copies of real-life jobs (J. Funke, 1993, in press; Kluwe et al., 1991; Strohschneider & Schaub, in press), this inference is at least questionable.

Clearly, if one wants to use CPS-based training scenarios to improve real-job performance, then one needs to make sure that objective system characteristics correspond to the training needs, that is to the cognitive requirements of the job. This, in turn, requires intensive analysis of the system behavior and job analyses of the real tasks (Patrick, 1992), both of which are, however, frequently not performed. Thus, the similarity of requirements for computer-simulated and real-world systems cannot be tested. Likewise, in many cases there is no justification for the use of a certain scenario as a training task, that is, the content validity of the training task is not assessed (Goldstein, 1991). A few task-specific CPS scenarios for training have been constructed, however, by developing the system model together with an expert group (Senge & Sterman, 1992) and with reference to a case study (Graham et al., 1992).

In discussing possible contributions of existing empirical studies of learning with CPS scenarios to personnel training in the workplace, it has to be taken into account that the existing studies differ in several characteristics, for example, in the theoretical background, the type of the simulated tasks and their requirements, and especially in the training objectives and, consequently, in their practical relevance. Training studies in the field of cognitive psychology are typically oriented toward *generalizable and transferable* knowledge, strategies, and performance (e.g. Dörner et al., 1983; Putz-Osterloh, 1990). Studies done from an engineering psychology perspective, in contrast, emphasize the acquisition of *system-specific* knowledge and performance for a certain complex technical system, and employ learning by doing methods (Hahn & Hesse, 1993; Kluwe et al., 1991). Thus, in the latter, transfer to other systems is less emphasized. Several studies have also been done in instructional psychology, using CPS scenarios in schools for teaching *declarative* (Preiß, 1992) or sometimes *procedural, domain-specific* knowledge (Leutner, 1992), but without taking special notice of performance in system control or of transfer.

Results of Learning and Training Studies

Not a single evaluation study of a personnel training program with a CPS scenario can be found in the literature with regard to the most important criterion of applied personnel training, namely improved performance on the job. On the other hand, several studies on learning in CPS scenarios have been reported that focus on system-specific knowledge acquisition and improved system control, or on the transfer of performance to other systems. Also, suggestions for comprehensive training programs have been made in CPS research as well as in instructional research that could potentially contribute to personnel training.

Considerable differences among learning and training studies exist in the characteristics of the systems used (e.g., the number of variables, the complexity, and abstractness; J. Funke, 1992). Thus, the assumption that a complete internal system representation has been established after training might be tenable only for small systems. In more complex systems, training may need to focus on the heuristic strategies that reduce complexity (Strohschneider & Schaub, in press) and the acquisition of a preliminary action base (Kluwe & Haider, 1990). Training times and schedules also vary widely, ranging from one single training period of one hour or less to 20 periods of an hour each (Kluwe, Misiak, & Haider, 1989). The results will be discussed in the order of the training methods used.

Effects of Practice in CPS Scenarios

Learning by Doing. In simulation-based training, participants are given the opportunity to try out decisions, and to realize their consequences, in ways that are similar to studies of learning by doing or exploratory learning with unknown systems. Learning by doing usually leads to improved performance on the same system (Kluwe et al., 1989) exceeding traditional learning by instruction or by demonstration (Beckmann, in press), although it does not always lead to improved explicit knowledge about the system (Kluwe & Haider, 1990). While transfer of learning by doing to real jobs has not yet been examined in the literature, the results regarding transfer to different systems are mixed. Transfer between systems sometimes occurs in both directions (Bakken et al., 1992), sometimes in only one direction (Putz-Osterloh, 1991; Putz-Osterloh & Lemme, 1987), and sometimes no transfer is observed (Putz-Osterloh & Haupts, 1990). The fact that the similarity between training and target systems is typically not defined in these studies, could well be the reason for the lack of transfer that is observed. In addition, the goals (e.g., knowledge acquisition, system control, prediction of system states) of the simulation task in training also need to be pointed out carefully, as different goals have been shown to determine which type of knowledge is acquired (J. Funke, 1992; Kluwe & Haider, 1990).

Flexibility Training. Training with a simulation anchors learning in a meaningful context, and may lead to situated learning (Resnick, 1989) and situation-specific knowledge. Confronting trainees with different scenarios that simulate different systems with systematically varied characteristics might promote transfer to different CPS situations and overcome the context dependency of cognitive skills. Schwarck (1986), however, found no transfer to a new target scenario after training with three different CPS scenarios. Breuer and Kummer (1990) also examined three CPS scenarios that were integrated with a curriculum of lectures in politics/economy, but reported only an increased self-assessed cognitive complexity of the trained pupils, rather than data on knowledge and performance changes. Thus, it remains unclear how exactly flexibility can be achieved through training.

Part-Task Training and Adaptive Training. Because learning by doing is more difficult in the presence of certain situational and system characteristics (e.g., intransparency of system connections, dynamic developments, and time-delayed feedback; for an overview see J. Funke, 1992), part-task training with subsystems and adaptive training with increasingly difficult systems (Lintern, 1991) might be an appropriate means of achieving learning as long as the structure of the original task is not distorted. Broadbent, FitzGerald, and Broadbent (1986), for instance, reported improved explicit knowledge and performance in the TRANSPORT system after part-task training. Also, three different formats of part-task training were superior to whole-task training in the computer-based simulation system SPACE FORTRESS (see Lintern, 1991, for an overview).

Tutorial Aids. Leutner (1992) reported the results of a series of six experiments in which different tutorial aids were added to learning by doing in two CPS scenarios. Giving informations by computer-aided instruction only improved domain-specific knowledge, but did not affect knowledge of the system structure and control performance in the scenarios. Particularly, automatic adaptive information was even less effective than permanently available background help facilities. On the other hand, detailed advice before each decision improved control performance on the scenario, but did not increase explicit system knowledge. Although verbal and graphical information about the system that was offered in advance of exploratory learning had generally no effect (J. Funke, 1983; Hesse, 1982; Leutner, 1992; Putz-Osterloh, 1981; Putz-Osterloh & Haupts, 1990), intensive graphical presentations of the system structure (Hübner, 1988; Latzina, 1990) and the use of graphics to display selected input- and output-data (Putz-Osterloh, Bott, & Köster, 1990) was superior to simple exploration.

Training General Strategies

General Problem Solving Strategies. Dörner et al. (1983) found no effect of pretraining (i.e., describing the characteristics of a system, possible failures, and decision strategies) on later performance on a complex cognitive system. In training studies based on the concept of cognitive complexity, Streufert, Nogami, Swezey, Pogash, and Piasecki (1988; see also Streufert & Swezey, 1986) significantly improved managers' performances on such higher competencies as the breadth of strategies used in a CPS scenario after training structural competence (e.g., of how to integrate thoughts and actions into overall conceptualizations) and the use of content specific strategies. Similarly, training general heuristics, self-reflections, and practicing different scenarios in a 4-hour session, Hofmann (1992) found significantly improved information search and decision strategies and better performance on the target scenario DISKO.

Metacognition. The metacognitive processes of monitoring and controlling problem solving steps and of establishing mental models have been the training objective of self-reflection training studies (Putz-Osterloh, 1983, 1985; Schwarck, 1986). So far, however, these studies have not demonstrated a training effect.

In summary, most of the existing learning and training studies have used a single training method to increase specific aspects of task performance. Generally, the empirical results have not been very convincing and are mixed at best.

Comprehensive Training Programs

Dörner (1989) proposed a type of flexibility training that uses a battery of different scenarios combined with individualized debriefings by experts. The goal of the approach is to increase the awareness of failures and to assure generalization of heuristics. Preiß (1992) discussed a program for teaching processes and structures of business companies and markets in vocational education. The program is oriented toward principles of traditional business games, and includes an introduction by video, an information booklet, a CPS scenario, several worksheets, and tutorials. Both Dörner's and Preiß's methods have not been empirically tested yet. In general, the effects of integrating several methods to teach CPS scenarios with other, general training methods, although proposed, have not yet been empirically tested.

Practical training applications that draw heavily on the system-dynamics approach (Forrester, 1961) to develop the *system thinking* of managers and to improve strategic management have been described by Senge and Sterman (1992). Senge and Sterman have avoided CPS scenarios with low content validity. Their method, using a practical complex management problem, trains the ability to build a mental model by mapping, testing, and improving participants' mental models using graphical software. Similarly, the *management flight simulator* approach (Bakken et al., 1992; Graham et al., 1992; Senge & Sterman, 1992) uses computer-simulated scenarios based on generic models or cases that are presented stepwise and are related to the issues of the specific industry setting of the participants. Principles of part/adaptive training, coaching/tutoring, and self-reflection are also included in this approach. Evaluation results have not yet been reported.

Further Aspects of Training Methods

Some, as of yet unaddressed, questions of training with CPS scenarios deserve mention. A central problem of the approach is how the generalization and transfer of cognitive skills can be achieved given that training of abstract strategies in a declarative mode seems hardly effective (Howell & Cooke, 1989; Larkin, 1989) and domain-specific training results in context-bound procedural knowledge (Anderson, 1987). Context-specific training, complemented by several decontextualizing activities (e.g., debriefing, varying scenarios) is recommended by many instructional psychologists (e.g., Adams, 1989; Collins, Brown, & Newman, 1989).

The typical training duration for the comprehensive training programs is one to several days. The duration is in line with the assumption that a lot of time is needed to improve performance that can be generalized. Indeed, Stern (1993) has recently criticized short-time training studies for wrongly indicating reduced transfer and no generalizability when both could be obtained with longer training.

Optimal fidelity lies somewhere between simulations too simplistic to transfer to reality and too complex to learn from. An inverted U-shaped curve is said to describe the relation between fidelity and learning (Alessi, 1988; Hays & Singer, 1989). Fidelity is a characteristic of the whole training situation, not of a simulated system alone, and its optimal level is moderated by the knowledge of the trainees, the training objectives, and the training domain. No empirical results relating the effects of the fidelity of CPS scenarios to training have been reported in the literature thus far.

SUMMARY AND CONCLUSIONS

Personnel selection and personnel training are two possible applications of computer-based CPS scenarios that originate from basic research in cognitive psychology. However, applications cannot simply be transferred or deduced from concepts and instruments of basic research.

Constructing CPS scenarios for personnel selection and training has frequently been more an art than a scientific activity. Existing techniques of job analysis often do not permit to exactly specify the cognitive requirements and training needs of jobs. In addition, missing links between formal system characteristics and cognitive demands of CPS scenarios make it difficult to systematically construct content valid scenarios.

CPS scenarios used as diagnostic tools share the typical methodological problems of other simulation-oriented instruments (e.g. reduced standardization caused by freedom of action, no test theory for dynamic systems, difficulties to construct equivalent instruments). Also, performance in the scenarios is measured at different levels and with different methodological foundation. Test-retest reliabilities typically range from the .40s to the .80s, split-half and parallel-test reliabilities of simultaneously presented scenarios run in the .70s and .80s. These coefficients are below those of psychometric tests, but they are at least comparable to the reliabilities of other simulation-oriented selection methods.

Concerning validity, neither the strategies applied in studies of construct validity nor the published results have been very consistent and convincing thus far. Also, the few studies of criterion-related validity are quite provisional and most of them lack adequate sample sizes as well as job-relevant measures of job performance. If one interprets the results cautiously, then the validity coefficients appear to run in the high .30s. These values are similar to the coefficients obtained for other simulation-oriented selection methods. Validity studies that avoid the shortcomings of the studies reviewed and focus on additional aspects, (e.g., incremental validity, the role of specific job requirements for validity, the fairness of CPS scenarios) are needed.

For personnel training, evaluation studies of training applications are at least as urgent as studies of selection methods. At this time, not a single evaluation study assessing job performance following training with a CPS scenario can be found in the literature. Consequently, hypotheses and recommendations of perhaps effective CPS training methods must be deduced from basic research on learning in CPS scenarios. This is made complicated by differing training objectives, system characteristics, and training methods among the studies.

Specific training methods based on practice on scenarios (e.g. learning by doing, part-task training, and tutorial aids) tend to produce training effects, but rather specific ones, that is, either improved knowledge or improved performance, depending on the training content. The training of general strategies has been even less effective. Some comprehensive training programs have been proposed that integrate specific and general trainings. Here, the initial context-specific training is followed by decontextualizing activities, in order to achieve transfer of cognitive skills. These training programs have training durations of up to several days, which appears necessary to achieve generalizable improvements.

The early enthusiastic stage of expectations about the potential applications for CPS scenarios is over. If we take a close look at the plain empirical results that have been reported over 15 years of research, then it is obvious that personnel selection and training with CPS scenarios are still in their infancy. CPS scenarios will probably need to be improved and adapted to selection or training applications step by step, based on better methods for job analysis, and controlled by strict evaluation studies. In any case, a lot of applied research will be necessary before CPS scenarios will become valuable parts of elaborated selection and training programs in human resource management.

ACKNOWLEDGMENTS

I am grateful to Peter Frensch and Joachim Funke for many helpful comments on an earlier draft.

REFERENCES

Adams, M. J. (1989). Thinking skills curricula: Their promise and progress. *Educational Psychologist, 24*, 25–77.

Alessi, S. M. (1988). Fidelity in the design of instructional simulations. *Journal of Computer-Based Instruction, 15*, 40–47.

Anderson, J. R. (1987). Skill acquisition. Compilation of weak-method problem solutions. *Psychological Review, 94*, 192–210.

Badke-Schaub, P. (1987). *Persönlichkeit und Problemlösen: Charakteristika des Verhaltens in komplexen Problemsituationen und Möglichkeiten der Prognose aufgrund von persönlichkeitsspezifischen Faktoren* [Personality and problem solving: Features of behavior in complex problem situations and prognostic potential by means of personality factors] (Memorandum Nr. 48, Universität Bamberg, Lehrstuhl Psychologie II).

Bakken, B., Gould, J., & Kim, D. (1992). Experimentation in learning organizations: A management flight simulator approach. *European Journal of Operational Research, 59*, 167–182.

Bartram, D. (1987). The development of an automated testing system for pilot selection: The Micropat project. *Applied Psychology: An International Review, 36*, 279–298.

Bass, B. M. (1954). The leaderless group discussion. *Psychological Bulletin, 51*, 465–492.

Beckmann, J. F. (in press). *Lernen und komplexes Problemlösen. Ein Beitrag zur Validierung von Lerntests* [Learning and complex problem solving. A contribution to validate learning potential tests]. Bonn, Germany: Holos.

Borman, W. C. (1991). Job behavior, performance, and effectiveness. In M. D. Dunnette & L. M. Hough (Eds.), *Handbook of industrial and organizational psychology Vol. 2* (pp. 271–326, 2nd ed.). Palo Alto, CA: Consulting Psychologists Press.

Borman, W. C., & Brush, D. H. (1993). More progress toward a taxonomy of managerial performance requirements. *Human Performance, 6*, 1–21.

Breuer, K., & Kummer, R. (1990). Cognitive effects from process learning with computer-based simulations. *Computers in Human Behavior, 6*, 69–81.

Broadbent, D. E., FitzGerald, P., & Broadbent, M. H. P. (1986). Implicit and explicit knowledge in the control of complex systems. *British Journal of Psychology, 77*, 33–50.

Collins, A., Brown, J. S., & Newman, S. E. (1989). Cognitive apprenticeship: Teaching the crafts of reading, writing, and mathematics. In L. B. Resnick (Ed.), *Knowing, learning, and instruction* (pp. 453–494). Hillsdale, NJ: Lawrence Erlbaum Associates.

Dörner, D. (1986). Diagnostik der operativen Intelligenz [Diagnosis of operative intelligence]. *Diagnostica, 32,* 290–308.

Dörner, D. (1989). *Die Logik des Mißlingens* [The logic of failures]. Reinbek, Germany: Rowohlt.

Dörner, D., Kreuzig, H. W., Reither, F., & Stäudel, T. (1983). *Lohhausen. Vom Umgang mit Unbestimmtheit und Komplexität* [Lohhausen. On dealing with uncertainty and complexity]. Bern, Switzerland: Hans Huber.

Eyferth, K., Schömann, M., & Widowski, D. (1986). Der Umgang von Psychologen mit Komplexität [On how psychologists deal with complexity]. *Sprache & Kognition, 5,* 11–26.

Forrester, J. W. (1961). *Industrial dynamics.* Cambridge, MA: MIT Press.

Fruhner, R., Schuler, H., Funke, U., & Moser, K. (1991). Einige Determinanten der Bewertung von Personalauswahlverfahren [Some determinants for the evaluation of personal selection procedures]. *Zeitschrift für Arbeits- und Organisationspsychologie, 35,* 170–178.

Funke, J. (1983). Einige Bemerkungen zu Problemen der Problemlöseforschung oder: Ist Testintelligenz doch ein Prädiktor? [Some remarks on the problems of problem solving research or: Does test intelligence predict control performance?]. *Diagnostica, 29,* 283–302.

Funke, J. (1992). *Wissen über dynamische Systeme: Erwerb, Repräsentation und Anwendung* [Knowledge about dynamic systems: Acquisition, representation, and use]. Berlin, Germany: Springer.

Funke, J. (1993). Computergestützte Arbeitsproben: Begriffsklärung, Beispiele sowie Entwicklungspotentiale [Computer-based work samples: Definition, examples, and future trends]. *Zeitschrift für Arbeits- und Organisationspsychologie, 37,* 119–129.

Funke, J. (in press). Erforschung komplexen Problemlösens durch computerunterstützte Planspiele: Kritische Anmerkungen zur Forschungsmethodologie [Research on complex problem solving by means of computer simulated games: Critical comments on research methodology]. In T. Geilhardt & T. Mühlbradt (Eds.), *Handbuch computerunterstützte Planspiele.* Stuttgart, Germany: Verlag für Angewandte Psychologie.

Funke, J., & Rasche, B. (1992). Einsatz computersimulierter Szenarien im Rahmen eines Assessment Center [Use of computer-based scenarios within an assessment center]. *Zeitschrift Führung+Organisation, 61,* 110–118.

Funke, U. (1991). Die Validität einer computergestützten Systemsimulation zur Diagnose von Problemlösekompetenz [On the validity of a computer-based simulation for the prognosis of problem solving competence]. In H. Schuler & U. Funke (Eds.), *Eignungsdiagnostik in Forschung und Praxis* (pp. 114–122). Stuttgart, Germany: Verlag für Angewandte Psychologie.

Funke, U. (1992). Die Validität einer eignungsdiagnostischen Simulation zum komplexen Problemlösen [The validity of a complex problem simulation in personnel selection]. In L. Montada (Ed.), *Bericht über den 38. Kongreß der Deutschen Gesellschaft für Psychologie in Trier 1992* (pp. 495–496). Göttingen, Germany: Hogrefe.

Funke, U. (1993). Computergestützte Eignungsdiagnostik mit komplexen dynamischen Systemen [Computer-based aptitude diagnosis with complex dynamic systems]. *Zeitschrift für Arbeits- und Organisationspsychologie, 37,* 109–118.

Funke, U., Krauß, D., Schuler, H., & Stapf, K. (1987). Zur Prognostizierbarkeit wissenschaftlich-technischer Leistungen mittels Personvariablen: Eine Metaanalyse der Validität diagnostischer Verfahren im Bereich Forschung und Entwicklung [On the predictability of scientific and technical performance by means of person variables: A metaanalysis of the validity of diagnostic instruments in the area of research and development]. *Gruppendynamik, 18,* 407–428.

Gatewood, R., Thornton, G. C., & Hennessey, H. W. (1990). Reliability of exercise ratings in the leaderless group discussion. *Journal of Occupational Psychology, 63,* 331–342.

Goldstein, I. L. (1991). Training in work organizations. In M. D. Dunnette & L. M. Hough (Eds.), *Handbook of industrial and organizational psychology,* Vol. 2 (pp. 507–619, 2nd ed.). Palo Alto, CA: Consulting Psychologists Press.

Graf, J. (Ed.). (1992). *Planspiele. Simulierte Realitäten für den Chef von morgen* [Business games: Simulated realities for tomorrow's leader]. Speyer, Germany: Gabal.

Graham, A. K., Morecroft, J. D. W., Senge, P. M., & Sterman, J. D. (1992). Model-supported case studies for management education. *European Journal of Operational Research, 59,* 151–166.

Hahn, C., & Hesse, F. W. (1993). Die Steuerung komplexer Systeme in der Intensivmedizin [Control of complex systems in intensive care]. *Zeitschrift für Arbeits- und Organisationspsychologie, 37,* 183–190.

Harris, M. M., & Schaubroek, J. (1988). A meta-analysis of self-supervisor, self-peer, and peer-supervisor ratings. *Personnel Psychology, 41,* 43–62.

Hasselmann, D. (1993). *Computersimulierte komplexe Problemstellungen in der Management-Diagnostik* [Computer simulated complex problems for management diagnosis]. Hamburg, Germany: Windmühle.

Hays, R. T., & Singer, M. J. (1989). *Simulation fidelity in training system design.* New York: Springer.

Hesse, F. W. (1982). Training-induced changes in problem solving. *Zeitschrift für Psychologie, 190,* 405–423.

Hofmann, W. (1992). *Trainierbarkeit komplexer Problemlösefähigkeit* [Trainability of complex problem solving ability]. Unpublished master's thesis, University of Hohenheim, Stuttgart, Germany.

Howell, W. C., & Cooke, N. J. (1989). Training the human information processor: A review of cognitive models. In I. L. Goldstein (Ed.), *Training and development in organizations* (pp. 121–182). San Francisco, CA: Jossey-Bass.

Hübner, R. (1988). Die kognitive Regelung dynamischer Systeme und der Einfluß analoger versus digitaler Informationsdarbietung [Cognitive regulation of dynamic systems and the influence of analogue versus digital presentation of information]. *Zeitschrift für Psychologie, 196,* 161–170.

Hübner, R. (1989). Methoden zur Analyse und Konstruktion von Aufgaben zur kognitiven Steuerung dynamischer Systeme [Methods for the analysis and construction of dynamic system control tasks]. *Zeitschrift für Experimentelle und Angewandte Psychologie, 36,* 221–238.

Hunter, J. E., & Hunter, R. F. (1984). Validity and utility of alternative predictors of job performance. *Psychological Bulletin, 96,* 72–98.

Keys, B., & Wolfe, J. (1990). The role of management games and simulations in education and research. *Journal of Management, 16,* 307–336.

Kluwe, R. (1990). Computergestützte Systemsimulationen [Computer-based system simulations]. In W. Sarges (Ed.), *Management-Diagnostik* (pp. 458–463). Göttingen, Germany: Hogrefe.

Kluwe, R. H., Misiak, C., & Haider, H. (1989). Erste Ergebnisse zu einem Modell der Steuerung eines komplexen Systems [First results pertaining to a model of human control of complex systems]. In D. Dörner & W. Michaelis (Eds.), *Idola fori et idola theatri. Festschrift aus Anlaß der Emeritierung von Prof. Dr. phil. et Dr. med. Hermann Wegener* (pp. 101–119). Göttingen, Germany: Hogrefe.

Kluwe, R., & Haider, H. (1990). Modelle zur internen Repräsentation komplexer technischer Systeme [Models for the internal representation of complex technical systems]. *Sprache & Kognition, 9,* 173–192.

Kluwe, R., Schilde, A., Fischer, C., & Oellerer, N. (1991). Problemlöseleistungen beim Umgang mit komplexen Systemen und Intelligenz [Problem solving performance when interacting with complex systems and intelligence]. *Diagnostica, 37,* 291–313.

Kreuzig, H. W., & Schlotthauer, J. A. (1991). Ein Computer-Simulations-Verfahren in der Praxis: Offene Fragen—empirische Antworten [Computer simulation in the application: Open questions—empirical answers]. In H. Schuler & U. Funke (Eds.), *Eignungsdiagnostik in Forschung und Praxis* (pp. 106–109). Stuttgart, Germany: Verlag für Angewandte Psychologie.

Kubinger, K. (1993). Testtheoretische Probleme der Computerdiagnostik [Test theoretical problems of computerized diagnosis]. *Zeitschrift für Arbeits- und Organisationspsychologie, 37*, 130–137.

Larkin, J. H. (1989). What kind of knowledge transfers? In L. B. Resnick (Ed.), *Knowing, learning, and instruction* (pp. 283–305). Hillsdale, NJ: Lawrence Erlbaum Associates.

Latzina, M. (1990). Problem solving: Using various dynamic model presentations. *Computers in Human Behavior, 6*, 97–113.

Leutner, D. (1992). *Adaptive Lernsysteme. Instruktionspsychologische Grundlagen und experimentelle Analysen* [Adaptive learning systems. Basics of instructional psychology and experimental analyses]. Weinheim, Germany: Psychologie Verlags Union.

Leutner, D. (in press). Computerunterstützte Planspiele als Instrument der Personalentwicklung [Computer-based simulations as instruments for personnel development]. In T. Geilhardt & T. Mühlbradt (Eds.), *Handbuch computerunterstützte Planspiele*. Stuttgart, Germany: Verlag für Angewandte Psychologie.

Lintern, G. (1991). Instructional strategies. In E. Morrison (Ed.), *Training for performance: Principles of applied human learning* (pp. 167–191). New York: Wiley.

Müller, H. (in press). Complex problem solving: The evaluation of reliability, stability, and some causal models. In R. Steyer, H. Gräser, & K. F. Widaman (Eds.), *Consistency and specificity: Latent state-trait models in differential psychology*. New York: Springer.

Obermann, C. (1991). *Problemlösesimulation "Airport"* [Problem solving situation "Airport"]. Göttingen, Germany: Hogrefe.

Obermann, C. (in press). Computergestützte Planspiele in der Mitarbeiterauswahl [Computer-based simulation games in personnel selection]. In T. Geilhardt & T. Mühlbradt (Eds.), *Handbuch computerunterstützte Planspiele*. Stuttgart, Germany: Verlag für Angewandte Psychologie.

Patrick, J. (1992). *Training: Research and practice*. London: Academic Press.

Preiß, P. (1992). Komplexität im Betriebswirtschaftslehre-Anfangsunterricht [Complexity in first-grade courses on economy]. In F. Achtenhagen & E. G. John (Eds.), *Mehrdimensionale Lehr-Lern-Arrangements* (pp. 58–78). Wiesbaden, Germany: Gabler.

Putz-Osterloh, W. (1981). Über die Beziehung zwischen Testintelligenz und Problemlöseerfolg [On the relationship between test intelligence and success in problem solving]. *Zeitschrift für Psychologie, 189*, 79–100.

Putz-Osterloh, W. (1983). Über Determinanten komplexer Problemlöseleistungen und Möglichkeiten zu ihrer Erfassung [On some processes determining the interaction with complex problems, and on the possibilities to assess these processes]. *Sprache & Kognition, 2*, 100–116.

Putz-Osterloh, W. (1985). Selbstreflexionen, Testintelligenz und interindividuelle Unterschiede bei der Bewältigung komplexer Probleme [Self-reflection, intelligence test scores, and interindividual differences in complex problem solving]. *Sprache & Kognition, 4*, 203–216.

Putz-Osterloh, W. (1990). Problemlösen [Problem solving]. In W. Sarges (Ed.), *Management-Diagnostik* (pp. 193–199). Göttingen, Germany: Hogrefe.

Putz-Osterloh, W. (1991). Computergestützte Eignungsdiagnostik: Warum Strategien informativer als Leistungen sein können [Computer-based aptitude tests: Why strategies can be more informative than performance data]. In H. Schuler & U. Funke (Eds.), *Eignungsdiagnostik in Forschung und Praxis. Psychologische Information für Auswahl, Beratung und Förderung von Mitarbeitern* (pp. 97–102). Stuttgart, Germany: Verlag für Angewandte Psychologie.

Putz-Osterloh, W. (1993). Complex problem solving as a diagnostic tool. In H. Schuler, J. L. Farr, & M. Smith (Eds.), *Personnel selection and assessment: Individual and organizational perspectives* (pp. 289–301). Hillsdale, NJ: Lawrence Erlbaum Associates.

Putz-Osterloh, W., Bott, B., & Köster, K. (1990). Modes of learning in problem solving: Are they transferable to tutorial systems? *Computers in Human Behavior, 6*, 83–96.

Putz-Osterloh, W., & Haupts, I. (1990). Diagnostik komplexer Organisations- und Ent-scheidungsstrategien in dynamischen Situationen: Validität und Anwendbarkeit [Diagnosis of complex strategies for organization and decision in dynamic situations: Validity and applicability]. *Untersuchungen des Psychologischen Dienstes der Bundeswehr, 25*, 107–167.

Putz-Osterloh, W., & Lemme, M. (1987). Knowledge and its intelligent application to problem solving. *German Journal of Psychology, 11*, 286–303.

Resnick, L. B. (1989). Introduction. In L. B. Resnick (Ed.), *Knowing, learning, and instruction. Essays in honor of Robert Glaser* (pp. 1–24). Hillsdale, NJ: Lawrence Erlbaum Associates.

Robertson, I. T., & Kandola, R. S. (1982). Work sample tests: Validity, adverse impact, and applicant reaction. *Journal of Occupational Psychology, 55*, 171–183.

Schaub, H. (1990). Die Situationsspezifität des Problemlöseverhaltens [The situational specificity of problem solving behavior]. *Zeitschrift für Psychologie, 198*, 83–96.

Schaub, H., & Strohschneider, S. (1992). Die Auswirkungen unterschiedlicher Problemlöseer-fahrung auf den Umgang mit einem unbekannten komplexen Problem [Effects of different experiences with problems on how to deal with an unknown complex problem]. *Zeitschrift für Arbeits- und Organisationspsychologie, 36*, 117–126.

Schippmann, J. S., Prien, E., & Katz, J. A. (1990). Reliability and validity of in-basket performance measures. *Personnel Psychology, 43*, 837–859.

Schönpflug, W. (1993). Applied Psychology: Newcomer with a long tradition. *Applied Psychology: An International Review, 42*, 5–30.

Schoppek, W. (1991). Spiel und Wirklichkeit—Reliabilität und Validität von Verhaltensmustern in komplexen Situationen [Game and reality—Reliability and validity of behavior patterns in complex situations]. *Sprache & Kognition, 10*, 15–27.

Schuler, H., Funke, U., Moser, K., & Donat, M. (in press). *Personalauswahl in Forschung und Entwicklung. Eignung und Leistung von Wissenschaftlern und Ingenieuren* [Personal selection in research and development]. Göttingen, Germany: Hogrefe.

Schwarck, J. Chr. (1986). *Trainingseffekte beim Lösen komplexer Probleme* [Effects of training in complex problem solving]. Frankfurt, Germany: Peter Lang.

Senge, P. M., & Sterman, J. D. (1992). Systems thinking and organizational learning: Acting locally and thinking globally in the organization of the future. *European Journal of Operational Research, 59*, 137–150.

Sonntag, K., & Schaper, N. (1992). Förderung beruflicher Handlungskompetenz [Development of professional competence]. In K. Sonntag (Ed.), *Personalentwicklung in Organisationen* (pp. 187–210). Göttingen, Germany: Hogrefe.

Stern, E. (1993). Kognitives Training: Was verändert sich? Fragestellungen, Methoden und neuere Ergebnisse [Cognitive training: What changes? Questions, methods, and recent results]. In L. Montada (Ed.), *Bericht über den 38. Kongreß der Deutschen Gesellschaft für Psychologie in Trier 1992* (pp. 975–977). Göttingen, Germany: Hogrefe.

Strauß, B., Hasselmann, D., & Hasselmann, G. (1993). Validitätsaspekte computergestützter Szenarien in der Managementdiagnostik [Aspects of validity for computer-based scenarios in management diagnosis]. In A. Gebert & U. Winterfeld (Eds.), *Arbeits-, Betriebs- und Organisationspsychologie vor Ort* (pp. 530–540). Bonn, Germany: Deutscher Psychologen Verlag.

Streufert, S., Nogami, G. Y., Swezey, R. W., Pogash, R. M., & Piasecki, M. T. (1988). Computer assisted training of complex managerial performance. *Computers in Human Behavior, 4*, 77–88.

Streufert, S., Pogash, R., & Piasecki, M. (1988). Simulation-based assessment of managerial competence: Reliability and validity. *Personnel Psychology, 41*, 537–557.

Streufert, S., & Swezey, R. W. (1986). *Complexity, managers, and organizations*. New York: Academic Press.

Strohschneider, S. (1986). Zur Stabilität und Validität von Handeln in komplexen Re-alitätsbereichen [On the stability and validity of complex problem-solving behavior]. *Sprache & Kognition, 5*, 42–48.

Strohschneider, S., & Schaub, H. (in press). Problemlösen [Problem solving]. In T. Geilhardt & T. Mühlbradt (Eds.), *Handbuch computerunterstützte Planspiele*. Stuttgart, Germany: Verlag für Angewandte Psychologie.

Süß, H. M., Beauducel, A., Kersting, M., & Oberauer, K. (1992). Wissen und Problemlösen. Zur Dissoziation von verbalisierbarem Wissen und Steuerleistungen beim komplexen Problemlösen [Knowledge and problem solving. On the dissociation between verbalizable knowledge and control performance in a complex problem solving task]. In L. Montada (Ed.), *Bericht über den 38. Kongreß der Deutschen Gesellschaft für Psychologie in Trier 1992* (pp. 347–348). Göttingen, Germany: Hogrefe.

Süß, H. M., Kersting, M., & Oberauer, K. (1991). Intelligenz und Wissen als Prädiktoren für Leistungen bei computersimulierten komplexen Problemen [Intelligence and knowledge as predictors of performance in solving complex computer-simulated problems]. *Diagnostica, 37*, 334–352.

Süß, H.-M., Oberauer, K., & Kersting, M. (1993). Intellektuelle Fähigkeiten und die Steuerung komplexer Systeme [Intelligence and control performance on computer-simulated systems]. *Sprache & Kognition, 12*, 83–97.

Tannenbaum, S. I., & Yukl, G. (1992). Training and development in work organizations. *Annual Review of Psychology, 43*, 399–441.

Thornton, G. C., & Cleveland, J. N. (1990). Developing managerial talent through simulation. *American Psychologist, 45*, 190–199.

Ulrich, H., & Probst, G. J. (1988). *Anleitung zum ganzheitlichen Denken und Handeln* [How to think and act wholistically]. Stuttgart, Germany: Haupt.

Wernimont, P. R., & Campbell, J. P. (1966). Signs, samples, and criteria. *Journal of Applied Psychology, 52*, 372–376.

PART FOUR

METHDOLOGICAL ISSUES IN RESEARCH ON COMPLEX PROBLEM SOLVING

CHAPTER TEN

Experimental Research on Complex Problem Solving

Joachim Funke
University of Bonn, Germany

INTRODUCTION

In the European tradition, experimental research on Complex Problem Solving (henceforth CPS) is relatively new; indeed, it was not the preferred mode of studying CPS when this research domain was introduced during the mid-1970s. This statement may sound somewhat surprising given that one of the most cited early German studies on CPS, the LOHHAUSEN study (Dörner, Kreuzig, Reither, & Stäudel, 1983) in which subjects were asked to perform the duties of the mayor of a small simulated city, was an experimental study in which a treatment factor (i.e., training schedule) was effectively manipulated. That this study was indeed an experimental study has often been overlooked because the experimental results were by far not as impressive as the low correlations between test intelligence and CPS scores that were reported by the authors (see, e.g., Dörner, 1980).

The experimental treatment in the Dörner et al. study consisted of two different types of training, (a) training where global information about strategic procedures was available to subjects, and (b), training where more concrete hints on strategic and tactical issues were given. Performance in the two training groups was compared to performance in a control group. The results demonstrated that although subjects in the treatment conditions judged the training sessions as helpful, the three groups did not differ on the dependent variables that captured the quality of system's control.

Soon after the new research domain CPS had been established, a theoretical discussion concerning the experimental approach to studying CPS began that has not ended to this date. Dörner (1989), on the one hand, pointed out that classical experimental methods, and especially tools like analysis of variance, are not useful when one wishes to understand the complex behavior of people operating on complex systems. Funke (1984), in contrast, has argued that experimental research within CPS is not a contradiction in terms.

In the following, I am concerned with how the experimental method can be, and has been, fruitfully employed to help us understand CPS. As previously stated (Frensch & Funke, this volume), CPS, at least in the European tradition, deals with problem solving of tasks that are novel, dynamic, complex, and intransparent. This discussion, therefore, is limited to experimental research utilizing tasks, mostly computerized, that meet these criteria. I do not discuss static tasks, for example.

In the first section, I summarize and discuss the pros and cons of the experimental approach to studying CPS. In the second section, I present a taxonomic scheme that categorizes most of the experimental work that has been performed to date, and discuss some experimental studies in detail to illustrate what has been achieved so far. In the final section, I draw conclusion regarding why, when, and how to conduct experimental studies in CPS research.

PROS AND CONS OF EXPERIMENTAL RESEARCH

In the first section, I describe a critique of the analytical approach that has been formulated recently, discuss some alternatives to ANOVA techniques, and describe the main features of the experimental approach as it has been used to conduct CPS research. I start with some provocative and critical remarks.

A Critique of the Analytical Approach

In a rather amusing paper, Dörner (1989) has illustrated his critique of the analytical approach to studying CPS (i.e., the experimental analysis of complex behavior) by using an example of strange green turtles that have invaded earth from outer space and have been found by human scientists. The scientists, of course, want to understand how the turtles behave. Unbeknownst to the scientists, the turtles' behavior can be described by a finite state automaton and is rather simple: they drive through pipes with little space shuttles and polish the tubes wherever they find dust. Sometimes the turtles appear to sleep; at other times, they behave restlessly as if they were searching for something special. They also react to light differentially: a red light makes them stop, a green one lets them go, etc. The researchers propose to analyze the turtles' behavior experimentally in a *turtle box* in order to find contingencies between the turtles' behavior and the degree of dust or type of light they encounter. Analysis of variance reveals that 15% of the variance in the turtles' behavior is due to the type of light the turtles encounter. If one uses the previous behavior of the turtles as additional predictor, one gains an additional 11% in variance explained.

Dörner's (1989) main argument is that the program behind the turtles' behavior, driven by a finite state automaton, cannot be detected by any experimental analysis that is based on the general linear model. Instead of aggregating and averaging over situations, one needs to very precisely describe the individual turtles' behavior, based on long periods of observation, if one wants to understand "what makes the turtles tick." Indeed, Dörner reports that it was one of the researchers' children who developed a good model of the turtles' behavior based on her long observation during playing with the turtles.

Alternatives to ANOVA Techniques

Dörner's provocative paper argues against the use of the experimental method in cases where the subjects under study show interaction phenomena. In these cases, only controlled single case studies in combination with computer simulations of the cognitive processes can reveal what is going on—according to Dörner. But is this really true?

Dörner's story, I argue, misrepresents experimental psychology and is a good example for how ANOVA techniques can be misunderstood. ANOVA is a tool for data analysis; it is not, nor was it ever intended to be, a research method. If one uses experimental designs in one's research, one need not rely on analysis of variance for data analysis. Confirmatory LISREL analysis, for example, can be a very powerful tool for testing causal assumptions. As far as I know, Müller (1993, in press) has been the first to use LISREL methods in the analysis of causal models involving CPS variables. Müller was interested in predicting subjects' control performance from their knowledge about the system. His study was designed according to the principles of latent state-trait theory (see Steyer, Gräser, & Widaman, in press). That is, at two different points in time, subjects' knowledge about the system and the quality of their control performance was measured on two independent, but formally identical systems. This design allows to distinguish state from trait influences. Figure 10.1 shows the causal model that fit Müller's (1993) data well.

The model depicted in Figure 10.1 shows a latent trait variable I that represents subjects' ability to identify the relations among the system variables. This ability directly influences the state variables for identification performance at time 1 (I_1) and time 2 (I_2); both, in turn, have direct and strong effects on the state variables for control performances at the corresponding time points, C_1 and C_2, which are moderately correlated.

My main point here is that the misuse of a specific data analysis technique cannot and should not be used as an argument against the use of experimental methods in general. A similar point has recently been made by Riefer and Batchelder (1988) who argue for the use of multinomial processing models of cognitive processes instead of classical ANOVA techniques in human memory research. They do not, and neither do I, argue against the use of the experimental method in general, however.

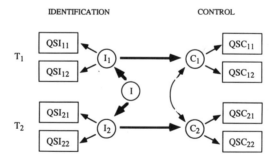

FIG. 10.1. Simplified LISREL model capturing the relation between system identification (manifest variable "Quality of System Identification," *QSI*) and system control (manifest variable "Quality of System Control," *QSC*). The indices stand for time of measurement (T_1 or T_2) and type of system. The latent variables "Identification" (*I*) and "Control" (*C*) also have time indices (adapted from Müller, 1993, p. 102).

Features of the Experimental Approach

Which approaches to examining CPS might a researcher choose? In addition to the experimental manipulation of variables, the researcher might decide to adopt a single-case analysis. The latter approach has as its goal the exact reconstruction of an individual solution approach to a given problem (see Kluwe, this volume). Or the researcher might attempt to construct an artificial system that reproduces subjects' behavior as accurately as possible (i.e., computer simulation of cognitive processes; see Dörner & Wearing, this volume). Although all of these represent reasonable approaches to studying CPS, I am concerned with the first possibility only, that is the experimental manipulation of variables that are deemed important for our understanding of CPS. Next, I shall discuss some pros and cons of the experimental approach.

Separation of Independent and Dependent Variables. One of the fundamental aspects of experimental research is the separation of independent (IV) and dependent variables (DV). IVs are variables that are experimentally manipulated; DVs are response variables that indicate the effects of the experimental manipulation. In principle, and when some assumptions (e.g., randomized allocation of subjects to treatments) are met, this setup allows for a causal interpretation such that the observed effects have been caused by the manipulation of the IVs. The separation of cause and effect in combination with a model that captures the relation between IVs and DVs constitutes the basis for causal explanations which is a high goal in any natural as well as social sciences.

However, some argue that the separation of cause and effect, or IVs and DVs, ignores the fact that for some systems such a differentiation is highly artificial. If one looks at a simple predator-prey-system in ecology, for instance, then it would be a mistake to claim that one of two species is the cause of the other's survival. In reality, both species depend highly on each other due to feedback loops in the system. As Brehmer and Dörner (1993, p. 178) put it, "Thus, in experiments with microworlds we have to give up the traditional focus on stimulus-response laws in favor of more cybernetic conceptions." However, even feedback loops can be described in terms of causes and effects and can thus be examined experimentally. There is therefore no convincing reason to assume that the study of complex systems cannot be approached experimentally.

Control of Manipulation. Closely related to the separation of cause and effect is the question of experimental control. For an experiment to be considered solid, one needs a strong degree of control over the treatment conditions. One of the problems with the control of the manipulation in

CPS research, however, is that typically only the starting values can be controlled in any given system. Once a subject has entered the first response, the subject moves through the microworld on an individual path. Due to the fact that, at least in complex microworlds, there exists a huge number of potential interventions for each simulation cycle, it is virtually impossible that two subjects follow exactly the same pathway through the system. Therefore, the *stimulus* cannot be controlled by the experimenter—the experimenter merely sets the stage for a subject who then follows an idiosyncratic path. Brehmer, Leplat, and Rasmussen (1991, p. 379) point out that "the traditional psychological idea of a strict causation from stimuli to responses must be abandoned, for in these experiments, stimuli are produced by the subjects."

Although I agree that experimental control, at least in a narrow sense, cannot be maintained in complex microworlds, I believe that Brehmer et al.'s conclusion is unwarranted. The loss of control does not invalidate the experimental approach. It does, however, require a more careful analysis of between-subjects effects. Because there exist different individual pathways through a system, one needs to make certain, for example, that the dependent variables are comparable across levels of the IV. One way of achieving this would be to partial the proportion of variance within a dependent variable that is due to the Eigendynamik of the system (see the following); this can be done, for instance, by running the simulation system without any intervention. Another way to achieve comparability across levels of the IV would be to *reset* a system more often and to give subjects a new chance with the same, or comparable, start values. Both of these procedures make the measurement of subjects' performance more reliable.

Replication. One of the criteria for solid experimental work is that an observed phenomenon can be replicated. This requirement distinguishes artifacts and epiphenomena from real, *true* phenomena. In psychological research, replicability is affected by the reliability of measurement. If one is interested in determining a person's IQ score, for instance, and if it is assumed that IQ is a stable trait that does not change much over time, then measures obtained at different points in time should not differ by much. The reliability of measures is thus a necessary requirement in experimental CPS research.

However, if one asks subjects twice to play the role of the major of the small city, for instance, one cannot expect the second performance to be equal to the initial performance. After all, subjects learn about the system during their interaction. Thus, it should not come as a surprise that studies on the reliability and stability of CPS measures all too often yield low scores (e.g., Hasselmann, 1993; Schoppek, 1991; Strohschneider, 1986; Süß, Kersting, & Oberauer, 1991, 1993; but see Müller, 1993; Putz-Osterloh, 1991), leading some to even argue that situation specificity is a characteristic feature of CPS (see Schaub, 1990), or worse, that unstable data is a reason for not working experimentally but, for example, to perform single-case analyses in order to gain some insight into what is going on.

From the viewpoint of an experimental psychologist, of course, it does not make sense to obtain reliability scores if there is no stable phenomenon. If one is interested in finding replicable phenomena, then one has to conduct better experiments. Data snooping, I believe, is, at best, useful for generating hypotheses. Hypotheses, however, can be generated by other means also.

Objectivity.   One of the advantages often claimed by proponents of the experimental method is the objectivity of the method. This means that different people all watching the same event should all come to the same conclusion about what has happened. In the case of experimental CPS research, this implies the use of measures that objectively capture a subject's knowledge and behavior. Notice that the existence of an experimental treatment effect does not necessarily imply that the subject is aware of the effect—what is important is that the treatment has an effect on the dependent variables.

Of course, one might argue, as some do, for a strong reliance on subjects' opinions about, and perceptions of, say, a microworld's demands (e.g., Putz-Osterloh & Bott, 1990; Schaub, 1993; Strohschneider, 1990). If subjects do not perceive any difference between two selected systems with respect to their cognitive demands, then the systems should be categorized as of equal difficulty, regardless of whether or not objective measures show significant differences (see the discussion between Funke, 1991, and Strohschneider, 1991a). The main point here is that subjective evaluations are assumed to be more important than any criterion variable.

I believe strongly that any reliance on the self-reports of subjects is mistaken. There are simply too many processes going on during CPS that, although they might never reach subjects' awareness, nevertheless affect CPS performance.

Summary

There are at least two different opinions concerning the adequacy of experimental methods for studying CPS (cf. Eyferth, Schömann, & Widowski, 1986). Some argue that such complex phenomena cannot be analyzed with classical experimental techniques but require different techniques, such as, for instance, cognitive modeling (e.g., Brehmer & Dörner, 1993; Dörner, 1989, 1992; Dörner & Wearing, this volume; Schaub, 1993; Strohschneider, 1991a). Others argue for the use of experimental techniques because of their central role in scientific progress (e.g., Funke, 1991, 1993; Hussy, 1985; Kluwe, this volume; Müller, 1993; Strauß, 1993). It appears that the controversy may, at least in part, be due to a misconception of what experimental methods really are. Experimental techniques are not only useful in testing a set of static assumptions; they can also be used to test dynamic process models.

A TAXONOMY OF VARIABLES THAT AFFECT COMPLEX PROBLEM SOLVING

Before describing examples of experimental studies, I will first introduce a taxonomic scheme in order to structure the research on CPS that has been performed. According to the taxonomy, three different factors affect CPS performance, namely person, situation, and system variables. The taxonomy was first presented in Funke (1986; later refinements in Funke, 1990) as an elaboration of Hussy's (1985) two-factor model. Hussy proposed a differentiation between person variables and problem variables. Funke's three-factor proposal was subsequently criticized by Strohschneider (1991a) and Strauß (1993). According to Strauß, the main controversy is one between a more operationally oriented position (the experimenter's view) as represented by Funke (1990), and a more subjective point of view (the subject's view) as represented by Strohschneider (1991a). Strauß himself argues for a two-fold taxonomy consisting of person factors and problem factors. I present next the original taxonomy from Funke (1990) with its three classes. The three factors are introduced first.

Person Factors

Person factors comprise competencies that a subject introduces into the CPS situation and competencies that a subject acquires during interaction with the situation. For example, subjects working with a certain simulation system may be experts in the simulated domain or may be novices (see, e.g., Reither, 1981). Also, subjects may learn more or less about the dynamics of a simulated scenario during their exploration and control of the system (see, e.g., Heineken, Arnold, Kopp, & Soltysiak, 1992).

Situation Factors

Situation factors include different experimental contexts in which a simulation system can be embedded. Situational context factors are independent from the used scenario. For example, subjects may be instructed to either passively observe a system or to actively make interventions (e.g., Funke & Müller, 1988), or subjects may be presented with a diagram describing the system's relations or not (e.g., Putz-Osterloh, 1981).

System Factors

System factors represent specific attributes of the used system, that are either formal or content related. For example, the same simulation system of an epidemic disease may be presented to subjects as simulating a harmless flu or as simulating a dangerous smallpox propagation (see Hesse, 1982). Independent of this semantic embedding, the task may vary on the situation factor as being transparent with respect to its interrelations, for example, or not.

Summary

Taxonomies are useful for structuring research domains. Traditionally, taxonomies in the area of problem solving have differentiated between well-defined and ill-defined problems in terms of their givens and goals (e.g., Reitman, 1965). In CPS, three main factors can be distinguished where each factor can be manipulated independently of all others. These three factors are the person, the given situation, and the system, or task, at hand.

**EXPERIMENTAL RESEARCH
ON COMPLEX PROBLEM SOLVING**

In the following, I discuss some experimental results for each of the above mentioned influence factors. The section is intended to demonstrate the merits of experimental research on CPS. Therefore, I discuss only a specific selection of studies and do not give a complete overview.

Studies on Person Factors

Studies exploring the effect of person factors on CPS tend to focus on test intelligence as one dominant and important person variable. In addition, comparisons between experts and novices and analyses on clinical groups and on strategic preferences belong into this category. Other person variables that have been explored theoretically as well as experimentally but are not discussed here because of space limitations, include self-reflection (e.g., Putz-Osterloh, 1985; Reither, 1981), value orientation (e.g., Reither, 1985), emotions (e.g., Dörner, Reither, & Stäudel, 1983; Hesse, Spies, & Lüer, 1983; Stäudel, 1987) and language (e.g., Roth, 1985; Roth, Meyer, & Lampe, 1991).

Test Intelligence. Strohschneider (1990, 1991b) has compared the predictive value of test intelligence for CPS performance under two different experimental conditions. All subjects operated an abstract system called VEKTOR first, and were then confronted with the semantically rich peace-corps worker simulation system, MORO. The *Berlin Intelligence Structure* test (BIS; see Jäger, 1982, 1984, for a detailed description) was used to assess subjects' intelligence. The BIS differentiates between two factors, a content-oriented component representing knowledge in three different modalities, and a process-oriented component representing four operative abilities. For the MORO system (Strohschneider, 1991b, Exp. 2), *all* of the seven subtest scales correlated significantly with a general measure of control performance; the same was found for the VEKTOR system with respect to six out of the seven subscales. Strohschneider concluded that test intelligence was indeed a significant predictor of CPS performance. Comparing the two systems, Strohschneider found that performance on the two was not correlated significantly. This indicates that a single CPS trait may not be responsible for performance under all conditions.

Süß, Oberauer, and Kersting (1993; Süß, Kersting, & Oberauer, 1993) also assessed the value of test intelligence for predicting CPS performance measures. In their study, the authors used the well-known system TAILORSHOP under intransparency conditions. All subjects were also asked to complete the intelligence test BIS. Using traditional measures of performance for the TAILORSHOP (total assets at the end of simulation and the number of simulated months with a revenue), the authors found no significant correlations with any of the BIS scales. Based on the assumption that the (unknown and therefore perhaps low) reliability of the CPS measures could have caused this zero-effect, the authors tried other ways of operationalizing the TAILORSHOP performance. In a task analysis, the authors discovered that two sub-goals were used by clever problem solvers that, unfortunately, conflicted with each other: shirt sales and profit margin. Due to system inherent characteristics, all subjects had a negative profit margin; lucky problem solvers, however, decreased this negative value and at the same time increased shirt sales. Because revenues are the product of sales and profit margin per shirt, clever problem solvers increased their losses despite the fact that they were using efficient strategies. When Süß, Oberauer, and Kersting (1993) constructed a new dependent measure, namely the *sum* of the increases in shirt sales and in profit margin, then the new measure of CPS quality correlated significantly with the BIS scale "capacity of information processing."

Taken together, the two studies demonstrate that intellectual abilities have predictive value for CPS results when certain conditions are met: (1) instead of using a global IQ measure, one needs to separate different components of intelligence of which the "capacity of information processing" appears to be the most promising predictor; and, (2) CPS quality has to be measured reliably—a condition which is rarely met. For more details on the role of intelligence in CPS, see Hörmann and Thomas (1989), Hussy (1989, 1991), Jäger (1984, 1991) and Beckmann and Guthke (this volume). A recent review on this topic is given by Kluwe et al. (1991).

Expert-Novice Comparisons. Reither (1981) was the first to validate the third-world scenario DAGU by comparing the control performances of experienced technical advisers, who had about ten years of practice in third-world countries (i.e., experts), and of postgraduate students who had just begun their first mission as development aid volunteers (i.e., novices). Both experts and novices worked on the system DAGU in groups of three. The main result of Reither's study was that experts showed a broader range of actions and a greater willingness to make decisions from the start, but also that experts used only standard strategies and were not able to adopt to changing task conditions. Reither calls this behavior the "blindness of the specialists" (see also Frensch & Sternberg, 1989). Despite these strategic differences between novices and experts, *both* groups performed terribly on the system, however. In both groups, the number of inhabitants of the simulated country had decreased dramatically after 20 simulated years, due to starvation. This finding leads to the (as of yet unanswered) question if either the experts did not acquire any usable knowledge during their ten years of practice, or if the simulated system did not capture reality in a valid manner.

Schaub and Strohschneider (1992) examined if managers and students act differently when dealing with the MORO scenario. In MORO, subjects have to take the role of a peace-corps worker in Africa. The authors reported that the managers' problem solving behavior was characterized by a more intensive exploration of the scenario and by a more cautious and adaptive way of adjusting to the demands of the task. On average, the managers achieved better results than the students. One potentially confounding factor in this comparative study was the age of the subjects, however. The managers were 25 years older than the students, on average, and, thus, had more life experience. Similar studies comparing students of economy with professors of that discipline on their performances on the TAILORSHOP scenario have been conducted by Putz-Osterloh (1987; see also Putz-Osterloh & Lemme, 1987). These studies are presented in more detail by Buchner (this volume).

Repeated exposure to a problem, of course, also produces a certain degree of expertise and should therefore lead to better problem performance and representation. This could indeed be demonstrated in a number of studies where subjects had to work on the same scenario for more than one simulation period (e.g., Dörner & Pfeifer, 1992; Funke, 1985; Heineken et al., 1992; Schmuck, 1992). In general, it seems fair to argue that knowledge is an important predictor of control performance (Funke, 1985; Putz-Osterloh, Bott, & Houben, 1988), although dissociations between the two variables in CPS situations have also been reported (see Berry & Broadbent, 1984; Broadbent, FitzGerald, & Broadbent, 1986; Hayes & Broadbent, 1988; for critical remarks see Haider, 1992, 1993; Sanderson, 1989). These dissociations are covered in more detail by Berry and Broadbent (this volume).

Clinical Groups. In a prospective longitudinal study, Fritz and Funke (1988; see also Fritz & Funke, 1990) compared the quality of CPS in pupils who had *minimal cerebral dysfunctions* (MCD) and in matched controls (CON). Working with the dynamic system OEKOSYSTEM, all subjects were asked to first explore and then to control the system. In terms of the quality of subjects' knowledge acquisition (as revealed by causal diagrams of the assumed structural relations), the authors found that the MCD group did not acquire significantly less knowledge than did the CON group. However, the strategies used differed markedly for the two groups. Subjects in the CON group used single variation interventions which tend to reveal the causal relations among variables three times more often than did subjects in the MCD group. With respect to the quality of system control, there was no significant group difference, although 20% of the subjects in the CON group reached the required goal state at least once, whereas almost none of the MCD subjects did.

Strategies. Schmuck (1992) used a self-constructed instrument to assess the degree to which subjects spontaneously exert executive control and compared subjects with high and low efficiency of executive control on their performances in the FIRE scenario. Subjects classified as highly efficient showed better performance from the start but also needed more time and made more interventions. These subjects also showed a greater variability in behavior than did subjects classified as low in efficiency (see also Krems, this volume). Schmuck argued that these strategic differences explain the low stability scores found in many CPS studies (a similar argument has been made by Ringelband, Misiak, & Kluwe, 1990). The explanation relies strongly on the assumption, however, that Schmuck's instrument allows a reliable differentiation between people who differ in efficiency, a fact that has yet to be demonstrated.

Vollmeyer and Holyoak (1993) have recently analyzed the strategies subjects use when exploring, controlling, and predicting an unknown complex dynamic system called BIOLOGY LAB. Subjects were categorized according to their exploration behavior as either (1) using a scientific strategy, (2) using systematic variations of a strategy, or (3) using unsystematic variations of a strategy. As expected, strategies (1) and (2) led to a better representation of the system and to a better prediction of system states than did strategy (3). Surprisingly however, no group differences were found for subjects' control performance. The authors interpret their result as indicating that different types of knowledge are necessary for the three different tasks (see also Reichert & Dörner, 1988, on the use of simple heuristics).

Putz-Osterloh (1993) also strongly recommends strategy analyses for the explanation of individual differences. Using the DYNAMIS microworld, she found significant improvements in structural system knowledge for subjects using efficient strategies for intervention, a finding that stands in direct contrast to the findings reported by Vollmeyer and Holyoak (1993).

Studies on Situation Factors

In studies exploring the role of situation factors on CPS, several variables have been experimentally manipulated, including the type of task, the effects of noise-induced stress, individual versus group problem solving, the transparency of system variables, and the type of the system presentation.

Type of Task. Funke and Müller (1988) conducted an experiment with the SINUS system in which the subjects' task was to first explore an unknown dynamic system for a given number of trials through either passive observation of another person interacting with the system or active intervention. Later, all subjects were asked to control the system such that given goal states were reached. The dependent variables in this study were the quality of knowledge acquisition and the quality of control performance. Results showed that active intervention led to better control performance but reduced the amount of verbalizable knowledge. Surprisingly, the observers, who were poor in control performance, constructed better causal diagrams showing the system variables; thus, they appeared to have acquired knowledge about the variables and their interrelations but not about how to control the system.

Berry (1991) performed a similar study using the SUGAR PRODUCTION and the PERSONAL INTERACTION tasks. In her Experiment 1, subjects had to first watch an experimenter interacting with the system and then to control the system by themselves. It seemed as if subjects did not learn anything through pure observation, neither on the control scores nor on the post-task questionnaires. In a second experiment, Berry found that learning by observation was however possible when the task was changed from a task with non-salient relations to a task with salient relations among the system variables. The effect of this modification was apparent on both diagnostic measures, on the quality of control performance as well as on the system knowledge as measured by a questionnaire (for more details, see Berry & Broadbent, this volume).

Stress. Dörner and Pfeifer (1992) tested the effects of noise-induced stress on CPS. Despite the fact that stress is certainly a person variable this study is subsumed under situation factors because the experimental conditions manipulated situational aspects. The authors used a version of the FIRE scenario developed by Brehmer and his associates (Brehmer & Allard, 1991; see also Brehmer, this volume). The subjects' task was to manage five different fires either under conditions of a stressful white noise or under quiet conditions. Time pressure was present in both conditions. At a global level, there was no difference between the two conditions with respect to their success and failure rates. A more fine grained analysis—looking at subjects' tactical decisions—revealed, however, that although stress did not affect the number of errors made, it did affect which types of errors were made (for a classification of CPS errors see, e.g., Dörner, 1991). For example, an incorrect dosage of fire fighting interventions and a more reactive type of behavior was characteristic of the stressed subjects.

Individual versus Group CPS. Köller, Dauenheimer, and Strauß (1993) compared group CPS to individual CPS. In a first session, all subjects worked individually on the scenario FUEL OIL DISTRIBUTION. Performance on the system was then used to classify subjects as either good or poor problem solvers. Then, in a second session, subjects worked on a very similar scenario called TEXTILESHOP either individually or in a dyad consisting of either two poor or two good problem solvers. It turned out that the individual problem solvers' performances were worse than the performances achieved by the dyads. For the latter, it did not seem to matter whether they were composed of good or poor problem solvers.

Leutner (1988) worked with pupils who had to deal with a derivative of the TAILORSHOP either as individuals or in groups of three persons. In distinction to the previously reported work it turned out here that knowledge acquisition was significantly higher for individuals than for groups but with respect to control performance there was no difference (for more details see Leutner, 1992).

Badke-Schaub (1993) analyzed problem-solving strategies of individuals and groups dealing with a model for the epidemic of AIDS. Subjects had to propose interventions to prevent the spreadout of the disease. Badke-Schaub found that groups have problems to define a common goal but have advantages in finding problem-relevant informations. Groups also produced more proposals for solutions but found it difficult to select one or more of these proposals.

Transparency. Putz-Osterloh and Lüer (1981; see also Putz-Osterloh, 1981) investigated the effect of transparency on problem solving quality in the scenario TAILORSHOP. One group received the system under conditions of intransparency; here, subjects were told only which interventions were possible but did not receive further information. The second group received a graphical representation of the relations among (almost all of) the system variables. After 15 simulated time cycles (i.e., months), subjects in the transparency condition had achieved better scores on the performance measure. In addition, the correlation between system performance and test intelligence was also moderated by transparency. Only under transparent conditions was a small but significant rank correlation between the two variables observed; under intransparency conditions, the correlation was zero. Putz-Osterloh and Lüer (1981) argued that the equivalence of the two tasks—the intelligence test and the CPS task—might have been much higher under transparency than under intransparency conditions. In the former case, both tasks shared the attribute that information was given to subjects who had to analyze it. In the latter case, CPS required additional information search procedures that were not necessary to complete the intelligence test. Although it may have been true for the Putz-Osterloh and Lüer study, Funke (1983) has shown empirically that this assumption does not generally hold: The moderating effect of transparency on the IQ-CPS relationship is lost in favor of a main effect of test intelligence if one selects a larger range of IQ values than those shown normally by student subjects.

In a recent study, Putz-Osterloh (1993) again manipulated the transparency of a system by presenting, or not presenting, a structural diagram of the system DYNAMIS. In this study, the experimental group which received the diagram was not superior to a control group without diagram on measures of task performance and strategy selection. But on a follow-up transfer task with a modified system, the experimental group outperformed the control group on both types of indicators. Putz-Osterloh concluded from these results that knowledge acquisition is not necessarily a prerequisite for good control. The strategies that are applied may be more important for predicting the quality of performance.

Information Presentation. Hübner (1987, 1988) performed an experiment in which 20 subjects had to control a simulated GAS ABSORBER. The system state was displayed either in an analog or a numerical format. With respect to the dependent variable *Quality of Control* it turned out that the analog group was significantly better and also needed less time than the group with numeric presentation.

Studies on System Factors

Experimental research manipulating system attributes has concentrated on the effects of the variables Eigendynamik, feedback delay, and semantic embedding.

Eigendynamik. In a series of experiments, Funke (1993) systematically varied several system factors, one of which was the *Eigendynamik* of the system (Exp. 2). Eigendynamik is present when a system changes its state at time t due to the values of some variables at time t-1 but does so independently of any input by the operator. In the extreme case, Eigendynamik means that a system changes over time despite the fact that no active intervention has occurred. Many natural systems show this property requiring an operator to anticipate the system's inherent changes due to the Eigendynamik (see, e.g., de Keyser, 1990). Funke (1993) has used the SINUS system, an artificial system simulating the growth of living creatures from a distant planet with three exogenous and three endogenous variables, to study the effect of Eigendynamik. There were three different conditions, a control condition with no Eigendynamik, and two conditions with different degrees of Eigendynamik. The results demonstrated that increased Eigendynamik yielded a decrease in the quality of system control although the quality of system identification remained unaffected by the manipulation. This pattern of findings suggests that the two dependent variables may tap different processes that are differentially affected by Eigendynamik.

Feedback Delays. Heineken et al. (1992) tested the effects of feedback delay on CPS by using a simple system called TEMPERATURE in which subjects had to control the temperature of an artificial system for 1.200 simulation cycles. Feedback concerning the quality of the intervention was either immediate or after little or much delay. In addition, half of the subjects were informed in advance which delay condition would be realized. Heineken et al. reported that, (a) the quality of system control decreased with increasing delay, and, (b) a priori information about the delay was not effective. Interestingly enough, even in the much-delay condition, subjects were—after a long period of time—able to control the system. This indicates that although feedback delay may influence the rate of learning, it does not appear to completely block the ability to master a time-delayed systems.

Other studies manipulating feedback delay have been performed by Funke (1985), Matern (1979), and, most notably, Brehmer (1990). Brehmer's research will not be presented here; instead the interested reader is referred to his chapter in this volume.

Semantic Embedding. Hesse (1982) has compared two different semantic embeddings for the same underlying system. EPIDEMIC simulates the spread of a disease in a small community. In one condition, subjects, as the managers of a local health service, were asked to care for people who had the flu. In the second condition, the disease was changed to a life threatening small-pox epidemic. The change in semantics changed subjects' behavior drastically; in the more "dangerous" situation, subjects tended to be, among other things, much more involved, and to take more time for making their decisions.

Another interesting study on the effects of semantic embedding has been reported by Beckmann (1995; see also Beckmann & Guthke, this volume). The author compared two semantic embeddings (CHERRY TREE vs. MACHINE) of the same system structure with respect to subjects' knowledge acquisition and control performances. In this experiment, the semantically rich embedding seemed to prevent problem solvers from using efficient analytic knowledge acquisition strategies.

Problem isomorphs in the sense of Hayes and Simon (1976) have also been used by Berry and Broadbent (1984; see also Berry & Broadbent, this volume), Funke and Hussy (1984), and by Huber (in press; see also Huber, this volume).

Studies on Interaction Effects

The interactions between person, situation, and system factors have been researched less frequently than the individual factors. One selected area concerns the interaction between person and situation variables.

Person and Situation.   Rost and Strauß (1993) analyzed the interaction between type of information presentation (numerically vs. graphically) and type of induced mental model (propositional vs. analog) using a simple simulation system called SHOP. Their study demonstrates the usefulness of interaction analysis in CPS research. The authors started with the assumption that the advantages of a certain presentation format (presentation of system information in numeric or in graphical form) would affect performance only if it corresponded to the format in which knowledge about the system was internally represented. The internal representation format was induced in this study in a short training session that either stimulated thinking about the system in terms of propositions (if-then statements) or in terms of a graphical network in which the nodes represented the variables connected by causal links, and the diameter of the nodes indicated the quantitative state of the variables. Rost and Strauß (1993) assumed that a propositional representation of system knowledge would best fit a numerical presentation and that the analog representation would best fit the graphical presentation. The central system variable in their scenario was *Money.* For each of the 25 simulation cycles, the dependent variable *Problem Solving Quality* was set to +1 if an increase in money had occurred, −1 in case of a decrease, and 0 in case of no change. The results of this rather interesting experiment are summarized in Figure 10.2.

The figure illustrates a significant disordinal interaction between type of presentation and type of training. The analog training condition showed large differences between the two presentation formats whereas the propositional training differences were much smaller for the two presentation formats. The interaction between person (i.e., representation format) and situation (i.e., presentation format) variables clearly indicates a necessity to go beyond main effects in the experimental analysis of CPS. Other work on interaction research has been done by Leutner (1988, 1992) within his studies

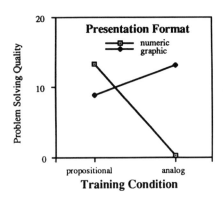

FIG. 10.2. Interaction between type of training and type of presentation format on problem solving quality (adapted from Rost & Strauß, 1993, p. 80).

on aptitude treatment interaction between pupils' ability and type of learning during CPS.

Summary

The short overview over experimental research conducted in the area of CPS illustrates that the different facets of the taxonomic scheme have not received equal attention by researchers. In addition, at least some preliminary conclusions turned out to depend on the selection of the facet under study. If one allows only for a variation in the person facet, one may indeed conclude that there are no situation effects and no effects due to system attributes on CPS. Clearly, studies that simultaneously manipulate at least two of the three mentioned facets are required because only they allow for the analysis of interactions between the different facets. To illustrate the importance of this argument look at the case of transparency: we know very clear about the moderating role of transparency with respect to the relation between CPS performance and test intelligence. Other examples discussed above demonstrate how interesting results can be produced within such multifactor experiments.

CONCLUDING REMARKS

What are the merits, the advantages, and the disadvantages of using the experimental method for exploring CPS? Do the findings presented above really *depend* on the use of the experimental method? Could we have come up with similar conclusions if we had used different techniques? From my very personal point of view, the presented examples demonstrate at least three main points.

First, the experimental method is useful, that is, CPS *can* be fruitfully explored experimentally. The assumption that this research area can, in principle, not be explored through well established analytical tools is simply not justified. The complexity of the research topic is independent of the complexity of the analysis used: complex systems can be studied with simple tools.

Second, the taxonomy presented is a useful one. There is overwhelming evidence for differential effects of person, situation, and system variables on measures of CPS knowledge and performance. One may, of course, discuss whether or not the three facets are independent, semi-independent, or related, but their usefulness for guiding research agendas should not be doubted.

And third, interaction studies are both useful and necessary. It is absolutely essential to conduct more interaction studies because the real story is in the interaction of various variables. One should keep in mind, of course, that interaction analyses are needed only to test interaction hypotheses, and not to test main effect hypotheses.

Are there any problematic aspects of the experimental approach to exploring CPS that must be dealt with? I believe there are, but I also believe that these problems are general problems of the research domain that are not a property of any particular analysis technique or method. I list four of these problems as follows:

The first problem concerns the *measurement of CPS knowledge and performance.* As I stated in the introduction to this chapter, adequate measurement of subjects' knowledge and performance in CPS situations represents a major hurdle that needs to be addressed and resolved before we can make any real progress toward understanding CPS. To this end, Hübner (1989), for instance, has proposed mathematical procedures for the operationalization of certain aspects of task performance. Kolb, Petzing, and Stumpf (1992) propose the use of operations research methods for the same purpose. I personally believe that real progress will not come from these propositions (which, however, may be very useful for certain purposes) but will only come from theoretical advances. Any good theory of CPS must prescribe the dependent variables and must outline how these variables can be measured. Additionally, a theory of the formal system itself may help to select important and reliable indicators of system performance.

The second problem concerns *generalizability and external validity.* Although the artificial systems currently used in our labs are much more complex than they were 20 years ago, we cannot necessarily assume that increased complexity has also led to improved generalizability. Dörner's attempt to bring complexity into the labs of the scholars of thinking and problem solving was successful—but has the situation really changed with respect to our understanding of real-world phenomena? I agree with Hunt

(1991, p. 391) who argues that "Geneticists have a theory that explains how one generalizes from inheritance in the fruit fly to inheritance in human beings. Cognitive psychology does not have a theory to explain how we move from game behaviors to behaviors in other situations."

The third problem concerns the *analysis of problem solving processes*. The experimental method has not been specifically designed for process analyses, although experimental treatments can help in testing assumptions about parameters and their assumed dependence on external factors (e.g., multinomial modeling; see Riefer & Batchelder, 1988). Thus, process models and experiments are not contradictory; they are complementary tools that help us understand CPS.

And finally, the *development of problem solving theories* is in a rather desolate condition. Developing a theory, or multiple theories, is the most difficult job to achieve—and yet at the same time the most necessary prerequisite for additional experimental research. A good theory prescribes and determines experimental research. Theoretical assumptions can be derived from everyday experiences, from cognitive modeling, or from single-case or field studies. Most, if not all, of the assumptions can be tested experimentally—but the experimental method does not in itself prescribe the development of theories.

In my own view, the experimental method will remain the method of choice for studying human CPS simply because no other method is as capable of providing decisive answers to clearly formulated questions. At the same time, however, it remains clear that progress in this difficult research area can be achieved only if different approaches work together to achieve insights into how people deal with complex problems.

ACKNOWLEDGMENTS

Preparation of this chapter was supported by a grant from the "Deutsche Forschungsgemeinschaft (DFG)" to the author (ref. no. Fu 173/1 and 173/2). Additional financial support by the European Community within the "Human Capital and Mobility" program is greatly acknowledged. Thanks to Axel Buchner, Peter Frensch, Lisa Irmen, Burkhard Müller, and Bianca Vaterrodt-Plünnecke for helpful comments on earlier versions of this chapter. Special thanks to Peter Frensch for improving the readability of this chapter.

REFERENCES

Badke-Schaub, P. (1993). *Gruppen und komplexe Probleme. Strategien von Kleingruppen bei der Bearbeitung einer simulierten Aids-Ausbreitung* [Groups and complex problems. Strategies of small groups in dealing with a computer simulated AIDS epidemic]. Frankfurt, Germany: Peter Lang.

Beckmann, J. F. (1995). *Lernen und komplexes Problemlösen. Ein Beitrag zur Validierung von Lerntests* [Learning and complex problem solving. A contribution to validate learning potential tests]. Bonn, Germany: Holos.

Berry, D. C. (1991). The role of action in implicit learning. *Quarterly Journal of Experimental Psychology, 43A*, 881–906.

Berry, D. C., & Broadbent, D. E. (1984). On the relationship between task performance and associated verbalizable knowledge. *Quarterly Journal of Experimental Psychology, 36A*, 209–231.

Brehmer, B. (1990). Strategies in real-time, dynamic decision making. In R. Hogarth (Ed.), *Insights in decision making. A tribute to Hillel J. Einhorn* (pp. 262–279). Chicago, IL: University of Chicago Press.

Brehmer, B., & Allard, R. (1991). Dynamic decision making: The effects of task complexity and feedback delay. In J. Rasmussen, B. Brehmer, & J. Leplat (Eds.), *Distributed decision making: Cognitive models for cooperative work* (pp. 319–334). New York: Wiley.

Brehmer, B., & Dörner, D. (1993). Experiments with computer-simulated microworlds: Escaping both the narrow straits of the laboratory and the deep blue sea of the field study. *Computers in Human Behavior, 9*, 171–184.

Brehmer, B., Leplat, J., & Rasmussen, J. (1991). Use of simulation in the study of complex decision making. In J. Rasmussen, B. Brehmer, & J. Leplat (Eds.), *Distributed decision making: Cognitive models for cooperative work* (pp. 373–386). New York: Wiley.

Broadbent, D. E., FitzGerald, P., & Broadbent, M. H. P. (1986). Implicit and explicit knowledge in the control of complex systems. *British Journal of Psychology, 77*, 33–50.

de Keyser, V. (1990). Temporal decision making in complex environments. *Philosophical Transactions of the Royal Society London, B327*, 569–576.

Dörner, D. (1980). On the difficulty people have in dealing with complexity. *Simulation & Games, 11*, 87–106.

Dörner, D. (1989). Die kleinen grünen Schildkröten und die Methoden der experimentellen Psychologie [Little green turtles and methods of experimental psychology]. *Sprache & Kognition, 8*, 86–97.

Dörner, D. (1991). The investigation of action regulation in uncertain and complex situations. In J. Rasmussen, B. Brehmer, & J. Leplat (Eds.), *Distributed decision making: Cognitive models for cooperative work* (pp. 349–354). New York: Wiley.

Dörner, D. (1992). Über die Philosophie der Verwendung von Mikrowelten oder "Computerszenarios" in der psychologischen Forschung [On the proper use of microworlds or "computer scenarios" in psychological research]. In H. Gundlach (Ed.), *Psychologische Forschung und Methode: Das Versprechen des Experiments. Festschrift für Werner Traxel* (pp. 53–87). Passau, Germany: Passavia-Universitäts-Verlag.

Dörner, D., Kreuzig, H. W., Reither, F., & Stäudel, T. (Eds.). (1983). *Lohhausen. Vom Umgang mit Unbestimmtheit und Komplexität* [Lohhausen. On dealing with uncertainty and complexity]. Bern, Switzerland: Hans Huber.

Dörner, D., & Pfeifer, E. (1992). Strategisches Denken, strategische Fehler, Streß und Intelligenz [Strategic thinking, strategic errors, stress, and intelligence]. *Sprache & Kognition, 11*, 75–90.

Dörner, D., Reither, F., & Stäudel, T. (1983). Emotion und problemlösendes Denken [Emotion and problem solving]. In H. Mandl & G. L. Huber (Eds.), *Emotion und Kognition* (pp. 61–81). München, Germany: Urban & Schwarzenberg.

Eyferth, K., Schömann, M., & Widowski, D. (1986). Der Umgang von Psychologen mit Komplexität [On how psychologists deal with complexity]. *Sprache & Kognition, 5*, 11–26.

Frensch, P. A., & Sternberg, R. J. (1989). Expertise and intelligent thinking: When is it worse to know better? In R. J. Sternberg (Ed.), *Advances in the psychology of human intelligence* (Vol. 5, pp. 157–188). Hillsdale, NJ: Lawrence Erlbaum Associates.

Fritz, A., & Funke, J. (1988). Komplexes Problemlösen bei Jugendlichen mit Hirnfunktionsstörungen [Complex problem solving by children with cerebral dysfunctions]. *Zeitschrift für Psychologie, 196*, 171–187.

Fritz, A., & Funke, J. (1990). Superhirn trotz Teilleistungsschwäche? [Master mind despite of cerebral dysfunctions?]. *Acta Paedopsychiatrica, 53,* 146–162.

Funke, J. (1983). Einige Bemerkungen zu Problemen der Problemlöseforschung oder: Ist Testintelligenz doch ein Prädiktor? [Some remarks on the problems of problem solving research or: Does test intelligence predict control performance?]. *Diagnostica, 29,* 283–302.

Funke, J. (1984). Diagnose der westdeutschen Problemlöseforschung in Form einiger Thesen [Assessment of West German problem solving research]. *Sprache & Kognition, 3,* 159–172.

Funke, J. (1985). Steuerung dynamischer Systeme durch Aufbau und Anwendung subjektiver Kausalmodelle [Control of dynamic systems by building up and using subjective causal models]. *Zeitschrift für Psychologie, 193,* 435–457.

Funke, J. (1986). *Komplexes Problemlösen—Bestandsaufnahme und Perspektiven* [Complex problem solving. Overview and perspectives]. Heidelberg, Germany: Springer.

Funke, J. (1988). Using simulation to study complex problem solving: A review of studies in the FRG. *Simulation & Games, 19,* 277–303.

Funke, J. (1990). Systemmerkmale als Determinanten des Umgangs mit dynamischen Systemen [System features as determinants of behavior in dynamic task environments]. *Sprache & Kognition, 9,* 143–153.

Funke, J. (1991). Solving complex problems: Human identification and control of complex systems. In R. J. Sternberg & P. A. Frensch (Eds.), *Complex problem solving: Principles and mechanisms* (pp. 185–222). Hillsdale, NJ: Lawrence Erlbaum Associates.

Funke, J. (1993). Microworlds based on linear equation systems: A new approach to complex problem solving and experimental results. In G. Strube & K.-F. Wender (Eds.), *The cognitive psychology of knowledge. The German Wissenspsychologie project. With commentaries by A. C. Graesser, A. Lesgold, and R. Kluwe* (pp. 313–330). Amsterdam: Elsevier Science Publishers.

Funke, J., & Hussy, W. (1984). Komplexes Problemlösen: Beiträge zu seiner Erfassung sowie zur Frage der Bereichs- und Erfahrungsabhängigkeit [Complex problem solving: Contributions to its conception as well as to the question of domain specificity and expertise]. *Zeitschrift für Experimentelle und Angewandte Psychologie, 31,* 19–38.

Funke, J., & Müller, H. (1988). Eingreifen und Prognostizieren als Determinanten von Systemidentifikation und Systemsteuerung [Active control and prediction as determinants of system identification and system control]. *Sprache & Kognition, 7,* 176–186.

Haider, H. (1992). Implizites Wissen und Lernen. Ein Artefakt? [Implicit knowledge and learning. An artifact?]. *Zeitschrift für Experimentelle und Angewandte Psychologie, 39,* 68–100.

Haider, H. (1993). Was ist implizit am impliziten Wissen und Lernen? [What is implicit within implicit knowledge and learning?] *Sprache & Kognition, 12,* 44–52.

Hasselmann, D. (1993). *Computersimulierte komplexe Problemstellungen in der Management-Diagnostik* [Computersimulated complex problems for the diagnosis of management abilities]. Hamburg, Germany: Windmühle.

Hayes, J. R., & Simon, H. A. (1976). The understanding process: Problem isomorphs. *Cognitive Psychology, 8,* 165–190.

Hayes, N. A., & Broadbent, D. E. (1988). Two modes of learning for interactive tasks. *Cognition, 28,* 249–276.

Heineken, E., Arnold, H.-J., Kopp, A., & Soltysiak, R. (1992). Strategien des Denkens bei der Regelung eines einfachen dynamischen Systems unter verschiedenen Totzeitbedingungen [Strategies of thinking in controlling a simple dynamic system under different deadtime-conditions]. *Sprache & Kognition, 11,* 136–148.

Hesse, F. W. (1982). Effekte des semantischen Kontexts auf die Bearbeitung komplexer Probleme [Effects of semantic context on problem solving]. *Zeitschrift für Experimentelle und Angewandte Psychologie, 29,* 62–91.

Hesse, F. W., Spies, K., & Lüer, G. (1983). Einfluß motivationaler Faktoren auf das Problemlöseverhalten im Umgang mit komplexen Problemen [Influence of motivational factors on problem solving performance in interacting with complex problems]. *Zeitschrift für Experimentelle und Angewandte Psychologie, 30,* 400–424.

Hörmann, H.-J., & Thomas, M. (1989). Zum Zusammenhang zwischen Intelligenz und komplexem Problemlösen [On the relationship between intelligence and complex problem solving]. *Sprache & Kognition, 8,* 23–31.

Huber, O. (in press). Decision behavior in a multistage investment task. *Acta Psychologica.*

Hübner, R. (1987). Eine naheliegende Fehleinschätzung des Zielabstandes bei der zeitoptimalen Regelung dynamischer Systeme [An obvious error in estimating the goal distance while performing time-optimal regulations of dynamic systems]. *Zeitschrift für Experimentelle und Angewandte Psychologie, 34,* 38–53.

Hübner, R. (1988). Die kognitive Regelung dynamischer Systeme und der Einfluß analoger versus digitaler Informationsdarbietung [Cognitive regulation of dynamic systems and the influence of analogue versus digital presentation of information]. *Zeitschrift für Psychologie, 196,* 161–170.

Hübner, R. (1989). Methoden zur Analyse und Konstruktion von Aufgaben zur kognitiven Steuerung dynamischer Systeme [Methods for the analysis and construction of dynamic system control tasks]. *Zeitschrift für Experimentelle und Angewandte Psychologie, 36,* 221–238.

Hunt, E. (1991). Some comments on the study of complexity. In R. J. Sternberg & P. A. Frensch (Eds.), *Complex problem solving: Principles and mechanisms* (pp. 383–395). Hillsdale, NJ: Lawrence Erlbaum Associates.

Hussy, W. (1985). Komplexes Problemlösen—Eine Sackgasse? [Complex problem solving—A dead end?]. *Zeitschrift für Experimentelle und Angewandte Psychologie, 32,* 55–77.

Hussy, W. (1989). Intelligenz und komplexes Problemlösen [Intelligence and complex problem solving]. *Diagnostica, 35,* 1–16.

Hussy, W. (1991). Komplexes Problemlösen und Verarbeitungskapazität [Complex problem solving and processing capacity]. *Sprache & Kognition, 10,* 208–220.

Jäger, A. O. (1982). Mehrmodale Klassifikation von Intelligenzleistungen: Experimentell kontrollierte Weiterentwicklung eines deskriptiven Intelligenzstrukturmodells [Multimodal classification of intelligence test performance]. *Diagnostica, 28,* 195–225.

Jäger, A. O. (1984). Intelligenzstrukturforschung: Konkurrierende Modelle, neue Entwicklungen, Perspektiven [Research on the structure of intelligence: Competitive models, new developments, perspectives]. *Psychologische Rundschau, 35,* 21–35.

Jäger, A. O. (1991). Beziehungen zwischen komplexem Problemlösen und Intelligenz—eine Einleitung. Zur ungebrochenen Vitalität einer mit "Lohhausen" aufgescheuchten Hydra [Relations between complex problem solving and intelligence—an introduction. On the unbroken vitality of a hydra which started with "Lohhausen"]. *Diagnostica, 37,* 287–290.

Kluwe, R. H., Schilde, A., Fischer, C., & Oellerer, N. (1991). Problemlöseleistungen beim Umgang mit komplexen Systemen und Intelligenz [Problem solving performance when interacting with complex systems and intelligence]. *Diagnostica, 37,* 291–313.

Köller, O., Dauenheimer, D. G., & Strauß, B. (1993). Unterschiede zwischen Einzelpersonen und Dyaden beim Lösen komplexer Probleme in Abhängigkeit von der Ausgangsfähigkeit [Differences between individuals and two-person groups in solving complex problems in relation to initial ability level]. *Zeitschrift für Experimentelle und Angewandte Psychologie, 40,* 194–221.

Kolb, S., Petzing, F., & Stumpf, S. (1992). Komplexes Problemlösen: Bestimmung der Problemlösegüte von Probanden mittels Verfahren des Operations Research—ein interdisziplinärer Ansatz [Complex problem solving: Determining the quality of human problem solving by operations research tools—an interdisciplinary approach]. *Sprache & Kognition, 11,* 115–128.

Leutner, D. (1988). Computersimulierte dynamische Systeme: Wissenserwerb unter verschiedenen Lehrmethoden und Sozialformen des Unterrichts [Computersimulated dynamic systems: Knowledge acquisition under different forms of teaching and types of social context]. *Zeitschrift für Entwicklungspsychologie und Pädagogische Psychologie, 20,* 338–355.

Leutner, D. (1992). *Adaptive Lehrsysteme. Instruktionspsychologische Grundlagen und experimentelle Analysen* [Adaptive teaching systems. A primer of instruction psychology and experimental analyses]. Weinheim, Germany: Psychologie Verlags Union.

Matern, B. (1979). Verzögertes Wirksamwerden von Eingriffen in der automatisierten Industrie—Konsequenzen für die Arbeitsgestaltung [Delayed effects of interventions in automatized industry—Consequences for work design]. *Sozialistische Arbeitswissenschaft, 23*, 224–228.

Müller, H. (1993). *Komplexes Problemlösen: Reliabilität und Wissen* [Complex problem solving: Reliability and knowledge]. Bonn, Germany: Holos.

Müller, H. (in press). Complex problem solving: The evaluation of reliability, stability, and some causal models. In R. Steyer, H. Gräser, & K. F. Widaman (Eds.), *Consistency and specificity: Latent state-trait models in differential psychology.* New York: Springer.

Putz-Osterloh, W. (1981). Über die Beziehung zwischen Testintelligenz und Problemlöseerfolg [On the relationship between test intelligence and success in problem solving]. *Zeitschrift für Psychologie, 189*, 79–100.

Putz-Osterloh, W. (1985). Selbstreflexionen, Testintelligenz und interindividuelle Unterschiede bei der Bewältigung komplexer Probleme [Self-reflections, intelligence test scores, and interindividual differences in complex problem solving]. *Sprache & Kognition, 4*, 203–216.

Putz-Osterloh, W. (1987). Gibt es Experten für komplexe Systeme? [Are there experts for complex problems?]. *Zeitschrift für Psychologie, 195*, 63–84.

Putz-Osterloh, W. (1991). Computergestützte Eignungsdiagnostik: Warum Strategien informativer als Leistungen sein können [Computer-based aptitude tests: Why strategies can be more informative than performance data]. In H. Schuler & U. Funke (Eds.), *Eignungsdiagnostik in Forschung und Praxis. Psychologische Information für Auswahl, Beratung und Förderung von Mitarbeitern* (pp. 97–102). Stuttgart, Germany: Verlag für Angewandte Psychologie.

Putz-Osterloh, W. (1993). Unterschiede im Erwerb und in der Reichweite des Wissens bei der Steuerung eines dynamischen Systems [Differences in the acquisition and extent of knowledge during the control of a dynamic system]. *Zeitschrift für Experimentelle und Angewandte Psychologie, 40*, 386–410.

Putz-Osterloh, W., & Bott, B. (1990). Sind objektive Systemmerkmale auch subjektiv als Anforderungen wirksam? [Are objective features of a system also effective as subjective demands?]. *Zeitschrift für Experimentelle und Angewandte Psychologie, 37*, 281–303.

Putz-Osterloh, W., Bott, B., & Houben, I. (1988). Beeinflußt Wissen über ein realitätsnahes System dessen Steuerung? [Knowledge acquisition and improvement in system control]. *Sprache & Kognition, 7*, 240–251.

Putz-Osterloh, W., & Lemme, M. (1987). Knowledge and its intelligent application to problem solving. *German Journal of Psychology, 11*, 268–303.

Putz-Osterloh, W., & Lüer, G. (1981). Über die Vorhersagbarkeit komplexer Problemlöseleistungen durch Ergebnisse in einem Intelligenztest [On whether results from a test of intelligence can predict problem solving performance]. *Zeitschrift für Experimentelle und Angewandte Psychologie, 28*, 309–334.

Reichert, U., & Dörner, D. (1988). Heurismen beim Umgang mit einem "einfachen" dynamischen System [Heuristics of coping with a "simple" dynamic system]. *Sprache & Kognition, 7*, 12–24.

Reither, F. (1981). About thinking and acting of experts in complex situations. *Simulation & Games, 12*, 125–140.

Reither, F. (1985). Wertorientierung in komplexen Entscheidungssituationen [Value orientation and decision making in complex situations]. *Sprache & Kognition, 4*, 21–27.

Reitman, W. R. (1965). *Cognition and thought: An information processing approach.* New York: Wiley.

Riefer, D. M., & Batchelder, W. H. (1988). Multinomial modeling and the measurement of cognitive processes. *Psychological Review, 95*, 318–339.

Ringelband, O. J., Misiak, C., & Kluwe, R. H. (1990). Mental models and strategies in the control of a complex system. In D. Ackermann & M. J. Tauber (Eds.), *Mental models and human-computer interaction. Volume 1* (pp. 151–164). Amsterdam: Elsevier Science Publishers.

Rost, J., & Strauß, B. (1993). Zur Wechselwirkung von Informationsdarbietung und mentalem Modell beim Umgang mit einem komplexen Problem [Interaction of information feedback and mental model in solving a complex problem]. *Sprache & Kognition, 12*, 73–82.

Roth, T. (1985). Sprachstatistisch objektivierbare Denkstilunterschiede zwischen "guten" und "schlechten" Bearbeitern komplexer Probleme [Statistically objectifiable differences in thought styles in the handling of complex problems]. *Sprache & Kognition, 4*, 178–191.

Roth, T., Meyer, H. A., & Lampe, K. (1991). Sprachgebrauch, Informationsstrukturierung und Verhalten in einer komplexen Problemsituation [Language use, cognitive differentiation, and behavior in a complex decision task]. *Sprache & Kognition, 10*, 28–38.

Sanderson, P. M. (1989). Verbalizable knowledge and skilled task performance: Association, dissociation, and mental models. *Journal of Experimental Psychology: Learning, Memory, and Cognition, 15*, 729–747.

Schaub, H. (1990). Die Situationsspezifität des Problemlöseverhaltens [The situational specificity of problem solving behavior]. *Zeitschrift für Psychologie, 198*, 83–96.

Schaub, H. (1993). *Modellierung der Handlungsorganisation* [Modeling of action regulation]. Bern, Switzerland: Hans Huber.

Schaub, H., & Strohschneider, S. (1992). Die Auswirkungen unterschiedlicher Problemlöseerfahrung auf den Umgang mit einem unbekannten komplexen Problem [Effects of different experiences with problems on how to deal with an unknown complex problem]. *Zeitschrift für Arbeits- und Organisationspsychologie, 36*, 117–126.

Schmuck, P. (1992). Zum Zusammenhang zwischen der Effizienz exekutiver Kontrolle und dem mehrfachen Lösen eines komplexen Problems [Efficiency of executive control processes and stability of behavior in repeated solving of complex problems]. *Sprache & Kognition, 11*, 193–207.

Schoppek, W. (1991). Spiel und Wirklichkeit—Reliabilität und Validität von Verhaltensmustern in komplexen Situationen [Game and reality—Reliability and validity of behavior patterns in complex situations]. *Sprache & Kognition, 10*, 15–27.

Stäudel, T. (1987). *Problemlösen, Emotionen und Kompetenz* [Problem solving, emotions, and competence]. Regensburg, Germany: Roderer.

Steyer, R., Gräser, H., & Widaman, K. F. (Eds.). (in press). *Consistency and specificity: Latent state-trait models in differential psychology*. New York: Springer.

Strauß, B. (1993). *Konfundierungen beim Komplexen Problemlösen. Zum Einfluß des Anteils der richtigen Lösungen (ArL) auf das Problemlöseverhalten in komplexen Situationen* [Confoundations in complex problem solving. On the influence of the degree of correct solutions on problem solving in complex situations]. Bonn, Germany: Holos.

Strohschneider, S. (1986). Zur Stabilität und Validität von Handeln in komplexen Realitätsbereichen [On the stability and validity of complex problem-solving behavior]. *Sprache & Kognition, 5*, 42–48.

Strohschneider, S. (1990). *Wissenserwerb und Handlungsregulation* [Knowledge acquisition and action regulation]. Wiesbaden, Germany: Deutscher Universitäts Verlag.

Strohschneider, S. (1991a). Kein System von Systemen! Kommentar zu dem Aufsatz "Systemmerkmale als Determinanten des Umgangs mit dynamischen Systemen" von Joachim Funke [No system of systems! Reply to the paper "System features as determinants of behavior in dynamic task environments" by Joachim Funke]. *Sprache & Kognition, 10*, 109–113.

Strohschneider, S. (1991b). Problemlösen und Intelligenz: Über die Effekte der Konkretisierung komplexer Probleme [Problem solving and intelligence: The effects of problem concreteness]. *Diagnostica, 37*, 353–371.

Süß, H.-M., Kersting, M., & Oberauer, K. (1991). Intelligenz und Wissen als Prädiktoren für Leistungen bei computersimulierten komplexen Problemen [Intelligence and knowledge as predictors of performance in solving complex computer-simulated problems]. *Diagnostica, 37,* 334–352.

Süß, H.-M., Kersting, M., & Oberauer, K. (1993). Zur Vorhersage von Steuerungsleistungen an computersimulierten Systemen durch Wissen und Intelligenz [On the predictability of control performance on computer-simulated systems by knowledge and intelligence]. *Zeitschrift für Differentielle und Diagnostische Psychologie, 14,* 189–203.

Süß, H.-M., Oberauer, K., & Kersting, M. (1993). Intellektuelle Fähigkeiten und die Steuerung komplexer Systeme [Intelligence and control performance on computer-simulated systems]. *Sprache & Kognition, 12,* 83–97.

Vollmeyer, R., & Holyoak, K. J. (1993, June). *Hypothesis-testing strategies in learning a complex dynamic system.* Paper presented at the Fifth Annual Convention of the American Psychological Society, Chicago, IL.

CHAPTER ELEVEN

Single Case Studies and Models of Complex Problem Solving

Rainer H. Kluwe
University of the Federal Armed Forces, Hamburg, Germany

INTRODUCTION

This chapter is concerned with the use of single case studies in problem solving research. Single case studies have been used to (a) test existing models of problem solving, and, (b) provide the basis for model development. As with any form of method, single case studies have both advantages and disadvantages. Potential disadvantages include premature generalizations, a lack of explication of the boundary conditions when hypotheses are examined, and a circularity that is caused by testing and developing a theory with the same set of data. The strengths of single case studies, in contrast, are that they provide rich data bases and allow access to process information. In this chapter, I shall argue that single case studies should not be considered alternatives to experimental group designs, but, rather, that the two methods should be applied for different purposes.

Methodological discussions in cognitive psychology range from the contributions of experimental designs, analyses, and methods for collecting data to issues of computer modeling and simulation (e.g., Ericsson & Simon, 1984; Kintsch, Miller, & Polson, 1984). This chapter is concerned with a specific methodological approach, namely single case studies. Compared to experimental group studies, the single case method is relatively rarely applied in psychological research on problem solving, although it is widespread in the context of computer modeling approaches.

Traditional experimental approaches to the study of complex problem solving (henceforth CPS) have recently been severely criticized (Dörner, 1992; Dörner & Lantermann, 1991; for a profound response to the criticisms see Herrmann, 1990), at least partly because they tend to use a specific type of problem solving task. Far too long, it is criticized, have tasks been selected that have not much in common with problem solving situations in every-day life (see also Anderson, 1993, p. 94). The Tower of Hanoi task may serve as the prototypical example of a task that lacks *ecological validity*. It has been argued that more complex and dynamic task environments should be studied, for example so-called *microworlds*, that is, scenarios that can be implemented on a computer. Computerized scenarios, however, cannot be studied with traditional experimental group studies. One of the reasons for this is that it is difficult to precisely control the experimental factors when computerized scenarios are used. Another reason is that process information is usually ignored in group studies (Dörner & Lantermann, 1991). Finally, it is argued that it is unlikely that complex task environments are represented internally in an uniform manner. That is, different individuals will develop rather different representations of the task. The heterogeneity of internal representations is a major obstacle when working with average data and when comparisons between individuals are made. More important, the internal representations presumably change over the course of acting in a complex environment, and one cannot expect that these changes occur in the same way for all subjects under study. Performance may thus be the result of rather different knowledge bases and strategies. Furthermore, although the problem states might be equal for all subjects at the beginning, after a few individual solution steps, different subjects will face rather different problem states. It is, therefore, hardly meaningful to analyze a problem solving study at the aggregate level.

Dörner (1992; Dörner & Lantermann, 1991), though not entirely rejecting experimental approaches, therefore argues strongly against the use of experimental designs in the traditional sense because experiments in the domain of CPS do not appear to capture the pattern of a problem solver's actions, goals, intentions, and decisions (but see J. Funke, this volume). Dörner, instead, recommends to develop theoretical models of the problem solving process with the aid of single case studies and computer simulations (see Dörner & Wearing, this volume).

Interestingly, Herrmann (1990) has recently pointed out that the controversy about the *right* approach to studying CPS is by no means new, and that it is in fact possible to perform meaningful experiments in complex domains. Complexity by itself, so says Herrmann, does not hinder the formulation of simple and empirical statements about the operation of the cognitive system: "The importance of theoretical innovations is very often due to the fact that new conclusions are derived from a complex description of a system that are simple and that can be examined" (Herrmann, 1990, p. 9, translated by the author). Thus, the assumed shortcomings of experiments are seen not as due to the experimental method itself, but as caused by a lack of understanding and a lack of theoretical analysis of the complex human activity (see also J. Funke, this volume).

There are good reasons to construct process models for the domain of CPS. Whether or not a process model may be constructed, however, does not depend on the type of task that is used. Rather, the construction of process models is affected by the research goals one chooses. Newell (1982), for example, has argued that process models are appropriate when the goal is to analyze and understand cognitive activity at the symbolic level. However, models of human problem solving also require empirical evidence, and this raises the question of which methodological approaches provide appropriate data for the development and the evaluation of models.

In cognitive psychology, process models of human problem solving are frequently accompanied by single case studies. The reasons for relying on data from individuals are manifold. First, single cases provide rich data bases of the cognitive activity and problem solving behavior of individuals. They provide a much more fine grained picture of the individual problem solving process than do average data. Furthermore, when appropriate methods for collecting data on line are applied, such as thinking aloud data or eye movements, then single case studies may provide information about the dynamics of the individual solution search. Finally, single case studies can reveal important individual differences.

SINGLE CASE STUDIES

In the following, we focus on the methodological procedure that is followed by researchers when they conduct single case studies in the CPS domain. The reader may want to keep in mind that I do not claim that the single case methodology is the only, best, or even most typical approach for studying CPS. The position taken here does not propagate single case studies as the appropriate method when studying CPS. Instead, it is asserted that the research goal and the research question determine the choice of methods.

Problems, in the present context, are considered complex if they contain many interrelated components, and if many different cognitive operations are necessary to achieve their solutions. Furthermore, problems are complex if they can be decomposed into subproblems, and if they carry a high degree of uncertainty due to the information load, dynamics, and opacity of the task environment (see Frensch & Funke, this volume).

Goals of Single Case Studies

The value of single case studies is often viewed as low; single case studies are rarely considered to be equivalent to *true* experiments. Irrespective of this view, there is a rather long tradition of single case studies in some disciplines of psychology, most notably in clinical psychology. Usually, these studies focus on outcome evaluation of specific intervention techniques. In this context, there exists a rich literature on the statistical analysis of single case data (Kazdin, 1982; Kratochwil, 1992).

When single case studies are conducted within the realms of research on CPS, the emphasis is not on specific interventions and on the evaluation of outcomes. Instead, the focus is on the individual's problem solving process, the analysis is qualitative rather than quantitative, and statistical tests are rarely applied. The main interest is in the cognitive processes that can be inferred from the collected data and that are assumed to underlie the observed solution behavior.

There are at least two different ways in which single case studies can be fruitfully employed in problem solving research. In the first approach, the starting point is a theory. Hypotheses are derived from the theory, and single cases are studied to test the theory. In the second approach, the starting point are single cases that are studied based on preliminary assumptions about the problem solving process. Here, assumptions regarding cognitive processes are derived from the study of single cases and are implemented in a model, which, in turn, is subjected to further investigations. Of course, the real-life research approaches will never be exact copies of these two alternatives but will typically contain components of both approaches.

Procedures for Single Case Studies

Dörner (1992), among others, has proposed the use of a research procedure where computer modeling and single case study are explicitly connected. According to Dörner, one should start out with the analysis of the problem solving behavior of individuals, that is, with single case studies. The data collected, in turn, provide the basis for developing a theory of problem solving. It is expected, of course, that the behavior of single individuals can be explained and analyzed in the context of a general theoretical system.

Notice that such a research procedure does not start out as a *tabula rasa*. Instead, the research procedure is anchored in a priori formulated theoretical assumptions about the possible structure and organization of subjects' problem solving procedures. This is a rather crucial requirement for the analysis of verbal data obtained in single case studies, and one that has been especially emphasized by Ericsson and Simon (1984). Dörner and Lantermann (1991) suggest to proceed as follows: (a) study a large variety of single cases, (b) derive hypotheses about the dependencies and determinants of problem solving processes, (c) implement hypotheses in a computer program, (d) generate *synthetic* behavior, (e) compare the *synthetic* and *empirical* performances, and, (f) in case of deviations, modify the model. Of course, this approach conceals some rather difficult steps, as, for example, inferring which cognitive processes underlie the observed performance and formulating a theory or constructing a simulation program. Also, one should not underestimate the difficult task of evaluating programs (Herrmann, 1990).

The main point of Dörner's proposal is that single case data contribute to model development and model evaluation. At least three important questions remain, however, that need to be addressed (Westmeyer, 1989): (a) when are single case studies to be preferred over group studies? (b) is it possible to reject hypotheses on the basis of single cases? and, (c) is it possible to generalize the results obtained in single case studies? All of these questions are addressed here.

With respect to the first question, there are several factors that influence the choice of single case versus group studies. For example, conducting a group study may be difficult when a sufficiently large homogenous sample of subjects cannot be formed, or when the experimental procedure is too time consuming, or is associated with high costs. Westmeyer (1989) has pointed out that single case studies and group studies are not alternatives. That is, it is not the case that one should prefer experimental group studies in general, and should proceed with single case studies only when the experimental approach is not feasible. Westmeyer argues instead that single case studies should not replace group studies because the two methodological approaches accomplish different research goals.

Types of Hypotheses

That the two methodological approaches accomplish different research goals becomes evident, for example, when one considers the type of hypothesis that is subjected to empirical investigations. Bunge (1967) has distinguished among eight different types of hypotheses (Westmeyer, 1989). For all types of hypotheses in which statements about single individuals are made, single case studies may be applied as a method. According to Bunge, this is possible when existential hypotheses or universal hypotheses are tested. Single case studies are thus appropriate when hypotheses are examined that make direct statements about single individuals. They are not appropriate when the hypotheses refer to classes of subjects or to fictitious statistical modal individuals (Westmeyer, 1989). In the latter case, that is, when statistical hypotheses are examined, group studies need to be conducted. Hypotheses that may be explored by single case studies include, for example: (a) indefinite existential hypotheses where some or all variables remain undetermined (e.g., "There are problem solvers that have difficulties solving complex problems" or "There are intelligent problem solvers that are not able to solve complex problems"), (b) quasi-general hypotheses that allow for exceptions (e.g., "Most problem solvers follow specific stages of knowledge acquisition when working on new problems" or "Performance increments when practicing problem solving can usually be described in terms of a power function"), (c) bounded universal hypotheses where the validity of the hypothesis is restricted to a specific type of problems (e.g., "The procedure of problem solvers when solving well-defined problems follows a sequence of steps as described by means-ends analysis"), and, (d) unbounded universal hypotheses (e.g., "The process of human problem solving follows a procedure described by the heuristic of means-ends analysis"). As far as I can see, the type of hypothesis is rarely considered when the benefits and disadvantages of single case and group studies are compared. Any decision concerning the selection of the one or the other approach requires, among other things, a consideration of which type of hypothesis is tested.

The Problem of Falsification

With regard to the falsification of hypotheses, Westmeyer (1989) argues that the result of one single case study is not sufficient to confirm universal hypotheses, although it is sufficient to reject such hypotheses. Thus, generalization on the basis of single cases is not possible when results are obtained that support the hypothesis, but may be possible when the results contradict the hypothesis. However, the validity of hypotheses that are established in the context of a theory is also constrained by boundary conditions that are not always made explicit. Single cases that disconfirm an universal hypothesis do not necessarily falsify an entire universal hypothesis. Rather, they may debilitate the hypothesis that was formulated and examined in the context of specific constraints. This position has been put forward, for example, by Ericsson and Simon (1984).

In single case studies, the concern is usually about one theory, not about alternative hypotheses. Ericsson and Simon (1984) deny a *sudden death* of theories, and emphasize the role of additional assumptions. The failure of a theory may be due to factors other than the theory itself. "Perhaps the fault does not lie in the theory, but in some of the auxiliary, methodological, and theoretical assumptions that have been made in the fitting process" (p. 285). That is, assumptions implicit in the theory may be wrong. Therefore, Ericsson and Simon propose that "the theoretical assumptions and presuppositions underlying the data analysis should be made explicit" (Ericsson & Simon, 1984, p. 286). The results of a single case study need to be related to the hypothesis examined, and thus can be interpreted as confirming or debilitating the hypothesis, if the additional implicit assumptions connected with the theory are taken into account.

The Problem of Generalization

The generalization of individual cases clearly raises important problems. One way to elude most, though not all, of the problems might be to follow a procedure suggested by Westmeyer (1989). First, establish a quasi-general hypothesis (e.g., "If two problems are similar, then performance on the second problem will be improved after the first problem has been solved"). Second, formulate a singular hypothesis (e.g., "Performance of subject A will be improved on problem y after the similar problem x has been solved"). And third, study single cases, and collect data about the individual problem solving processes; and (d) if the result supports the singular hypothesis, then it also supports the quasi-general hypothesis.

Note that in order to extend the validity of the hypothesis, it is necessary to design a series of direct and systematic replications of single case studies, selecting different subjects and applying different tasks. Then, group studies may follow. In this context, single case studies gain an important function, namely a *filter* function (Westmeyer, 1989). That is, single case studies guide decisions about which experimental factors might be essential for group studies.

In the following, four examples of single case studies that have been reported in the literature are discussed. The first group of studies contains two cases in which single case studies were used to examine already existing models. The work by Bhaskar and Simon (1977) and by Anderson (Neves & Anderson, 1981; Anderson, 1982) is considered here. The second group of studies is concerned with the case where theoretical generalizations are based on the results from single case studies. Here, the work by Shrager and Klahr (1986) and by Kluwe and coworkers (Kluwe, 1991) will be discussed. In each case, the goal of the study was to model the information processing steps that underlie complex human problem solving.

The four studies were selected to illustrate how single case studies can be applied in cognitive scientific research. The focus of the discussion concerns the function of the single case study and the relation between computer model and single case data.

SINGLE CASE STUDIES AND THE TESTING OF MODELS

Bhaskar and Simon (1977)

Bhaskar and Simon (1977) report the results of a study on problem solving in the domain of thermodynamics. While existing theories of human problem solving have been largely developed on the basis of laboratory tasks (e.g., Newell & Simon, 1972), Bhaskar and Simon's goal is to extend an existing theory to tasks that require a large amount of domain-specific knowledge. The authors' research strategy combines a single case study, that is, a thorough analysis of the thinking aloud protocol of one subject, with the development and test of a simulation program. Verbal data obtained from one subject who was instructed to think aloud while solving a physical problem are analyzed in order to examine a theory about human problem solving that is implemented in a computer program. The specific version of the program, SAPA (Semiautomatic Protocol Analysis) that is investigated in the study, is characterized by the authors as a "hybrid between a program (a theory of behavior in the usual sense) for simulating the human subject and a program for coding this thinking-aloud protocol automatically" (Bhaskar & Simon, 1977, p. 197).

SAPA analyzes thinking aloud protocols, but is, at the same time, described as a *weak* theory of the human problem solving process. SAPA is based, at least to some extent, on the theory of human problem solving developed by Newell and Simon (1972). An unbounded universal hypothesis is guiding the data analysis, according to which the processes that are implemented in the program can be precisely identified in the verbal protocol of the human subject. Referring to the program as both a theory and a simulation of human problem solving processes, Bhaskar and Simon postulate that the individual protocol of verbalizations "can be encoded in terms of a definite fixed set of basic processes, and that these processes will usually follow one another in certain sequences" (Bhaskar & Simon, 1977, p. 202). The program guides and formalizes the encoding process in which the individual protocol and the encoding of the system are compared sentence by sentence. Deviations of the empirical data from the theory (e.g., incomplete or inaccurate processes) become evident in the course of coding the protocol. Interestingly, the authors expect that "to the extent that the *normal* process sequence is not followed by the subject, this will be revealed by the choices the coder is forced to make" (Bhaskar & Simon, 1977, p. 202).

The data obtained from the case study may provide support for the hypothesized cognitive processes and for their sequence, or they may debilitate the assertions inherent in the program. The criterion used to evaluate the hypotheses is the amount of overlap between the problem solving procedure as it is implemented in the program and the subject's observed procedure. The authors want to avoid any quantitative analysis of the goodness of fit but suggest that the degree of fit is given by the amount of overlap of the sequence of steps in the encoded protocol with the sequence of lines in the protocol of the subject.

The status of the program and the function of the single case study in this paper remain, however, unclear. Although the program is characterized as a theory of human problem solving, it is emphasized that the goal is explicitly not to test the theory, but that the program is used "as a tool to help us induce what his actual progress is" (Bhaskar & Simon, 1977, p. 207). On the other hand, however, the results obtained with this procedure are interpreted as supporting the theory: "Examination of encoding in terms of these criteria shows that SAPA does indeed provide a zeroth-order approximation to the subjects behavior . . ." (p. 213). Deviations are registered but are not interpreted as weakening the theory. The individual protocol of verbalizations provides data that do not support SAPA but that appear to debilitate the simulation program as a theory of human problem solving. There are erroneous steps in the individual solution procedure that are not predicted by the program and that cause deviations from the theoretical general procedure. In addition, planning steps exhibited by the subject are not "anticipated by the SAPA program" (Bhaskar & Simon, 1977, p. 212). Despite these inconsistencies, the authors conclude that their analysis reveals a consistent solution process that might be best described as a form of means-ends analysis that is modified, however, by the knowledge of the individual. It is stated that means-ends analysis is not specific for problems of this type, and finally even that the "subject does not use means-ends analysis quite consistently" (Bhaskar & Simon, 1977, p. 213). Irrespective of these results, a generalization is suggested across task environments, according to which the procedure followed by the subject is similar to those that can be observed in task environments that have less rich semantic content.

The study by Bhaskar and Simon (1977) is an example of a single case study that is conducted in the context of the development of a theory. There is a preliminary theory that is implemented as a computer program. It is assumed, thereby establishing an unbounded universal hypothesis, that the problem solving behavior of human problem solvers follows a series of steps that is organized by the principle of means-ends analysis. This hypothesis is examined by analyzing the verbal data of one subject, that is, in terms of a singular hypothesis. A criterion is provided for judging the similarity between program and data.

The amount of overlap obtained is accepted as satisfactory although there are deviations. The criteria for rejecting or accepting the model, or parts of it, remain unspecified. Finally, the theory is accepted as a *zeroth order* theory of human problem solving.

There remains some ambiguity about the authors' statement that the single case study is not conceived of as a test of their theory. It is difficult to judge what the empirical results really mean because SAPA is characterized in two ways. Thus, the single case study may serve different purposes. First, SAPA is described as a theory to be examined; but, second, with regard to the data collected, it is applied to deduce the actual behavior of the subject, and is thus conceived of as a tool to describe individual behavior. The question remains: were single case data used to examine and modify SAPA, or were they used to generate a description of the individual information processing procedure based on preliminary theoretical assumptions provided by SAPA? Although the goal may not have been to test SAPA as a theory of human problem solving behavior, the use of concepts such as degree of fit and validity suggests the examination of a theory. The interpretation of the results finally includes generalizations to the nature of the solution processes in other than semantically rich domains.

The main problem of this study that should have become evident, is the fact that data are encoded on the basis of a model and that at the same time these data are applied to examine the model.

Anderson (1982)

Both Anderson (1982) and Neves and Anderson (1981) refer to the results from single case studies in the context of their development of a theory of skill acquisition. The theory, implemented as a computer simulation program, provides descriptions of processes for encoding task environments, for the generation of solution procedures, and for the speedup of solution procedures with practice. The research combines theory development with the analysis of data obtained from single cases. That is, the theory is, to some extent, based on the observation of subjects who solve problems repeatedly, but is also guided by existing theoretical considerations derived from the ACT* model (Anderson, 1983) and earlier work performed by Fitts (1964).

In the study reported by Neves and Anderson (1981; see also Anderson, 1982), three subjects worked on 150 geometry proofs. The subjects' task was to provide justifications for proofs in a proof system that had been developed by the authors.

Dependent variables are the total time for solving a problem, the average number of steps needed to solve the problem, and the time per step, where a step refers to a command that is executed at the computer. The relation between the dependent variables and the cognitive mechanisms remains hypothetical: "We thought time per step would reflect speedup on the problem due to such automatic factors as composition; we thought number of steps per problem would reflect other factors in addition to composition such as strategy modifications. We were interested in how these factors combined to yield an overall power law" (Neves & Anderson, 1981, p. 75). In general, the function of the study is described as an "experiment looking at the effects of practice" (p. 74).

Average data from three subjects are reported and shown in a log-log, performance X practice, plot. The obtained shape of the practice curve provides empirical support for a general assumption that was originally introduced by Newell and Rosenbloom (1981). There, the so-called power law of practice was described as a general empirical finding in research on skill acquisition.

However, Neves and Anderson also report that at a less aggregated level, the functions from one subject were fit better by exponential functions than by power functions. This finding reflects a faster speedup than is predicted by the power law, but according to Neves and Anderson (1981), this result does not invalidate their theory. The findings obtained with the three subjects are described as indicating a "rather broad spectrum of changes (that) underlies the systematic improvement of subjects," referring to strategy changes and "other kinds of optimization" (Neves & Anderson, 1981, p. 78).

A central assumption concerns the speedup function, "However, our main point here is that in our task there seem to be many processes speeding up faster than a power law. When these are combined, they better approximate a power law. Thus, we do not think that the fact that overall speedup better fits a power law refutes the psychological validity of the composition process as one of the underlying mechanisms producing the speedup" (Neves & Anderson, 1981, p. 78). It is not quite evident how one arrives at this general conclusion because the speedup follows an exponential function only for one out of the three subjects. Nevertheless, this result is used to maintain the assumption that composition speeds up faster, that is, exponentially (as indicated by the practice-related changes for the variable time per step). The data from the two remaining subjects in this study do not seem to support this assumption, although at the aggregate level, they do not invalidate it either. The use of the power function as a criterion for examining and evaluating the model proves to be a quite liberal criterion, and allows the authors to maintain their assumption regarding the exponential speedup of component processes.

The data from the same three subjects are referred to by Anderson (1982) when he describes his model of skill acquisition in more detail. Here, selected episodes from the thinking aloud protocols are related to important components of the learning model. The mechanism of compilation, for example, is illustrated by excerpts from the protocol of one subject. The goal is to show that there is a speedup in the application of postulates, that *piecemeal application* is eliminated, and, furthermore, that there is a *dropout* of verbal rehearsal. The latter is taken "as evidence that the student is no longer calling a declarative representation of the problem into working memory " (p. 382).

Another example refers to the claim "that knowledge in a new domain always starts out in declarative form and is used interpretatively" (Anderson, 1982, p. 375). An example of an interpretive system in ACT*, that is, of problem solving procedures that interpret the problem statement and instruction, is developed and is rather loosely related to the collected data: "It captures important aspects of the behavior of my three high school students on this problem" (p. 375). It remains open, though, what exactly has been observed and which verbal data are the basis of this inference. The verbal protocols, here, serve less the purpose of inferring cognitive mechanisms than of illustrating and justifying particular mechanisms that are implemented in the program.

The same single case study that was described initially (Neves & Anderson, 1981) as an experiment looking at the effects of practice, is subsequently characterized by Anderson (1982) as an "experimental test" of the theory of skill acquisition. The goal is to examine the following general hypothesis derived from the theory, "both number of productions and time per production should decrease as a power function of practice" (p. 402).

Referring to the same log-log plots as Neves and Anderson (1981), Anderson (1982) claims that the "experiment does provide evidence that underlying a power law in complex tasks are power laws both in number of steps applied and in time per step" (p. 402). This result provides additional empirical support for the general hypothesis that speedup of practice on cognitive tasks follows a power function as suggested by the analysis provided by Newell and Rosenbloom (1981). It does not, however, add substantial support for the skill model. Earlier, in Neves and Anderson (1981), the exponential speedup of underlying component processes, that is, of composition, had been emphasized. Here, it is concluded "that in our task there seem to be many processes speeding up faster than a power law" (p. 178).

It should be noted that Anderson (1982), in contrast to Neves and Anderson (1981), makes explicit some of the constraints for which the validity of the power law hypothesis is claimed. Assumptions concerning the relation between dependent variables and components of the model are discussed critically (p. 402).

Again, as with Bhaskar and Simon (1977), the function of the empirical data that have been obtained from single case studies remains unclear in the studies by Neves and Anderson (1981) and Anderson (1982). The same single case study is applied in slightly different ways, first, to look at the effects of practice, and second, to test a theory. Segments of the verbal protocols from single cases are used selectively to make model assumptions more plausible. In the 1981 version, the authors rely rather strongly on the data from one of the three subjects, thus deriving support for the exponential speedup assumption in the composition mechanism. In the later (1982) version, the evaluation is focusing on the resulting power function, a rather liberal criterion. Thus both, the obtained log-log functions for average data as well as the reported exponential functions for one subject are judged as providing empirical evidence for assumptions implemented in the model. The critical point in the studies is the selection and interpretation of the dependent variables because this establishes the association between model and data. Anderson (1982) makes his assumptions explicit with regard to this point. The underlying conjectures may be debatable, but it seems reasonable to maintain them as long as there are no better alternative interpretations.

THE DEVELOPMENT OF MODELS BASED ON SINGLE CASE STUDIES

Shrager and Klahr (1986)

The work by Shrager and Klahr (1986; Shrager, 1987) is concerned with *instructionless learning*. An essential attribute of this situation is that learning occurs without any assistance. As an example of instructionless learning take a learning situation in which an individual wants to find out how a complex device works. Shrager and Klahr's study was directed at the analysis of the learning process and of the main learning mechanisms that guide the acquisition of knowledge about a device.

Shrager and Klahr studied seven subjects who where instructed to find out how a rather complex, programmable toy worked. Subjects were asked to think aloud while interacting with the device, and had no domain-specific knowledge about the toy at the outset. The protocol of each subject thus contained verbal data, key presses, and the states and behaviors of the device. After an initial exploration phase, subjects were asked to explain how the toy worked to the experimenter. One of the subjects' protocols is provided as an example. Based on the protocol data, Shrager and Klahr (1986) provide a "coarse-grained description of the learning process," in which two stages of the process of knowledge acquisition are distinguished: an initial orientation phase and a systematic investigation phase. In addition, a distinction among different types of acquired knowledge is proposed. The different types of knowledge are exemplified by selected protocols in order to support their plausibility.

Shrager and Klahr make explicit the theoretical presuppositions regarding which information is assumed to be inherent in the protocols. Boundary conditions of this type are rarely provided and discussed in published single case studies. The analysis of what is learned is based entirely on the subjects' protocols. On the basis of the protocols, the authors establish generalizations that have the status of first degree inductions, such as ". . . there tend to be elements that are acquired earlier and some that are acquired later" (p. 168), or "most of the relevant knowledge is eventually acquired" (p. 168). As an important result of the analysis of the verbal data, it is reported that there are entire passages in the protocols in which subjects presumably analyze their incorrect hypotheses; this may engender new assumptions and the formulation of more correct hypotheses. Examples of the protocols are provided in order to increase the plausibility of this interpretation.

Also, a comprehensive theory of instructionless learning is provided that incorporates the recorded data as well as theoretical assumptions regarding which heuristics are used for hypothesis formation, the design of experiments, and the analysis of the results.

In general, it is assumed that subjects "form hypotheses and design experiments to confirm them" during the course of knowledge acquisition, and that subjects make predictions about the behavior of the device. Also, it is inferred from the protocols that "systematic investigation of the device follows cycles composed of hypothesize-experiment-observe" (p. 172). Evidence for these bounded universal hypotheses is offered in the form of selected examples from the protocols. It is not clear, however, how well the assumptions fit the verbal and behavioral data for all seven subjects.

Finally, the authors propose a set of cognitive mechanisms that presumably underlies the observed performance of their subjects operating an unknown device without assistance. It is claimed that the inferences drawn (with respect to the time course and the mechanisms of knowledge acquisition) are valid not only for the particular subjects and the device studied. A step toward a second degree induction is taken and a quasi general hypothesis is established, "syntactic, semantic, and model knowledge are likely to play a role in most reasoning about complex systems" (p. 176). Furthermore, it is assumed that the mechanisms for hypothesis construction, and the planning and execution of experiments "will be found in all instructionless contexts" (p. 177). This hypothesis is quasi general because it allows for exceptions. The possible costs of interacting with a device are introduced here as a restriction: low costs are related to a high rate of interaction. That is, when taking the interaction into account, the hypothesis is assumed to be especially valid for "low cost" devices.

With regard to the spectrum of learning behavior that is accounted for by their analysis, the authors refer to two fully analyzed protocols. They claim that for a specific phase of the learning process, namely the investigation phase, utterances and keystrokes could be categorized into episodes that supported the hypotheses.

Hypothesis formation and development are essential cognitive mechanisms in the obtained protocols, although they are not stated explicitly in the protocols (". . . we infer them from the broader context of the subject's behavior" [p. 177]). Shrager and Klahr discuss the possibility that their own inferences might be wrong, but eventually judge the coverage of hypotheses as "fairly good" (p. 178), and argue that the inferred hypotheses are supported by the verbal and behavioral data. Again, we encounter here the problem of using one data base for two purposes: first, to make inferences about cognitive mechanisms, and second, to derive support for the inferred mechanisms.

With regard to the status of the resulting theory for instructionless learning, the authors claim that their study is the beginning of a process where an "empirical basis for formulating a coherent theory" for instructionless learning is developed (p. 179). The theory is formulated in terms of a computer program (Shrager, 1987).

The research procedure that we encounter here is essentially inductive, that is, the developed theoretical framework includes a set of quasi-general hypotheses about the learning process and its mechanisms that has been derived from protocols obtained in single case studies. There is no empirical evidence, however, for the derived universal hypotheses as this would require additional empirical tests.

The crucial point in analyses of this type is the transition from individual protocol data to universal hypotheses about cognitive mechanisms. Inferences made by the researcher about cognitive mechanisms are difficult to justify and to explain. References to illustrative parts of verbal protocols may make inferences more plausible, but they cannot replace strong empirical tests. The development of stable simulation programs and subsequent empirical tests are clearly necessary to demonstrate the claimed validity of such inferences.

Kluwe, Haider, and Misiak (1990)

Kluwe, Haider, and Misiak (1990; Kluwe et al., 1989) followed the research procedure that has been proposed by Dörner (1992; Dörner & Lantermann, 1991). The starting point here were single cases studies that were followed by the analysis of verbal and behavioral data guided by preliminary theoretical assumptions. The analyses of the single case studies provided a base for model development in terms of a simulation program. Finally, the model was evaluated by comparing generated "synthetic" data with collected empirical data.

One of the interesting issues in the domain of CPS is how knowledge is acquired and used. This question, among others, was studied by Kluwe et al. (1989; 1990)through five extensive single case analyses. Subjects' task was to operate a linear, time discrete, time invariant system that was implemented on a computer. Subjects were instructed to try to reach target values provided by the experimenters, and to keep the difference between target values and system state as small as possible. The system contained independent subsystems that differed with respect to connectivity and dynamics. The task met the criteria for a CPS task that were outlined above, namely, an uncertainty due to information load, opacity of the task environment, and imponderable effects of inputs. Subjects were not told anything about the attributes of the system; they, thus, had no domain-specific knowledge. Also, there was no specific knowledge necessary to control the system because the system, and thus the control task, was not presented as a meaningful scenario. Instead, system variables were given artificial names. Each subject operated the system for ten sessions at two sessions per day. Subjects' inputs were registered on line. Verbal data were obtained by asking subjects to give a naive person information about the important attributes of the system and about how to operate the system.

The analysis of the behavioral and data was guided by general assumptions that had been derived from other studies in this domain as well as from existing cognitive theories. Singular hypotheses were established that referred to the particular system and the subjects of the study: (a) subjects would improve their control performance over the course of practice, (b) subjects would acquire knowledge about the relations among the variables of the system (so-called "structural knowledge"), and, (c) subjects would develop groupings of system variables based on the observed behavior of the variables (e.g., dynamic variables).

An analysis of the behavioral data clearly supported the first assumption (i.e., assumption a). However, the obtained time course for the improvement in control performance had not been anticipated. We found an initial decrease in the quality of control performance that was followed by a rather sudden improvement and continuous high control performance thereafter.

With regard to assumptions (b) and (c), the data revealed the following findings for all five subjects: Neither the verbal nor the behavioral data provided any evidence for the acquisition and use of structural knowledge. Subjects rarely verbalized any knowledge they might have had about the relations among the variables. They developed, however, chunks of variables. Chunks were based on the dynamic attributes of the variables, that is, the variable changes following inputs. These groupings were derived from verbal statements but were also found in the input pattern of the subjects. That is, groups of variables with similar control attributes were monitored and controlled together.

These results are not in accordance with the assumption that "structural knowledge" is necessary to act successfully in complex task environments. At least for the particular control task we used, structural knowledge was not necessary to reach the goal state because subjects did not need to develop a deep understanding of the internal structure of the system. It does, of course, not make much sense to construct structural knowledge when there is no necessity to acquire such knowledge. Still, there may be other tasks for which the development of structural knowledge is a prerequisite for successful performance (e.g., tasks requiring failure detection and failure diagnosis).

In order to more thoroughly explore this null-finding, a simulation program was developed. The procedure followed Newell (1982), and is illustrated in Figure 11.1. From the single case studies, bounded universal hypotheses were derived: (a) performance improves with practice, (b) knowledge that is acquired and used does not contain information about the interconnections among system variables, and, (c) over the course of practice, groupings of variables are developed based on the dynamic behavior of the variables. The validity of these hypotheses was claimed in the context of specific conditions. These refer to the method of knowledge assessment that was used (teaching back protocols), to the behavioral data selected and their analysis (e.g., the expectation that knowledge chunks are reflected in subjects' input patterns), the control task, and the formal characteristics of the system. However, the boundary conditions for the hypotheses were not explicitly stated. Based on the data obtained at the knowledge level, inferences were made to hypothetical data structures and processes (Kluwe, 1993).

The construction of the process model was an additional step in the research procedure to acquire more insight into the processes and data that were hypothesized to underlie the performance of subjects in single case studies. The problem space implemented in the program included information about the system: the variables, values of variables, target values, differences between target values and variable states, and inputs.

Production rules were constructed that captured the monitoring of the system states (i.e., for selecting variables), controlled the input (i.e., for

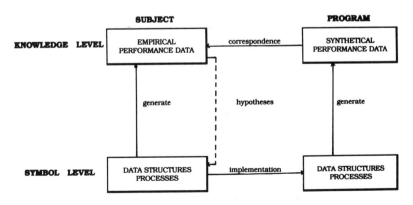

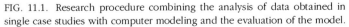

FIG. 11.1. Research procedure combining the analysis of data obtained in single case studies with computer modeling and the evaluation of the model.

changing the values of variables), categorized the variables according to their dynamic behavior, determined probabilities for the selection of variables, and monitored the dynamic behavior of the variables. Parameters were constructed that determined the categories of variables with respect to the variables' dynamic behavior, the number of variables taken into account when monitoring the system, and the priorities when applying rules.

The evaluation of the program followed several steps (Kluwe, 1993): First, it was examined if the program acted and performed as expected. The dynamic behavior of the program was analyzed when the system monitored the system state and performed inputs. Singular hypotheses guided this part of the investigation. For example, it was expected that the program would monitor difficult variables more frequently and would perform more inputs on such variables compared to inert variables. This assumption was derived from the observation of individual subjects. Several assumptions of this type were examined and led to results that confirmed the established hypotheses.

In a second step, synthetic subjects were systematically compared with selected single cases. For example, the parameters of the program were changed according to parameters obtained for subjects in the single case study. The performances of the program and of the empirical subjects were then compared (a somewhat similar procedure has been used by Reichert & Dörner, 1988; there, a simulation was described that was based on assumptions derived from group studies, however).

The evaluation of the program at this level provided rather satisfactory results, although it should be noted that the criteria for judging the performance of the program and comparing the program with empirical data were not explicitly discussed. To do so would have required, for example, that the regions of acceptance and rejection were stated more precisely.

In a third step, more than 50 synthetic subjects were generated by varying the parameters of the program. A subsequent cluster analysis did not separate synthetic and empirical subjects with respect to performance, monitoring, and control inputs.

Note that the program was not provided with so-called *structural knowledge*, that is, knowledge about the interconnections of the variables. The basic procedure of the program was to apply rules for discriminating between variables according to their dynamic behavior, and for grouping variables.

The performance of the program was clearly in the range of the empirically obtained performance data. In addition, it could be shown that the performance of the program improved over the course of "practice" in a manner similar to that of human subjects.

On the basis of these results, it was suggested that problem solving for this type of task may be successful when one relies on knowledge about input-output associations, rather than on structural knowledge. In fact, system solutions can be reached on the basis of rules that consider a few attributes of each variable separately. As a result of this research, we are inclined to maintain the bounded universal hypothesis about knowledge and system control that complex system control is sometimes successful even when it is not accompanied by knowledge about the internal structure of the system. Knowledge about the responses of system variables to inputs is acquired and used, as is knowledge about the groupings of variables with respect to their behavior. The hypothesis allows for exceptions by taking into account the type of the control task selected and the goal followed.

The generalization is based on data from single case studies and is to some extent supported by the performance of a simulation program that was developed on the basis of single case analyses. Nevertheless, the model clearly needs further experimental testing. For example, it would be necessary to analyze which type of knowledge is acquired when the goals are changed within the same system. It is hypothesized that individuals when acting in complex environments do not acquire *the* knowledge about the system. Rather, which knowledge is acquired is, to a large extent, dependent on the goals that are established by the individual or by the instruction. When the goals allow the problem solver to act at the level of simple input-output relations, then it is not necessary for the individual to acquire deep knowledge about the structural and causal relations. This implies that a lack of expressible deep knowledge should not be mistaken as a deficit of the individual when shallow knowledge is sufficient to solve a task.

The shortcomings of this particular study are similar to those discussed earlier. The model (i.e., the simulation program) is developed on the basis of data obtained from single cases; the evaluation of the model is performed, however, using the same data. Furthermore, the generalization of findings, that is, the established universal hypotheses, lack empirical support. Also, there are important constraints for the validity of the hypotheses that are not made explicit.

CONCLUSIONS

The controversy between using experimental methodology or using single case studies in conjunction with computer modeling to explore human CPS is by no means a new one (Herrmann, 1990). The complexity of the phenomenon by itself does not provide enough of a reason to favor the modeling and single case methodology a priori. Instead, one has to take into account that there are different research goals. The individual research questions and research goals should determine the selection of the *right* methodological approach.

In this chapter, single case studies are viewed as one step, among other steps, in a comprehensive research process that is directed at the development of models. There are roughly two groups of single case applications: (a) the development of models of human problem solving based on single case data, and, (b) the evaluation of models by deriving and testing hypotheses in single case studies. The former research procedure relies to a considerable extent on induction and is directed at deriving general statements about human problem solving. The latter procedure is predominantly directed at the goal of providing empirical evidence for hypotheses by analyzing data from single cases.

In all studies that were discussed in this chapter, the application of the single case methodology was associated with theoretical frameworks or models, or at the least with preliminary theoretical assumptions. This is in accord with the characteristics of single case analyses discussed by Ericsson and Simon (1984). Ericsson and Simon even deny that data from single cases can ever be used in the absence of a theoretical framework. They also point out, however, that collecting data before any hypotheses are formulated is by no means a worthless approach: "The common view that hypotheses must be formulated before experiments are run in order for the data to have value as evidence is simply false. However, *how much* credence we should place in them on the basis of the evidence may depend on whether or not they were thought of first" (Ericsson & Simon, 1984, p. 283). Clearly, not always does an elaborated theoretical system exist to generate hypotheses that are worthwhile of being investigated. There will always remain some states during the research process where the hypotheses established for, and derived from, single cases are quite isolated. Bunge (1967), for instance, points out that all empirical generalizations "are isolated during their infancy," and are "presystematic and pretheoretical." The hypotheses are not yet "entrenched in some system either as axioms (starting-points) or as theorems (logical consequences)" (p. 238).

The use of single case analyses in the context of computer modeling raises serious problems, some of which are summarized below:

(a) Hypotheses that enter empirical tests and hypotheses that are derived from empirical tests are always constrained by specific additional presuppositions and assumptions. These assumptions concern, among others, the methods for collecting data, the dependent variables, the methods used in the modeling, and the criteria for judging the similarity between the performance of the program and human performance. It is rarely the case that these aspects are made explicit. Positive examples are provided, however, by Anderson (1982; the discussion of the relation between dependent variables and the skill model) and by Shrager and Klahr (1986; e.g., the discussion of verbal data). This step is simply necessary to justify the acceptance and rejection of hypotheses, especially in the case of a lack of support or of negative empirical evidence.

(b) There is a tendency among researchers, when testing and developing models, to selectively focus on those components or on those verbalizations that provide some support for the established hypotheses. Also, universal hypotheses are formulated rather easily, without specifying the constraints under which their validity is claimed. In this context, a distinction that was originally proposed by Bunge (1967), may be made between first and second degree induction. As an example, one can proceed from a statement that was derived from one observed case, "Subjects when solving this novel complex task x follow the knowledge acquisition stages a, b, c" via second degree induction to the statement, "When solving novel complex tasks, the process of knowledge acquisition follows stages a, b, c." This type of generalization is frequently found in single case studies. In most studies, however, there is no empirical support for such a statement. Bunge (1967) views this type of empirical induction, that is, the generalization of observed cases, rather critically, and states that its usefulness has been "grossly overestimated by philosophers" (p. 244). Empirical inductions in the sense of conjectures that are based on cumulative experience, for example multiple single cases, "are scientifically uninteresting precisely because they do not go far beyond experience. The most important conjectures are gained on the basis of little or no experience of the preconceptual kind: they are not solutions to recurring empirical problems but to new problems of a conceptual kind" (p. 245). This position is not shared here because the process of research is conceived of as a repeated cycle. Single case analyses are just intermediate steps in the process of theory development, and do not exclude the possibility of posing original problems and of inventing entirely new hypotheses. "A single verbal protocol is not an island to itself, but a link in a chain of evidence, stretching far into the past and the future, that gradually develops, molds, and modifies our scientific theories" (Ericsson & Simon, 1984, p. 280).

(c) Especially when models are tested, there is a tendency to provide selected episodes from individual protocols in order to illustrate components of the model and to increase the plausibility of the assumptions implemented in a program. Needless to say, which episode are selected depends on the researcher, a procedure that is difficult to examine and to justify. Although this is by no means an unusual procedure as Ericsson and Simon (1984) point out, "Protocol analysis sometimes consists largely of extracting examples of concepts or processes from the verbalization as evidence for theories that predict them . . . the contribution of such examples to the credibility of a theory depends on what alternative explanations are available" (Ericsson & Simon, 1984, p. 287), there is the danger that such illustrative episodes are mistaken as empirical evidence.

(d) In many single case studies, both theory development and testing uses the same data. Researchers in the area are well aware of this problem. The resulting theory "may appear to reflect mainly hindsight—pulling out of the data the hypotheses that have been implicitly hidden in it by the data interpretation process. This is the core of validity in the criticisms sometimes leveled against computer simulation of thinking, although it hardly justifies the extravagant and usually false claim that if you are given a verbal protocol, you can always write a computer program that will simulate it" (Ericsson & Simon, 1984, p. 286).

The danger of circularity, according to Ericsson and Simon (1984), is relatively minor if the coding of the protocol is objective and reproducible and if the model is parsimonious. However, it is clearly desirable to test the model by applying data from other subjects in the domain or from other task domains. That is, the theories developed on the basis of single case data can and need to be subjected to experimental tests, as has been done, for instance, in the case of Anderson's model of skill acquisition. It is of interest that most of the authors discussed above describe the status of their models as preliminary and as requiring additional empirical support. Thus, the value of single case studies may be especially high during the early stages of model development and evaluation.

In general, perhaps the most important contribution of single case studies occurs during those initial states in the research process when careful observation is required, a procedure that is frequently practiced in other disciplines. Lorenz (1973), for example, emphasizes this aspect, that is, the careful and precise description of behavior and procedures. This can be achieved in the context of extensive single case studies, and it may provide the researcher with knowledge and with some preliminary understanding of the observed behavior and procedures. Such a step might prove to be especially useful in very complex domains. As a consequence, really new problems may be posed and simple hypotheses may be established that can later be examined empirically.

REFERENCES

Anderson, J. R. (1982). Acquisition of cognitive skill. *Psychological Review, 89,* 369–406.
Anderson, J. R. (1983). *The architecture of cognition.* Cambridge, MA: Harvard University Press.
Bhaskar, R., & Simon, H. A. (1977). Problem solving in semantically rich domains: An example from thermodynamics. *Cognitive Science, 1,* 193–215.
Bunge, M. (1967). *Scientific Research I.* Berlin: Springer.
Dörner, D. (1992). Über die Philosophie der Verwendung von Mikrowelten oder "Computerszenarios" in der psychologischen Forschung [On the proper use of microworlds or "computer scenarios" in psychological research]. In H. Gundlach (Ed.), *Psychologische Forschung und Methode: Das Versprechen des Experiments* (pp. 53–87). Passau, Germany: Passavia Universitätsverlag.
Dörner, D., & Lantermann, E. D. (1991). Experiment und Empirie in der Psychologie [On experiments and empirical data in psychology]. In K. Grawe, R. Hänni, N. Semmer, & F.

Tschan (Eds.), *Über die richtige Art, Psychologie zu betreiben* (pp. 37–58). Göttingen, Germany: Hogrefe.

Ericsson, K. A., & Simon, H. A. (1984). *Protocol analysis: Verbal reports as data.* Cambridge, MA: MIT Press.

Herrmann, T. (1990). Die Experimentiermethodik in der Defensive? [The experimental method on the defensive?]. *Sprache & Kognition, 9,* 1–11.

Kazdin, A. E. (1982). *Single-case research design.* New York: Oxford University Press.

Kintsch, W., Miller, J. R., & Polson, P. G. (1984). *Methods and tactics in cognitive science.* Hillsdale, NJ: Lawrence Erlbaum Associates

Kluwe, R. H. (1991). Zum Problem der Wissensvoraussetzungen für Prozeß- und Systemkontrolle [On hidden knowledge for process control and system control]. *Zeitschrift für Psychologie. Supplement, 11,* 311–324.

Kluwe, R. H. (1993). Knowledge and performance in complex problem solving. In G. Strube & K. F. Wender (Eds.), *The cognitive psychology of knowledge* (pp. 401–423). Amsterdam: Elsevier Science Publishers.

Kluwe, R. H., Haider, H., & Misiak, C. (1990). Learning by doing in the control of a complex system. In H. Mandl, E. de Corte, N. Bennett, & H. F. Friedrich (Eds.), *Learning and instruction* (Vol. 2.1, pp. 197–218). Oxford: Pergamon Press.

Kluwe, R. H., Misiak, C., & Haider, H. (1989). Modelling the process of complex system control. In P. Milling & E. Zahn (Eds.), *Computer-based management of complex systems* (pp. 335–342). Berlin, Germany: Springer.

Kratochwill, T. R. (1992). Single-case research design and analysis: An overview. In T. R. Kratochwill & J. R. Levin, (Eds.), *Single-case research design and analysis* (pp. 1–15). Hillsdale, NJ: Lawrence Erlbaum Associates.

Lorenz, K. (1973). The fashionable fallacy of dispensing with description. *Naturwissenschaften, 60,* 1–9.

Neves, D. M., & Anderson, J. R. (1981). Knowledge compilation: Mechanisms for the automatization of cognitive skills. In J. R. Anderson (Ed.), *Cognitive skills and their acquisition* (pp. 57–84). Hillsdale, NJ: Lawrence Erlbaum Associates.

Newell, A. (1982). The knowledge level. *Artificial Intelligence, 18,* 87–127.

Newell, A., & Simon, H. A. (1972). *Human problem solving.* Englewood Cliffs, NJ: Prentice-Hall.

Newell, A., & Rosenbloom, P. S. (1981). Mechanisms of skill acquisition and the law of practice. In J. R. Anderson (Ed.), *Cognitive skills and their acquisition* (pp. 1–56). Hillsdale, NJ: Lawrence Erlbaum Associates.

Reichert, U., & Dörner, D. (1988). Heurismen beim Umgang mit einem "einfachen" dynamischen System [Heuristics of coping with a "simple" dynamic system]. *Sprache & Kognition, 7,* 12–124.

Shrager, J. (1987). Theory change via view application in instructionless learning. *Machine Learning, 2,* 1–30.

Shrager, J., & Klahr, D. (1986). Instructionless learning about a complex device: The paradigm and observations. *International Journal of Man-Machine Studies, 25,* 153–189.

Westmeyer, H. (1989). Wissenschaftstheoretische Grundlagen der Einzelfallanalyse [Philosophy of science for single case analysis]. In F. Petermann (Ed.), *Einzelfallanalyse* (pp. 18–35) (2nd ed.). München, Germany: Urban & Schwarzenberg.

PART FIVE

CONCLUSIONS

CHAPTER TWELVE

Expertise in Complex Problem Solving: A Comparison of Alternative Conceptions

Robert J. Sternberg
Yale University

INTRODUCTION

One does not have to read many Agatha Christie novels to recognize Hercule Poirot's expertise as a detective. Expertise in the solution of complex problems has always held a certain fascination for us, as shown by the fact that so many novels, TV series, and other forms of dramatic production have been built around characters who are experts in solving complex medical, legal, family, or other problems. In real life, true experts hold a similar fascination. Few laypeople would have doubted the expertise of Einstein as a physicist. Hence, they would not have doubted anything he said about physics, no matter how skeptical his fellow scientists might have been of particular claims that he made. At a lesser level, but still relevant, we depend on the expertise of lawyers, doctors, and other professionals when we seek their consultations, and at times put our lives in their hands.

What, exactly, is it that makes an *expert* problem solver? Psychologists have been studying expertise since the beginning of the century, although under a variety of different labels. For example, the studies of intelligence of Binet and Simon (1905) can be seen as studies of intellectual expertise, and many other studies in psychology equally could be viewed from the standpoint of the study of expert behavior. The modern study of expertise under its own name began in earnest about 30 years ago (DeGroot, 1965) and continues through to the present day.

Curiously, very few of the studies of expertise in complex problem solving take seriously the question of just what is an expert. For the most part, investigators have taken a task selected for reasons that are not always altogether clear, and then defined expertise operationally in terms of outstanding performance on that task. Often, outstanding performance has been compared to nonoutstanding performance in order further to clarify the foundations of expertise. Such operational definitions are functionally useful, but do not come face to face with the question of just what constitutes an expert. That is the question I will address here.

A major goal in this analysis is to compare the conceptions of expertise proposed by European investigators, as exemplified by those in the present volume, with those proposed by American investigators, as exemplified by the majority of the contributions in Sternberg and Frensch (1991). But I also try to place these various contributions into a more general framework that encompasses all of the various conceptions of expertise—those that overlap across international borders and those that do not.

In this chapter, I briefly consider 10 different views of expertise. First, however, I open with general comments regarding some of the basic similarities and differences between the European and American perspectives. I then take a more principled approach to understanding expertise in problem solving, namely, in terms of the 10 points of view.

The first four views are ones that have been generally held at one time or another, in the literature. These views include the (a) general-process view, according to which experts are people who solve problems by different processes from those used by nonexperts, or who use the same processes more effectively than do nonexperts; (b) quantity-of-knowledge view, according to which experts simply know more than do nonexperts; (c) knowledge-organization view, according to which experts organize their knowledge more effectively than do nonexperts; (d) cognitive-complexity view, according to which experts are somehow cognitively more complex in the information they can process, perhaps because of superior working-memory capacity. The next four views are based on the triarchic theory of intelligence (Sternberg, 1985), but correspond to intuitions people have had as to what constitutes an expert. These conceptions include superior (e) analytical ability in solving problems, which may be seen as the ability to use effectively the knowledge one has; (f) creative ability, which involves creating new knowledge on the basis of knowledge one already has; (g) automatization, according to which experts do things more adeptly and automatically than do nonexperts; and (h) practical ability, which involves "knowing the ropes" or knowing how to get ahead in one's field of endeavor. The ninth (i) view is based on implicit theories, or people's conceptions of a construct. This ninth, labeling view holds that an expert is an expert by virtue of being labeled as such. Finally, I present a tenth, synthetic view (j), which combines elements of the others that have already been considered earlier. On this view, expertise is a prototype, and is rarely reached in its purely prototypical form. Rather, people have aspects of expertise, namely, the other nine aspects that will have been considered in this article.

AMERICAN AND EUROPEAN VIEWS OF EXPERTISE IN COMPLEX PROBLEM SOLVING

The American View

All of American research in psychology has its roots in European philosophy and psychology, whether one traces back these roots to ancient Greece (the work of Plato and Aristotle) or to 19th-century Europe (the work of Wundt, carried over to the United States by Titchener and others). But Americans have prided themselves on having diverged from the European forebears, and William James rather than Wilhelm Wundt is usually viewed as the *father* of American psychology.

Oddly enough, therefore, the dominant contemporary American approach to complex problem solving clearly originated in research conducted in Europe, not in the United States. This research was the pioneering work of DeGroot (1965) on expert chess players, which was later extended by Chase and Simon (1973). The main impact of this work was to shift thinking about expertise from a point of view emphasizing general information processing (Miller, Galanter, & Pribram, 1960; Newell, Shaw, & Simon, 1958) to one emphasizing the preeminence of knowledge (Chase & Simon, 1973). Typical American work has compared experts versus novices in the performance of tasks requiring high levels of professional expertise. Whereas early work, such as that of Chase and Simon or of Reitman (1976), emphasized games, later work switched in emphasis to what were viewed in the United States as more serious professional pursuits, such as physics (Chi, Glaser, & Rees, 1982; Hegarty, 1991; Larkin, 1983; Larkin, McDermott, Simon, & Simon, 1980; McCloskey, 1983), electronics (Lesgold & Lajoie, 1991), computer programming (Adelson, 1981; Card, Moran, & Newell, 1983; Kay, 1991), and mathematical calculation (Ashcraft, 1982; Brown & Burton, 1978; Groen & Parkman, 1972; Resnick, 1982; Siegler & Shrager, 1984).

Not all American research on problem solving followed the approach of expert–novice differences in technical problem solving. For example, Gick and Holyoak (1983) and Gentner (1983) initiated productive and long-lasting programs of research on analogical problem solving. Wagner and Sternberg (1985) initiated a program of research on nontechnical managerial problem solving, and Voss et al. (1983) started looking at problem solving in the social sciences, in particular, international relations, rather than in the natural sciences. But the study of differences between experts and novices in the natural sciences and mathematics has predominated in American research.

As Hunt (1991) has pointed out, the view of expertise that has emerged from this research is "one of a problem solver who has memorized a huge number of tricks of the trade, rather than one who has developed a single powerful strategy for reasoning. Local optimality acquired at the expense of global consistency" (p. 394). In sum, Americans have primarily studied expertise in knowledge-rich domains, and have attributed expertise to greater knowledge about these domains.

The American approach has several strengths. One is a tradition of careful experimental study. Another is the close observation of true experts at work. A third strength is the awakening to the fact that one cannot be an expert in a field without knowing a lot about the field. The cognitive psychology of the 1960s might well have given one the impression that expertise in the absence of extensive knowledge was, in fact, possible.

Over the years, I have developed several concerns about the American approach to research on complex problem solving, an approach that at times I have found to be discouraging.

First, there is something nonprofound about showing that the difference between experts and novices is that experts know more than do novices. I have sometimes commented only half in jest to student audiences that if they want to establish a solid career in cognitive psychology, they should pick out experts and novices in something, and show that the experts know more than the novices—for sure they will get a publication somewhere. When a central finding in a literature becomes something one's grandmother could have told one, we need to be concerned.

I don't wish to trivialize the American research. Of course, it has gone well beyond simply saying that experts know more than do novices. But at heart, what has been said is largely an elaboration of that basic statement. Is that the best we have to offer? Is it even always true? For example, Adelson (1984) and Frensch and Sternberg (1989) have shown circumstances in which knowledge can interfere with expertise, and Sternberg and Lubart (1991) have argued that creative problem solving often requires one to avoid the entrenchment that can come with a lot of knowledge about a domain.

Second, why are we Americans studying physics expertise anyway? What percentage of Americans (or Europeans, for that matter) become physicists, or actually even ever study physics? The number is small and diminishing— even the top physicists in the United States are having trouble finding jobs! The American approach has emphasized the intensive study of extremely specialized pursuits. Obviously, the underlying assumption is that what is learned about expertise in these specialized pursuits will generalize to other pursuits. But will it? Do everyday people think like physicists? I, at least, doubt it. Most people can hardly understand a physics course, or even intuitive physics (McCloskey, 1983).

Third, studying experts does not guarantee that one is studying the experts at what actually makes them experts. For example, one can certainly give expert physicists textbook problems to solve, and compare their strategies and mental representations to those of novices. But expert physicists don't solve textbook problems for a living; nor do expert mathematicians solve arithmetic computation problems, or expert computer programmers debug other people's programs. My point is that even if we have studied the right people, we have often studied them doing the wrong tasks. We need not only study experts, but study these experts doing the tasks that render them experts.

Fourth, there has been relatively great attention focused on group differences between experts and novices, but relatively little attention focused on individual differences among experts. If we look at great scientists or writers or artists, for example, we will find that they do not all succeed in the same way. It is not clear that there is any common thing that makes them an expert, any more than there is a common thing that makes a game a game (Wittgenstein, 1953). To consider some examples of expert *psychologists*, for example, Tversky and Kahneman achieved success in part by coming up with ideas for very simple experiments that just about anyone might have thought of—but didn't; Endel Tulving achieved renown in part by coming up with experimental findings that were the opposite of what anyone might have expected; Jean Piaget achieved success by devising the most nearly complete theory of cognitive development ever proposed, and backing the theory with ingenious if not always airtight experiments; and so on. Without considering individual differences, it is difficult fully to understand expertise.

Fifth, even American psychologists have voted with their feet. For the most part, promising graduate students in recent years have decided to pursue specializations in cognitive psychology other than that of complex problem solving. The work on problem solving has not captured their imagination, or their research. Of course, one could argue that the study of complex problem solving has traditionally been on the periphery of cognitive psychology. It has. But 10 years ago, who was studying parallel models of cognition? Practically no one. Today, many graduate students in the United States are pursuing the study of connectionist models. The study of learning, moribund after the demise of behaviorism, has been revived. Cognitive neuropsychology, a tiny area 20 years ago, is probably the hottest area in cognitive psychology today. When an area captures the imagination of a generation, students pursue it. Complex problem solving has not captured their imagination, at least in the United States.

Finally, whether one likes the predominant American approach or not, one cannot help thinking that there must be something more. Is an expert nothing more than someone who has spent countless hours learning patterns? In the extreme, scholars such as Ericsson have argued that virtually anyone can become an expert at virtually anything if they just put enough time into learning and practice (e.g., Ericsson & Staszewski, 1989). Ericsson, of Swedish origin, represents the American philosophy even more extremely than do Americans—the philosophy that everyone is equal means that everyone can do anything that anyone else can do.

In my opinion, this line of research, like much of that on giftedness, is flawed by the absence of control groups. The researchers study the successes, but not the enormously larger number of failures. For every supersuccess in musical, artistic, athletic, or other performances, there are hundreds and perhaps thousands of would-be musicians or artists or football players who never made it to the top, and were never heard from again. Most people never make it to the greatest musical conservatories or art academies—not because they don't put in the time, but because they don't have the talent. Even with talent, a person needs to work very hard to achieve success in complex performances. But without the talent, hard work is unlikely to lead to the heights. We need to separate our American philosophy from honest or at least realistic psychology. In my opinion, we haven't.

The European View

But for a small though extremely significant and unfortunate accident of history, I would have been born in Austria (or perhaps not born at all!). Reading the essays in this volume, I can see advantages. I believe that although there are problems with the European approach, it deals with some fundamental questions that American research scarcely addresses. Moreover, it is probably more in the tradition of the classical work on problem solving initiated by the Gestalt psychologists (e.g., Duncker, 1945; Köhler, 1925; Luchins, 1942; Maier, 1930, 1931) than is the American work.

As noted by Frensch and Funke (this volume), there are two principal approaches in the European tradition to studying expertise in complex problem solving. One approach was largely initiated by Broadbent (1977) in England, the other by Dörner (1987) in Germany. The key difference between the two traditions is that in the former, one is able to specify a precise rule via a mathematical formula that would optimize problem solving, whereas in the latter, the problems are so complex that it is questionable whether we could ever devise any mathematical or even computer simulation that would clearly optimize performance. What the two approaches have in common, however, is that one can give the problems to anyone of at least roughly average intelligence and get them to solve the problems. In the American tradition, in contrast, many of the problems that are used in physics or computers would go well beyond the knowledge base of the ordinary person in the street.

The contributions in this volume can be roughly sorted in terms of the two traditions. Buchner provides an excellent review of the various specific problems that have been used in the two traditions, which is why I do not repeat this review of problems here. He also usefully points out the importance of looking at individual differences in problem solving, something that is certainly neglected in the American tradition. Dörner and Wearing (the latter of whom, I am proud to say, was my junior-year advisor at Yale before he inconveniently decided to accept a full professorship at Melbourne), of course, concentrate on Dörner's own approach, initiated with the Lohhausen problem. Brehmer's fire-fighting simulation is closer to the German tradition, except that the progress of the simulation is time-driven rather than subject-response-driven. Although Berry and Broadbent make some changes from earlier theoretical positions, their person control and whale tasks are in the English tradition. And so on. I have read few edited books with uniformly excellent chapters—this is one of those few books.

There are several attractive features of the European approach, as represented in this volume, that are in general not shared by the American approach, some of which I discuss here.

A first feature is that almost anyone can be a subject. The Europeans are studying how problems are solved by people in general, not just by the small fraction of one percent of people who are physicists or molecular biochemists, or whatever. Thus, from the standpoint of population generalizability, the European research seems to apply in its outcomes to far more people.

A second feature is that the problems are about life in general. On the one hand, most people don't get to be mayor of a town, as in Lohhausen, or to run a city TRANSPORTATION SYSTEM (Broadbent, 1977). On the other hand, these problems in management are similar to ones tens of thousands of managers face as they run their companies, and in many ways reflect the myriad variables that people face as they run their lives. Thus, in terms of task generalizability as well as population generalizability, the European research seems to go further.

A third attractive feature is that, in combination, the British and German approaches look both at problems that are so hopelessly complex that it would be exceedingly difficult or impossible to specify an optimal formula (the German approach) and at problems whose optimal solution can be characterized by a mathematical function so that it is possible to compare people's performance to the optimal (the English approach). By studying both kinds of problems, we learn more about problem solving than we would by studying only simpler or only more complex problems. The American research, on the other hand, has often looked at problems that don't even resemble those that the experts in their fields truly face. As noted earlier, what makes an expert physicist has little or nothing to do with the physicist's ability to solve textbook-like problems.

Finally, the Europeans have paid much more attention to individual differences than have the Americans. American cognitive research was in part a reaction to the psychometric tradition (see Sternberg, 1977), and perhaps for this reason, Americans doing problem-solving (and other cognitive) research have often avoided the study of individual differences with a passion. In contrast, several of the chapters in this volume, namely, those of Berry and Broadbent, Beckmann and Guthke, Krems, U. Funke, J. Funke, and Kluwe pay close attention to individual differences, and other chapters at least mention the issue.

Despite the attractive general features of the European approach, there are some drawbacks, as there are to any research. The ones I have observed in this volume are the following.

First, despite the attractiveness of the paradigms, it would be difficult to specify any large set of principles of problem solving that have emerged from the work. In fact, the American work may have yielded more general principles (especially the work of Holyoak on analogies). If we were to try to state a list of generalizations about problem solving, the list would probably not be long.

Second, the cost of using very complicated problems is that it is difficult to get a consensus as to what constitutes a reliable and valid way of scoring. When we find, for example, that variables related to Lohhausen performance do not relate to performance on conventional tests of ability, we have to worry about the reliability and validity of the measures, a concern echoed in the fine chapter by Beckmann and Guthke. Indeed, as these authors point out, it is difficult to know even how to assess reliability and validity adequately.

Third, the approach is more task-centered than one might desire. Much of the review of literature in the various chapters, such as Buchner's, centers around the tasks and what one can do with them. Ultimately, we would hope to organize our search for understanding of problem solving around theoretical rather than task-based constructs. The European approach has not yielded the kinds of more general theories of problem solving that have emerged in the United States, say, out of the work of Newell and Simon (1972). Indeed, although the work was not initiated in the correlational tradition, it often ends up being primarily an analysis of the post hoc correlations of various indices of performance with outside measures, say, of intelligence or extraversion. It would be nice if the correlations were predicted on the basis of some general theory of problem solving.

Fourth, the approach may be spinning itself out. After a spate of exciting and forward-moving research projects, the rate of development of the paradigm seems to be decreasing. This slowing is typical of maturing paradigms. It may be that the time will be coming when new paradigms need to make themselves felt. The chapter by Huber on the investment task and parallel BREEDING LIZARDS TASK seems to be an effort in this direction.

The American and European approaches are complementary rather than contradictory. To a large extent, they look at different aspects of complex problem solving. I don't believe one approach is uniformly better than the other, but rather that neither approach succeeds in addressing all of the question one might ask about complex problem solving, or in particular, what makes an expert problem solver. At the same time, we have to realize that no one approach to anything answers all possible questions.

Although the European and American approaches differ in some significant respects, they have one fundamental thing in common: Both seek to elucidate just what constitutes an expert problem solver. What are the various views of the expert problem solver that emerge from the research that has been done on complex problem solving? That is the question I address in the next section.

RECEIVED VIEWS OF EXPERTISE

The General-Process View

The pioneering work of Newell, Shaw, and Simon (1958) and Miller, Galanter, and Pribram (1960) shifted much of the emphasis in American experimental psychology from stimulus–response theories of behavior to cognitively based theories. Instead of treating the mind as a black box that mediated between stimuli and responses to stimuli, psychologists started to treat the processes of thought as being of interest and as being knowable in their own right. Cognitive psychologists studied the processes used to solve various kinds of problems, the strategies into which these processes were combined, and the latencies and error rates of these various processes. Implicitly, the notion of expertise was that an expert differed from a novice in variables such as these—in which processes and strategies were used, and in the speed and accuracy with which the processes were executed.

Consider, for example, a game such as chess. It seems obvious that an expert would have to think about chess in a way which was different from a novice. The expert could pick excellent moves after considering only a few possibilities, suggesting that his or her strategy was quite different from the novice, who would not recognize these excellent moves as being excellent. Perhaps the expert saw farther into the possible futures of the game, or considered more possible alternative moves, or simply had a clever method for selecting the better moves. Whatever the difference, the information-processing view provided welcome relief from the stimulus-response view, in that it actually considered what went on in the expert's head, rather than merely considering antecedents and consequences.

The view of expertise as based on superiority in general information processing was consistent with a view of intelligence that was developing at the time, namely, that more intelligent problem solvers are fundamentally superior information processors. A wide variety of studies was showing that more intelligent people could process information more efficiently than could less intelligent people (e.g., Eysenck, 1986; Hunt, 1978; Jensen, 1982; Sternberg, 1977). Raaheim (1974) suggested that intelligent people might be better able to cope with relative novelty, in general, and others, such as Guthke (1985) suggested that general learning potentials might be a key to understanding intelligence.

Thus, intellectual expertise might consist of the ability efficiently to process information in a variety of tasks that anyone could do, given time, whereas specific forms of expertise might consist of the ability to process domain-specific information either faster or more accurately than could novices. The idea that there might be this conceptual link between general intelligence and the more specific abilities needed for domain-specific expertise was an attractive one, because it placed various kinds of cognitive expertise within a single rubric. But certain research, described below, suggested that this view might be, at best, incomplete, and at worst, wrong.

Knowledge-Based Views

The Quantity-of-Knowledge View. The study of expertise was revolutionized when first DeGroot (1965) and then Chase and Simon (1973) discovered that the difference between experts and novices in chess did not appear in their mental processing of information at all. Chase and Simon required both expert and novice chess players to remember configurations of chess pieces on chessboards that were exposed for brief periods of time. Perhaps the key difference between expert and novice chess players was in their ability to encode and then remember information, so that the experts would do much better on this task than would the novices. The experts did do better, but only when the chess pieces were arranged in a sensible configuration with regard to the game of chess. When the pieces were arranged in a random configuration that would never occur in a game of chess, the experts remembered no better than did the novices. These results were inconsistent with the view that the experts somehow processed information in general in a manner that was different than that of the novices. Rather, the results suggested that whatever the difference, it was specific to chessboard configurations. Chase and Simon suggested that the advantage of experts over novices was due to their having stored in memory tens of thousands of sensible configurations of chess pieces that potentially occur in games. They could recognize these configurations, and thereby encode them easily. To novices, on the other hand, the sense of a configuration looked no different from the nonsensical ones, and thus, they had no edge in remembering the sensible ones. They had no stored chess patterns to which to relate the given information. Other studies soon replicated the effect in other situations (e.g., Reitman, 1976) and suggested that the difference between experts and novices in knowledge was not limited to chess.

At one level, the findings of Chase and Simon were very exciting. At another level, they were less so. The Chase and Simon findings failed the *grandmother test*, by which a psychological finding gains interest if it is a finding that would not be obvious in advance to one's grandmother. The finding that experts know more than novices is not one of the great surprises of the century. It is hard to imagine how they would not know more. To the extent that the finding was exciting, however, it was not because experts knew more, but because the difference in knowledge seems to be causally related to their expertise.

From an educational point of view, these findings were perhaps disquieting. There has always been a strong conservative faction of educators and parents that has believed that the best education is the one that stuffs the most facts into children's heads. The modern emphasis on developing the thinking skills (Baron & Sternberg, 1987) has no place in this conservative point of view. If anything, teaching for thinking can get in the way of teaching for knowledge, because it wastes time that might otherwise be used in stuffing in more facts. But it soon became apparent that although quantity of knowledge might be necessary for expertise, it almost certainly was not sufficient.

The quantity-of-knowledge view, as far as I can tell, has had much more impact on American thinking than on European thinking. Perhaps it is in part a result of the kinds of problems studied. Americans have tended to study problems requiring a rich knowledge base for their solution, whereas Europeans have tended more to study problems that require little specific prior knowledge. Moreover, there seems to be a cultural difference in assessment between the two continents. The kinds of multiple-choice tests of factual knowledge that have been so popular in the United States have never taken hold in Europe (most fortunately).

Perhaps paradoxically, the everyday styles of scholars on the two continents do not mirror their emphases in problem-solving research. If I may be permitted anecdotal and speculative observations, I will briefly comment on a difference I have observed in presentation styles across the two continents. European researchers, especially German ones I have heard present orally, go to great lengths to show the importance of the scholarly antecedents of their work. American researchers often have only the briefest literature reviews when they open their talks, and sometimes none at all. Moreover, they as often as not don't know the literature they are not citing! There is even a difference in promotion systems for advancement in scholarship. In Spain, for example, faculty members undergo a rigorous examination for promotion to Catedratico that requires the faculty members to show both broad and deep knowledge and understanding of the work in their field. In the United States, the last examination of this kind anyone in academia takes is the doctoral qualifying exam, if the individual even takes such an exam. Promotions depend largely on published scholarship, and usually to a lesser extent on teaching (with more emphasis on teaching in the smaller, teaching-oriented colleges). Thus, for reasons I can't claim to understand, the emphases in research seem at variance with the cultural emphasis in academia.

The Organization-of-Knowledge View.   Studies of experts in physics by Chi, Glaser, and Rees (1982), Larkin, McDermott, Simon, and Simon (1980), and others suggested that, at least in the understanding of experts in physics, quantity of knowledge was not the most useful construct. Chi and her colleagues, for example, found that experts in physics sorted physics problems in a way that was different from the way that novices sorted the same problems. Experts tended to sort problems in terms of a deeper, more fundamental conceptual structure, whereas novices tended to sort them in terms of a more superficial surface structure. These results and others suggested that the difference between groups was not only in the amount of knowledge they had, but in how they organized that knowledge. Experts organize knowledge more according to its deep structure, novices according to its surface structure. Indeed, novices might not even be able to distinguish the deep structure from the surface structure, a sign of their not deeply understanding the material in their field of interest. Many other studies reviewed in Chi, Glaser, and Farr (1988), Hoffman (1992), and Sternberg and Frensch (1991) also suggested that organization of knowledge is at least as important as amount of knowledge in differentiating experts from novices in a variety of different disciplinary areas.

The organization-of-knowledge view is more interesting than the quantity-of-knowledge view, both conceptually and educationally. It suggests that there is more to expertise than just knowing more. One has to know how to organize what one knows. An expert could not simply memorize a book on a given topic or a series of encyclopedia entries, because the organization would not be one that he or she could exploit in order to do tasks effectively in the domain in which expertise is sought.

In order concretely to understand the difference between the two points of view, consider two people who study the French language. One of these hypothetical people memorizes an English–French–English dictionary as well as a book of French grammar. The other has spent 15 years in France and has had to communicate with French people, but never has memorized any entries in a dictionary nor even read a book of grammar in more than a cursory way. Which individual is more likely expertly to communicate in French? Clearly the second. Although the first person may have an enormous quantity of information, the information is inert. She is unlikely to know when or how to use the information, and thus it is available, but inaccessible for use. The second person may actually have fewer items of information stored, but the information that is stored is encoded in a way that makes it readily accessible and usable. The result is that the second person is far more likely to be an expert communicator in French than is the first.

The difference between these two points of view is not limited to the learning of languages. Consider an aspect of mathematics such as algebra. Memorizing formulas and principles of algebra does not make an expert in algebra. The student who seeks to receive an A in the course by memorizing all the information he can get his hands on may well end up failing instead. A second student who memorizes nothing, but who understands how to use principles of algebra that he has acquired in the course of his problem solving, is much more likely to achieve expertise in algebra. Thus, the organization-of-knowledge viewpoint again seems to be the more useful one.

Clearly, in order to organize information well, one must first have information to organize. During the 1960s, a rash of new curricula appeared in the sciences and mathematics, devoted to teaching children to think in these disciplines. For the most part, these methods did not enjoy long-term success because they placed great emphasis on thinking concepts, but insufficient emphasis on children's learning the concepts in the first place. In order to think well, one first needs concepts with which to think.

The quantity-of-knowledge and especially the organization-of-knowledge points of view were attractive because they placed expertise within a framework that was becoming very popular within the study of cognitive development in general. According to this framework, preferred by Chi (1978), Siegler (1978), Keil (1989), and others, cognitive development centered largely around the acquisition and organization of information. On this view, Piaget (1972) was incorrect in his emphasis on general information processing. What distinguishes the more cognitively mature individual from the less cognitively mature one is the possession of a greater amount of knowledge and the superior organization of this knowledge. The work of these psychologists suggested that children's failure in a variety of tasks was not due actually to their inability to process information, but rather to their lack of knowledge needed for various tasks that they might seek to do. Thus, cognitive expertise became an advanced form of cognitive development within a specific domain. Just as one could develop cognitively at a general level and thus reach a level of higher maturity, so could one advance in a more specific domain, and achieve cognitive expertise in that domain.

The organization-of-knowledge view, like the quantity-of-knowledge view, is much more entrenched in the United States than in Europe, for much the same reasons described before. Americans have used the kinds of problems that require organization of a large knowledge base; Europeans generally have not. But there is a point of view conceptually related to the organization-of-knowledge that is more prevalent in Europe than in America, the cognitive-complexity view.

The Cognitive-Complexity View

The basic idea of this view is that expert problem solvers are somehow cognitively more complex than are novices. This is the point of view that has been championed in the United States by Streufert (e.g., Streufert & Streufert, 1978), who, ironically, is European; in Canada by Pascual-Leone (1970), who is also European, and in Europe by many of the contributors to this volume, whether they use the term or not. For example, Dörner and Wearing refer to the need to build up a mental representation of the system to be managed. In order to build up such a complex representation, one needs to be able to hold it in working memory (which is why some theorists, such as Pascual-Leone, have emphasized the importance of working memory to cognitive complexity). Beckmann and Guthke discuss the importance of learning to problem solving, but in order to learn as complex a system as Lohhausen, say, one must be able to learn to handle very complex information.

Ceci (1990) has recently argued that cognitive complexity provides a key to understanding complex performances that do not seem to be mediated by IQ. For example, in his studies of bettors at the race track, Ceci found that the best bettors were able to construct complex implicit multiple-regression formulas to predict winners of races; but scored an average of only 97 on intelligence tests. In order to be an expert, one not only needs to know a lot about a field, such as horse racing, but also needs to be complex enough to be able to process the network of information required to perform well.

TRIARCHIC CONCEPTIONS OF EXPERTISE

The view of expertise presented here is based on a triarchic theory of human abilities (Sternberg, 1985). Psychologists are sometimes satisfied with theories that astound laypeople either with their simplicity or with their complexity. For example, on the side of simplicity is Jensen's (1972) notion that the psychological basis of intelligence lies in a person's ability rapidly to solve choice-reaction-time tasks, in which one of two lights flashes, and the subject in turn must press one of two buttons. On the side of complexity are complicated-production-system models such as those proposed by Klahr (1984). But there seem to be theories of intermediate complexity that are easier to grasp and that are more plausible, in some respects, than the theories at the extremes of either simplicity or complexity.

The knowledge-basis views of expertise seem to be lacking in many of the aspects of expertise that fit into our everyday notions of what makes an expert. For example, to consider two fictional characters, Perry Mason was not an expert lawyer nor Philip Marlowe an expert detective simply because the one or the other knew a lot about lawyering or detecting, or even because each had organized the information he had acquired in an effective or streamlined way. Rather, it was their ability to process information—to extract from it clever inferences that would leave their readers in the dark—that distinguished these experts. The information that they used was available to any reader. What distinguished these experts from mere novices? Consider some possibilities.

Analytical Ability

Drawing of inferences goes beyond quantity and organization of knowledge—it requires effective use of knowledge. Experts seem to be able to infer things from information that novices could not infer. For example, the expert weather forecaster is able to infer what kinds of weather patterns are likely to follow from climatic trends, whereas a novice could have the same information and infer little or nothing from it about the future. The expert psychotherapist can take the results of psychological tests and interviews and infer the nature of a psychological disorder, whereas a novice would be more likely to make a wrong inference than a right one.

A true expert seems not only to have a great deal of knowledge, but also knows how to use the knowledge he or she has to analyze new information as it is acquired. On this point of view, organization of knowledge is only important to the extent that it permits a person to analyze information more effectively. It is not the organization per se that matters, but the utility of this organization in promoting analysis. An expert is not just a store house of facts; he or she is someone who knows how effectively to exploit the facts that are stored. On this view, cognitive psychologists might be faulted in their heavy use of memory paradigms, which seem to place the locus of expertise in memory. Cognitive psychologists have always felt comfortable studying memory, and perhaps it is therefore not surprising that the remembering of knowledge would become so key to their notion of expertise. We are reminded of how, if a carpenter is given a hammer, he is certain to find something to hammer. The hammer of cognitive psychologists in this case has been the study of the learning, organization, and recall of information. The expert witness in court, for example, would be of little use if he or she were able only to recite facts. The expert witness is expected to use his knowledge base to analyze the information presented to the court, and it is his superiority in performing this analysis that lends him his credibility as an expert.

All of the problems discussed in the chapters of this book require analytical thinking for their solution. Basically, one has to analyze the problem and how to solve it. The particular analytical demands of the individual problems differ. Some place more emphasis on quantitative analysis, others on quali-tative analysis. Some of the problems are transparent, in the sense that there is a structure that can be known, whereas others are not. When the problems are not transparent, analysis requires the construction of a mental model that represents as many aspects of the problem as one is able to understand, at least to some extent. A person who was unable to analyze the problems could be many things, but not an expert problem solver.

Creative Ability

The view of expertise involving analytical ability may seem right as far as it goes, but it seems not to go far enough. Agatha Christie's detectives, Hercule Poirot and Miss Marple, did not just analyze the information that they were given; they seem to have had creative insights that took informa-tion that other people saw in one way, but that they saw in another. Some-how, they were able to redefine the problems at hand, and thereby reach ingenious and insightful solutions that never occurred to others. In the lan-guage of our own investment theory of creativity (Sternberg & Lubart, 1991), creative people redefine problems in order to "buy low and sell high"—they come up with ideas that go against the crowd, convince the crowd they are right, and then move on to the next unpopular idea.

The processes of insight that creative people use correspond to what I have referred to as *selective encoding, selective combination,* and *selective compari-*

son (Davidson & Sternberg, 1984; Sternberg, 1985). A selective-encoding insight is one in which a person realizes the relevance of some information at the same time that she screens out as irrelevant other information. This filtering is critical in many kinds and perhaps all kinds of expertise. The expert lawyer needs to know which facts and which laws are critically relevant in the case at hand, and which may sound like they apply but they do not. The expert doctor needs to know what symptoms are critical in leading to a diagnosis, and which of the many tests that she might perform are ones that will be helpful in making a diagnosis, given a certain set of symptoms. The expert detective needs to zero in on the critical clues for deciding who is the guilty party. Many clues are irrelevant, and others may actually be misleading in the search for the guilty party. The expert mathematician seeking to do a proof needs to know which of the many postulates and theorems of mathematics are relevant to the proof, and which are not. Selective-encoding insights, thus, provide one basis for going beyond the information given.

Selective combination involves combining information in ways that may not be obvious to other people. Again, selective combination seems crucial in many forms of expertise. The lawyer needs to know how to combine the facts in order to yield a plausible case. The doctor needs to know how to combine the symptoms and the test results to lead to a diagnosis. A detective needs to know how to combine the facts to lead to a plausible scenario that might have led a certain person to commit a crime. The mathematician needs to know not only which postulates and theorems are relevant, but how to combine them in a logical order that makes for a mathematical proof. A person who identifies useful information but cannot combine it effectively cannot fully be an expert.

Finally, the expert needs selective comparison as well. Selective comparison involves applying all the information acquired in another context to a problem at hand. It is here that acquired knowledge becomes especially important, both with respect to quantity and organization. But again, it is not the knowledge per se that matters but the ability to exploit it effectively, to know when to apply it as well as when not to. A lawyer needs to know when past legal precedents are relevant and when they are red herrings. Similarly, a doctor needs to know when symptoms are genuinely similar to those of a past case and thereby suggest the same diagnosis, and when they are different enough only to seem to lead to the same diagnosis. Selective comparison may be viewed as a kind of analogy-forming, where an analogy is drawn between the present situation and some situation from the past.

The idea that experts need to go beyond analysis to synthesis—to some kind of creative form of thought—fits well with other things we know. For example, in academic disciplines, the true experts in a field are not considered to be the ones who have taught courses on subject matter for many years and thus may have memorized what everyone else has done, but people who have made creative theoretical and empirical contributions to a given field. The most distinguished experts are usually the people who have advanced the field, not merely those who have learned where the field happens to be at a given time. The same would be true in other disciplines. In art, for example, the expert is not merely someone who can imitate the work of a famous artist, but someone who is well able to analyze the work of other artists, or who creates original art work of his own. In literature, one could be viewed as an expert either by virtue of superior criticism of literary work or by superior production of such work. But merely memorizing literary works and being able to retrieve them is not likely to be the basis for the recognition of a person as an expert. Thus, it appears that some kind of creative or synthetic contribution can be important, in addition to or instead of an analytical one.

If I have a concern about both the European and the American approaches to problem solving, it is that the creative aspect of problem solving has been largely ignored. The Americans are perhaps more at fault, because they are the ones who have chosen to focus on the experts in domains such as physics, mathematics, and the social sciences. What makes a truly great physicist is not the ability to solve the textbook-like problems that characterize a high school or introductory college physics course—it is the ability to generate novel and important theories (in the case of the theoretical physicist) or experiments (in the case of the experimental physicist). Similarly, the great mathematician is one who generates novel and important proofs, and the great psychologist one who generates novel and important theories and experiments. The American research concentrates on what may be the least important aspects of true expertise, and by studying fairly trivial tasks with respect to what experts do, ends up with theories that may emphasize some of the less important aspects of expertise. To the extent that professors at my institution are expert *psychologists*, it is not because they could get a perfect score on a difficult multiple-choice or fill-in-the blanks test on the findings in their field!

Of course, creativity is very difficult to study, and even recent attempts (see Sternberg, 1988) have only scratched the surface. But European researchers on problem solving have shown their willingness to study very complex tasks and processes. I would hope they would thus be willing to shift more of their emphasis away from the analytical and more toward the creative aspects of complex problem solving. Both aspects are important, but the lion's share of attention has certainly gone to the former.

Automatization

Experts seem not only to do more than can novices, they seem to do it more easily—more effortlessly. For example, an expert driver drives almost automatically, and makes driving look easy, as does an expert dancer with respect to dancing, or an expert violinist with respect to playing the violin. Performances that seem easy for this person are impossible for the novice, even when he or she expends great effort. Similarly, the expert speaker of French or any other language speaks automatically, whereas the novice speaks in a halting and insecure manner. Experts have automatized many of the aspects of performance that for novices required controlled processes (Shiffrin & Schneider, 1977).

Automatization offers a further advantage to the expert. Presumably, humans have limited-capacity systems for processing information. It is widely agreed that controlled processing is resource-consuming, whereas automatic processing consumes few resources at all. By having much of their information processing automatized, experts free their cognitive resources for dealing with novel aspects of a situation. For example, a person who can hardly read German is in no position to make sophisticated inferences about a text written in German, whereas a person who has automatized the basic bottom-up comprehension skills of German will be in a better position to make these inferences. A person who is just learning to drive is more susceptible to accidents because he needs to spend many of his resources trying to manage the various aspects of driving a car, leaving him without the resources to cope with sudden perilous situations that may develop. An expert driver, on the other hand, has more resources available to devote to a sudden perilous situation. Thus, automaticity promotes or at least permits the use of higher levels of analysis and synthesis, and thus promotes expertise.

Automatization has not played a major role in studies or theories of problem solving, either in Europe or in the United States. In the case of the Europeans, the lack of emphasis is no surprise. Europeans have generally presented their subjects with relatively novel problems, whose solution could not have been automatized in advance. In the case of the Americans, the lack of emphasis is surprising. Here's why.

Expert game players, who have been studied extensively in the United States, virtually automatically exclude some kinds of moves without being aware they are doing so. It is perhaps this aspect of performance that is so difficult to simulate on a computer, and that has led to most expert chess-playing programs being brute-force programs that consider millions of moves that an expert would never consider. As another example, an expert scientist knows automatically many aspects of design and analysis, freeing processing resources for dealing with the relative novelty in conceptual problems (Sternberg, 1985). The undergraduate or beginning graduate student does not enjoy this level of automatization, and often devotes so many mental-processing resources to the relatively routine aspects of experimental work that he or she does not have that many resources left over to cope with novelty. To understand why experts can deal with more interesting problems than novices, we have to understand all of the uninteresting parts of problem solving that they can ignore, but the novice cannot.

Practical Ability

A true expert does not operate in a social vacuum. In any field of endeavor, advancement requires a knowledge of how the field operates, and how successfully to navigate within it. A business executive, for example, might have excellent analytic and creative skills, but without practical savvy and understanding of how corporations really function, these analytic and synthetic abilities are likely to remain unused or useless. Even in the ivory tower of academia, advancement to successively higher levels of expertise requires the knowledge of the ins and outs of publication, teaching, gaining tenure, obtaining grants, and the like. Similarly, no matter what are the analytical or synthetic abilities of a great lawyer such as the American fictional character Perry Mason, Mason could not have succeeded if he did not understand how courts and criminals work. The detective, similarly, does not operate in an abstract world, but rather has to have the practical savvy for knowing what leads can be pursued and what ones cannot be.

The general point here is that experts seem to have practical as well as analytic and synthetic abilities. They get to where they are not only on the basis of abstract abilities, but on the basis of their being able to apply these abstract abilities within the constraints of the field in which they work. Many a potentially brilliant writer or artist or scientist has probably never seen the limelight precisely because of a failure to understand how her field truly functions. Probably no one could argue that this kind of practical ability or common sense is sufficient for expertise, but for many kinds of expertise, it appears at least to be a necessary condition. Its necessity arises from our own necessity of operating within real, practical constraints rather than solely within ideal and hypothetical ones.

Our own research (e.g., Sternberg & Wagner, 1993; Sternberg, Wagner, & Okagaki, 1993; Wagner & Sternberg, 1986) has shown the importance of practical intelligence to real-world problem solving. We have found, for example, that managers who excel in managerial problem solving make extensive use of their ability to acquire and use tacit knowledge—what one needs to know to succeed in an environment that one is not explicitly taught and that often is not even verbalized. Moreover, this ability is not related to intelligence as measured by conventional psychometric tests. Moreover, tests of practical intelligence correlate better with job performance than do tests of academic intelligence. Even professors of psychology, another group we have studied, need tacit knowledge for success. They need to know, for example, how to get a job, how to keep a job, how to build a reputation, how to get funded in their research, how to get articles accepted by journals, and so on. We have found in our research that scores on tests of tacit knowledge predict success in academic psychology as well as in business. Clearly, practical intelligence is an important part of true expertise in a field.

I am surprised and a bit disappointed that investigators of problem solving have not devoted more attention to the practical aspects of job performance. The kinds of problems that have been studied in Europe are certainly more practical than those that have been studied in America. But the tacit-knowledge aspects of these problems have not been much studied. For example, to be a politician at any level—whether mayor or member of Parliament— one has to know how to "grease the wheels"—how to get things done in a way that one can only learn on the job. Greasing the wheels often means getting to know the right people, knowing how to handle them, knowing when to act and when not to, and so on. The kind of tacit knowledge I am talking about cannot be represented by a mathematical algorithm, and probably can't even be programmed into a computer simulation—at least, not easily. Yet, it is key for real expertise. Politicians don't get reelected if they don't have it. Academics don't get permanent positions. Lawyers don't get partnerships. And so on. They may have all the analytical and creative abilities needed for success; without the practical abilities, they disappear from the professional scene, usually sooner rather than later.

A LABELING CONCEPTION

When all is said and done, even cognitive psychologists who take a broader cognitive approach to the study of expertise probably will not fully understand the concept of expertise if they do not look at social factors as well. To some extent, expertise is a matter of labeling. From this point of view, a person is expert because he or she is labeled as such.

People are designated as *expert witnesses, expert chess players,* or *expert photographers* because they meet certain organized criteria for designation as an expert. These criteria may differ from one field to another, and they may be loosely and even inconsistently applied from one case to another. But when we talk about expertise as it occurs in the real world, labeling is probably key. A doctor becomes an *expert* when he or she receives a certification to practice. We know that there is wide variation in the true expertise of various doctors, but once certified, they all have equal opportunities to be labeled as experts. We even consult them as experts, hoping that the ones we pick will be ones whose knowledge and ability to use that knowledge match their credentials. Their entitlement to the label of *doctor* identifies them as experts, and they are treated as such, almost without regard to their particular cognitive accomplishments. The same can be said for lawyers or Ph.D.s or people in any number of fields. Having received the credentials, they become *instant experts,* regardless of their cognitive capabilities.

Some people may resist the notion that labeling has anything to do with expertise. It is important to distinguish exactly what it does have to do with, which is the way in which people use the concepts of expertise, more or less independently of any cognitive antecedents that we might create. One can dismiss such factors as *merely* socially psychological. But the danger here, as is always true in cognitive psychology, is that in formulating theories of cognition, one will become detached from what happens in the real world, as opposed to what happens in some ideal world that cognitive psychologists might create in their laboratories. To an extent, expertise is a labeling phenomenon and this phenomenon needs to be taken into account as well as the cognitive ones.

Labeling is not just a social phenomenon, but is also a cognitive one. One has to decide to apply the label, or not to. And decision making is something that cognitive psychologists study. When all is said and done, labeling may have at least as much to do with who is designated as an expert as does any kind of problem-solving or other cognitive expertise. Personally, I would like to see cognitive psychologists study how people decide whether to apply the label of *expert* or not. I believe they might be in for some surprises. For example, the labeled experts in the mind of the public have little to do with these labels in the minds of academics. The *expert psychologists* in the United States, in the view of laypeople, are those who appear on television shows or write newspaper columns or popular books. The most esteemed experts in academia are often people with whom the lay public is unfamiliar. Of course, we can dismiss their opinions as unimportant. But then, we must apply equal scrutiny to our own labeling. Why do we label the superior researcher as the expert, and not the superior communicator to the public? Labeling phenomena bear study, by both cognitive and social psychologists.

EXPERTISE AS A PROTOTYPE

My own point of view in writing this chapter is not to promote one or another of these views as expertise, but rather to promote the view that expertise, like other constructs, is a prototype (Neisser, 1976; Rosch, 1973). It comprises all of the aspects described previously, and probably others as well. Certainly, in specific domains, expertise may have aspects that do not apply in other domains. For example, the expert dancer needs a level of coordination and stamina that would not apply to the expert theoretical physicist. People are not really experts or nonexperts, but rather are experts in varying degrees. Their degree of expertise will depend on the extent to which they fulfill the criteria described above both singly and jointly. The more of each attribute they have, and the larger their share of attributes, the more likely they are to be *experts*. Obviously, the labeling criterion is different in kind from the others, and may well depend on them to a certain degree. These criteria are by no means independent, nor are they even fully mutually exclusive. Rather, they represent correlated aspects of expertise. A multidimensional representation would thus have oblique rather than orthogonal axes.

The view of expertise as a prototype implies that within a given domain, people have a shared conception of what an expert is. The attributes of the prototype may differ somewhat from one domain to another. For example, the expert clinical psychologist might be viewed primarily as one who makes accurate diagnoses and then provides psychotherapy that maximizes the probability of a cure; in biology, the expert might be someone who does top-flight research on the nature of life; in theoretical physics, the expert might be someone who devises theories that compellingly account for large, important problems about the physical universe, and so on. A given field may have several alternative prototypes. For example, the expert academic psychologist might be viewed quite differently from the expert clinical psychologist: Research quality and productivity would be seen as far more important in the academic domain than in the clinical domain.

Prototypes of expertise can vary over time and space. For example, as the study of economics becomes more quantitative, knowledge and ability to use econometric techniques might increase in importance in the prototype of the economic expert. Moreover, the expert economist in a socialist country might be a rather different person from that in a capitalist country. Thus, prototypes are dynamic rather than static.

Prototypes also differ across groups making the judgments. As noted previously, the lay public and academic psychologists have very different prototypes of the *expert psychologist*. Of course, academic psychologists would view their prototype as the *correct* one, but so would the lay public. And when they hear that the academic psychologist's contribution to the study of problem solving is to show something they are quite sure they already knew, their certainty that they are right may be reinforced. There is no single prototype of the expert across groups making judgments. And even within the mind of a single person, there may be conflict. In judging an academic as an expert, how much emphasis do we place on different types of scholarly contributions? Speaking for myself, there are some people whom I view as experts on some days, and as semi-charlatans on others!

Although people may judge expertise against one or more prototypes of what an expert is, we are fortunate that not everyone who is knowledgeable about and adept in a field conforms to any single prototype. As people with different kinds of qualifications emerge and show that they can be knowledgeable about and productive in a field, we find that we need to broaden our view of expertise in order to allow for the diversity of skills that can lead to outstanding performance.

In conclusion, expertise is a multifaceted phenomenon. To a large extent, it is a cognitive phenomenon, but it is not exclusively a cognitive one. One needs to take into account as well the social conditions under which the label of expertise is granted. Expertise involves both general and specific processes, as well as knowledge and the ability to organize it. Research on problem solving, wherever it takes place, needs to take into account the many aspects of prototypes of expertise in order fully to understand what makes an *expert problem solver.*

There have been, and will continue to be, alternative approaches to how one should elucidate the characteristics of the expert. Europeans have tended to emphasize *everyday* problems, but have split among themselves in just what kinds of problems should be studied. Some investigators have preferred highly complex problems where an optimal algorithm could not possibly be specified; others have preferred simpler yet challenging problems where there is a specifiable optimal route to solution, usually expressed in terms of a mathematical equation. Americans have tended to prefer problems requiring technical expertise. Almost certainly, we need to study all of these kinds of problems in order to understand complex problem solving. There is no one right kind of problem to study, any more than there is any right kind of problem. Ultimately, we will need to integrate what seem now like separate lines of research into a basis for a single, unified theory of problem solving. Newell and Simon (1972) made an attempt to do so more than 20 years ago. A new integrated theory will have a much richer data base on which to draw.

ACKNOWLEDGMENTS

Research for this article was supported under the Javits Act Program (grant No. R2O6R00001) as administered by the Office of Educational Research and Improvement, U.S. Department of Education. Grantees undertaking such projects are encouraged to express freely their professional judgment. This article, therefore, does not necessarily represent the positions or policies of the government, and no official endorsement should be inferred.

REFERENCES

Adelson, B. (1981). Problem solving and the development of abstract categories in programming languages. *Memory and Cognition, 9,* 422–433.

Adelson, B. (1984). When novices surpass experts: The difficulty of a task may increase with expertise. *Journal of Experimental Psychology: Learning, Memory, and Cognition, 10,* 483–495.

Ashcraft, M. H. (1982). The development of mental arithmetic: A chronometric approach. *Developmental Review, 2,* 213–236.

Baron, J. B., & Sternberg, R. J. (Eds.). (1987). *Teaching thinking skills: Theory and practice.* New York: Freeman.

Binet, A., & Simon, T. (1905). Méthodes nouvelles pour le diagnostic du niveau intellectuel des anormaux. *L'Année psychologique, 11,* 245–336.

Broadbent, D. E. (1977). Levels, hierarchies, and the locus of control. *Quarterly Journal of Experimental Psychology, 29,* 181–201.

Brown, J. S., & Burton, R. R. (1978). Diagnostic models for procedural bugs in basic mathematical skills. *Cognitive Science, 2,* 155–192.

Card, S. K., Moran, T. P., & Newell, A. (1983). *The psychology of human-computer interaction.* Hillsdale, NJ: Lawrence Erlbaum Associates.

Ceci, S. J. (1990). *On intelligence . . . More ore less.* Englewood Cliffs, NJ: Prentice-Hall.

Chase, W. G., & Simon, H. A. (1973). The mind's eye in chess. In W. G. Chase (Ed.), *Visual information processing* (pp. 215–181). New York: Academic Press.

Chi, M. T. H. (1978). Knowledge structure and memory development. In R. S. Siegler (Ed.), *Children's thinking: What develops?* (pp. 73–96). Hillsdale, NJ: Lawrence Erlbaum Associates.

Chi, M. T. H., Glaser, R., & Farr, M. J. (Eds.). (1988). *The nature of expertise.* Hillsdale, NJ: Lawrence Erlbaum Associates.

Chi, M. T. H., Glaser, R., & Rees, E. (1982). Expertise in problem solving. In R. J. Sternberg (Ed.), *Advances in the psychology of human intelligence* (Vol. 1, pp. 7–75). Hillsdale, NJ: Lawrence Erlbaum Associates.

Davidson, J. E., & Sternberg, R. J. (1984). The role of insight in intellectual giftedness. *Gifted Child Quarterly, 28,* 58–64.

DeGroot, A. D. (1965). *Thought and choice in chess.* The Hague: Mouton.

Dörner, D. (1987). On the difficulties people have in dealing with complexity. In J. Rasmussen, K. Duncan, & J. Leplat (Eds.), *New technology and human error* (pp. 97–109). New York: Wiley.

Duncker, K. (1945). On problem solving. *Psychological Monographs, 58*(8).

Ericsson, K. A., & Staszewski, J. J. (1989). Skilled memory and expertise: Mechanisms of exceptional performance. In D. Klahr & K. Kotovsky (Eds.), *Complex information processing: The impact of Herbert A. Simon* (pp. 235–267). Hillsdale, NJ: Lawrence Erlbaum Associates.

Eysenck, H. J. (1986). The theory of intelligence and the psychophysiology of cognition. In R. J. Sternberg (Ed.), *Advances in the psychology of human intelligence* (Vol. 3, pp. 1–34). Hillsdale, NJ: Lawrence Erlbaum Associates.

Frensch, P. A., & Sternberg, R. J. (1989). Expertise and intelligent thinking: When is it worse to know better? In R. J. Sternberg (Ed.), *Advances in psychology of human intelligence* (Vol. 5, pp. 157–188). Hillsdale, NJ: Lawrence Erlbaum Associates.

Gentner, D. (1983). Structure-mapping: A theoretical framework for analogy. *Cognitive Science, 7,* 155–170.

Gick, M. L., & Holyoak, K. J. (1983). Schema induction and analogical transfer. *Cognitive Psychology, 15,* 1–38.

Groen, G. J., & Parkman, J. M. (1972). A chronometric analysis of simple addition. *Psychological Review, 79,* 329–343.

Guthke, J. (1985). Ein neuer Ansatz für die rehabilitationspsychologisch orientierte Psychodiagnostik—das Lerntestkonzept als Alternative zum herkömmlichen Intelligenztest [A new approach in psychodiagnostics from the viewpoint of rehabilitation psychology—The learning test concept as an alternative to the conventional intelligence test]. In K. H. Wiedl (Ed.), *Rehabilitationspsychologie* (pp. 177–194). Stuttgart, Germany: Kohlhammer.

Hegarty, M. (1991). Knowledge and processes in mechanical problem solving. In R. J. Sternberg & P. A. Frensch (Eds.), *Complex problem solving: Principles and mechanisms* (pp. 253–285). Hillsdale, NJ: Lawrence Erlbaum Associates.

Hoffman, R. R. (Ed.). (1992). *The psychology of expertise: Cognitive research and empirical AI.* New York: Springer-Verlag.

Hunt, E. B. (1978). Mechanics of verbal ability. *Psychological Review, 85,* 109–130.

Hunt, E. (1991). Some comments on the study of complexity. In R. J. Sternberg & P. A. Frensch (Eds.), *Complex problem solving: Principles and mechanisms* (pp. 383–395). Hillsdale, NJ: Lawrence Erlbaum Associates.

Jensen, A. R. (1972). *Genetics and education.* London: Methuen.

Jensen, A. R. (1982). The chronometry of intelligence. In R. J. Sternberg (Ed.), *Advances in the psychology of human intelligence* (Vol. 1, pp. 255–310). Hillsdale, NJ: Lawrence Erlbaum Associates.

Kay, D. (1991). Computer interaction: Debugging the problems. In R. J. Sternberg & P. A. Frensch (Eds.), *Complex problem solving* (pp. 317–342). Hillsdale, NJ: Lawrence Erlbaum Associates.

Keil, F. C. (1989). *Concepts, kinds, and cognitive development.* Cambridge, MA: MIT Press.

Klahr, D. (1984). Transition processes in quantitative development. In R. J. Sternberg (Ed.), *Mechanisms of cognitive development.* San Francisco: Freeman.

Köhler, W. (1925). *The mentality of apes.* London: Routledge & Kegan Paul.

Larkin, J. (1983). The role of problem representation in physics. In D. Gentner & A. L. Stevens (Eds.), *Mental models* (pp. 75–100). Hillsdale, NJ: Lawrence Erlbaum Associates.

Larkin, J., McDermott, J., Simon, D. P., & Simon, H. A. (1980). Expert and novice performance in solving physics problems. *Science, 208,* 1335–1342.

Lesgold, A., & Lajoie, S. (1991). Complex problem solving in electronics. In R. J. Sternberg & P. A. Frensch (Eds.), *Complex problem solving* (pp. 287–316). Hillsdale, NJ: Lawrence Erlbaum Associates.

Luchins, A. S. (1942). Mechanization in problem solving. *Psychological Monographs, 54*(6).

Maier, N. R. F. (1930). Reasoning in humans: I. On direction. *Journal of Comparative Psychology, 10,* 115–143.

Maier, N. R. F. (1931). Reasoning in humans: II. The solution of a problem and its appearance in consciousness. *Journal of Comparative Psychology, 12,* 181–194.

McCloskey, M. (1983). Intuitive physics. *Scientific American, 248*(4), 122–130.

Miller, G., Galanter, E., & Pribram, K. (1960). *Plans and the structure of behavior.* New York: Holt.

Neisser, U. (1976). *Cognition and reality: Principles and implications of cognitive psychology.* San Francisco: Freeman.

Newell, A., Shaw, J. C., & Simon, H. A. (1958). Elements of a theory of human problem solving. *Psychological Review, 65,* 151–166.

Newell, A., & Simon, H. A. (1972). *Human problem solving.* Englewood Cliffs, NJ: Prentice-Hall.

Pascual-Leone, J. (1970). A mathematical model for the transition rule in Piaget's development stages. *Acta Psychologica, 32,* 301–345.

Piaget, J. (1972). *The psychology of intelligence.* Totowa, NJ: Littlefield Adams.

Raaheim, K. (1974). *Problem solving and intelligence.* Oslo: Universitetsforlaget.

Reitman, J. S. (1976). Skilled perception in Go: Deducing memory structures from inter-response times. *Cognitive Psychology, 8,* 336–356.

Resnick, L. B. (1982). Syntax and semantics in learning to subtract. In T. P. Carpenter, J. M. Moser, & T. A. Romberg (Eds.), *Addition and subtraction: A cognitive perspective* (pp. 136–155). Hillsdale, NJ: Lawrence Erlbaum Associates.

Rosch, E. (1973). On the internal structure of perceptual and semantic categories. In T. E. Moore (Ed.), *Cognitive development and the acquisition of language* (pp. 112–144). New York: Academic Press.

Shiffrin, R. M., & Schneider, W. (1977). Controlled and automatic human information processing. II: Perceptual learning, automatic attending, and a general theory. *Psychological Review, 84,* 127–190.

Siegler, R. S. (1978). The origins of scientific reasoning. In R. S. Siegler (Ed.), *Children's thinking: What develops?* (pp. 109–149). Hillsdale, NJ: Lawrence Erlbaum Associates.

Siegler, R. S., & Shrager, J. (1984). A model of strategy choice. In C. Sophian (Ed.), *Origins of cognitive skills* (pp. 229–293). Hillsdale, NJ: Lawrence Erlbaum Associates.

Sternberg, R. J. (1977). *Intelligence, information processing, and analogical reasoning: The componential analysis of human abilities.* Hillsdale, NJ: Lawrence Erlbaum Associates.

Sternberg, R. J. (1985). *Beyond IQ: A triarchic theory of human intelligence.* New York: Cambridge University Press.

Sternberg, R. J. (1988). *The triarchic mind: A new theory of human intelligence.* New York: Viking.

Sternberg, R. J., & Frensch, P. A. (Eds.). (1991). *Complex problem solving: Principles and mechanisms.* Hillsdale, NJ: Lawrence Erlbaum Associates.

Sternberg, R. J., & Lubart, T. I. (1991). An investment theory of creativity and its development. *Human Development, 34,* 1–31.

Sternberg, R. J., & Wagner, R. K. (1993). The g-ocentric view of intelligence and job performance is wrong. *Current Directions in Psychological Science, 2*(1), 1–4.

Sternberg, R. J., Wagner, R. K., & Okagaki, L. (1993). Practical intelligence: The nature and role of tacit knowledge in work and at school. In H. Reese & J. Puckett (Eds.), *Advances in lifespan development* (pp. 205–227). Hillsdale, NJ: Lawrence Erlbaum Associates.

Streufert, S., & Streufert, S. C. (1978). *Behavior in the complex environment.* Washington, D.C.: Winston.

Voss, J. F., Greene, T. R., Post, T., & Prenner, B. (1983). Problem solving skill in the social sciences. In G. Bower (Ed.), *The psychology of learning and motivation: Advances in research theory* (Vol. 17, pp. 165–213). New York: Academic Press.

Wagner, R. K., & Sternberg, R. J. (1985). Practical intelligence in real-world pursuits: The role of tacit knowledge. *Journal of Personality and Social Psychology, 49,* 436–458.

Wagner, R. K., & Sternberg, R. J. (1986). Tacit knowledge and intelligence in the everyday world. In R. J. Sternberg & R. K. Wagner (Eds.), *Practical intelligence: Nature and origins of competence in the everyday world* (pp. 52–83). New York: Cambridge University Press.

Wittgenstein, L. (1953). *Philosophical investigations.* New York: Macmillan.

Author Index

Subject Index

A

Action regulation, 38-40, 70, 95, 96
Adaptation, 214
Adaptive testing, 189, 192
Algorithms, 12
Ambiguity, 119
Analysis of variance, 244-246
Analysis
   dependency, 67
   whole-part, 67
Assessment center, 220
Attention, 115, 129
Automatization, 297, 312, 313

B

Barriers, 7, 18, 22
Betting game, multistage, 153
Business games, 107

C

Candle problem, 202
Causal diagram analysis, 45, 193,
   255
Chunking, 50, 52
Clinical groups, 137, 251, 254
Closure
   flexibility of, 203
   speed of, 203

Cognitive complexity, 297, 308,
   309
Cognitive modeling, 249
Cognitive processes, 16-18, 272,
273, 276, 277
Cognitive variables, 20
Comparability
   of complex problems, 183, 184
   of CPS and intelligence, 30, 34,
     35, 178, 185
Compensation, 106, 113, 114, 127
Competence
   epistemic, 86, 87
   heuristic, 39, 86, 87, 92
Complexity, 14, 18, 22, 29, 46, 47,
   66, 71, 168-170, 204, 206, 213,
   232, 244, 271, 272
Computer program, debugging,
   202, 204, 206, 213
Computer simulation, 41, 6, 71, 95,
   135, 245, 247, 276, 283, 285
Confirmation bias, 206, 209, 210
Control, cognitive, 204
Control performance, 33-35, 132,
   133, 135-137, 143, 147, 148,
   181, 185, 192-197, 200, 234,
   244, 246, 253-255, 270, 284,
   287
Control performance, measure, 160-
   162, 164-166, 248, 252, 261